History in the Age of Vikings
Volume 3

Introduction by Mark Bussler
Editing and Layouts by Ephraim Durnst
Based on the works of Paul B. Du Chaillu
Cover design by Mark Bussler

www.CGRpublishing.com

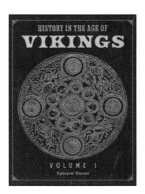

History in the Age of Vikings:
Volume 1

1904 St. Louis World's Fair:
The Louisiana Purchase Exposition
in Photographs

How to Draw Womens' Eyes:
Inspired by Classic Illustrations
Volume 1

Introduction

HISTORY IN THE AGE OF VIKINGS: VOLUME 3

by Mark Bussler

Writer Paul B. Du Chaillu concluded his multi-volume work on Viking history with a celebratory tome about conquest, fighting, and expeditions. We wonder if he saved his favorite stories for last because, in these pages (spread throughout no less than six chapters!), we learn about the Battles of Brávöll and Dúnheidi, Ragnar Lodbrok, King Halfdan, the first Jarls of Normandy, the Battle of Brunanburgh, King Svein, King Olaf, Knut, Harald Hardradi, and much more.

Chapter XVII, titled Champions and Berserks, is especially interesting and filled with the kinds of flair and drama that modern audiences might expect from the Vikings. "To be considered the foremost champion or Kappi was the greatest ambition of every warrior; and to attain this proud position was no easy task among so many men who were equally brave and perfectly reckless of their lives and thoroughly skilled in the handling of weapons."

Following a section on poetry, which was regarded as "a gift from the gods" to perpetuate their great deeds in song and verse, Du Chaillu regales us with a favorite descriptive passage "The aim of every champion was to become a Berserk… When within sight of their foe Berserks wrought themselves into such a state of frenzy that they bit their shields and rushed forward toward the attack, throwing away their arms of defense, reckless of every danger, sometimes having nothing but a club, which carried with it death and destruction."

Additionally, this third volume of Viking history brings us much beautiful jewelry, rings, necklets, belts, necklaces, furniture, doorways, and more, reminding readers that the Vikings were not only among the world's foremost warriors years but also leaders in art, craftsmanship, poetry, and culture.

As with the previous volumes, we endeavored to restore this fascinating series for future generations to enjoy and educate. Images have been, where necessary, enlarged and cleaned up from the contemporary master print.

Mark Bussler

- Bussler is the writer of T*he World's Fair of 1893 Ultra Massive Photographic Adventure* series, *The White City of Color, 1915 San Francisco World's Fair in Color, 1904 St. Louis World's Fair: The Louisiana Purchase Exposition in Photographs*, and more. He is also president of CGR Publishing, cover designer, and lead restoration engineer.

Enlarged image from page 103.

Table of Contents

VOLUME 3

Enlarged images from page 99.

Enlarged images from page 99.

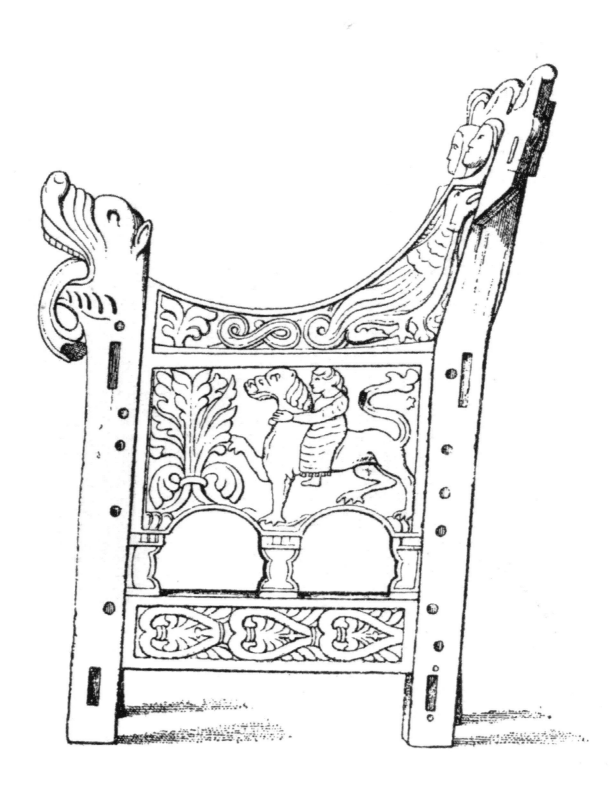

9

CHAPTER I.

THE FLEETS OF THE NORTHMEN.

Maritime power of the North—Their huge fleets—Good harbours—Strategical skill—Size of some of their fleets—Fleets accompanied by provision ships.

NOTHING can give us a greater insight into the maritime power of the North than the accounts we read, here and there in the Sagas, of the fleets gathered together for the purpose of war and invasion. The number of the vessels is quite remarkable, but seeing that the finds corroborate so much that is told us in the Sagas, there is no reason to doubt the truthfulness of their statements as regards the magnitude of the fleets, and the vessels were far from being as small as have been imagined.

From the Sagas we learn that the aim of every chief was to be powerful at sea; every bondi was owner of one or more craft. They were born seamen, but were also trained to fight on land. They surrounded themselves with warlike retainers, and with these made distant expeditions to win honour and booty. These men were also soldiers, and good horsemen. As we see that in every great land battle the warriors came from all parts of the Northern lands, it must be concluded that the same took place in regard to their invasions of foreign countries. Only in a very few instances have we accounts of the Norsemen being defeated at sea by the fleets of the countries they attacked; even in these rare instances their combats took place with a very small number of vessels compared with the powerful fleets of their enemies, who were either Frisians or their own people who had settled in England.

Fortunately, Frankish and old English chronicles, which are quite independent of those of the North, help to corroborate the general truthfulness of the Eddas and Sagas, and from them we have several accounts of the number of vessels which sailed up the Seine, the Rhine, the Elbe, and the Weser, or went to England.

The largest fleet that ever met in the North was that which assembled for the battle of Bravöll; though the number of vessels is not mentioned, we read that the Sound was covered with vessels. This fleet reached from Kjöge to Skanör, so that, if the account is trustworthy, people could walk as on a bridge from Zeeland over the Sound, a distance of some twenty miles. Sigurd Hring had 2,500 (3,000) ships to oppose him.[1]

The maritime expeditions of the Northmen to distant lands were undertaken with a great deal of care and foresight; the men were under strict discipline, and were attired with the greatest splendour. It would be a mistaken idea to think that the Northmen started on these voyages without any previous knowledge of the country they were to invade, or of the shores where they were going to land, or that they sailed with no definite object. Their previous knowledge of these far-off lands was no doubt gained in trading, and it was only after being thoroughly well acquainted with the geography of the part to be attacked that they ventured on their invasion.

Many of the places in foreign countries mentioned in the Sagas where the Norse fleets were safely moored and sheltered against storm, are to this day good harbours, and if others are no longer so it is because the shores of those coasts have been subjected to changes which are still taking place. The geographical positions of the rivers they ascended were well chosen; they knew what size of vessel to take there, and though their operations seemed to be detached, we find that their fleets were in communication with each other, and that their armies could assist one another in case of need, crush the enemy between the rivers they had ascended, or between them and the sea. In a word, their tactics showed considerable boldness and strategical skill, which generally left them a way of retreat, if necessary, to their vessels or to some island. Though the Sagas give us a good and vivid idea of the Norse mode of warfare at sea, they are very incomplete in regard to the description and details of the land expeditions, and we have to go to the Frankish chronicles in order to see the manner in which they attacked or besieged a city. From these we learn that the ships ascended the rivers as far as possible; if anything stopped the navigation, a canal was made or the vessels were drawn along the shore, and the obstacle thus passed. The Norsemen took possession of all the large islands, fortified them, and wintered there; and there they kept their spoils of war or plunder. They also brought cavalry in their ships, a fact proved by the Bayeux tapestry.

It is said that Harald Blátönn (blue tooth) went to Norway with a fleet of 700 (840) ships.

"Then King Harald summoned a host from his entire kingdom. Hákon jarl was with him, and Harald Grænski, son of Gudraud Björnsson, and many other powerful men, who had fled from their estates in Norway on account of Gunnhild's sons.

"The King of Denmark sailed from the south into Vikin with 700 ships,[1] and there all the inhabitants came under his rule; and when he reached Túnsberg, large numbers gathered to him.

"King Harald gave to Hákon jarl all the men who had come to him in Norway; and made him ruler over the seven fylkis of Rogaland, Hördaland, Sogn, Firdafylki, Sunnmœri, Raumsdal, Nordmœri"[2] (Olaf Tryggvason, c. 24, 2 Fms. I.).

---

[1] Heimskringla says 600 ships.

[2] The English chronicles mention numerous instances of large fleets descending on various parts of the coast, of which the following are a few:—

In the year 860, in the time of Ethelred a large fleet came to the land, and the crews stormed Winchester.

In the year 893 the Danish army came, from the east westward to Boulogne, and their war ships. They landed at the mouth of the Limne with 250 ships (this is in the eastern part of Kent).

In the year 894 the Danes among the Northumbrians and East Anglians gathered 100 ships and went south to besiege Exeter.

In the year 927 King Anlaf entered the Humber with a vast fleet of 615 sails.

In the year 993 Olave, with 93 ships, came to Staines.

In the year 994 Olave and Sveyn (Olaf of Norway and Svein of Denmark) came to London with 94 ships.

In the year 1006 a great fleet came to Sandwich and ravaged wherever it went. It returned in winter to the Isle of Wight; the distress and fear in the land were extreme. £36,000 and provisions was paid as tribute to the invaders.

In the year 1009, Thurkills came with his fleet to England, and after him another innumerable fleet of Danes, the chiefs of which were Hemming and Ailaf.

In the year 1069 the sons of Svein came from Denmark with 240 ships into the Humber.

In the year 1075 200 ships came from Denmark under Knut, son of Sweyne and Hecco, but did not dare to risk a battle with King William. After plundering in York they went to Flanders.

The Frankish chronicles give an account also of various fleets:—

EGINHARD.

In the year 810 the emperor (Charlemagne), then at Aix-le-Chapelle, planned an expedition against King Godfrey. He suddenly received the news that a fleet

Knut the Great had gathered a fleet of 1,200 vessels [1] for an attack on Norway.

"King Knut called to mind many things with which he charged King Olaf, as follows: That he captured his nephew Hakon, and let him take oath to him, and then seized the kingdom and drove him from the land; that he also took possession of the land which for a long time had been tributary to the Danish kings; that he had ravaged in the country of King Knut. So he went east from England with a great host to Denmark, reached the Limafjord, and thence sailed to Norway with 1,440 ships, for he had raised a general levy both in Denmark and England. Arriving at Agdir, he proceeded northward along the coast, and held meetings with the bœndr; he was acknowledged as king wherever he went, and he did not stop until he came to Nidaros" [2] (Fagrskinna, c. 104).[3]

When fleets went on distant expeditions, special vessels called *vistabyrding* (provision ships) followed them. Butter, the hard bread still used, dry, smoked, or salted meat, formed the stock of eatables, and there are many instances where ale and beer are mentioned.

---

of 200 ships coming from the country of the North had landed in Frisia, and ravaged all the islands adjacent to their shores.

In the year 845 Eurick, king of the Northmen, advanced against Louis in Germany with 600 vessels along the river Elbe.

In the year 850 Rorik, the nephew of Harold, who had recently left the service of Lothair, taking with him an army of Northmen, comes by the Rhine and the Watal with a multitude of ships, devastating Frisia, the island of Batavia, and other neighbourhood places.

In the year 852 the Northmen arrived in Frisia with 252 ships; after having received much silver they go elsewhere.

In the year 852 Godfrey, son of Harold the Dane, formerly baptized at Mayence, under the reign of the Emperor Louis, left Lothair and went to find his people. Afterwards having assembled a powerful force, he attacks Frisia with a multitude of vessels, and then enters the territory bordering on the river Scheidt.

In the year 857 the Danish pirates invaded the city of Paris and set fire to it. Here there must have been an enormous fleet.

In the year 861 the Danes, who had lately burned the town of Terouanne, came back under their chief Weland from the country of the Angles with more than 200 ships.

In the year 865, from Attigny Charles marched an army against the Northmen, who had entered the Seine with 500 ships. (We find at the same time Northmen on the Loire.)

[1] This means actually 1,440, as every hundred was equal to 120.

[2] Unfortunately some of the facts which we would like to know are missing in the Northern records in regard to the size of the fleet which came to England, with the son of Ragnar Lodbrok; but from what old English chronicles tell us, and from the depredations committed by them, we may assume that their number must have been very great. The same may also be said about the fleets of Svein and Knut.

[3] Cf. also Olaf Tryggvason's Saga, i. 89; Fornmanna Sögur.

From the Eddas and Sagas we gain an insight into their mode of warfare at sea. The accounts given of some of their combats are so vivid and precise, that we could almost imagine ourselves to be eye-witnesses of those terrific and bloody conflicts which, even to this day, stand unparalleled in the annals of maritime warfare for the length of their duration, the fierceness and obstinacy of the attack or defence, the number of ships or men engaged, and the carnage that took place.

For centuries these people remained undisputed masters of the sea. In their case, as in that of the ruling nations of to-day, it was their navy that enabled them to conquer, settle, and colonize other lands. If we call these men pirates, we must also apply the name to the English, French, Spaniards, Dutch, &c., because they have taken possession of countries against the will of the inhabitants, just as in the United States the land of the Indians has been gradually taken away from them. Civilisation was aggressive in ancient times, as it is to-day.

Enlarged image from page 156.

CHAPTER II.

MODE OF NAVAL WARFARE OF THE NORTHMEN.

Sea fights—Standard and shield burgh—Method of fighting—Use of grappling irons—Choice of the crew—Boarding of ships—Battle at the river Helga —Custom of strengthening ships' sides before a combat—Rowers protected by shields—Use of stones as weapons—Harbours protected by cables— The war levy.

FROM the numerous sea-fights described in the Sagas, we see that the most important and decisive part of the struggle took place near the prow and stem of the ship. Here the strongest and most valiant men were always stationed,[1] among them the standard-bearer of the chief or king, round whom they were ranged in battle order, and formed the *skjald-borg* (shield-burg).

"During the winter King Harald had a large dragon made and fitted out very splendidly. He placed on it his hird and Berserks. The stem defenders were the most carefully selected, for they had the king's standard. That part aft of the prow near the pumping-room (*austr-rum*) was called rausn (fore-castle). It was manned with Berserks Only those who surpassed others in strength and bravery and all kinds of skill got into the hird of King Harald. Only with such men was his ship manned, and he had then a large choice of hirdmen out of every Fylki" (Harald Fairhair's Saga, c. 9).

In a sea-fight between Hakon Herdibreid and King Ingi:

"Hakon went on board the east voyage [2] Knörr, and a shield-burgh was put round him there, but his standard remained on board the longship where he had been."[3]

Before the fight it was the custom to sound the horns and hoist the standards, and to tie the stems of the ships together, so that each line formed an unbroken whole ; sometimes several

---

[1] They were called *Stafnbúar*, stem or prow men.
[2] East voyage = voyage in the East

Baltic (Russia, &c.).
[3] Cf. also Olaf Tryggvason's Saga, c. 115.

anchors seem to have been employed for this purpose, as it is said that they were used to hold the ships together during the battle. When they came to the attack, the men sought to drag the ships of the enemy closer by means of grappling-hooks (*stafnlé*) and anchors. Eirik Jarl decided the battle of Svold by attacking the outermost ships of Olaf Tryggvason. As soon as one ship was cleared of men, he loosened its fastenings.

" It was then customary when men fought on board ships to tie them together and fight in the prows" (Harald Fair-hair's Saga, ch. 11).

In the celebrated battle of Svold most violent and **fatal** was the defence on the Long Serpent among the forerooms-men and the stem-defenders (see pp 192–3).

After leaving Norway Olaf steered the Long Serpent himself, and the crew was so carefully chosen that no man who was older than sixty or younger than twenty was to be on board, and they were picked also with regard to valour and strength. The king's hirdmen were first chosen, composed of the strongest and bravest men from the country and foreign lands.

" Ulf the red carried King Olaf's standard, and was placed in the front (prow) of the Serpent together with Kolbjörn Stallari, Thorstein Oxfoot, Vikar of Tiundaland. the brother of Arnljót Gellini. The following men were on the forecastle (rausn) in the bows :—Vakr Raumason Elfski, Bersi the Strong, An the archer of Jamtaland, Thránd the Hardy of Thelamörk, and Úthyrmir (Unsparing), his brother. From Hálogaland were :—Thránd the Squinting, Ögmund Sandi, Hlödvir (Louis) the Long of Saltvik, Harek the Keen. From the inner part of Thrandheim were :—Ketil the Tall, Thorfinn the Dashing, Hávar of Orkadal and his brothers. The following were in the foreroom :—Björn of Studla, Börk of Firdir, Thorgrim Thjódólfsson of Hvin, Asbjörn and Orm, Thórd of Njardarlög, Thorstein the white of Oprustadir, Arnor of Mœri, Hallstein and Hauk of Firdir, Eyvind Snake, Berg-thor Bestil, Hallkel of Fjalir, Olaf Dreng (good warrior), Arnfinn of Sogn, Sigurd Axe, Einar of Hördaland, Finn, Ketil of Rogaland, Grjótgard the nimble. The following were in the Krapparum [1] :—Einar Thambarskelfir (he was not

---

[1] The narrow room, the third room or space from the stern.

up to the standard being only eighteen winters old), Thorstein Hlifarson, Thórólf, Ivar the Starter, Orm Hood-nose, and many other very famous men were on the Serpent, though we cannot name them. Eight men were in every *half-room* (sixteen in one room), selected one by one. Thirty men were in the foreroom. People said that the picked men on board surpassed other men as far in fineness and strength and bravery as the Long Serpent surpassed other ships. Thorkel Nefja, the king's brother, steered the Short Serpent, Thorkel the Wheedler and Jostein, the king's uncles, the Trana; both these ships were very well manned. Eleven large ships left Thrandheim with Olaf, also twenty-seaters and smaller ships and store-ships (*vistabyrding*)" (Olaf Tryggvason's Saga (Heimskringla), c. 102).

When the crew felt that they were unequal to the contest by being boarded, they then cut the ropes that tied them to other ships, and tried to avoid the coming danger.

"The king's men attacked the jarl's ship and almost got up on it. When the jarl saw his danger he called to the men in the forepart of the ship to cut the ropes (by which the ships were fastened together) and let them loose; they did so. The king's men threw their grappling hooks on the club-formed beaks of the prow, and thus held them fast. Then the jarl bade the men in the prow cut off the beaks, which they did. Einar Thambarskelfir had laid his ship on the other side of the jarl's, and cast an anchor into the prow of the jarl's ship, and thus they got out on the fjord" (St. Olaf's Saga, c. 48).

"At this time there was a great war in Norway; Harald Lúfa, the son of Halfdan Svarti (black), was subduing the country. . . . . When he came to Hördaland a mass of warriors met to fight him. . . . . Both sides had many men. This was one of the greatest battles in Norway; most Sagas mention it, for there came men from the whole country, and many from other countries, with a great number of Vikings. Önund laid his ship at the side of that of Thorir Chinlong, which was nearly in the middle of the fleet. King Harald with his ship attacked that of Thorir Chinlong, who was known as the greatest berserk and very valiant. There ensued the severest fights on both sides. The king urged his berserks to attack; they were called Ulfhednar (the wolf-skin coats), and no weapons wounded them; and when they rushed forward nothing withstood them. Thorir defended himself very manfully and fell on his ship with great valour; it was cleared of men from stem to stern, and as the ropes were cut it drifted backward between the others. The king's men then attacked the ship of Önund; he was in the fore part of the ship, and fought bravely. The king's men said: ' That man fights hard in the stem ; let us give him some mark in memory of his having been in the battle.' Önund was standing with one of his feet on the side of the ship, and as he dealt a man a blow a spear was thrust at him ; as he parried the blow he bent backwards, when one of the king's stem-defenders cut off his leg below the knee, after which he could fight no more. The greater part of the men on his ship fell. Önund was carried on board the ship of Thrand, the son of Björn and brother of Eyvind Eastman ; he was against King Harald, and lay on one side of Önund's ship. After this the main fleet broke into flight. Thrand, and the other Vikings who were able to, got away and sailed westward. Önund, as well as Balki and Hallvard Súgandi (gush of wind), went with him. When he was healed he afterwards walked with a wooden leg ; from this he was called Önund tree-foot while he lived " (Gretti's Saga, c. 2).

We see that at that period expeditions to and from the west were common.

The battle at the river Helga (Sweden) is thus described :—

" One evening the spies of Onund saw Knut sailing not far off. Önund let a war blast be blown. His men took down their tents, armed themselves, and rowed out of the harbour (at the mouth of the river) and eastwards along the coast ; they laid their ships side by side and tied them together, and made ready for battle. Önund sent spies ashore to tell Olaf, who had the dam broken and let the river into its bed. He then went down to his ships in the night. When Knut came off the harbour, he saw the host of the kings ready for battle. It seemed to him it would be too late in the day to begin a battle, as the whole of his host was not ready. His fleet needed much space for sailing, and there was a long way between his foremost and hindmost ship, and the outermost and the one next to the land. There was little wind. When he saw the Swedes and Northmen had left the harbour, he went in with such ships as could get room there, but the greater part of his host lay out on the sea (outside the harbour). Next morning, when it was almost day, many of their men were on land, some talking, others at their games. They suspected nothing until the water rushed down upon them like a torrent ; large timbers followed, and were driven against their ships ; these were damaged, and the water flowed all over the fields ; the men on land, and also many of those on the ships, lost their lives. All who could, cut their anchor-ropes, and the ships drifted in great disorder. The large dragon, on which the king was, floated out with the current; it was not easy to move it with oars, and it drifted out to the fleet of the kings. When they recognized it, they at once surrounded it. As the ship had sides as high as the walls of a burgh, and many chosen and well-armed men were on board, it was not easy to capture it. After a short time Ulf jarl came up with his ships, and the battle began. Thereupon the host of Knut gathered from all sides. Then Olaf and Önund saw that they had gained as much advantage as was then possible; they pulled back and got loose from the host of Knut, and separated the fleets. Because this attack had not been as Knut had ordered, he did not row after them; they began to array the ships and make themselves ready. When they had separated, and each fleet was mustered, the kings counted their men, and found that they had not lost many; they saw also that the odds would be so great if they waited till Knut had made ready all his great host, and attacked them, that there was little hope of victory. They decided to row with all their ships eastward along the coast " (St. Olaf, c. 106).[1]

Before the conflict the sides of the ships were strengthened by *viggyrdil* (war-girdle) or *vigfleki* (war-hurdle).

" King Sverri was at Bergen (Björgyn) with his host, and all his ships lay ready and war-girdled at the gangways" (Sverri's Saga, c. 52).

When King Svein of Denmark was pursuing King Harald with an overwhelming force,

" He (Harald) bid the men lighten his (ship) by throwing overboard malt, wheat, and pork, and to cut holes in the ale-barrels: this helped awhile. Then he had *viggyrdils*, vats, and empty barrels, as well as the prisoners of war, thrown into the sea " (Harald Hardradi's Saga, c. 35).

" We will carry out on the boards (i.e. the sides of the ship) *vigfleki*, and defend ourselves as best we can, but not attack them " (Flateyjarbok).

A man with his shields protected the rowers from the missiles of the enemy; but in spite of this, many were often killed.

---

[1] Cf. also St. Olaf, 185, 186 ; Njala, c. 30.

Three men were generally stationed in each *half-room*, one for rowing, one for protecting the rower, and one for fighting.

Erling Skakki said to King Ingi: "If we now attack them and row against the current, and have three men in every *half-room*, then one must row, the other protect him, and we shall then have not more than one-third of our host in the fight" (Hakon Herdibreid's Saga, c. 6).

"When the men on board the jarl's ships began to fall and get wounded, and the line of men on their gunwales got thin, King Olaf's men went on board. Their standard was carried on board the ship next to the jarl's, and followed by the king himself" (St. Olaf's Saga, ch. 48).

Stones were extensively used in sea fights.

Svein Ulfsson,[1] King of Denmark, fought a battle outside Árós (Aarhus) against King Magnus of Norway, of which it is said,

"Svein's men armed themselves and tied together their ships. There at once ensued a hard battle. . . . They fought in the stems. Only those who stood there could reach to use their swords; those who stood in the fore-room used *kesjas* (a kind of lance), and those still farther aft shorter javelins or large arrows; some threw stones with slings, while those who were aft of the mast used bows" (Magnus the Good, c. 31).

"A battle was fought at the mouth of the Gauta river between the kings Ingi and Hakon; there were thrown down on them *kesjas* (spears), and stones so large, that they were forced to retreat" (Hakon Herdibreid's Saga, c. 2).

Cables were stretched across the mouths of rivers or harbours, in order to prevent the ships of the enemy from entering.

"Olaf went to Saudungssund and lay there; he stationed one ship on each side of the Sound, and had a thick cable stretched between them. Hakon jarl (son of Eirik who was son of the famous Hakon jarl) rowed shortly after into the Sound with a manned skeid. He thought that two trading vessels were in the Sound, so rowed into it between them. Olaf's men drew the cable under the middle of the keel of the skeid, and hauled it with windlasses; as soon as it touched the skeid its stern was lifted,

---

[1] *Svein Ulfsson* was the son of Ulf jarl and Astrid, the sister of Knut the Great. He carried on long war against King Magnus the Good, and at last was acknowledged as King of Denmark. This was about the middle of the 11th century.

and the prow plunged forwards so that the sea came in ; the ship was filled and upset " (St. Olaf's Saga, c. 28).

The country was divided into *skipreida*, or ship levy districts, in Norway, and no doubt there were similar divisions in the other countries of the Northmen. Every skipreida had to build, equip, and man a certain number of ships, some more than others.

Leidangr was the term applied to a levy of men, ships, and money. A levy when necessary was effected in the following manner.

" When a ship has been loosened from its fastenings and a man has not come in to his half-room then his oar shall be raised (= stand with its blade into the air), and witnesses called that he is liable to pay a fine of three marks (merkur). If a man goes on board another ship than the one he should go to he shall row in the expedition of the levy and (besides) pay the fine " (Gulath, 301).

" Olaf summoned a Thing in the town (Nidarós). He made it known to all people that he wanted to have a levy that summer from the country ; he wanted a certain number of men and ships from each Fylki ; he stated how many ships he wished to have from the fjord (Trondhjemsfjord). Then he sent word southwards and northwards along the coast and inland, and summoned men for war. He had the Long Serpent launched, and all his other ships, small and large " (Olaf Tryggvason's Saga, c. 107, Heimskringla).

" Hakon Jarl had also equipped his men, intending to do warfare, and had twelve large ships. After Gull Harald had departed, Hakon Jarl went to the king and said : ' Now we may go on the expedition, and nevertheless have to pay the fine for default in the levy (leidviti). Now Gull Harald will slay Harald Gráfeld, and then take the kingship in Norway ' " (Olaf Tryggvason's Saga, vol. i., Fornmanna Sögur).

Leidviti was the tax which was paid instead of the leidangr, when the latter was not needed, being originally the fine for neglecting to participate in leidangr. It was also paid by the one who took part in the warfare, but on the wrong ship. It seems to be the latter which the jarl refers to—a warfare with loss, in consequence of lack of forethought.

CHAPTER III.

SEA BATTLES.

The battle of Svold—The battle of the Jomsvikings.

THE two most famous sea-fights which are related in the Sagas are those of *Svold* and *Jomsvikings;* the former of which took place between Olaf Tryggvason against King Svein of Denmark, Olaf of Sweden, and Eirik jarl of Norway. When Olaf Tryggvason had left *Vindland* (the land of the Wends), and was returning to Norway, his enemies were waiting in ambush in order to attack him, and thus was fought the battle of Svold.

"Svein King of Denmark, Olaf King of Sweden, and Eirik jarl lay under the island with all their host. The weather was fine and the sunshine was bright. All the chiefs went up on the island, and many of the host with them. When they saw that very many of the ships of the North-men sailed out to sea they were very glad, for their host grumbled at lying there so long, and some had lost all hope of the King of Norway's coming. Now they saw a large and splendid ship sailing, and both the kings said: 'This is a large and exceedingly fine ship; it must be the Long Serpent.' Eirik jarl answered: 'This is not the Long Serpent, which must look larger and grander, though this is a large and fine ship.' It was as the jarl said. Styrkár of Gimsar owned the ship. Shortly after they saw another much larger ship, which had a head on its prow. King Svein said: 'This must be the Long Serpent; let us now go to our ships and not be too slow in attack.' Eirik jarl replied: 'This cannot be the Long Serpent, though it is finely fitted out.' It was as he said, for it belonged to Thorkel Nefja, King Olaf's brother; but he was not on board himself. And now they saw another large and fine ship. King Svein said: 'There you can see the king's ship.' The jarl replied: 'Certainly this is a large and splendid ship, but the Serpent must be much grander.' Close upon it came a fourth large ship. The two last were owned by two men of Vikin,

Thorgeir and Hyrning, the king's brothers-in-law ; but they did not steer the ships, for they were on the Long Serpent with King Olaf. A little while after appeared a fifth, much larger than any of the preceding. King Svein said, laughing : 'Now is Olaf Tryggvason afraid, for he dares not sail with the head on his dragon.'[1] Eirik jarl replied : 'This is not the king's ship ; this one I know well, as well as the sail which is striped ; it belongs to Erling Skjalgsson. of Jadar ; let them sail on, for I tell you truly that there are warriors on board, whom, if we go into battle with Olaf Tryggvason, it is better not to have, but to miss in his fleet, than to have it manned as it is, for I think Erling himself steer it.' It was not long after these five large ships and all the small ones of the fleet had sailed past them that they recognised Sigvaldi jarl's ships, which turned in towards the island. They saw there three ships, and one of these was a large headship (i.e. a ship having a head on the stem) ; then said King Svein : 'Let us now go to the ships, for here comes the Long Serpent.' Eirik jarl answered : 'Many other large and splendid ships have they besides the Long Serpent, but few have yet sailed past ; let us still wait.' Then many said : 'Now we may see that Eirik will not fight against Olaf Tryggvason, and dares not avenge his father ; and this is such a great shame that it will spread over all lands, if we lie here with such a large host, and Norway's king sails with his handful of men past us and out to sea.' Eirik jarl became very angry at their words, and asked all to go to the ships, saying : 'I expect, though the Danes and Swedes now question my courage much, that both of them will be less at their ease before the sun goes down into the sea to-night than I and my men.' When they went down they saw four large ships sailing, one of which was a dragon-ship much ornamented with gold. Many men said that the jarl had spoken the truth. Here now sails the Long Serpent, and it is a very large and fine ship ; no long ship is similar to it in beauty and size in the northern lands. It is not strange that the king is widely renowned, and is so great as to have such grand things made. King Svein arose and said : 'High shall the Serpent carry me to-night. Him will I steer.' Eirik jarl added : 'Even if King Olaf Tryggvason had no larger ship than the one we just now saw ; King Svein would never win it from him with the Dana host alone.' But these large head ships they thought to be the Long Serpent, the first was the Tranan (the crane), and the second the Ormrinn Skammi (the short serpent). The men crowded to the ships, and pulled down the tents, and the

---

[1] This refers to a general superstition.

chiefs arranged the host for attack, and it is said that they threw lots who should first attack Olaf's own ship, the Long Serpent. Svein King of Denmark drew the lot to attack first, and Olaf King of Sweden and Eirik jarl last, if they needed it ; and it was agreed between the chiefs, King Svein, King Olaf, and Eirik jarl, that each should become owner of one-third of Norway if they slew King Olaf; while he who first got up on the Serpent should own all the booty there was on board, and each should own the ships which he himself captured and cleared of men. Eirik jarl had a very large Bardi which he used to have on Viking expeditions ; there were beaks on the top of both stem and stern, and below these was a thick iron plate which covered the whole of the stem and stern all the way down to the water.

" When the chiefs had talked thus between themselves they saw three very large ships, and following them a fourth. They all saw a large dragon's head on the stem, ornamented so that it seemed made of pure gold, and it gleamed far and wide over the sea as the sun shone on it. As they looked at the ship they wondered greatly at its length, for the stern did not appear till long after they had seen the prow [1] ; then all knew and no one gainsaid that this was the Long Serpent. At this sight many a man grew silent, and fear and terror crept into the breast of the host. This was not strange, for the great ship carried death for many men. Then said Eirik jarl : 'This famous ship is befitting such a king as Olaf Tryggvason ; for it is true of him that he excels other kings as much as the Long Serpent does other ships.'

" When Sigvaldi jarl had let down the sails on his ships and rowed up to the island, Thorkel Dydril on the Tranan and other ship-steerers who went with him saw that he turned his ships towards the island ; they lowered their sails and followed him. Thorkel shouted to Sigvaldi, asking why he did not sail. The jarl replied he would wait there for King Olaf. They let their ships float until Thorkel Nefja arrived with the Short Serpent and the four ships which followed him ; they also lowered their sails, and let their ships float, waiting for the king.

" The fleet of the kings lay inside the harbour, so that they could not see how large a host they had ; but when King Olaf sailed towards the island and saw that his men had lowered their sails and waited for him, he steered towards them and asked why they did not go on. They told him that a host of foes was before them, and requested him to flee. The king

---

[1] The Serpent glided past the point of the island slowly.

stood on the lypting while he heard these tidings, and said to his men : ' Let down the sail as quickly as possible, and some of you put out the oars to take the speed off the ship. I will rather fight than flee, for never yet have I fled from battle ; my life is in God's power, but never will I take to flight, for he is not a true king who in fear flies from his foes.' It was done as the king said, and the Serpent ran in front of the ships, and the men of the other ships brought them ahead by pulling with their oars. Then the entire host of the kings rowed out from under the island ; and the chiefs were very glad when they found that King Olaf had fallen into their ambush.

" When King Olaf Tryggvason and his men saw that the sea was covered far and wide with the war-ships of their foes, a wise and valiant man, Thorkel Dydril, his uncle, said : ' Lord, here is an overwhelming force to fight against ; let us hoist our sails and follow our men out to sea. We can still do so while our foes prepare themselves for battle, for it is not looked upon as cowardice by any one for a man to use forethought for himself or his men.' King Olaf replied loudly : ' Tie together the ships, and let the men prepare for battle and draw their swords, for my men shall not think of flight.' The chiefs arranged the host for attack, and it is said that they threw lots, who should first attack Olaf's ship, the Long Serpent. Svein drew the lot to attack first, then Olaf and Eirik jarl last if it was needed.

" King Olaf signalled by horn to lay the eleven ships together which he had there. The Long Serpent was in the middle, with the Short Serpent on one side and the Crane on the other, and four other ships on each side of them. But this ship-host, though he had large ships, was only a small detachment compared to the overwhelming host which his enemies had. He now missed his host, as it was likely.

" King Olaf's men now tied together the ships as bid ; but when he saw that they began to tie together the stems of the Long Serpent and the Short Serpent, he called out loudly : ' Bring forward the large ship ; I will not be the hindmost of all my men in this host when the battle begins.'

" Then Ulf the red, the king's standard bearer and his stem defender, said : ' If the Serpent shall be put as much forward as it is larger and longer than the other ships, the men in the bows will have a hard time of it.' The king answered : ' I had the Serpent made longer than other ships, so that it should be put forward more boldly in battle, and be well known in fighting and sailing, but I did not know that I had a stem defender who was both red and faint-headed.' Ulf replied :

'Turn thou, king, no more than back forward in defending the lypting than I will in defending the stem.' The king had a bow in his hand, and laid an arrow on the string and aimed at Ulf. Then Ulf said : 'Do not shoot me, lord, but rather where it is more needed, that is at our foes, for what I win I win for thee. May be you will think your men not over many, before the evening comes.' The king took off the arrow and did not shoot.

"King Ólaf stood on the lypting of the Serpent, and rose high up; he had a gilt shield and a gilt helmet, and was very easily recognised. He wore a short red silk kirtle over his coat of mail. When he saw that the hosts of his foes began to separate, and that the standards were raised in front of the chiefs, he asked : 'Who is chief of that standard which is opposite us?' He was told that it was King Svein with the Danish host. The king said: 'We are not afraid of those cowards, for no more courage is there in the Danes than in wood-goats ; never were Danes victorious over Northmen, and they will not conquer us to-day. But what chief follows the standards which are to the right?' He was told that it was Olaf the Swede, with the Svia host. The king added : ' Easier and pleasanter will the Swedes think it to sit at home and lick their sacrifice bowls[1] than to board the Long Serpent to-day under your weapons, and I think we need not fear the horse-eating Swedes ; but who owns those large ships to the left of the Danes?' 'It is,' they said, 'Eirik jarl Hakonsson.' King Olaf replied : 'This host is full of high-born men whom they have ranged against us ; Eirik jarl thinks he has just cause for fighting us, it is likely we shall have a hard struggle with him and his men, for they are Northmen like ourselves.' Then the kings and the jarl rowed at King Olaf. . . . The horns were blown, and both sides shouted a war-cry, and a hard battle commenced. Sigvaldi let his ships row to and fro, and did not take part in the battle.

"The battle raged fiercely, at first with arrows from cross-bows and hand-bows, and then with spears and javelins, and all say that King Olaf fought most manfully. . . .

"King Svein's men turned their stems as thickly as they could towards both sides of the Long Serpent, as it stood much further forward than the other ships of King Olaf; the Danes also attacked the Short Serpent and the Crane, and the fight was of the sharpest, and the carnage great. All the stem-defenders on the Serpent who could fought hand-to-hand, but King Olaf himself and those aft shot with bows and used

---

[1] Sacrifice lasted longer in Sweden than in Norway or Denmark.

short swords (handsax), and repeatedly killed and wounded the Danir.

"Though King Svein made the hardest onset on the Northmen with sixty ships, the Danish and Swedish hosts nevertheless were incessantly within shooting distance; King Olaf made the bravest defence with his men, but still they fell. King Olaf fought most boldly, he shot chiefly with bows and spears, but when the chief attack was made on the Serpent he went forward in hand-to-hand fight, and cleft many a man's skull with his sword.

"The attack proved difficult for the Danes, for the stem-defenders of the Long Serpent and on the Short Serpent and the Crane hooked anchors and grappling-hooks on to King Svein's ships, and as they could strike down (upon the enemy) with their weapons, for they had much larger and higher-boarded ships, they cleared of men all the Danish ships which they had laid hold of. King Svein and all who could get away fled on board other ships, and thereupon they withdrew, tired and wounded, out of shooting distance. It happened as Olaf Tryggvason guessed, that the Danes did not gain a victory over the Northmen.

"It happened to the Swedes as to the Danes, that the Northmen held fast their ships with grappling-hooks and anchors, and cleared those they could reach. Their swords dealt one fate to all Swedes whom they reached with their blows. The Swedes became tired of keeping up the fight where Olaf with his picked champions went at them most fiercely. . . . Men say that the sharpest and bloodiest fight was that of the two namesakes before Olaf and the Swedes retreated. The Swedes had a heavy loss of men, and also lost their largest ships. Most of the warriors of Olaf the Swedish king were wounded, and he had won no fame by this, but was fain to escape alive. Now Olaf Tryggvason had made both the Danes and Swedes take to flight. It all went as he had said.

"Now must be told what Eirik Jarl did while the kings fought against Norway's king. The Jarl first came alongside the farthest ship of King Olaf on one wing with the Járnbardi (iron-board), cleared it, and cut it from the fastenings; he then boarded the next one, and fought there until it was cleared. The men then began to jump from the smaller ships on to the larger ones, but the Jarl cut away each ship from the fastenings as it was cleared.

"The Danes and Swedes then drew up within shooting distance on all sides of King Olaf's ships, but Eirik Jarl lay continually side by side with one of them in hand-to-hand fight; and as the men fell on his ship, other Danes and Swedes took their places. Then the battle was both hard and sharp and many of King Olaf's men fell.

"At last all Olaf's ships had been cleared except the Long Serpent, which carried all the men who were able to fight. Eirik Jarl then attacked the Serpent with five large ships. He laid the Járnbardi alongside the Serpent, and then ensued the fiercest fight and the most terrible hand-to-hand struggle that could be. . . .

"Eirik Jarl was in the foreroom of his ship, where a shield-burgh was drawn up. There was both hand-to-hand fight and spear-throwing and every kind of weapon was thrown, and whatever could be seized by the hand. Some shot with bows or with their hands, and such a shower of weapons was poured upon the Serpent that the men could hardly protect themselves against it. Then spears and arrows flew thickly, for on all sides of the Serpent lay warships. King Olaf's men now became so furious that they jumped upon the gunwales in order to reach their foes with their swords and kill them, but many did not lay their ships so close to the Serpent as to get into the hand-to-hand fight, most of them thought it hard to deal with Olaf's champions

"The Northmen thought of nothing but continually going forward to slay their foes, and many went straight overboard; for out of eagerness and daring they forgot that they were not fighting on dry ground, and many sank down with their weapons between the ships. . . .

"King Olaf Tryggvason stood on the lypting of the Serpent, and chiefly used during the day his bow and javelins; and always two javelins at a time. It was agreed by all, both friends and foes, who were present, and those who have heard these tidings told with the greatest truth, that they have known no man fight more valiantly than King Olaf Tryggvason. King Olaf surpassed most other kings, in that he made himself so easily known in the battle that men knew no example of any king having shown himself so openly to his foes, especially as he had to fight against such an overwhelming force. The king showed the bravery of his mind, and the pride of his heart, so that all men might see that he shunned no danger. The better he was seen and the greater lack of fear he showed in the battle, the greater fear and terror he inspired.

"King Olaf saw that his men on the fore part of the ship frequently raised their swords to strike, and that the swords cut badly. He cried out: 'Why do you raise your swords so slowly? I see they do not bite?' A man replied: 'Our swords are both dull and broken, lord.' The king then went down from the lypting into the foreroom and unlocked the high-seat chest, and took therefrom many bright and sharp swords, which he gave to his men. As he put down his right hand they saw that blood flowed out of the sleeve of the coat-of-mail, but no one knew where he was wounded.

"Hard and bloody was the defence of the foreroom men and the stem-defenders, for in both those places the gunwale was highest and the men picked. When the fall of men began on the Serpent, it was first amidships, mostly from wounds and exhaustion, and men say that if these brave men could have kept up their defence the Serpent would never have been won.

"When only a few were left on the Serpent around the mast amidships, Eirik Jarl boarded it with fourteen men. Then came against him the king's brother-in-law, Hyrning, with his followers, and between them ensued a hard struggle, for Hyrning fought very boldly. It thus ended that Eirik Jarl retreated on to the Bardi; but of those who had followed him, some fell, and some were wounded; and Hyrning (Thor image) and Eirik Jarl became much renowned from this fight. . . .

"Eirik Jarl took off the Bardi the dead and wounded, and in their stead brought fresh and rested men, whom he selected from among Swedes and Danes. It is also said by some that the Jarl had promised to let himself be baptized if he won the Serpent; and it is a proof of their statement that he threw away Thor and put up in his place a crucifix in the stem of the Bardi. When he had prepared his men, he said to a wise and powerful chief who was present, Thorkel the high, brother of Sigvaldi Jarl: 'Often have I been in battles, and never have I before found men equally brave and so skilled in fighting as those on the Serpent, nor have I seen a ship so hard to win. Now as thou art one of the wisest of men, give me the best advice thou knowest how the Serpent may be won.' Thorkel replied: 'I cannot give thee sure advice thereon, but I can say what seems to me best to do. Thou must take large timbers, and let them fall from thy ship upon the gunwale of the Serpent, so that it will lean over; you will then find it easier to board the Serpent, if its gunwale is no higher than those of the other ships. I can give thee no other advice, if this will not do.' The Jarl carried out what Thorkel had told him. . . .

"When Eirik Jarl was ready he attacked the Serpent a second time, and all the Danish and Swedish host again made an onset on King Olaf Tryggvason; the Swedes placed their prows close to the Serpent, but the greatest part of the host was within shooting distance of the Northmen, and shot at them incessantly. The Jarl again laid the Bardi side by side with the Serpent, and made a very sharp onslaught with fresh men ; neither did he spare himself in the battle, nor those of his men who were left.

"King Olaf and his men defended themselves with the utmost bravery and manliness, so that there was little increase in the fall of men on the Serpent while they were fresh ; they slew many of their foes, both on the Járnbardi and on other ships which lay near the Serpent. As the fight still went against Eirik Jarl, he hoisted large timbers on the Bardi, which fell on the Serpent. It is believed that the Serpent would not have been won but for this, which had been advised by Thorkel the high.

"The Serpent began to lean over very much when the large timbers were dropped on one gunwale, and thereupon many fell on both sides. When the defenders of the Serpent began to thin, Eirik boarded it and met with a warm reception.

"When King Olaf's stem-defenders saw that the Jarl had got up on the Serpent, they went aft and turned against him, and made a very hard resistance ; but then so many began to fall on the Serpent, that the gunwales were in many places deserted, and the Jarl's men boarded them ; and all the men who were standing up for defence withdrew aft to where the king was. Haldór (a poet) says that the jarl urged on his men.

"It is said that Thorstein Uxafót was in the foreroom aft by the lypting,[1] and said to the king, when the Jarl's men came thickest on board the Serpent : 'Lord, each man must now do what he can ?' 'Why not ?' answered the king. Thorstein struck with his fist one of the Jarl's men, who jumped up on the gunwale near him ; he hit his cheek so hard that he dropped out into the sea, and at once perished. After this Thorstein became so enraged, that he took up the sailyard and fought with it. When the king saw this, he said to Thorstein : 'Take thy weapons, man, and defend thyself with them ; for weapons, and not hands alone or timber, are meant for men to fight with in battle.' Thorstein then took his sword, and fought valiantly. There was still a most fierce fight in the foreroom, and King Olaf shot from the lypting javelins or spears, both hard and often. When he saw that Eirik Jarl had come into the foreroom of the Serpent, he shot at him with three short-handled *kesjas* (a kind of spear), but they did not go as usual (for he never missed his aim when shooting), and none of these *kesjas*

---

[1] As a rule the foreroom (*fyrirrúm*) seems to have been before the mast, but on the Long Serpent this was not the case, as we can see from the above sentence, for there it was immediately in front of the *lypting* (poop).

hit the Jarl. The first flew past his right side, the second his left, and the third flew on to the forepart of the ship above the Jarl's head. Then the king said: 'Never before did I thus miss a man; great is the Jarl's hamingia (luck); it must be God's will that he now shall rule in Norway; and that is not strange, for I think he has changed the *stem-dweller* on the Bardi. I said to-day that he would not gain victory over us, if he had Thor in the stem.'

" As many of the Jarl's men had got up on board the Serpent as could be there, and his ships lay on all sides of it, and but few remained for defence against such a host. In a short time many of King Olaf's champions fell, though they were both strong and valiant. There fell both the king's brothers-in-law, Hyrning and Thorgeir, Vikar of Tiundaland, Úlf the red, and many other brave men, who left a famous name behind.

" Kolbjörn Stallari (Marshal) had defended the stem during the day with the other stem-defenders; he had weapons and clothing very much like King Olaf, and he had dressed so because he thought that, if necessary, as it now was, he might save the life of the king. When the most valiant of the king's men in the foreroom began to fall, Kolbjörn went up on the lypting to the king. It was not easy to tell them apart, for Kolbjörn was a very large and handsome man. There was then such a thick shower of weapons in the lypting, that the shields of King Olaf and Kolbjörn were covered all over with arrows. But when the Jarl's men came up to the lypting, it seemed to them that so much light came over the king that they could not see through it, yet when the light vanished they saw King Olaf nowhere" (Olaf Tryggvason's Saga, Fornmanna Sögur, ii., 299–332).

The Battle of the Jomsvikings arose out of a vow made by Sigvaldi, at the *arvel* given by King Svein Tjuguskegg (forked beard) for Strut Harald Jarl, that he would rule Norway.

" The Jomsvikings went northward along the coast, plundering and ravaging wherever they landed. They made great coast raids, slew many men, and often burned towns; all, who heard of them and could flee, fled. When they were at Úlfasund, off Stad, it is said that they and Hakon jarl heard of each other. They sailed twenty sea-miles northward from Stad, and entered the harbour at Hereyjar, and laid all their fleet therein. Then they were in want of food again, and Vagn Ákason went on his skeid to the island Höd, not knowing that the jarl lay in the bay, near the island. Vagn landed.

They went up, wishing to make a shore raid if they could. They happened to meet a man driving three cows and twelve goats. Vagn asked for his name. He said it was Úlf. Vagn said to his men : 'Take the cows and the goats and slaughter them, and any other cattle you may find here, for our ship.' Úlf asked : 'Who commands the men on board this ship?' 'Vagn Ákason,' was the answer. Úlf said : 'I think there are, not very far from you, bigger cattle for slaughter than my cows or goats.' Vagn said : 'If thou knowest anything about the journey of Hakon jarl tell us, and, if thou canst tell us with truth where he is, thy cows and goats are safe ; what knowest thou about him ?' Úlf answered : 'He lay with one ship late yesterday night inside of the island Höd, in Hjörungavag, and you can slay him when you like, for he is waiting for his men.' Vagn said : 'Then all thy cattle are safe ; come on board our ship, and show us the way to the jarl.' Úlf said : 'That is not right for me, and I will not fight against the jarl, but if you wish I will show you the way into the bay ; and, if I go on board, you must promise to let me go when you see your way into the bay.' Úlf went on board early in the day, and Vagn, as quickly as he could, went back to Hereyjar, and told Sigvaldi and the Jomsvikings the news that Úlf told.

"The Jomsvikings made themselves ready as if they were to go into a most fierce battle, though Úlf said it was not needed. When they were quite ready they rowed towards the bay. It is said that Úlf thought they would see more ships there than he had told of. When the ships came into sight, Úlf jumped overboard and wanted to swim to the shore and not wait for his reward. When Vagn saw this he wished to give him what he deserved, snatched a spear and threw it after him ; it hit him in the middle and killed him. All the Jomsvikings rowed into the bay, and saw that it was covered all over with warships. There were more than three hundred ships, snekkjas and skeids and trading-ships. The Jomsvikings at once arrayed their ships. Hakon and his sons saw the Jomsvikings come, and at once unfastened their ships and said which were to fight against which. It is told that the upper end of Hjörungavag is to the east, and its mouth to the west ; three rocks, one larger than the two others, stand in the bay ; they are called Hjörungs, and the bay is named from them. There is a reef in the middle of the bay at the same distance from the shore in three directions. An island called Primsigd is north of the bay, and Harund is south of it, off Harundarfjord.

"The Jomsvikings arrayed their ships thus : Sigvaldi laid his ship in the middle, Thorkel the high, his brother, laid his next thereto; Búi the stout and Sigurd Kápa, his brother, had theirs in the one wing of the array, and Vagn Ákason and Björn the British in the other. Hakon jarl determined who should fight against these champions, and in most places three were placed against one. As to their array, Svein, son of Hakon, was placed against Sigvaldi; three chiefs were arrayed against Thorkel the high, Yrjaskeggi, Sigurd Steikling, Thórir Hjört (stag); two were with Svein Hakonarson against Sigvaldi, Gudbrand of Dalir, and Styrkár of Gimsar. Against Búi were Hallstein Kerlingabani, and Thorkel Leira and Thorkel Midlang (iendirmen). Against Sigurd Kápa were Ármód of Önundarfjord and his son Árni. Against Vagn Ákason were Eirík jarl Hakonarson, Erling of Skuggi, and Ögmund the white, whose hand Vagn cut off. Against Björn the British were Einar the little, Hávard Uppsjá, and Hallvard of Flydrunes, Hávard's brother; Hakon himself was not arrayed against any one, but had to support the whole line and command it.

"The fleets closed, and Hakon jarl was with his son Svein to support him against Sigvaldi. A most fierce fight began, and one could find no fault with the onset or attack of either; it is told that it went equally with Sigvaldi and Hakon and Svein, so that neither moved backwards. Then Hakon jarl saw that Búi had forced back a long way some of the northern wing of their array, and those who fought against him drew back with their ships, and thought it better to retreat; he followed up, nevertheless, and dealt heavy blows; they were ill-treated by him, and he was dangerous to men in the battle. The Jarl saw that the fight was equal with Eirík and Vagn in the southern wing. Eirík went thence with his own ship, and his brother Svein with another, up to Búi and fought against him, and put the wing in line again, but could do no more. Hakon meanwhile fought against Sigvaldi, and when Eirík came back to the southern wing Vagn had forced back many of Eirík's ships, which had retreated and had been separated, so that Vagn went through the line and attacked them fiercely. Eirík became very angry when he saw this, and boarded the skeid which Vagn steered valiantly with his Járnbardi. They came alongside of each other and fought again, and never had the fight been harder than then. Vagn and Áslák Hólmskalli jumped on board Eirík's Járnbardi from their skeid, and each went along the side of the ship, and Áslák dealt blows on both sides, so to speak, as also did Vagn, and they cleared their way so that all fell back. Eirík saw that these men were so fierce and mad that this would not last long, and that the Jarl's help must be got as quick as possible. Áslák was bald and had no helmet on his head, and exposed his bare skull; the weather was bright, clear, and warm, and many took off their clothes on account of the heat, and wore only their armour. Now Eirík goaded his men on, and they made an attack on Áslák, and struck his head with swords and axes, thinking it would be most dangerous to him as his head was bare. Nevertheless it is said that the weapons rebounded from his skull, whether they were swords or axes, and did not cut, and sparks flew from the skull at the blows. Whatever they did, he went forward fiercely, and cleared his way by many hard and heavy blows, slaying many a man. Vigfús, son of Vígaglúm, caught up a large beaked anvil which lay on the deck of the Járnbardi, on which he had previously rivetted the guards of his sword as they had been unfastened; he struck at Áslák so that its beak sank into his head; Áslák could not withstand that, and at once fell dead. Vagn went along the other side, and cleared his way, dealing blows on both sides and wounding many; then Thorleif Skúma ran to meet Vagn, struck at him with his club, and hit his helmet; the blow was so strong that the skin under the helmet was grazed, and Vagn leant over and staggered towards Thorleif, and at the same time thrust his sword at Thorleif; then he leapt from the Járnbardi, and came down standing on his skeid, and none made a harder onset than he and all his men. Nevertheless he and Áslák had killed so many on the Járnbardi, that Eirík put men from other ships on it till it was fully manned, as he thought it needful; and a very fierce fight followed. Then Eirík saw that Hakon with his array had landed, and there was some pause in the battle. . . .[1] The sky began to darken in the north, and a dark and black cloud glided up from the sea, spreading quickly; it was about noon. and the cloud soon spread all over the sky, and a shower of hail followed at once, and the Jomsvikings had all to fight with their faces against the hail, which seemed to be followed by lightning and thunder-claps. This hail-shower was so terrible, that some of the men could do no more than stand against it, as they had previously taken off their clothes on account of the heat. They began to shiver, though they fought boldly enough. It is said that Hávard Höggvandi, Búi's follower, was the first who saw Hördabrúd in the host of Hakon jarl, and many with second sight,[2] and even those who had no second sight, saw. When the hail-shower abated a little, they also saw that an arrow flew from each finger of the Troll, 'M'tch' as it seemed to them, and always hit and killed a man. They told Sigvaldi and others; and Hakon and his men

---

[1] Part is here omitted, referring to the sacrifice of Hakon's son. See Vol. I., page 367, "Sacrifices."

[2] A man who can see supernatural beings.

made the hardest onset they could when the shower burst and while it lasted. Then Sigvaldi said : 'It seems to me that it is not men whom we have to fight to-day, but the worst Troll (fiends), and it requires some manliness to go boldly against them, though it is clear that men must take heart as they can.' It is told of Hakon, that when he saw the shower abate and it was not as violent as it had been, he once more invoked Thorgerd and her sister Irpa, saying that he had made himself deserving by sacrificing his son for victory. Then the hail-shower burst on them again, and when it began Havard Höggvandi saw that two women were in Hakon jarl's ship, and that they did the same as he had seen the one do before. Sigvaldi said : 'Now I will flee, and all my men shall do so, for it is worse than when I spoke of it before, as there was but one Trollwoman then, but now there are two, and I will not stand it any longer ; our excuse is that we do not flee from men, though we draw back ; but we did not vow to fight against fiends.' He (Sigvaldi) turned away his ship, and shouted to Vagn and Búi to flee as quickly as they could. When he unfastened his ship and shouted, Thorkel Midlang jumped from his ship on board Búi's, and at once struck at Búi. In the twinkling of an eye he cut off his lower lip and the whole of his chin downward, so that it fell on the ship, and Búi's teeth flew off at the blow. Búi said when he got the wound : 'The Danish woman in Borgundarhólm will not be as fond of kissing me, even though I get home now.' Búi struck at Thorkel ; the deck was slippery from blood, so that Thorkel fell at the shield-row when he tried to escape the blow, which hit him in the middle, and cut him in two at the gunwale. Immediately after this Búi took one of his gold-chests in each hand, and jumped overboard with them ; neither he nor the chests came up or were seen thereafter. Some say that when Búi stepped on the gunwale to jump overboard he spoke these words : 'Overboard, all Búi's men.' Sigvaldi left the fleet, and did not know that Búi was gone overboard, and shouted to Vagn and Búi's to flee, as he was about to do. . . . Sigvaldi was cold from the shower, and began rowing to warm himself, while another man sat at the rudder. When Vagn saw Sigvaldi he flung a spear at him, thinking it was he who sat at the rudder, but Sigvaldi was rowing, and the man at the rudder was hit. As Vagn flung the spear from his hand he said to Sigvaldi that he should die as the meanest of men. Thorkel the high, Sigvaldi's brother, went away with six ships as soon as Sigvaldi was dead, and so did Sigurd Kápa, for his brother Búi was gone overboard, and he could wait for him no longer. They both thought they had fulfilled their vows, and went home to Denmark with twenty-four ships. All who could leave the remaining ships jumped on board Vagn's skeid, and there they defended themselves very valiantly till it was dark; then the battle ended, and very many were still on their feet in Vagn's skeid. Hakon jarl was overtaken by night and could not make a search as to how many were alive or likely to live in the ships, so he had a watch set during the night that no man should escape from them, and they took all the rigging down. Then Hakon rowed to the land, and pitched tents; they thought they had reason to boast of the victory. Then they weighed the hailstones in order to prove the power of Thorgerd and Irpa; it was well proved, for it is told that each hailstone weighed one eyrir, and they were weighed in scales. Thereafter the wounds of the men were dressed, and Hakon jarl and Gudbrand of Dalir watched during the night" (Jomsvikinga Saga, c. 41–44).

From the following account we see that these men of old knew how to die, and how the spirit of chivalry seemed to have departed from the land, though Eirik, the son of Hakon, at last stopped the bloodshed which had taken place. After the defeat of the Jómsvikings by Hakon jarl, eighty of the men who had not been captured landed on a skerry, and suffered great privations from the cold.

"Now it is to be told that Vagn and Björn the British talked of what they should do; Vagn said. 'There are two choices: to stay here in the ship till daybreak, and then be captured and that is not pleasant, or go ashore, and do them what harm we can, and then try to escape.' They all made up their minds, took the mast and the sailyard, left the ship and floated on them, eighty men together, in the dark. They wanted to get on land, and came to a skerry, and thought they were ashore. Many were very exhausted, and ten wounded men died there in the night, and the other seventy lived though many were much tired; and they could get no farther; they stayed there during the night. It is said that when Sigvaldi had fled the shower ceased, and all lightning and thunder, and the weather was cold and quiet during the night while Vagn was on the skerry till it was daylight.

"Shortly before day Hákon's men were dressing their wounds, and had been at it the whole night, beginning as soon as they landed, because so many were wounded. They had almost finished it, when they heard the twang of a bowstring in a ship, and an arrow flew from Búi's ship, and hit the side of Gudbrand, Hákon's kinsman; it was enough, and he died at once. The jarl and all thought this a great loss, and began preparing his body as well as they could, having no means to do it with. It is said that a man stood at the door of the tent. When Eirik went into it he asked: 'Why dost thou stand here, or why dost thou look as if thou wert dying; or art thou wounded?' It was Thorleif Skúma. Eirik said: 'I see thou art near to death.' Thorleif answered: 'I am not sure that the sword-point of Vagn Ákason did not hit me a little yesterday, when I struck him with the club.' The jarl sad: 'Badly has thy father kept his stock in Iceland if thou must die now.' Einar Skálaglamm heard what the jarl said, and made a stanza. . . . Thereupon Thorleif fell down dead.

" When it was light the jarl at once went to search the ships, and came on board Búi's ship, and wanted first of all to know who had shot in the night, thinking that that man deserved to be ill-treated. When they got on board they found one man, little more than breathing; it was Hávard höggvandi (the slashing), Búi's follower, sorely wounded, as both his feet were cut off below the knees. Svein Hákonarson and Thorkel Leira went to him; when they came, Hávard asked: 'How is it, boys; was anything sent from the ship this night ashore to you or not?' They answered: 'Certainly there came something; didst thou send it?' He said: 'I will not deny that I sent it to you; did the arrow hurt any man when it stopped?' They answered: 'It killed the man whom it hit.' He said: 'That is good; and whom did it hit?' 'Gudbrand the white,' they answered. 'He said: 'I did not succeed, then, in what I wished; I meant it for the jarl; nevertheless I am glad that a man was hit whose death is a loss to you.' Thorkel Leira said: 'Let us not look at this dog, but kill him as soon as we can.' He struck at him, and others ran thereto and cut him with weapons, and beat him till he was dead. Before that they had asked his name, and he told them.

"They went ashore after that, and told the jarl whom they had killed; that the man had been more than a common monster, and they had seen by his words that his character did not make him a better man. Then they saw that very many men were on the skerry; the jarl told them to go out to them and bring them all to him, as he wanted to have their lives in his power. The jarl's men went on board a ship, and rowed out to the skerry; few men there were able to fight, on account of wounds and cold, nor is it told that any one defended himself; they were all taken by the jarl's men ashore to him; they were seventy. Then the jarl had Vagn and his men led up on land, and their hands were tied behind their backs, and they were bound with one rope, one at the other's side, not loosely. The jarl and his men took their food, and sat down to eat; he wanted to have them all beheaded leisurely and in no hurry that day.

"Before they sat down to eat, the ships and the property of the Jómsvikings were taken ashore, and carried to the poles. Hákon and his men divided among themselves all the property, and the weapons; they thought they had won a great victory as they had got all the property captured from the Jómsvikings, and they boasted very much. When they had eaten enough, they walked out of the war-booths to the captives, and it is said that Thorkel Leira was appointed to behead them all. First they talked to the Jómsvikings, and asked whether they were as hardy men as was said; but it is not told that the Jómsvikings gave them any answer.

"It is next stated that some sorely wounded men were untied from the rope; Skopti Kark and other thralls had hold of it, and guarded them. When they were untied the thralls twisted sticks[1] in their hair; first three wounded men were led forward in that way, and Thorkel went to them and cut off each head; then he asked his own companions if they had seen him shudder at this work, 'for it is told,' said he, 'that any man shudders if he beheads three men one after the other.' Hákon answered: 'We do not see that thou hast shuddered at this, though it seemed so to me before thou didst it.'

The fourth man was led out of the rope, and a stick twisted in his hair, and he was led to where Thorkel beheaded them; he was much wounded. When he came Thorkel asked, before he struck, how he thought of his death. He answered: 'Well think I of my death; it will be with me as with my father; I shall die.' Thereupon Thorkel cut off that man's head, and thus his life ended. The fifth was untied from the rope and led thither; when he came, Thorkel said: 'How likest thou to die?' He said: 'I remember not the laws of the Jómsvikings, if I am afraid of my death or speak a word of fear; once must every man die.' Thorkel struck him. They wanted to ask every man before he was slain, and try whether they were as fearless as was told, and if no man spoke a word of fear they thought it proved. The sixth was led forward, and a stick twisted in his hair. Thorkel asked the same as before; the man said he liked well to die with a good fame, 'while thou, Thorkel, wilt live with shame.' He struck the blow. Then the seventh was led thither, and Thorkel asked the same. The man said: 'I like very much to die, but

---

[1] This practice was probably due to their not using a block; so that the head was held for the blow as described in the Saga.

strike me quickly; I have a belt-knife in my hand. We Jómsvikings have often talked of whether a man knew any-thing (had some consciousness) after his head had been cut off very quickly; it shall be a sign that I will stretch forth the knife if I know anything, else it will fall down.' Thorkel struck; the head flew off, but the knife fell down. The eighth was taken, and Thorkel asked the same. He said he liked it well, and when the death-blow was coming he said, 'Ram!' Thorkel stopped the blow, and asked why he said this. He answered: 'There will not be too many rams for the ewes which you, the jarl's men, named yesterday when you got wounded.' 'Thou art the greatest wretch,' said Thorkel, and dealt him the blow. The ninth was untied; Thorkel asked the same. He said: 'I like well my death, as do all my companions; but I do not want to be beheaded like a sheep, and I will sit for the blow; strike me face to face, and look carefully whether I wince in any way, for we have often talked of that.' This was done; he sat with his face to Thorkel, who walked to him and smote in his face; he did not wince, except that his eyelids sank down when death came over him. The tenth was led forward. Thorkel asked him the same. He said: 'I should like thee to wait while I arrange my breeches.' 'I grant thee that,' said Thorkel. When he had done, he said, ' Many things do not go as one hoped; I thought I should get into the bed of Thora, Skagi's daughter, the jarl's wife.' Hákon jarl said: 'Behead that man as quickly as thou canst; he has long had bad intentions.' Thorkel cut him. . . .

"Then a young man was led forward; he had much hair, yellow as silk. Thorkel asked the same. He said: 'I have lived the finest part of my life, and such men have now lost their life a little while ago that I do not care to live: I do not want thralls to lead me to the death-blow, but one who is no less a man than thou; it is easy to get that man, and he shall take hold of my hair, and pull away my head so that my hair does not become bloody.' A hirdman came, took the hair, and wound round his hand; Thorkel raised his sword, and intended to strike him as hard and quick as he could. He struck; but when the young man heard the sword whistling in the air, he pulled away his head strongly, and so it happened that the blow hit the man who had hold of his hair, and Thorkel cut off both his arms at the elbows. The young man jumped up, and said as a joke: 'What fellow is owner of the hands in my hair?' Hákon jarl said: 'The men who are still in the rope will do us great mischief; slay him as soon as you can; he has brought a great mishap on us, and it is clear that all of them who are living ought to be slain as soon as possible, for they are too hard for us to deal with, and their bravery and hardihood have not been exaggerated.' Eirík said to his father : 'We want to know, father, who they are before they are all slain ; what is thy name, young man ?' 'Svein,' answered he. 'Whose son art thou,' asked Eirík, 'and what is thy kin ?' He said : 'My father was called Búi, the stout, son of Veseti, on Borgundarhólm. I am of Danish kin.' 'How old art thou ?' said Eirík. 'If I live this winter I am eighteen winters old,' said he. Eirík said : 'Thou shalt live this winter, if I have my will, and not be slain.' He took him into peace, and into the company of himself and his men. When Hákon saw this, he said : 'I do not know what thou art thinking of, as thou savest a man who has caused us so much shame and digrace as this young man ; he has done us most harm, but nevertheless I like not to take him out of thy hands, and thou shalt have thy will this time.' Thus Eirík had his will. Hákon said to Thorkel : 'Behead the men quickly Eirík answered : 'They shall not be beheaded before I have first spoken with them, and I want to know who each of them is.'

"A man was untied from the rope when he said this ; the rope got a little entangled round his feet, so that he was not quite loose. This man was of large and handsome shape, young, and bold-looking. Thorkel asked him how he liked to die. 'Well,' said he, 'if I might first fulfil my vow.' Eirik jarl asked : 'What is thy name ? And what is thy vow, which thou desirest specially to fulfil before thou diest ?' He answered : 'My name is Vagn ; I am son of Áki, son of Palnatoki, of Fyen ; so I have been told.' Eirík said : 'What vow didst thou make, as thou sayest thou wouldst like to die if thou hadst fulfilled it according to thy will ?' 'I made the vow,' said Vagn, 'to get into the bed of Ingibjorg, the daughter of Thorkel Leira against his will, and that of all her kinsmen, and slay Thorkel if I came to Norway, and much do I lack if I cannot perform this before I die.' 'I will prevent thy doing this before thou diest,' said Thorkel. He rushed toward him and struck at him, holding his sword with both hands. Björn the British, Vagn's foster-father, kicked him with his foot away from the blow quickly. Thorkel missed Vagn, and hit the rope with which Vagn was tied and cut it asunder. Now Vagn was loose, and not wounded. Thorkel stumbled when he missed the man, and fell ; the sword dropped out of his hands. Bjorn had kicked Vagn so strongly that he fell, but he lay not a long time, and soon jumped up. He seized Thorkel's sword and gave him a deadly blow. 'Now I have fulfilled one of my two vows,' said Vagn, 'and I feel a great deal better than before.' Hákon said: 'Do not leave him loose long; slay him first, for he has done us much harm.' Eirik said: 'You shall not slay him, if I have my will, before you slay me; I take him away.' Hákon said: 'Now I need not meddle with this; thou wilt have thy way alone, kinsman.' Eirik said: 'Vagn is a good man-bargain (=acquisition), father, and I think it a good bargain to let him take Thorkel's place and honour; Thorkel might expect what happened to him, for now it is proved which often is said that "a wise man's guess is a prophecy"; thou sawest already to-day that he was death-fated.' Eirik took Vagn into his power, and then he was in no danger; Vagn said: 'I will accept life from thee, Eirik, only on condition that all my comrades who are living are given their lives; otherwise we will all go the same way, we comrades.' Eirik said: 'I will speak to thy comrades, but I do not refuse what thou askest.' Eirik went to Björn the British, and asked who he was, or what was his name. He answered 'Björn.' 'Art thou the Björn who fetched the man in King Svein's hall so boldly?'[1] 'I know not,' said Björn, 'that I fetched him boldly, but nevertheless I took the man away.' 'What didst thou seek,' said Eirik, 'in coming hither, old man, or what induced thee, bald and white haired, to come on this journey? It is true that all straws want to sting us, the Noregs-men, since even the men who are off their feet on account of old age came hither to fight us. Wilt thou receive thy life from me, for I think a man as old as thou ought not to be slain.' Björn answered: 'I will receive my life from thee on condition that the lives of my foster-son Vagn, and of all our men who are living are spared.' 'That shall be granted to all of you,' said Eirik, 'if I have my will, which I shall have.' He went to his father, and entreated him to spare the lives of all the living Jómsvikings, which the jarl granted him; and they were all untied, plighted faith was given to them, and they were taken into peace. It was arranged by Hákon and Eirik so that Björn the British went to the bu of Hallstein Kellingarbani. Five landed men were slain, beside Hallstein. Vagn Ákason went to the Vik with Eirik's consent, and before they parted Eirik said to him that, regarding his wedding with Ingibjörg, Thorkel's daughter, he might do what he liked. When Vagn came to Vik, he went to Ingibjörg, and stayed there during

---

[1] Allusion to an incident when Björn after a fight in King Svein's hall went in alone again to fetch one of his men who had been left inside.

the winter. The next spring he left, and kept faithfully all he had promised Eirik. He went home to his farms in Fyen, and for a long time afterwards managed them; he was thought to be a man of great deeds, and many famous men have sprung from him. It is told that he took Ingibjörg home with him.

"Björn the British went to Bretland, and ruled it as long as he lived, and was looked upon as a most brave man" (Jomsvikinga Saga, ch. 45, 47).

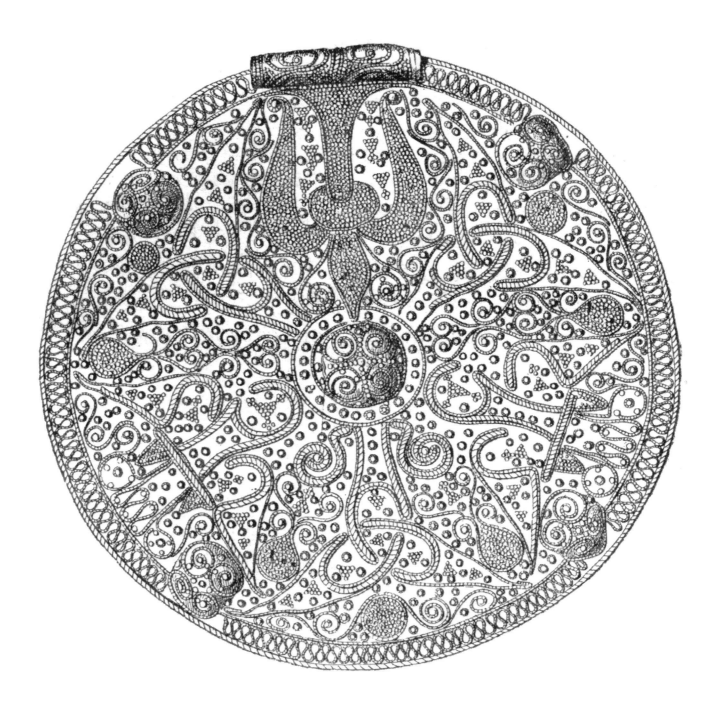

CHAPTER IV.

TRADERS AND TRADING-SHIPS.

Wide extent of trading expeditions—Commercial activity of the people—
Fairs—Immunity of trading ships from capture—Classification and name
of merchant vessels—Trade a high calling—Kings as traders—Laws
regulating trade — The earliest medium of exchange — Method of
reckoning—Weights and measures—Arabic and other coins and objects
—Insurance.

THE people of the North were, from very early times, great
traders, and as such undertook long voyages, as is seen from
the finds of the earlier iron age, and from many accounts in
the Sagas; this ancient trait in their character is still seen in
their descendants.

Their trading expeditions extended far south through the
present Russia, to the Black Sea, the Tigris and Euphrates,
and as far east as Samarcand; while with their ships they
traded to the seas of Western Europe and into the Mediterranean.

"Thórólf had a large seagoing ship; in every way it was
most carefully built, and painted nearly all over above the
water-line; it had a sail with blue and red stripes, and all the
rigging was very elaborate. This he made ready, and ordered
his men-servants to go with it; he had put on board dried
fish, skins, tallow, gray fur and other furs, which he had from
the mountains; all this was of much value. He sent it westward to England to buy cloth (woollen) and other goods he
needed. They went southward along the coast, and then out
to sea; when they arrived in England they found a good
market, loaded the ship with wheat and honey, wine and cloth,
and returned in the autumn with fair winds" (Egil's Saga).

"From England (London) Gunnlaug sailed with some
traders to Dublin. King Sigtrygg Silk-beard, son of Olaf
Kvaran and Queen Kormlöd then ruled in Ireland"[1] (Gunnlaug Ormstunga, c. 8).

---

[1] Cf. also Ólaf Tryggvason, Fornmanna Sögur. i.

"In the spring, after the Jómsviking battle, the Jarl summoned before him many chiefs east in the country. Thither also came at the Jarl's summons the brothers Jóstein and Karlshöfud, sons of Eirik of Ofrustad. There was also a man, by name of Thórir Klakka, a great friend of the Jarl. He was accustomed to go on Viking expeditions in the summer, but sometimes he went on trading journeys, and therefore he knew many countries" (Olaf Tryggvason, c. 51 (Heimskringla)).

"Some time after King Sverrir held a Thing in Björgyn (Bergen) and spoke: 'We thank all English men who bring hither wheat and honey, flour or cloth, for coming; we thank also all men who bring hither linen, wax or kettles. We will also name those who have come from the Orkneys, Hjaltland, Faroes, Iceland, and all who bring into this country things useful for it'" (Fornmanna Sögur, vii.).

He goes on to say that the Germans coming there bring wine and teach men to be drunkards.

"King Ólaf had proclaimed the Christian law in Vikin, in the same manner as in the northern part of the country; and it progressed rapidly, for the people of Vikin were much better acquainted with Christian customs than the men in the north, for both in winter and summer there were many Danish and Saxon traders. The men of Vikin also went much on trading journeys to England and Saxland, or Flæmingjaland (Flamland, Flandres) or Denmark; but some went on Viking expeditions, and stayed during winter in Christian lands" (St. Olaf, c. 62).

There were regular places where fairs were held for the barter of wares without fear of molestation, at which the same peace reigned as at the Thing or temple, their inviolability apparently being acknowledged by all. Booths were built in these places, to which native and foreign merchants came, and goods—furs, skins, costly cloths, garments, grain, slaves, &c., &c. —were sold or exchanged.

"Melkorka's son Olaf sailed to Ireland, and, as he was about to land, his headman, Örn, said: 'I do not think we shall meet with a good reception here, for this is far off from harbours and those trading-places where foreigners have peace'" (Laxdæla, c. 21).

48

"Next summer Thránd went with trading men south to Denmark, and reached Haleyri in the summer. There were very many people gathered, and it is said that thither come more people than to any other place in Nordrlönd (the northern lands) while the fair lasts. At that time King Harald Gormsson, called Blátönn (blue tooth), ruled Denmark. King Harald was at Haleyri in the summer, and many men with him. Two of the king's hirdmen who were there with him are mentioned; one was called Sigurd, the other Hárek. These brothers always went round the town, and wanted to buy the best and largest gold ring they could get. They entered a booth which was very finely arranged; a man sitting there received them well, and asked what they wished to buy. They said they wanted to buy a large and good gold ring. He answered there was a good choice of them. They asked for his name, and he called himself Hólmgeir Audgi (the wealthy). He set forth his costly things, and showed them a heavy gold ring which was very costly, and valued at so high a price that they did not know whether they could get so much silver at once as he wanted, and asked him to delay it till next morning, to which he assented.

"The king and others perceived that silver had been stolen from them, so the king issued a proclamation that no ships were to sail as long as matters stood thus. This seemed to many a great disadvantage, as it was, to stay there longer than the fair lasted. Then the Norwegians had a meeting among themselves to take counsel. Thránd was at the meeting, and said: 'The men here are very helpless.' They asked: 'Dost thou know a plan?' 'Certainly I do,' he said. 'Then give us thy advice,' they said. 'I will not do that gratuitously.' They asked what he demanded, and he answered: 'Every one of you shall give me one eyrir of silver.' They said that was a great deal, but it was agreed that every man there should give him half an eyrir at once, and the other half if he was successful. The next day the king had a Thing, and said that the men should never go thence until this theft was discovered. Then a young man with long red hair, freckly and rather ugly of face, began to speak, and said: 'The people here are rather helpless.' The advice-givers of the king asked what advice he had to give. He answered: 'It is my advice that every man here present give as much silver as the king demands, and when that is put into one place, then pay the loss of him who has suffered, and let the king have the rest as a gift of honour. I know that he will use well what he gets; let not people stay here weatherbound, such a multitude as here is assembled, to such a great disadvantage.' The assembled quickly accepted

P 2

this, and said they would willingly give silver to honour the king rather than stay there to their disadvantage. This plan was adopted, and the silver collected" (Færeyinga Saga, c. 3).

The trading ships, with very few exceptions, were free from the attacks of the Vikings, as plundering a merchant vessel at sea seems to have been considered unmanly. They were unlike the war vessels which we have described, and the general name given to these Kaup-skip (trading ships) shows that the distinction was easily recognised. They were neither ornamented with dragons nor with shields, and the war pennant was missing.

We find them mentioned under their different names— viz., Knörr, Kugg, Byrding (ship of burden), Vistabyrding (provision ships), and Haf-skip (deep-sea ship); there were also smaller or less important ones, among them even ferry-boats. Byrdings (ships of burden), the real cargo-carrying vessels, are frequently mentioned.

"One day when Ásmund was rowing through a Sound, a byrding sailed towards them; it was easily recognised, for it was painted on the bows with white and red; the sail was striped" (St. Olaf, 132).

Trade was considered a high calling. Even the sons of kings did not despise it; Harald Fairhair's son Björn was a great Farman (seafarer) and Kaupman (trader, merchant).

"King Harald's son, Björn, ruled over Vestfold, and resided chiefly in Túnsberg, but seldom engaged in warfare. To Túnsberg came many traders, both from around Vikin and from the country to the north, from the south from Denmark and Saxland. King Björn also had trading-ships sailing to various countries, and thus procured himself precious things, and other goods which he needed. His brothers called him trading-man, or faring-man. Björn was wise and quiet, and was thought likewise to be a good chief" (Fornmanna Sögur, vol. i.).

Even kings sometimes entered into partnership with traders. Ingimund, who had fought on the side of Harald Fairhair, but who had settled in Iceland, came to Norway.

"Gudleik Gerski (of Gardariki) was a native of Agdir; he was a great and rich trader and seafarer, who went on trading journeys to various countries; he often went to Gardariki, and therefore was called Gudleik Gerski. One spring he prepared his ship, as he wanted to go to Gardariki in the summer. King Olaf sent him word that he wished to see him. When Gudleik came, the king said he wished to enter into partnership with him, and asked him to buy for him costly things that were rare in Norway. Gudleik promised to do as he wished. . . . In the summer Gudleik went to Hólmgard, and there bought excellent *pell* (costly cloth), which he intended for clothes of rank (tignarklœdi) for the king, and costly skins, and an exceedingly fine table-service (bord-búnad)" (St. Olaf, 64). [1]

"Ingimund then said: 'Here I will show you, my lord, two bear-cubs, which I captured in Iceland, and I wish that thou wouldst accept them from me.' The king thanked him, and promised that he would grant him permission to take timber. During the winter they exchanged many presents, and in the spring his ship was loaded with the cargo which he chose, and the best timber that could be got. The king then said: 'I see, Ingimund, that hereafter thou wilt not any more come to Norway. Thou wilt need more timber than one ship can carry; here some ships are lying; choose which of them thou likest.' 'Choose for me, lord, that one which will bring most luck.' Ingimund replied. 'I will, as I know best,' said the king. 'Here is one called *Stigandi*,[2] which bites the wind better than any ship (sails better), and is more prosperous, too, and that I will select for thee; it is not large, but fine.' Ingimund thanked him for the gift, and departed for Iceland, where he soon arrived, and was received with joy by all." (Vatnsdæla Saga, c. 16).[3]

"Eyvind (an Icelander) became a trader, and went to Norway, and thence to other countries, and stopped in Mikligard (Constantinople), where he obtained great honours from the Greek king, and remained some time" (Hrafnkel's Saga).

"This summer a ship came from Norway to the Faroes; the steersman was called Rafn; his kin was in Vik, and he owned a house in Túnsberg. He constantly sailed to Hólmgard, and was called Hólmgardsfari. The ship came to Thórshöfn; when

---

[1] Cf. St. Olaf, c. 143.
[2] Stigandi = the stepping one.

[3] Cf. Hróa Thátt; Flateyjarbók, ii.; Landnamabók, iii.

the traders were ready to go it is said that Thránd of Gata came there one morning in a skúta and spoke to Rafn privately, saying he had two young thralls to sell him. Rafn said he would not buy them before he saw them. Thránd led forward the two boys with the hair shaved off, in white garments; they were fine looking, but swollen in the face from grief. When he saw the boys Rafn asked: 'Are not these the sons of Brestir and Beinir, whom you killed a short while ago?' 'Certainly, I think so,' said Thránd. 'They will not come into my hands,' said Rafn, 'for property.' 'Then let us both yield,' said Thránd; 'take here two marks of silver which I will give thee if thou takest them away with thee, so that they henceforth will never come to the Færoes.' He poured the silver into the lap of the steersman, counted it, and showed it to him. Rafn liked the silver well, and it was agreed that he should receive the boys. He sailed when he got a fair wind, and landed where he wished in Norway east at Túnsberg; he stayed there during the winter, and the boys with him, and they were well treated" (Færeyinga Saga, c. 8).

In hard years the exportation of grain was forbidden.

"At Ömd, in Thrándarnes, lived a chief named Ásbjörn. He had three feasts every winter, as was the custom of his father. Then the crops began to fail and bad years came, and his mother wanted him to omit some or all of the feasts; but he would not, and bought corn or had it given to him as a gift. One summer he could get no more corn. It was said from the south of the country that King Ólaf forbade to carry corn, malt and meal from the south northwards. Then Ásbjörn went on his ship with twenty men, and sailed southward till they came to Ögvaldsnes. Ásbjörn asked the king's steward, who lived there, if he would sell corn. He told them that the king had forbidden the selling of corn from the south to the north. Then Ásbjörn got corn from the thralls of the chief Erling Skjálgsson, who was the brother of Ásbjörn's mother. The king's steward went with sixty men out on Asbjörn's ship, and took the corn and his sail besides, and gave him another bad sail. Ásbjörn slew the steward some time after, when Ólaf was at a feast in the steward's house" (St. Olaf's Saga, c. 123).

Weights and balances were known to the Norse from very early times, as the finds prove; and their standard of measurement was the ell.

The earliest medium of value used as coin was the Baug (ring), which is mentioned in Rigsmál, and in the earlier laws. We find that the reckonings were by marks and aurar. One

Fig. 998.—⅓ real size.
Spiral rings of gold, used as money; found at the bottom of the Vammelo, Södermanland. Weight, about $1\frac{1}{10}$ lbs.

Fig. 999.—Real size.
Spiral rings; weight about $2\frac{1}{2}$ oz. Norway.

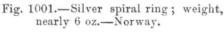

Fig. 1000.—Spiral ring found with three other smaller spiral rings, and two fragments; weight, nearly 3 oz.—Norway.

Fig. 1001.—Silver spiral ring; weight, nearly 6 oz.—Norway.

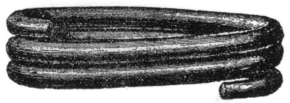

Fig. 1002.—Spiral ring, found with fourteen bracteates of gold, of four different patterns, &c. Weight, $3\frac{1}{2}$ oz.—Norway.

mark was 8 aurar (1 oz.); one eyrir was divided into eight ortugar, and one ortug into ten or sixty penningar; this latter

Fig. 1003.—Iron weight, real size, inlaid with bronze, weighing 4¾ oz. —Götland

Fig. 1004.—Iron weight, real size, inlaid with bronze, weighing slightly over ½ oz. —Rosenbys, Götland.

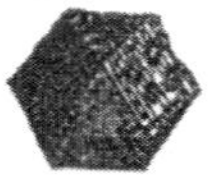

Fig. 1005.—Bronze weight, real size, found in the black earth, Björkö.

Fig. 1006.—One of ten weights found with balance. Real size.

Fig. 1008. The tongue of the balance.

Fig. 1007.—Bronze scales, ⅓ real size.—Vaxala, Upland. Later iron age.

Fig. 1009.

Bronze balance, with remains of bronze chain attached to it, found in a round mound, with a pincette of bronze, a bronze ornament for a drinking-horn, four or five clay urns, &c. ½ real size.—Norway. Earlier iron age

is sometimes mentioned as being of gold; it was customary to weigh the medium of exchange.

A man named Karl of Mœri was sent by King Olaf the saint

to the Faroes to collect taxes due to him. Leif, son of Össur, took the tax (silver) which Thránd had collected, "and poured it out on his shield" to Karl. They looked at the silver. Leif said:

Fig. 1010.—Spiral silver ring, used probably as money, ⅔ real size, found with a little cup, 1,923 Arabian coins, &c.—Vamblingö, Götland.

Fig. 1011.

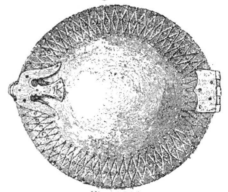

Fig. 1012.
Box, with top open, ⅔ real size, in which there was a scale, ten beads, and two ornaments of silver.—Petes, Götland.

Fig. 1013.
Hook of iron. ⅓ real size.

Fig. 1014.
Weight of iron. ⅓ real size.

With these were found two moulds of bronze, five unfinished fibulæ, ornament for a drinking cup, part of a bridle, a chain all in bronze, an iron key, the handle of which is of bronze, a blacksmith's pince (nipper), and another weight of iron, &c.—Smiss, Götland.

" ' We need not look long at this silver; here is every penning better than the other, and we want to have this silver; get thou, Thránd, a man to look on while it is weighed.'

Thránd answered that he thought it best that Leif should look at it on his behalf. Leif and the others then went out, and a short way from the booth they sat down and weighed the silver. Karl took the helmet from his head, and poured the silver which was weighed into it" (Færeyinga Saga, c. 46).[1]

As in the Greek, Roman, and earlier Byzantine periods, so in the Viking age, the island of Gotland stands foremost as the commercial centre of the North, as is proved by the number of coins discovered, showing that she kept the supremacy of trade for some ten or twelve centuries. The numerous English coins found there and in Sweden, show that the Swedes, and the

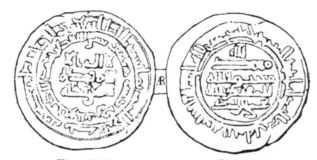

Fig. 1015.   Fig. 1016.
Arabic coin called Kufic, coined in 903 in Samarcand.—Götland. **Real size.**

Fig. 1017.   Fig. 1018.
Kufic coin of silver, date 742–743. Real size. Found in the cemetery of Fredriks-hald, Sweden, where another Kufic coin and two silver bracelets had previously been found.

people inhabiting the islands of the Baltic, were a seafaring people, and were constantly engaged in trading and warlike expeditions to England; in a word, they must have formed a great part of the host that made warfare in Western Europe. The runic stones which have been raised to the memory of those who have died in foreign lands are found almost if not entirely in Sweden.

Norway has produced fewer coins than the other Scandinavian

---

[1] Cf. Gretti's Saga, c. 98.

countries, but this may be owing to their having been melted, as jewels of silver are far more common there than elsewhere.

After the Roman and Byzantine era the Arabic period begins. Trade still followed the ancient channel through the present Russia. Thousands of Arabic coins of silver, besides probably, silver ornaments, to which the name of Kufic [1] has been given, struck in the countries ruled by the Arabians,

Fig. 1019.—Silver cup.—Götland. ½ real size.

Fig. 1020.—Silver vase.—Götland. ⅔ real size.

found their way north from Bokhara, Samarcand, Bagdad, Kufa, &c., &c., the earliest dating from 698, the latest 1010 after the Christian era. Coins of gold are exceedingly rare; the greater number of these belong to the ninth and the first half of the tenth century, that is to say, between 880 and 955. From that time a great number of silver ornaments appear in the North.

Norway has not as yet proved rich in Arabic coins. Of Kufic

---

[1] Kufa, as we know, was situated on one of the branches of the Euphrates, south of Bagdad, and was for a while the seat of the Caliphs.

only about seventy have been found, ranging in time from the year 742 to 952. These coins are the more interesting in that not only the names of the rulers, but of the cities, which then existed, where they were coined, are given; many are of the Samanid dynasty. More than twenty thousand have been

Fig. 1021.—Ornaments round pedestal.—Götland.

Fig. 1022. Fig. 1023.
Ornaments fastened to the bottom of a vase, representing two four-footed animals, one of which is eating the fruit growing upon a tree.—Götland. ⅔ real size.

found in Sweden and Götland; some of these, perhaps, came from Spain. They were probably brought by the ships which made voyages to the Mediterranean.

The two vases on p. 219 were found with Arabic coins and seven other silver vessels, and are probably of Arabic origin.

Frankish coins (800 to 850) have been found in Sweden of the time of Pepin, Charlemagne, and Louis le Debonnaire. In Norway of Charlemagne, Louis le Debonnaire, Pepin, son of Louis le Debonnaire, of Lothair, Louis' son.

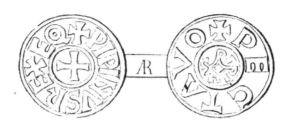

Fig. 1024.   Fig. 1025.

Frankish coin. Real size. Struck at Poictiers for Pepin, King of Aquitaine, either Pepin I. (817–838), or Pepin II. (845–864). Found with eight other Frankish coins. At the same place were found seven other Frankish coins, some Arabic coins, fragments of silver objects, &c.—Vestergötland.

Fig. 1026.   Fig. 1027.

Frankish coin—ninth century—of silver. Real size. Louis (Ludovic) le Debonnaire. Found in the upper part of a round tumulus, with burned bones, a pair of oval fibulæ of bronze, a bronze key, a silver pin, beads, &c., and other silver coins, four of which were of Louis le Debonnaire type, one of Charlemagne, the other of Coenwulf, of Mercia (796–818). The coins are pierced, and seemed to have been surrounded, in part, at least, with a bronze ring, and must have been worn as hanging ornaments —Norway.

More than twenty thousand English coins [1] have been found in Sweden and the island of Götland, fifteen thousand belong-

---

[1] Among the English coins found in Sweden, and now in the royal collection in Stockholm, are of—

Edward I.
Ethelstan.
Sihtric, of Northumberland.
Coin with the name of St. Peter.
Edgar.
Edward II.
Ethelred II.
Knut.
Harold I.
Harthacnut.
Edward Confessor.
Harold II.
King Sihtric, of Dublin, 989–1020.

English coins found in Norway of—

Coenwulf, of Mercia (796–819).
Ceolwulf, his son (819–821).
Northumbrian (Styca).
Eawred (808–840).
Archbishop Wulfred, of Canterbury (803–829).
Ethelred.
Canute the Great.
Edgar.
Edward the Martyr.
From the beginning of the eleventh century.
King Sigtrygg Silkiskegg.

ing to Ethelred's time (998–1016); this number is not surpassed in Britain itself, and the harvest still continues in the North. A number came no doubt through the channel of trade, and others probably from the Danegeld, Ethelred having thus paid more than 167,000 lbs. of silver; part of this war-booty fell to the lot of the Swedes and Danes.

Coins of the ninth and the earlier part of the tenth century,

Fig. 1028.   Fig. 1029.

Old English silver coin, eleventh century, beginning of King Knut's reign. Real size. Found under a large stone, by a landslip, with about 1600 silver coins, mostly English, many German, some Swedish, Danish, Bohemian, and Kufic.—Norway.

Fig. 1030.

Silver coin of Knut the Great, used as a hanging ornament. Real size.— Blekinge, Sweden.

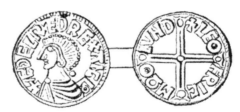

Fig. 1031.   Fig. 1032.

Silver coin of Ethelred. Real size. Found near Stockholm, with 737 Arabic, German, and old English coins, and one coin of the Swedish king, Olaf Skautkonung, some fragments of silver bracelets, &c. —Upland, Sweden.

are extremely rare, though England was much ravaged by the northern countries. I think no coins have been found thus far in Sweden before Alfred's date, and only three date before 950, but new discoveries may in time bring others to light. In Denmark only a few hundred English coins have been found; of the time of Ethelred and his successors about three thousand in Norway.

The earliest English and Frankish coins, strange as it may appear, have only been found in Sweden and Norway, but even these do not amount to more than fifty or sixty; none have been discovered in Denmark, and previously to the years 780 to 800, no specimen of Merovingian or English coins have been found in the North.

The number of German is very great, and more than fifty thousand have been found in Sweden and the island of Götland; they date chiefly from the middle of the tenth to the middle of the eleventh century, and are sometimes found to the number of one or two thousand together.[1]

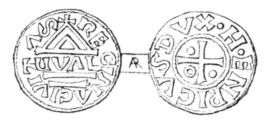

Fig. 1033.   Fig. 1034.

German silver coin of Henry of Bavaria, end of tenth century.—Gotland. **Real size.**

The intercourse with the Byzantine empire which had taken place in the earlier centuries continued for a long time, and a great number of Northmen entered the service of the Byzantine or Greek emperors, as seen in the Sagas.

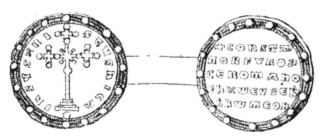

Fig. 1035.   Fig. 1036.

Byzantine coins (948–949). Real size. Struck by the emperors Constantine X. and Romanus III. Found with a necklace, 15 bracelets, 2 buckles, 2 spiral bracelets, 3 perfect and 360 imperfect Arabic coins, all of silver, and all of which were under an iron dish.—Björko, Upland.

---

[1] Among the great finds of coins are those of Findarfoe, in Götland, which had more than 3,000 German coins, besides English and others. Another in Johanneshus, in Blekinge, Sweden, which, besides a mass of ornaments and jewels of silver, contained over 3,400 German coins of the tenth and eleventh century. The German coins had been struck for German emperors, kings, princes, archbishops, bishops, &c., &c., and belong to Bohemia, Bavaria, Swabia, Lorraine, Franconia, the modern Saxony, Frisia, the Netherlands, &c. There are also coins of cities, those of Cologne being the most numerous, and even coins for Northern Italy. Most of these coins are derived from places along the rivers of Germany, especially the Rhine. The most common are those of Otto III. and his grandmother Adelheid, who reigned during the minority of her grandson (991–995).

A bog find in Norway proved very rich in gold objects, Arabic, Byzantine, Frankish, and there were also found English coins and other objects.[1]

Fig. 1037.—Border enlarged.

Fig. 1038.—Bog find.—Fibula of gold inlaid, ⅔ real size, found in a bog, with coins. —Norway.

Fig. 1039.—Silver wire bracelet, real size, found with four rings and seventeen beads, nine of which are of different pattern, three Arabic coins, three rings of silver, one of gold of twisted wires, &c., &c., at Hejsland, Halfhem parish, Götland.

---

[1] Among the coins were nine Kufic, eight of which were of gold, and one of silver, all of Abbasides Caliphs, from 760 to 840; four Byzantine coins of gold, of Valens, Mauricius, Constantine, Copronymus, and Michael III.; a gold coin of Louis le Debonnaire; two coins of silver-gilt of his sons Lothair and Pepin, a silver-gilt coin of Archbishop Wulfred, of Canterbury, 803–829. With these was a large treasure of gold and jewels, among which were two neck-rings, three bracelets, rings, charms, and an object, probably a *reliquary*, having a Christian inscription in Greek, numerous charms and ornaments, one of which was ornamented with an antique gem, and others with garnet beads, &c., &c., all of gold; some objects were silver-gilt; gold chains, &c., &c.

Fig. 1040.—Gold fibula, real size, inlaid with coloured glass, in a copper box in the ground, with over 4,000 coins, German, English, &c., two Swedish coins, Anund Jakob (son of Olaf Skautkonung), five necklaces, nine bracelets, two finger rings, &c., &c.—Blekinge, Sweden.

Fig. 1042.—Box of bronze found in a mound, Nordrup, Zealand, with a silver fibula, glass, &c.

Fig. 1041.—Ring, real size, with charms representing a sword, a spear head, &c., and some Arabic coins.—Öland.

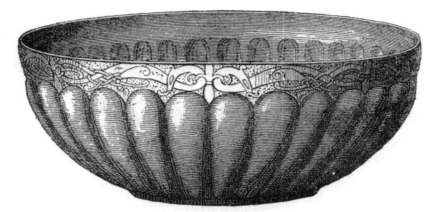

Fig. 1043.

Fig. 1044.
Bottom of vessel.

Silver vessel, with inside, bottom, and border gilt, found with three bracelets, thirty-one fragments of ingots, rings, 500 German and English coins, &c.—Lilla Valla, Götland.

Fig. 1045.—Bronze box, ¼ real size, containing fragments of ornaments, coins, two coins of Olaf Skotkonung and several hundreds English and German coins, &c.—Findarfve, Götland.

Fig. 1046.—Bracelet of silver, ½ real size, with small rings, four of which have Arabian coins wrapped round them.—Kullaberg, Scania.

Fig. 1047.—Fibula of silver, $\frac{2}{3}$ real size, figures in relief, embellished with Niello, found with Arabic coins.—Herestad, Scania.

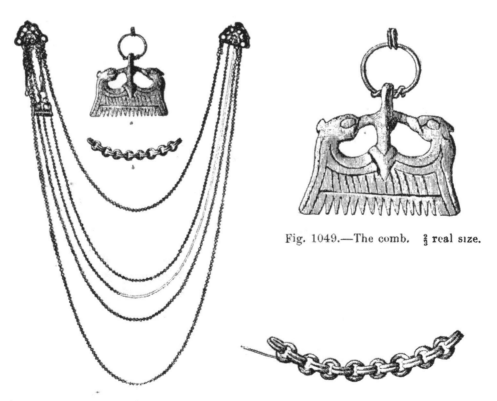

Fig. 1049.—The comb. $\frac{2}{3}$ real size.

Fig. 1048.—Chain of bronze, $\frac{1}{10}$ real size, with comb attached.—Lake Mälar.

Fig. 1050.—Real size of chain.

Q 2

65

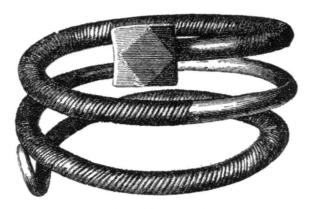

Fig. 1051.—Spiral silver bracelet, ⅔ original size, found with three similar bracelets, Arabian coins, &c.—Sandby, Öland.

Fig. 1052.—Bracelet of silver, ¾ real size, found with coins, &c., near Eskilstuna, Södermanland.

Fig. 1053.—Massive silver bracelet, ¾ real size, found under an old stable, with two other bracelets, Arabic, German, and old English coins, &c.—Undrom, Angermanland.

Fig. 1054.—Bracelet of silver, ¾ real size.—Eskilstuna, Södermanland.

Fig. 1055.—Neck-ring of twisted silver wire, found with the massive silver bracelet.

Fig. 1056.—Bracelet of solid silver, real size, found with four other silver bracelets and forty-six Arabic coins of silver, &c.—Thalings, Götland.

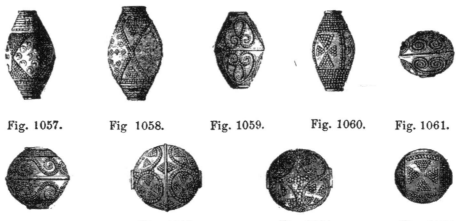

Fig. 1057.   Fig 1058.   Fig. 1059.   Fig. 1060.   Fig. 1061.

Fig. 1062.   Fig. 1063.   Fig. 1064.   Fig. 1065.
Beads of silver found with bracelet, p. 224.—Hemse, Götland.

Fig. 1066.   Fig. 1067.
Bead of green glass, real size.—Hemse.   Bead of glass mosaic, real size.—Hemse.

Fig. 1068.—Fibula of bronze inlaid with silver and gilt. Found in a mound in Hemse, Götland.

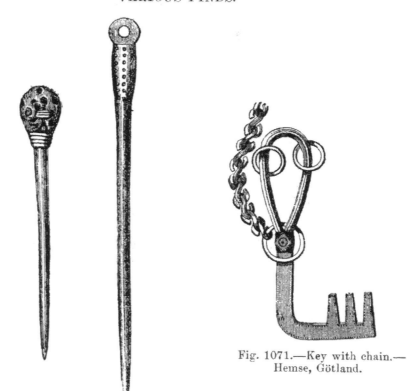

Fig. 1071.—Key with chain.—
Hemse, Götland.

Fig. 1069.   Fig. 1070.
Pins found in a cairn.—
Hemse, Götland.

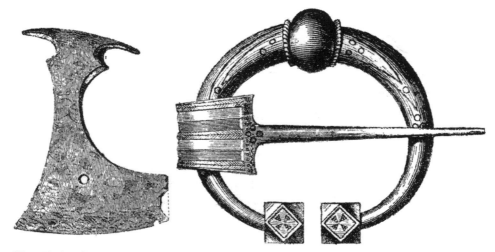

Fig. 1072.—Iron axe, with a round   Fig. 1073.—Bronze buckle or fibula, found in
hole in the blade.—Hemse. Götland.   a small cairn at Hemse, Götland.

Hemse find, Götland.   At this place are found several small coins with unburnt
   bodies.   Among the objects found besides those represented above, were several
   basins of bronze, number of bronze fibulæ, a great number of amber, crystal,
   and glass beads, several keys, bone combs, several clay urns, buckle of bronze, a
   fragment of a stone with runic character, several charms, iron axes, knives, pins,
   &c.   The only coins found were one Arabic coin, and two German coins of the
   10th and 11th centuries.

Fig. 1074.—Semi-circular ornament of silver with small rings at both ends.—
Fölhagen, Götland.

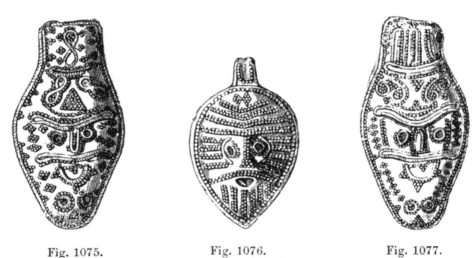

Fig. 1075.   Fig. 1076.   Fig. 1077.
Three of twelve snake-shaped necklace ornaments, real size.—Fölhagen, Götland.

Fig. 1078.—Bracteate.—Fölhagen, Götland.

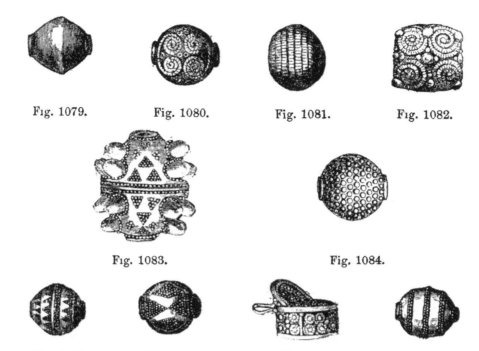

Fig. 1079.　　Fig. 1080.　　Fig. 1081.　　Fig. 1082.

Fig. 1083.　　　　　　Fig. 1084.

Fig. 1085.　　Fig. 1086.　　Fig. 1087.　　Fig. 1088.

Silver beads, real size, together with coins, &c., in a box in the earth, by a working man while digging a ditch, at Fölhagen, Götland, near the Monastery de Roma, from a lot of 49 beads of thirteen different patterns.

Fölhagen ground find, Götland. The objects were in a copper box, which however could not be taken whole, and contained, besides some of the objects represented above, an ingot of chemically pure gold, 8 bracelets of silver, 835 Kufic coins (971), 400 German coins, the latest from Otto III. before 1002 ; 4 English coins of Aethelred, and many other jewels.

Insurance companies were known from early times.

" Damages are to be paid if a disease comes among a man's cattle so that one-fourth or more of his cattle dies; then the men of the Hrepp shall pay the loss. The man shall call five of his neighbours to him during the next half month after the disease has ceased, in order to value his loss. He shall tell them his loss and show them the flesh and the skin of the dead cattle. Thereupon he shall take an oath before them that his loss is as great as they estimated it, or more. Then at a meeting he shall tell how great they valued his loss to be and the bœndr shall pay him one-half of the loss " (Gragas, i. 458.)

" There are also three rooms in the house of every man which are to be paid for if they are burnt. The first is stofa (sitting-room), second is hall (eldhus), the third is the pantry where women prepare food. If one owns both eldhus and skali he shall at a meeting in the spring say whether he wants people rather to be answerable for the eldhus or the skali " (Gragas, i. 459).

"Only the value of the clothes or things which a man owned and used every day shall be paid. If food is burned it shall be paid. The value of costly things or wares shall not be paid. A man's losses shall not be made good to him more than three times" (i. 460).

We have in the following passage an early reference to the great fair of Novgorod:—

"One summer Harald (Fair-hair) called to him his dearest favourite, Hauk hábrök (= high-breech), and said : 'Now I am free from all warfare and hostility in the land, and will lead a life of ease and pleasure. I will send you into Eastern lands this summer to buy for me some things that are costly and rare here.' Hauk said he should be obeyed in this as in other things, and the king allowed his men to go to various countries. Hauk departed with one ship and a good body of followers, and arrived east to Hólmgard (= Novgorod) in the autumn as the fair began, and went into winter quarters. Thither had come many people from various lands, among them were the champions of King Eirek from Uppsalir, Björn blueside and Salgard serk (= shirt), overbearing and wronging everybody. One day Hauk walked through the town with his men to buy some costly things for his lord Harald, when he came to where a man of Gardariki was sitting ; he saw a costly cloak all over adorned with gold. This he bought, left and went for the money. Before this, the same day, Björn had wanted to buy this cloak for the King of the Swedes, and its value was given. After Hauk had gone, the servant of Björn came and told the trader that Björn must, of course, get the cloak, but he said the matter was settled. The servant told Björn. Then Hauk came with the money for the cloak, paid all, and took it away" (Flateyjarbok, i. 577).

CHAPTER V.

DEBTS AND ROBBERY.

Stringency of laws on debt—An insolvent debtor the property of the creditor
—Redemption of debtor—Robbery and burglary—Robbery with violence
—Robbery without violence — Punishments — Irreclaimable thieves—
Laws on theft.

NOTHING could show more plainly that, apart from the profession of *Vikingry*, the people carried on their commercial transactions in a very honourable way, than the fact that the laws on debt were very stringent, and that robbery, arson, adulteration of food, &c., were punished most severely, and in some cases put the offender outside the pale of the law.

In regard to debts and the right of the creditor, some customs which had become law seem to be of high antiquity.

When a debtor could not pay, he had to come to the Thing and offer his person to his kinsmen, if they would pay the debt; first to the nearest kinsman; then, if he would not, he could offer himself to any of the others. If none of the kinsmen would have him, he belonged to his creditor till he had paid the debt by work or otherwise.

A woman who was a debtor could not offer herself without the consent of her kinsmen.

The owner of the debtor could use him as his thrall as long as the debt was not paid, but the debtor had the rétt to which he was born in regard to all other men. His master could beat him. but was not allowed to sell him unless he paid a fine of forty marks, or unless he ran away, when he became a real thrall. The debtor could also give his child for a higher debt than three marks.

If he did not stay with his creditor, he was allowed half a month to go through the Fylky and try to get the debt paid. If the creditor wanted only the money and not the person, he could offer the debtor to his kinsmen; or, if they would not buy him, the creditor could sell him to any one in the country, though not as a common thrall, and not for a higher amount than the debt.

If the debtor would not work and was obstinate, then the creditor could take him to the Thing and offer him to the kinsmen of the debtor to redeem; if they would not, the creditor could kill or maim him.

"A debtor shall be taken to the Thing. He shall first be offered to his kinsmen, and first to the nearest one if he wants him, or to the one to whom he prefers to sell him. No one is allowed to take a woman thus for the sake of debt, unless with the consent of her kinsmen. . . . He (the creditor) shall not drive him to work with blows unless he cannot get his debt from him. The man has no rétt towards him (the master) and his wife and all his thralls and each to the other. If others beat him the master has equal rétt on him as on his steward; the debtor owns the rest of his rétt according to his birth, and his rétt shall be the same as if he had no debt. . . . If a man sells a debtor like a slave he is liable to pay 40 marks, unless he has run away from his creditor, and the same must every one pay who sells a free man. . . . A family-born man may give his child for debt if he does it at the Thing or at the alehouse or at church, for 3 marks and not more. . . . If the debtor is obstinate to the creditor and will not work for him, he shall be brought to the Thing and offered to his kinsmen to redeem him. If they will not the creditor can maim him on the upper or lower part of the body" (Gulath. Law, 71).

Robbery (Rán) was viewed from a different point, according as more or less violence was employed in its commission.

Búrán (burglary) committed with armed force was considered the worst form, and was *útlegdarverk* (outlawry-work). Robbery of a whole farm was punished with outlawry, and the owner sent an arrow to the men of the Herad that night to pursue the robber. If when he was caught he returned the property, he had to pay indemnity to the king. If robbers defended themselves they were unholy, and no weregild was paid for them if they were killed.

"If men attack a bondi and rob his farm and take 3 cows or more, or 3 cows' value, then it is *búrán*. If the bondi owns only 3 cows, it is *búrán* if one is taken away. An arrow shall be sent, and each carry it to the other or pay a fine.[1] If they are pursued and found with the cattle and give them back, the leader pays 40 marks, and each of his men 3 marks. If they do not they are all outlaws " (Frostath., v. 14).

" In the second place, if a man finds another in his *búr*[2] who has gathered there a burden of property and clothes, he may slay him if he likes. He shall go to his neighbours and show them the slain man, and use their evidence at the arrow-thing. In the third place, if a man finds another in his sheep-house or cow-stall tying his cattle and trying to lead them away, he may slay him if he wants " (Gulathing Law, 160).[3]

Handrán was the term applied to robbery without violence of property out of the hand. Such a robber also was unholy, and could be killed without indemnity.

" It is *hand-robbery* if a man tears out of the hand of a man what he holds in it, or tears anything off his back. This is also liable to greater outlawry " (Vigslodi, c. 3).
" If a man commits hand-robbery on another, and he proves it by witnesses, then the robber is liable to pay 3 marks. If the robber runs away with the thing (robbed), and the owner runs after him and slays him, then he falls as an outlaw " (Gulath., 143).

The value of the stolen thing was appraised, and if it was worth an *örtug*, or more, then the thief was to be outlawed and slain, for he had forfeited his life.

If a man stole something of less value than an *örtug*, he was a *torf man*,[4] and was made to run the gauntlet while those present threw at him whatever they had handy ; if he got away alive he was thereafter without rétt.

" If a man steals on trading-journeys he makes himself a *götu-thjóf* (gauntlet-thief). His head shall be shaved and tarred, and (eider) down be taken and put on it. Then all the crew shall make a road for him and stand on both sides, and he shall run to the wood if he can. Every one present shall throw a stone or a stick after him, and whoever does not throw is liable to pay 9 *örtugar* "[5] (Bjarkey Law, 146).

---

[1] *Baug.*
[2] A place for provisions, still common in Norway. See ' Land of the Midnight Sun,' vol. i , p. 419.
[3] Cf. also Frostath. xiv. 12, 13.

[4] Literally a man of turf and tar ; *i.e.* equivalent to one who was tarred and feathered.
[5] Cf. also Gulath. 253 ; Frostath. xii. 12.

If the stealing of the very smallest thing occurred, even of less value than a *thveit*, the theft was called *hvinnska* (pilfering), and the thief was ever thereafter called *hvinn* (pilferer), and had no rétt.

" If a man steals less than a *thveit* he shall be called *hvinn* all his life and have no rétt " (Bjarkey Law, 147).

Any one who stole fruit or plants from a garden or farm could be beaten and deprived of his clothes.

" If a man goes into the leek-garden or the angelica-garden of another he has no rétt, though he is beaten and struck, and all his clothes are taken off him " (Frostath., xiv. 14).

The act of stealing food in order to sustain life was not, however, punished.

" Next is this, that no man shall steal from another. Nevertheless it must be remarked that the man who gets no work to live by, and steals food to save his life for the sake of hunger, then this theft must not be punished at all " (N. G. L., ii., 168).

Any one who had been caught stealing three times was held irreclaimable, and it was considered less expensive to the state to rid society altogether of such offenders than to imprison them.

" The man who can get work to live on and steals the amount of an *eyrir*, and has not done it before, shall be brought to the Thing and redeem his hide with 3 marks of silver. If he steals as much a second time he shall redeem his hide with 6 marks of silver. If he does not he shall lose his hide, and a key shall be put on his cheek. If he steals as much the third time he shall lose his hide, and the king shall take 6 marks of silver from his property if he has so much. If the same man steals oftener he is to be slain " (N. G. L., ii. 168).

Minors **were not** held responsible for their acts, but if the thief was a woman of good family, she was sent out of the country ; if a native thrall, he was beheaded ; if a foreign thrall, his master could beat him within five days ; if a native bondwoman or a freed woman (free but born of slaves), she was severely punished.

" If a woman of good family steals, she shall be sent from the country to another king's realm. If a minor steals, it shall be paid back. If a native thrall steals, his head shall be cut off, or his master shall deny it with *séttareid*.[1] If a foreign thrall, or the son of a foreigner, his hide shall be flogged, or his master shall have him flogged within five days. . . . If a man's freedwoman (*leysingja*) or a native bondwoman steals, one of her ears shall be cut off, the second time her other ear shall be cut off, the third time her nose shall be cut off; then she is called *stúfa* and *núfa*, and may steal as much as she likes " (Gulath. 259).

If a high-born man induced a slave to commit robbery, he and not the slave was punishable.

" If a freedman and a thrall committed a theft together, the freedman alone was regarded as the thief, for, says the law, he who steals with another's thrall steals alone" (Gulath. 261).

The removal of boundary stones was considered theft.

" If a man takes up standing boundary stones and lays them down in an another place and moves them into the land of his neighbour, then he is a thief" (Gulath. 264).

According to the Gulathing Law bargains were made void in case of *fals*, or cheating, and the cheater was fined 3 marks.

" No man shall sell to another that in which there is fraud or deceit. If a man sells sand or dirt instead of meal or butter, with which he covers the sand or dirt, the fine is 3 marks " (Gulath. 40).

To use the property of another man without his permission was called *fornœmi*[2] if it was a ship, a horse, or snow-shoes, and it was punished by indemnity to the owner, the special name for which was *áfang*. If he refused to pay the indemnity his act was robbery.

---

[1] An oath.
[2] The law term for plundering another man's property.

The king neither received nor paid áfang, as his things could be used by other people, and he could use other people's things.

"No man shall take the ship or horse of a man except with the leave of the owner. If he takes it he shall pay one eyrir and a half. If the owner finds him on the ship or horse and asks áfang it is well if he will pay. If he will not, the fine is doubled, and a *ranbaug* (robbery-fine) is to be paid to the king" (Gulathing, 92).

Spoiling the property of another was called *spellvirki* (spoiling-deed); if the damage was more than half a mark the owner received damages according to the valuation, and doubtless also according to his rétt. If the spoiler would not pay he was outlawed.

"No man shall spoil another man's things. If he spoils so much that the loss amounts to half a mark it is a *spoiling-deed*, of all which is valued as much as half a mark. If a man cuts off the tail of another's horse so high that he cuts some of its skin, then it is a spoiling-deed. If a man makes a cut into the side of a ship, fore or aft, worth half a mark, it is a *spoiling-deed*"[1] (Gulathing, 96).

---

[1] Frostath. Law, x. 46, applies this to other cattle also.

CHAPTER VI.

HALLS AND BUILDINGS.

Vast size and beauty of some buildings—Wood the only material used—Halls —Durability of the wooden structures—Carved doorways—Use of tapestry—Walls adorned with shields—The seats—Positions of the guests—Carved benches—Houses and rooms—Women's apartments— Open hearths—Use of turf as fuel—Representations of episodes from the sagas.

FROM the Eddas and Sagas we sometimes get a vivid conception of the vast size, beauty, and magnificence of some of the buildings of the Vikings in their home in the North.

The only **material mentioned in their** construction **is** wood.

Each prominent man or chief lived on his estate with his family, followers, and servants. The collection of buildings they occupied was called *bær ;* [1] they were of different styles, and varied in number according to the power, wealth, and taste of the owners, and often seem to have been far apart from each other ; every house was known by a different name. These buildings appear to have been built so as to form a quadrangle, the front facing an open space or grass plot called *tún,* the whole being surrounded by a fence called gard,[2] through which the entrance was by a gate, "*grind,*" or gateway, "*hlid.*"

"Raudulf lived in the days of King St. Olaf in the Austrdal (Österdal valley), when the king was journeying round the land and forcing people to embrace Christianity. He sent his sons to King Olaf, and invited him home to a feast. It was rather late in the day when the king came to Raud, with two hundred men ; he saw high and well-closed fences, and when they came

---

[1] Bœr or Bu, meant a dwelling-place occupied by a single family.

[2] The name gard, gaard, still signifies all the buildings of a farm.

to the gate it was open, but nevertheless well guarded. . . .
When the king rode in, Raud bondi stood there with his sons
and many people. Raud received him and his men well; they
alighted from their horses. The king asked the bondi : 'Is
this fine house which I see here in the enclosure a church?'
The bondi answered : 'It is my sleeping-house, which was
built this summer, and is now just finished;' the whole roof
of the house was shingle-covered, and tarred. Then they
went to the sitting-room, and the king saw that it was very
large; it was roofed with planks and tarred" (Fornmanna
Sögur, v. 331).

The finest buildings were called *holl* (hall), and were only
built by kings, chiefs, or jarls.[1] Another building, called *sal*,[2]
seems to have been the same as the hall, as it was built for the
reception of guests. Here and there we have descriptions of
halls belonging to prominent chiefs, richly ornamented with
carvings, which sometimes represented the deeds of warriors;
and were it not for some of these mementoes, which have been
rescued from oblivion and decay, we might doubt that the art
of carving had been carried to such perfection as it was.
Walls, doors, beds, seats, &c., are mentioned as being richly
carved.

"Olaf Höskuldsson had a hall made in Hjardarholt larger
and more magnificent than people had before seen; on the
wall and on the ceiling famous Sagas were carved with such
skill that the hall was thought to be far more splendid when
the hangings were taken down" (Laxdæla, c. 29)

"It was customary at that time to have large halls at the
bœr, at which the people sat before long fires in the evening;
tables were placed in front of the men, who afterward slept
alongside the walls, away from the fires. During the daytime
the women carded and spun wool in these halls" (Gretti's Saga,
ch. xv.).

Some of the churches and farm-houses built in the beginning
of the Christian era, and some of the doors, testify to the
durability of their wooden structures.

---

[1] Hrolf Kraki, 34, 40; Jomsvikinga Saga, 5, 22; Volsunga, 3; Half's Saga, 12; Egil, 8.

[2] The *sal* is also called *Disarsal*, a building for sacrifices to the Disir.

DOORWAYS.

The carved doorways with illustrations from the Eddaic songs must have been taken from buildings of a far earlier date than the churches, but it is impossible to tell the date. Some of the carvings are from two inches in depth to a line.

Only in two places are stone-built (*steinhöll*) halls mentioned.

" Gunnhild, Queen of Norway, said to Ögmund (one of her men) : ' Show them (Rút and his men) the way to my house, and make a good feast for them there.' Ögmund went with them to a stone-hall, covered with the finest tapestry" (Njala, ch. 3).[1]

King Atli sent an invitation to the sons of Gjuki, Gunnar and Högni, brothers of Gudrun, his wife.

Atli sent
Early to Gunnar,
A man skilled in riding;
Knefród was he called;
He came to the burgh of Gjuki
And to the hall of Gunnar,
To the benches around the fire,
And to the well-loved beer.

There the warriors drank
Wine in the foreign hall,
Silent and hiding their fear;
They feared the wrath of the Hunar;
Then shouted Knefród,
The southern man,
With a chilling voice,
Sitting on a high bench—

" Atli sent me to ride
Hither on his errand
On a horse chafing the bit
Through the unknown dark forest
To bid you both, Gunnar,
To come to the bench
With eagle-beaked helmets
To call on him."

We own seven halls
Full of swords;
Of each of these
The guards are of gold;
I know my horse is best,
My sword the sharpest;
My bow adorns the bench,
My brynjas are of gold,
My helmet and shield are the whitest.
(Atlakvida.)

The scene depicted **on the** door-jambs on the following page is thus described :—

" King Atli urged his host to make a fierce assault; they fought hard, but the Gjukimgar made an attack so violent that he retreated into the hall, and they fought inside very sharply. Many fell, and at last all the men of the brothers (Gunnar and Högni) were slain, so that they two alone were alive; but before that many a man went to Hel by their weapons. King Gunnar was attacked, and because of overwhelming force was captured and fettered. Thereupon Högni

---

[1] Cf. also Heimskringla.

R 2

Fig. 1089.   Fig. 1090.
Door-jambs, Osstad Church, Sœtersdal.   Height, 6 feet ; width, 1¾ feet.

fought with great valour and manliness, and killed twenty of King Atli's greatest champions; he threw many into the fire which had been kindled in the hall; all agreed that such a man could hardly be found, but nevertheless at last he was overpowered and taken. King Atli said: 'It is a great wonder that so many have been slain by him here; cut out his heart, and that shall be his death.' Högni answered: 'Do as thou likest, I will gladly bear what you do, and you shall see that my heart is not afraid, I have stood hard things before. I liked to go into trials while unwounded, but now I am badly wounded, and you will yet have your will on me.' The counsellor of King Atli said: 'I have better advice; let us rather take the thrall Hjalli, but spare the life of Högni; that thrall is death-fated, live he ever so long he will always be as bad as now.' The thrall heard this and screamed loudly, and ran away to where he thought he was safe. He said he was to suffer on account of their fight, and that it was undeservedly; that the day was evil on which he was to die and give up his swine-keeping. They seized him and threatened him with a knife; he cried loudly before he felt its point.

"Högni did what is unusual in such personal peril, interceded for the thrall's life, saying he did not want to hear his screaming, and that he preferred to be the sufferer himself; the thrall was glad to get his life. Högni and Gunnar were both put in fetters. Atli bade Gunnar tell where the gold was, if he wished to live. He answered: 'I will sooner see the bloody heart of my brother Högni.' They seized the thrall a second time, and cut his heart out, and showed it to King Gunnar. He said: 'Here you may see the heart of Hjalli the coward, and it is unlike the heart of Högni the brave, for now it trembles much, but it trembled twice as much when it lay in his breast.' They went to Högni, urged by King Atli, and cut out his heart, but such was his strength of mind that he smiled while he suffered this torture, and everybody wondered at his firmness; and the deed is ever since held in remembrance. They showed to Gunnar the heart of Högni the brave, who said: 'It is unlike the heart of Hjalli, for now it quivers little, but less while it was in his breast; thou wilt lose thy life, Atli, as we do now. I alone know where the gold is, for Högni cannot tell thee now. I was sometimes going to tell it while both of us lived, but now I am left to myself; the Rhine shall keep the gold, rather than the Hunar wear it on their arms. King Atli told them to take away the prisoner, and it was done. Gudrun with some men went to Atli, and said: 'Mayest thou fare as ill as thou didst keep thy word to me.'

Fig. 1091.——Carved doorway, Sauland's Church, Thelemarken.   Height, 13 feet ;
width, 7¾ feet ; height of door, 7½ feet ; width of door, 2⅓ feet.

"King Gunnar was put into a pit in which were many snakes, and his hands were tied firmly. Gudrun sent him a harp; he showed his art, and played on it with great skill, striking the strings with his toes. He played so well and wonderfully that few thought they had heard the harp played so well with hands, and he continued this idrott until all the snakes fell asleep except a large hideous viper, which crawled to him, and pierced into his body with its snout till it reached his heart; and there he lost his life with great prowess" (Volsunga Saga, c. 37).

The halls had two doors, one for the men, the other for women;[1] many of them, which were often covered with designs in ironwork and runic inscriptions, must have been extremely beautiful. Sweden is especially rich in them. The church door of Versås, represented on the next page, is undoubtedly of great antiquity, as the svastica is found upon it.

The walls of the halls were hung with tapestry, made by the wives and daughters of the family, often representing the deeds of their forefathers or those of their lord; the carvings on the walls were occasionally very fine. An idea of the vast size of these festive halls can be gleaned from the number of guests and attendants they could hold. Some walls were adorned with shields put so closely together that they overlapped each other; many were inlaid or ornamented with gold and silver, which must have added to the brilliancy of the scene.

"King Knut began his journey to Borgundarhólm (Bornholm), where Egil had made a grand feast for him; he went to this with a large hird.[2] There he had a hall as large as a king's, hung all over with shields" (Flateyjarbók iii., p. 401).

"King Harald Sigurdarson came to the chief Aslák, and invited himself to his house. Aslák went to meet him, and received him very well. The king and his men were shown in to a hall and seated; it was covered with shields and most splendidly adorned in all respects"[3] (Flateyjarbók iii., p. 401).

Once Thorfinn (an Icelandic poet) sat on an easy chair before King Olaf. The king said to him:

---

[1] "The land-owner shall pay the value of the land at the *Karldyr* (men's door)." Gragas ii.

[2] Bodyguard.

[3] Cf. also Njala, 117.

" ' Make a song, Scald, about that which is drawn on the hangings.' Thorfinn looked at them, and saw that Sigurd slaying Fafnir was embroidered on them " (Flateyjarbók iii.).

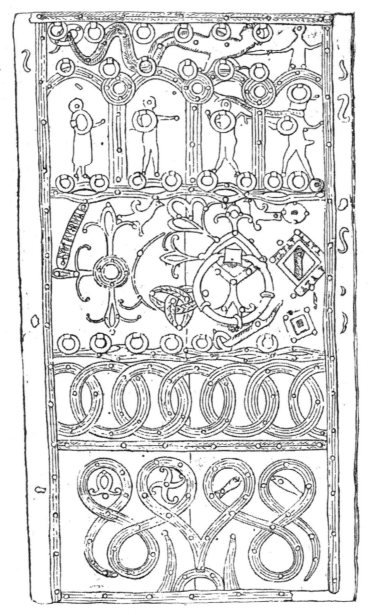

Fig. 1092.—The Church-door of Versås, Vestergötland. Representation of Sigurd slaying the serpent Fafnir : Runic inscription, *Asmutr Kärthi Dyrr* = Asmund made the door ; and svastica.

The halls were used for feasts,[1] and were built east and west, the long walls running north and south ; along the latter were the benches, and in the middle of each of these were the *hásæti*

---

[1] The banqueting halls were called *veitsluskali.*

or high-seats, also called *Ondvegi* or *Ondugi*, because the two seats were opposite each other (*Ond* = opposite, *vegi* = way). The most important benches were the *œdri bekk*, which ran along the northern wall, and the high-seat or the chief seat in the hall, which stood facing the sun, and was for the use of the master of the household, who never allowed any one else to use it. The long bench which ran along the southern wall was called "*úœdri bekk*" (the lower bench); the high-seat on this bench was called *annat ondvegi*, *nordr ondvegi* and *ondvegi a hinn uœdra bekk*, and was opposite to the other high-seat. To be placed in this *ondvegi* was the highest honour that could be shown to any one, and consequently this place was only assigned to most prominent men. The nearer the place on the benches assigned to any one was to the high-seat, the greater the honour; the places farthest away, near the doors, were the lowest.

"Thorkel Hák (an Ice-lander) had been abroad and became renowned in

Fig. 1093.—Door of Faaberg's Church, 9 feet high, 3 feet wide. Only three doors of the same kind (with iron-work) are preserved.

foreign countries . . . he went out to Sweden and became the companion of Sörkvir, and they ravaged the coast of the Baltic. East of Balagardssida, Thorkel, when going to get water one evening, met a *finngalkn* (a kind of dragon monster), which after a prolonged struggle he slew. Then he

Fig. 1094.—Door from Vånga Church, Ostergötland, Stockholm Museum.

went east to Adalsysla, where he also slew a flying dragon; afterwards he went back to Sweden. thence to Norway, and then to Iceland. He had these great feats carved above his locked bed, and on a chair in front of his high-seat. He was called Thorkel Hák because he spared no one, either in words or deeds, with whomsoever he dealt " (Njala, 120).

The seats on the *œdri bekk* were however more prominent than those on the lower bench. Next to the king, on the upper bench, on the right sat the under-kings or other prominent men.

On some occasions at a later period we find that to the left sat the queen with her women in the order of their rank, for the places of the women were then upon the long bench to the left of the king, and to the right of the other *ondvegismen*, the place of the men being on the left of the ondvegi.

Hildigunn wishing to make preparations **to receive** her kinsman Flosi, said :

" ' Now all my men-servants shall stand outside when Flosi rides into the yard, and the women shall clean the rooms, and put up the hangings and prepare the high-seat for him " (Njala, ch. 116).

The high-seat was often wide enough to hold two or three persons. Sigurd jarl of the Orkneys invited Gilli jarl of Sudreyjar (Hebrides) and Sigtrygg, king in Ireland, for Yuletide.

" Men were so seated that King Sigtrygg sat in the middle of the high-seat, and each of the jarls on either side of him. The men of Sigtrygg. and Gilli jarl sat on the inner side, and Flosi and Thorstein Siduhallson on the outer side of Sigurd jarl. The hall was full " (Njala, c. 154).

There were also, in some halls, transverse benches, called *Pall* or *Thverpall* (cross-benches) ; on these the women sat. In such cases the middle seat was the most prominent, and the lowest seat was at the end of the bench in the corner [1] : the word was used as a term of contempt.

" It was the custom of Gunnar and Njal to give feasts to each other once every winter in turns for friendship's sake. Now Gunnar had to stay with Njal, and went to Bergthorshval with Hallgerd. Helgi (son of Njal) and his wife were not at home. Njal received them well. When they had stayed there for a while Helgi and his wife Thórhalla came home. Then Bergthóra (Njal's wife) walked with Thórhalla up to the cross-bench (women's bench), and said to Hallgerd : ' Thou shalt give up thy seat to this woman.' She answered : ' I will not

---

[1] Njala 120 ; Fornmanna Sögur.

Fig. 1095.—Door, with knob of iron inlaid with silver, from Valthjofsstad Church, Iceland (now in the Copenhagen Museum).

move, for I do not want to be a corner-woman. I shall have my way here.' Then Thórhalla sat down" (Njala, c. 35).

The high-seats, which **were** cushioned, were often very beautifully carved with arms on both sides, and two pillars called Ondvegisulur, which were both carved and painted.

Only in extraordinary cases were there more than two high-seats, but we are told that Ingjald Illrádi, in order to receive the guests at his *arvel* after his father's death, built a new hall with seven high seats.

"Thordis and Bödvar went up on to the roof of the hall, took away the window covering to let the smoke out, and looked about the hall; they saw that the chair of Grima stood in the middle, and that Thór, seated, with his hammer, was carved on the chair-posts, but they did not see Thormod" (Fostbrœdra Saga).

To sit on the footboard in front of the king was to show submission; and it seems to have been usual when a subject **was** invested with the title of jarl to sit thus before the ceremony of investiture began.

"One day when King Magnus sat in his high-seat, and had many men with him, Svein Ulfsson sat on the footboard in front of the king. The king said: ' I will make known to the chiefs and all people my intention, which I want carried out. Svein Ulfsson, a man prominent both by his birth and deeds, has come to me here. He has become my man, and plighted me his word. You know that all the Danes have become my men this summer, and the land is without a chief; when I am gone, it is, as you know, often attacked by the Vendians, Courlanders, and others from Austrveg (eastern lands) and by the Saxar also. I promised to give them a chief to defend and rule the land. I see no man so well fitted for it in every respect as Svein Ulfsson. By his kin he is a chief. Now I will make him my jarl, and give into his hands Danaveldi to rule over while I am in Norway, as Knut the great made his father Úlf jarl chief over Denmark while he was in England. . . .' He rose, took a sword and fastened it on Svein's belt; then he took a shield and fastened it on his shoulder; then he put a helmet on his head and gave him the name of jarl, and those grants in Denmark which his father Úlf jarl had had there before. Then a shrine with holy things was brought, on which Svein laid his hands, and took oaths of allegiance to King

Magnus, who thereupon led him into the high-seat with himself" (Magnus the Good's Saga, ch. 24).

A great change was made in the position of the high-seat in later times by Olaf Kyrri (the Quiet), King of Norway (1067–1093), who placed it at the inner end of the hall where the cross-bench stood, instead of being in the centre of the long benches.

The benches were so made as to allow the guests to place at their backs, along the wall, their shields and swords, &c.

Fig. 1096.—Chair with five distinct rows of runes. The uppermost inscription gives the name of the owner of the chair—Thorunn Benedikt's daughter. On the front part of the seat are carved the twelve signs of the Zodiac, and above these their names in Latin, with runes; underneath them are inscribed in runes the Latin names of the twelve months.

"It was an old custom in Norway, Denmark, and Sweden to have doors at each end of the hall in king's residences and feasting halls, with the king's high seat on the middle of the long bench facing toward the sun. The queen sat on the left hand of the king, and the seat was then called *Ondvegi* (high-seat); the seats next to this on both sides were the most dignified for men and women, while the one next to the door was the least. The most high-born, old and wise man, was the king's counsellor, as it was then the custom of kings to have wise men who knew ancient examples and customs of their forefathers, but the counsellor sat on the northern bench opposite the king, on what was called the lower high-seat; there were also women on his right hand, but men on his left. It was then the custom for chiefs to carry the ale over the fire, and drink to the man sitting in the opposite high seat, and it was a great honour at that time to be toasted by the king.

"King Olaf had a raised bench placed in his feast halls, and put his high seat on the middle of the cross bench. He

Fig. 1097.—Chair from the Church of Grund, Iceland. Height, 39 inches; width, 30½ inches; depth, 17 inches. These two chairs are now in the old Northern Museum of Copenhagen. The seats, which are but little ornamented on the back, show that they were intended to be placed along a wall, and were undoubtedly covered by cushions. The lower part of the chair forms a box, with a small lid in the seat; on the upper part of its back, and on both the side-pieces, are inscriptions in later runes.

arranged his pages and candle boys in front; he also had a candle held in front of every high-born man who sat at his table, and a page holding a table cup before each; he had also chairs (stools) for his marshals and other wise men" (Fagrskinna, c. 219, 220).

A few seats, which have been saved from destruction, are beautifully carved with subjects from the Sagas.

Fig. 1098.—Inner side of the back. Gunnar in the snake pit. (Volsunga saga.)

Fig. 1099.—Back of the seat. $\frac{1}{19}$ real size.

Side view of chair. $\frac{1}{19}$ real size.

Fig. 1100.

Fig. 1101.

Carved bridal chair, formerly in Hitterdal Church, Thelemarken, Norway. Now on the farm of Hove. Showing the shape of hats worn and Gunnar in the snake-pit.

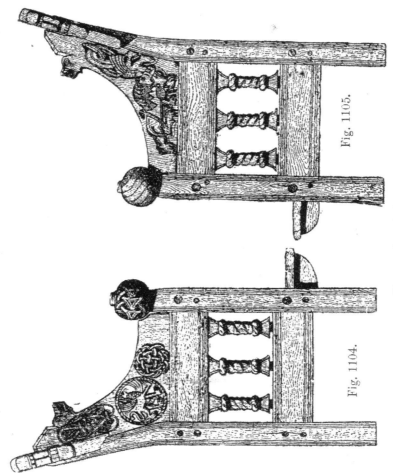

Fig. 1105.

Fig. 1104.

Chair. $\frac{1}{15}$ real size.

This carving may be explained by two different interpretations. The woman between the two horsemen may be Brynhild and the ring that which the gods got from the Dverg Andvari for a ransom for Otr, and which he predicted would always bring misfortune to its owner; or she may be Gudrun confiding to the messenger of Atli a ring, warning Gunnar and Hogni of their danger.

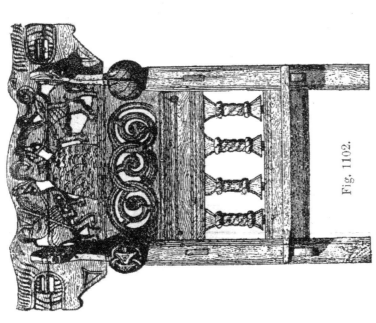

Fig. 1102.

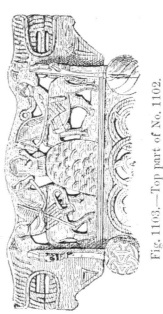

Fig. 1103.—Top part of No. 1102.

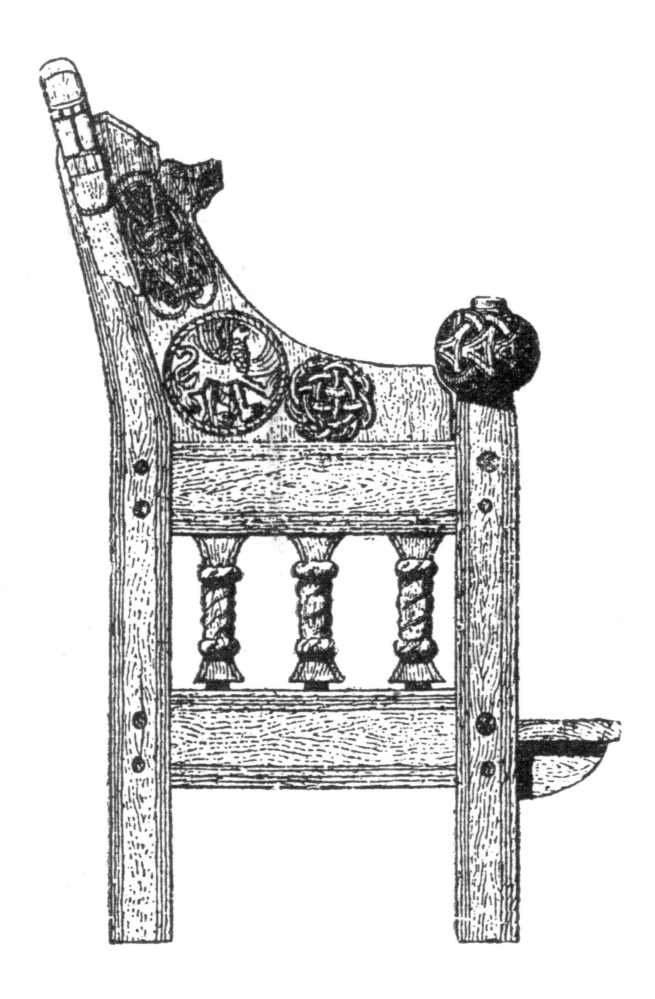

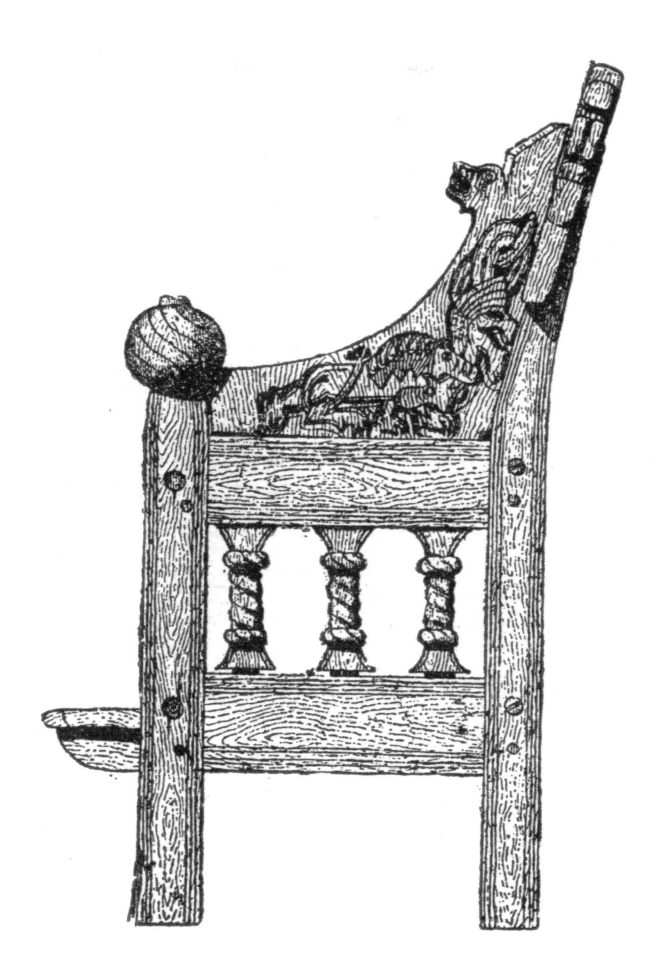

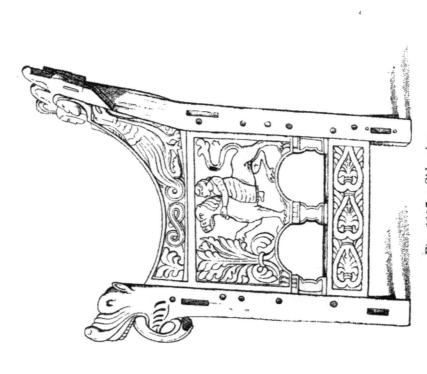

Fig. 1107.—Side view.
Chair supposed to have belonged to an old church, in Bö, Norway.

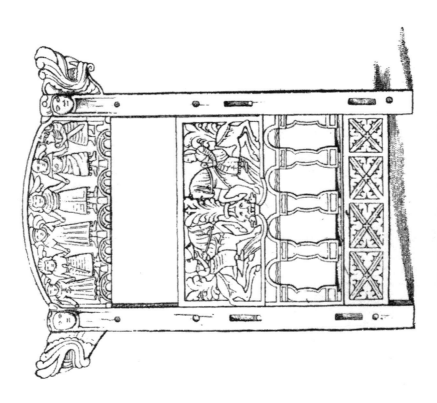

Fig. 1106.—Front view of chair.

One of the principal houses was the *skali*, or *eldhús*,[1] an oblong and quadrangular building, with a door at one, sometimes at both ends, intended for daily life and for feasting.

The *skemma*, *dyngja*, *stofa*, and *herbergi* were separate rooms, or buildings, sometimes used as sleeping apartments, where the

Fig. 1108.—Front view.

Chair carved with warriors fighting, with helmets on their heads. The helmets are similar to those of the Bayeux tapestry.

women of the household dwelt or remained during the daytime with their maids or attendants, and occupied themselves with

---

[1] The *skali* is often called the drinking or the sleeping *skali*. Orkneyinga, 18, 70, 115; Gisli Sursson, 29; Droplaugarsona Saga, 18, 28; Fornmanna Sögur, i. 288, 292; Kormak, 58; Fostbrœdra, 13; Njala, 78; Gunnlaug xi.

The *eldhús* meant a hall or chief room, where fires were kept. Gisli Sursson, 14, 15, 97; Eyrbyggja, 98; Laxdæla, 54.

s 2

all kinds of work.[1] Sometimes the *skemma* was built away
from other houses, and was then called *utskemma*. Where
there was a loft the lower room was called *undir-skemma*. In
such rooms the light came from window openings, and no fire
could be lighted.[2]

The *stofa*, which was usually occupied by women,[3] was large

Fig. 1109.—Side view of chair.
Warrior, with open helmet, slaying a dragon —Vaage, Gudbrandsdal, Norway.

or small; sometimes it was intended for a sleeping apartment.
At the royal residence in Nidaros, St. Olaf built a large
hirdstofa (king's men's house), with doors at both ends, for

---

[1] *Dyngja*—cf. Egil, 159; Gisli Sursson,
15; Njal, 66; Kormak, 10; Bjorn Hitdk,
68. *Skemma*—Færeyinga, 259; Gisli
Sursson, 7; Kormak, 228; Islendinga
Sögur, ii. 28. *Herbergi* seems to have
been a general term for any kind of room.

[2] Harald Hardradi, 70.
[3] Færeyinga, 41; Islendinga Sögur,
ii. 250; Fostbrœdra, 164. A *bad-stofa*,
or bath room, is mentioned. Eyrbyggja,
Forn. Sogur xiii. In St. Olaf's Saga, 82,
the *stofa* is said to be in the loft.

meals and general intercourse; a large *svefnskali* (sleeping house); and also a large *stofa*,[1] in which he held his *hirdstefna* (king's men's meetings). The common entrance led first into the *forstofa* (lobby), and then into the house proper; both were provided with doors, which could be locked. Sometimes the door was fastened on the inside with a *slagbrand* (bar).

Fig. 1110.—Back view of chair.
Warriors fighting on horseback.

The lofts, which consisted of rooms in the upper part of the *skali*, were frequently used as bedrooms, and were lighted by *loft-glugg* [2] (loft openings). Outside the loft there was, at least on one side, a *svalir* (balcony),[3] which was reached by an outside stairway. The loft generally had no communication with the *undir-skemma*.

---

[1] A house of the latter kind was also called *málstofa* (speaking-house) (Harald Hardradi's Saga, c. 45.
[2] Ingi's Saga, 28; Egil's Saga, 236;

Njal, 114, 199; Fms., 85; Ynglinga, St. Olaf, 116.
[3] Magnus the Good's Saga, c. 13.

When *Fjölnir* assisted King Frodi in Denmark, he was given a loft-room as a sleeping apartment; in an adjoining loft-room the flooring had been removed, in order to fill the large mead-vat standing in the *undir-skemma*. During the night *Fjölnir* went out, and as he had to return along the *svalir* to his room, he made a mistake as to the door, and fell down into the mead-vat.[1]

The beds (*hvila, rekkja*) were placed round the walls, inside the benches, and consisted of straw, the covering being the clothes worn in the daytime, and over the head a *feld* (fur cloak) was placed.

The buildings had windows, sometimes called light-holes, covered with a membrane, instead of glass, sufficiently large to enable a man to creep through them. The material used was the after-birth membrane, enclosing the foetus of the cow, which was stretched over the light-hole. This when dried is almost as transparent as glass, and can, for a certain time, resist the rain. It is still in use in some out-of-the-way places in Iceland; in the Sagas it is called *Skjall*, and the window is called *Skja*.

"Also if men sit in houses with *skjá* (light-holes) in them, it is so light inside that all men indoors recognise each other" (Konungs Skuggsja, p. 47).

There was no ceiling within the roof; the smoke from the open hearths on the floor, which covered the inside with soot, escaped through the *Ljori,* of which there was at least one, and which also admitted light.[2]

"Olaf Tryggvason burnt the hall of the seid-man Eyvind Kelda who escaped through the *Ljóri* (the light-hole in the roof)" (Olaf Trygg. c. 69).

We find that turf was occasionally used as fuel.

"Einar sailed westward to Shetland, and many men joined him. After that he went southward to the Orkneys, against Kalf Skurfa and Thorir (Treskegg). There a great battle was fought, and both the Vikings were slain.

> ' He gave Treskegg to the Trölls;
> Torfeinar slew Skurfa:
> He conquered the islands.'

---

[1] Yngl. Saga, c. 14.　　　　　[2] Ynglinga Saga, 34.

" After that he conquered the islands, and became a powerful chief.   He was the first man to cut turf from the ground for

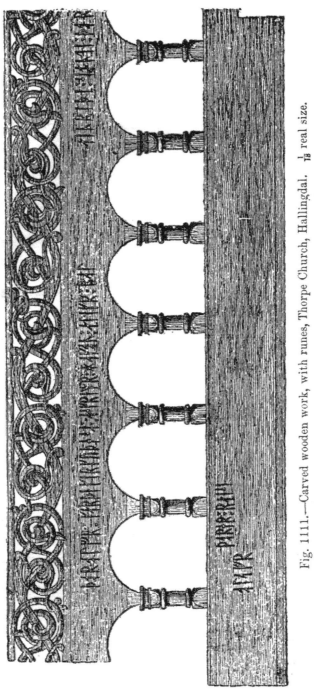

Fig. 1111.—Carved wooden work, with runes, Thorpe Church, Hallingdal. $\frac{1}{18}$ real size.

fuel at Torfnes (Turfness) in Scotland, for fuel was scarce in the islands " (Flateyjarbók, vol. i., p. 223).

Fig. 1112.—Doorway, Flaa Church, Hallingdal; 11½ feet high, 5½ feet broad.
Height of door, 8 feet; width of door, 2¼ feet.

Fig. 1113.—Doorway, Tuft Church, Sandver. Height, 11¼ feet; height of door,
7 feet; width of carving, 5½ feet; width of door, 2½ feet.—Norway.

Fig. 1114.—Carved doorway.—Portal of Opdal Church in Numedal, Norway, with representation of Gunnar in the snake-pit with his hands tied on his back. Height of sculptured part, 8 feet; breadth of sculpture, 5⅙ feet; height of door, 6¾ feet; width of door, 2½ feet.

Fig. 1115.

Fig. 1116.

Door-jambs of Hyllestad Church, Sætersdal. Height, 7 feet; width, 1¾ feet. Representation of seven episodes from the *Volsunga Saga*—Regin forging a sword; Sigurd trying it; Sigurd piercing the snake Fafnir; Sigurd roasting the heart of Fafnir; Sigurd's horse *Grani*; Sigurd slaying Regin; and Gunnar in the snake-pit playing the harp with his toes.

Fig. 1117.   Fig. 1118.
Door-jambs in Faaberg Church, Gudbrandsdal, about 7½ feet long.

Fig. 1119.

Fig. 1120.

Door-jambs in Lardals Church, Jarsberg. Height, 6⅙ feet; breadth of broader plank, 1⅓ feet. Representation of the skin of Regin's brother in the shape of an otter, and Sigurd slaying Fafnir.

Fig. 1121.   Fig. 1122.
Door-jambs, Ulvick Church, Hardanger ; 8 feet high ; nearly 2 feet wide.

Fig. 1123.   Fig. 1124.
Door-jambs, Hyllestad Church, Sætersdal ; 7 feet high, 1⅔ feet wide.

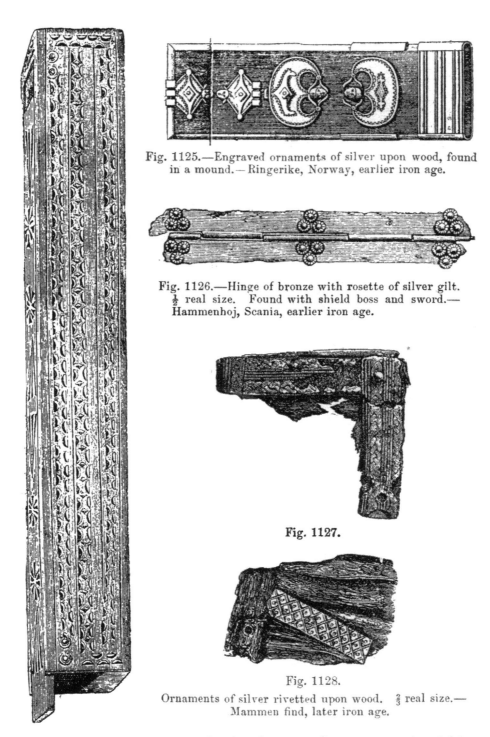

Fig. 1125.—Engraved ornaments of silver upon wood, found in a mound.—Ringerike, Norway, earlier iron age.

Fig. 1126.—Hinge of bronze with rosette of silver gilt. ½ real size. Found with shield boss and sword.—Hammenhoj, Scania, earlier iron age.

Fig. 1127.

Fig. 1128.

Ornaments of silver rivetted upon wood. ⅔ real size.—Mammen find, later iron age.

Fig. 1129.—A unique specimen of a box in extraordinary preservation (of box-wood), found in a mound, with a bronze kettle containing two ribs, one of a cow, the other of a dog. In the box was a large needle of bronze, fragments of a small silver ornament. At the ends are seen traces of bronze nails. $\frac{9}{10}$ real size.—Norway, earlier iron age.

We see in smaller objects (as on p. **112**) how highly finished were the carvings in the earlier iron age.

When a house was built the people inquired if the ground be lucky or unlucky in the new house. They measured the length and breadth repeatedly, and then they carefully examined if all the measurements were the same. If the measurements grew longer they thought it foreboded an increase of well-being for the dwellers; if the opposite they thought it foreboded a decrease in the well-being of the persons.

Ogmund went to Iceland from Norway.

" He measured the ground for his house. It was a belief that if the measurement was the same when it was tried repeatedly, then the well-being of the man whose measuring-yard grew too short would decrease, but increase if it grew longer. The measurement was performed three times and the yard was too short."

CHAPTER VII.

FEASTS, ENTERTAINMENTS.

Conviviality of the Northmen—Recital of poems and sagas at the feasts—
Music—Arrangement of the hall—Splendour of the table decorations—
Plainness of the food—Order of precedence—The custom of drawing lots
for places of honour—Entertainment of the guest by high-born maidens
—Presents given at the end of the feast—Heavy drinking—Viking
customs—Manners at table—General hospitality of the people—Waiting
at table.

IN reading the Sagas we are particularly struck at the number
of feasts which marked the life of the Northmen. Every
event the least above the common was celebrated in this
fashion, a fashion which has by no means disappeared from
among the Norsemen's descendants. On the occasion of such
feasts, the houses and halls were prepared in the most elaborate
manner; tapestry and embroidered cloths were hung on the
walls, and spread over the benches. Poems and Sagas were
recited, and music was also occasionally introduced. Among
other stringed instruments, the Sagas mention as used at
feasts, were, besides the harp, the *fidla* (probably fiddle) and
gigja (also probably a kind of fiddle).

In some cases as soon as the dishes had been put on the
table the enjoyment of the repast was heightened by music.

"When King Olaf of Sweden came to the table he asked
where lawman Emund was. On hearing that he was at home
at his lodgings, he said: 'Go after him, he shall be my guest
to-day.' Thereupon the dishes were brought in, and afterwards players with harps and gigjar entered" (St. Olaf's Saga,
c. 96).

Harald Fairhair and Eirik Eymundsson of Sweden were
at a feast with the powerful bondi Áki in Vermaland.

"Áki owned a large and old feast-hall; he had a new hall
made; it was as large as the other, and very well made; he
had it covered all over with new hangings, and the old hall

with old ones. When the kings came to the feast, Eirik with his hird was seated in the old hall, and Harald with his men in the new hall. All the table service was arranged so that Eirik and his men had old vessels and horns, though they were gilded and well ornamented. Harald and his men had only new vessels and horns; they were all ornamented with gold, painted with images and bright like glass. The drink on both sides was very good " (Harald Fairhair's Saga, c. 15).

A young Icelander, Brand, went to Norway with two of his friends. They visited Harek, who was high-born, but very ill-tempered.

" One day he (Harek) went up to Brand with a large drinking-horn, and asked him to drink it with him; but Brand refused,

Fig. 1130.——From Bayeux tapestry, showing drinking-horns, bowls, &c., similar to those of the finds.

saying: 'I have not got too much sense, but I do not drink away that which I have, and it seems to me thou wilt need all thine also'" (Ljósvetninga Saga, c. 8).

" When King Olaf approached the farm-servants ran ahead, to the farm and into the house, where Ásta, his mother, sat with her women. They told her of the king's journey, and that he would soon be there. Ásta rose at once, and bade men and women prepare for him in the best manner. She set four women to take the fittings of the *stofa*, and quickly arrange the hangings and the benches. Two men spread

T 2

straw on the floor, two brought in the *trapiza* (table at the entrance to the hall), and the *skap-ker* (a vat from which ale was put in cups); two placed the tables, two the food (two she sent away from the house), and two carried in the ale; all the others, both men and women, went out into the yard. Messengers went to King Sigurd to take him his *tignarklædi* (clothes of rank) and his horse, which had on a gilt saddle, and the bit was gilt all over and enamelled. Four men Ásta sent in four different directions throughout the district, inviting the high-born men to a feast, in order to welcome her son. All who were there were dressed in their best clothes, and to those who had none suitable she lent clothes " (St. Olaf's Saga, c. 30).

In contrast with the splendour of the table decorations, the food was often plain, for cooking had not attained a high standard.

Ölver, a húskarl (free servant) of the chief Thórir, and Egil with twelve men when on a journey came to Bárd, a steward of King Eirik's, in Atley.

" Bárd said: ' Now we will put the tables for you, I know you will like to go to sleep, you are tired.' Ölver liked this well. Then tables were set and food given to them, bread and butter, and large bowls filled with curds were set forward. Bárd said: ' It is a great pity that there is no ale here, so I cannot entertain you as well as I would like. You must help yourselves to what there is.' They were very thirsty, and swallowed the curds in large draughts. Then Bárd had buttermilk brought in, and they drank it " (Egil's Saga, c. 43).

" King Olaf and all his men stayed with his father, Sigurd Syr, awhile. Sigurd gave them as fare on alternate days fish and milk, meat and ale " (St. Olaf's Saga, c. 33).

Great care was taken at the feasts to seat guests according to their proper rank, as precedence was thought very much of.

" The Icelandic chiefs Olaf Höskuldsson and Usvifr continued their friendship, though there was some rivalry between the younger men. That summer Olaf held a feast half a month before winter: Usvifr had also prepared one on the first winter-nights. Each invited the other, with as many men as he thought proper. Usvifr went first to the feast of Olaf, and at the appointed time came to Hjardarholt; his daughter Gudrun

Fig. 1131.—Iron knife, ⅜ real size, in a mound with burnt bones, an iron comb, fragments of two urns destroyed by fire, &c.—Norway.

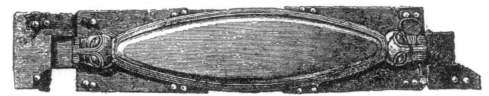

Fig. 1132.—Sharpening stone made fast with bands of bronze, ½ real size, found in a large tumulus with a shield boss of iron, several arrow-heads of iron, a large fibula of bronze, &c.—Norway.

Fig. 1133.—Knife of iron, ½ real size, found in a stone cist, with a double-edged iron sword, two spear-heads, &c., and a skeleton.—Cairn, Öland.

Fig. 1134.

Fig. 1135.

Scabbard of bronze, ⅔ real size, found in a tumulus mound inside a skeleton, with iron knife, ½ real size, Rikirde, Götland.

End of horn.

Fig. 1136.   Fig. 1137.

Bronze drinking-horn, the rim ornamented with a band of silver with figures in repoussé work.

Fig. 1138.—Ornament of bronze for a drinking-horn, found with a little gold bead.—Götland.

Fig. 1141.

Fig. 1139.—Fragment of drinking horn of bronze.—Norway.

Fig. 1142.

Fig. 1140.—Spoon of Elk horn, $\frac{2}{3}$ real size, found in the black earth in Björko, Sweden.

Silver ornament for knife (real size), found with a bronze kettle containing burnt bones, a gold ring, and two small silver ornaments.—Romsdal, Norway.

Fig. 1143.—Ornamentation drinking-horn of bronze, found with two other fragments of drinking horns, &c.

with her husband Bolli and his sons were with him. The next morning, as they walked along the hall, a woman stated how the women should be seated; at this time Gudrun stood opposite to the bed where Kjartan Olafsson slept. Kjartan was dressing, and put on a scarlet kirtle; he said to the woman who had spoken about the seats, for no one was quicker to answer than he: 'Hrefna shall sit in the high-seat, and be most honoured in every respect while I am alive.' Gudrun had always before sat in the high-seat at Hjardarholt and elsewhere. She heard this, and looked at Kjartan and turned pale, but said nothing" (Laxdæla, c. 46).

The guests sometimes drew lots for the place of honour.

Two brothers, Hreidar and Ivar, had a Yule-feast at Nes, in Vors, in Norway.

"Twelve guests were to sit together, and lots were drawn about who should sit next to Astrid, the daughter of Vigfus hersir; Eyjolf, an Icelander who was on a visit, always drew the lot to sit at her side; no one noticed that they talked more to each other than other people; but many said it would end in her becoming his wife. The feast was magnificent, and the people were sent away with gifts" (Vigaglum's Saga, c. 4).

Men and women sometimes went in pairs to the festive board, and sat together on the same seat. The pride of the high-born girls was very great, and none but brave **men** could claim the privilege of leading them to their **seats**. Occasionally the women drank together with the men.

"Egil and his brother Thórólf were on a Viking expedition, and went to Halland. As they did not ravage there, Arnfid jarl invited them to a feast, and they went, with thirty men from their ships. Before the tables were put up, the jarl said that the seats would be allotted there; that men and women should drink together, as many as could, but those who were without companions should drink by themselves. They placed the lots in a cloth, and the jarl picked them out. He had a very handsome daughter, then well full-grown. The lots fell so that Egil should sit at her side that evening . . . . Egil rose and took her seat. When the men sat down in their places, the jarl's daughter sang:—

What wilt thou do, lad, in **my** seat?	Thou didst not see the raven in the autumn
For seldom hast thou given	Croak over the heap of carrion;
A wolf warm flesh;	Thou wert not where
I want to be seated alone.	Shell-thin edges met.

"Egil took hold of her and seated her at his side; and sang :—

I have gone with a bloody blade	We made angry battle ;
And with a sounding spear	Fire played about the seats of men.
So that the wound-birds followed me,	We let the bloody corpses
There was hard onset on the Vikings,	Fall asleep in the town-gates.

"Then they drank together, and were very merry that evening, and the next day too. Then the Vikings went to their ships, and they separated from the jarl in friendship and exchanged gifts" (Egil's Saga, c. 48).

Sometimes **high-born maidens entertained their guests** alone.

Hjalti, Gizur, and Óttar, the skalds of St. Olaf, **went to** Sweden in order to reconcile the king to St. Olaf.

"They went one day to the house of the king's daughter Ingigerd; she sat and drank with many men. She received them well, for they were known to her. . . . They sat there the greater part of the day and drank; she put many questions to Hjalti, and asked him to come often and talk with her. He did so" (St. Olaf's Saga, c. 71 (Heimskringla)).

At the end of a feast presents were given to the guests.

Thorgeir, the famous Godir (lawman), who accepted Christianity on the people's behalf at the Althing A.D. 1000, made a feast.

"After the feast Thorgeir gave large gifts. He gave his kinsman Finnbogi five stud-horses, dandelion yellow in colour. It was said that they were the best horses in Nordlendinga-fjordung (the northern quarter of Iceland)" (Finnboga Saga, c. 23).

When Harald Fairhair came to Halogaland, great feasts were prepared for his reception on his own farms among his lendirmen or powerful bœndr. The feast that Thorolf prepared was so magnificent, that the king was jealous of it.

"The king had nearly three hundred men when he came to the feast, but Thórólf had five hundred men already there. Thórólf had prepared a large corn-barn, and set benches in it; there they drank, for no other room was large enough for them all to be in it together. Shields were hung all round the room. The king sat down in a high-seat. When the room was full from one end to the other, he looked round and got red in his face, but said nothing, and they felt that he was angry. The feast was splendid, and all the provisions were of the best. The king was not very merry, and stayed there for three nights, as he intended. On the day the king was about to leave, Thórólf went to him and asked him to go down with him to the beach. The king went. There the dragon ship which Thórólf had had made was floating, with tents and all outfittings. Thórólf gave it to the king, and asked him to consider that so many guests had been invited to do him honour, and not to compete with him. The king took this well" (Egil's Saga, c. 11).

Very many Sagas give instances of the heavy drinking at these feasts.

The Norwegian chief Thórólf Skjálg was at warfare one summer, and in the autumn when he came home he made a great feast.

"His foster-son Rögnvald said to the cup-bearers, that if men got very drunk in the beginning the feast would be considered a great feast, and told them to carry as much drink in as they could. Then Rögnvald burnt the hall, and the men in their beds were so drunk that they did not awake till the flames were playing round them, and they were burnt" (Olaf Tryggvason's Saga, 145 (Fornmanna Sögur)).

"When King Granmar heard of this (King Hjörvard's arrival) he sent men to him and invited him to a feast with all his men. He accepted this, for he had not ravaged in King Granmar's realm; when he came to the feast there was a great entertainment. In the evening, when the toasts were to be drunk, it was the custom for kings who ruled in the land and for their guests to drink in pairs at feasts in the evening, each man and woman together, as far as possible, the old ones keeping by themselves. It was the law of Vikings, even if they were at feasts, to drink in parties. King Hjörvard's high-seat was prepared opposite King Granmar's, and all his men sat on that bench. King Granmar told his daughter Hildi-gunn to make herself ready and carry ale to the Vikings. She was the most beautiful of women. She took a silver cup, filled it, and went before King Hjörvard and said: 'Hail, all Ylfingar, to Hrolf Kraki's memory'; she drank half of it and handed it to Hjövrard. He took the cup and her hand with it, and said she must come and sit at his side. She answered that it was not Viking custom to drink in pairs with women.

"Hjörvard said that he would rather make a change in the Viking laws in order to drink in pairs with her. Then she sat down, and they spoke of many things in the evening" (Ynglinga Saga, c. 41).

Next day King Hjörvard demanded her in marriage from Granmar, and was successful in his suit (Ynglinga Saga, c. 41).

In the earliest times that the manners at table of such heavy drinkers should have been rather **coarse** is not surprising.

"The champion Bödvar went into the hall of Hrolf Kraki, and sat down near the door. When he had been there for a short time he heard a noise from the corner next to it, and saw that a man's hand, very black, extended from a large heap of bones which lay there. He walked up to it and asked who was in the heap of bones; he was answered, timidly: 'I am called Hött, good Bökki.'[1] Bödvar said: 'Why art thou here? and what art thou doing?' Hött answered: 'I make me a shield-burgh, my good Bökki.' Bödvar took hold of him and pulled him out of the heap of bones. Hött shouted loudly: 'Now thou wantest me to be killed; I had prepared myself so well for defence before, and now thou hast torn my shield-burgh asunder. . . .' Bödvar took him and carried him out of the hall to a lake in the neighbourhood; and few saw it, and he washed him all over his body. Bödvar then went to the seat he had been sitting in before, and led Hött with him, and seated him at his side. Hött was so frightened that all his limbs trembled, but he thought nevertheless that this man was going to help him. Evening approached and the men came into the hall, and the champions of Hrólf saw that Hött was seated on the bench, and they thought the man who had done that had been rather shameless. Hött had a dismal look when he saw his acquaintances the hirdmen, for he had only met with unkindness from them; he wished greatly to live and go back to his bone-heap, but Bödvar held him so that he could not run away. . . . The hirdmen threw first small bones across the floor to Bödvar and Hött; Bödvar pretended not to see this. Hött was so frightened that he took neither food nor drink, expecting to be hit every moment; he said to Bödvar: 'My good Bökki, now a large joint-bone is going to hit thee, and it is meant to harm us.' Bödvar told him to be silent, and parried it with the hollow of his hand; he got hold of the joint-bone, with the leg attached,

---

[1] Pet name of Bödvar.

and threw it back at the man who cast it, and into his face, so strongly that he was slain. The hirdmen became much alarmed. The news reached King Hrolf and his champions in the castle that a tall man had come to the hall and killed one of the hirdmen, and they wanted him to be slain. The king asked if the hirdman had been killed without cause. ' Almost so,' they said. When he heard the truth, he said : ' The man shall not be slain ; you have got into a bad habit of throwing bones at harmless men ; it is a disgrace to me, and a great shame for you to do such things. I have often spoken of this before, but you have taken no heed ; call the man whom you have now assailed, that I may know who he is.' Bödvar came before the king, and became his hirdman " (Hrolf Kraki's Saga, c. 43).

It was a great recommendation for a man, when it could be said that his house afforded accommodation to every one. Hospitality was a leading trait in the character of the people. In the code of conduct known as Havamal (see p. 401) we see that the stranger must be well received, and the Sagas give some remarkable examples of the generous hospitality of the people, among them that of Geirrid, who had emigrated from Norway to Iceland :—

" Geirrid settled in Borgardal, inside Alpta fjord. She caused her house to be built across the high-road, so that all were obliged to ride through it. A table set with food, which was given to every one who wanted it, always stood ready.[1] Owing to this she was looked upon as a high-minded woman " (Eyrbyggja, c. 8).

" Some winters later, Hörd Grimkelson, with his wife Helga, Sigurd, foster-son of Torfi, Helgi Sigmundarson, and thirty men, landed at Eyrar, in Iceland. At that time Hörd was thirty winters old ; he had then been abroad for fifteen winters in succession, and had got much property and honour. Illugi the red, from Hólm, came to the ship, and invited him and all his men to stay with him, and did everything most honourable to them. Hörd took this well, and thought it a good invitation ; he went to him with twenty-five men, and they were treated with ale all the winter, with the greatest liberality " (Hörd's Saga, c. 19).

There are several passages in the Sagas from which we see that the usual length of time for a visit was three days.

---

[1] Cf. also Landnama, Part ii. 6.

When Einar, the poet, went to Iceland, he called on Egil, who was not at home.

" Einar waited three nights for him ; as it was not customary to make a visit longer than three nights, he prepared to go away " (Egil's Saga, c. 82).

The waiting at the tables was performed by servants, called *skenkjarar* (fillers), who filled the horns from the *skapker*, and carried them round ; even women of rank on special occasions filled the horns for the guests and brought them to them.

After a feast, it was the custom for the host to provide those of his guests who required them with horses and all necessaries for their journey home.

CHAPTER VIII.

DRESS OF MEN.

Luxury in dress—Material used—Popular colours—Everyday dress—Various garments—Belts of silver and gold—Cloaks—Trailing gowns—Shoes—Plaids — Gloves — Hats—Moustaches and beards—Hair worn long—Fashions—Splendour of chiefs' accoutrements.

THE finds as well as the Sagas, which are confirmed by the Bayeux tapestry, show that from a very early period the people of the North dressed with great luxury; but, with the exception of the complete garments of the bog finds, only fragments of wearing apparel belonging to the iron age have been discovered, which in most instances are thoroughly discoloured.

In the Sagas we have only partial descriptions of the dress worn by men and women, and though many names of pieces of clothing are mentioned, very little light is otherwise thrown upon the subject.

The material used for clothing seems to have been the same for both sexes—linen, wool, silk, skins, and furs. Among the costly materials mentioned is "*pell*" which is supposed to be like velvet. The materials were sometimes seamed with gold and silver thread, or embroidered. It was the custom to have a border on many of the clothes called *hlad*, which was either a band, ribbon, or a kind of lace.

Blue, red, green, scarlet, and purple, were the colours most in favour; grey was the colour for everyday use, and white *vadmal*, a coarse or thick woollen stuff, was the distinctive clothing for slaves.

The trousers were worn at a very early time, as we have seen from the Bog finds, and were kept in their proper place by a belt round the waist, and had the socks knitted on to them, over which were shoes. Over the linen and woollen shirts was the coat of mail. Over the shoulders a cloak was worn, resembling that of the Romans or Greeks, with a fringe or border at the sides. These cloaks were fastened by fibulæ. The costumes of the Bayeux tapestry agree with the descriptions of the Sagas.

The every-day dress of Geirmund is thus described :—

"He usually dressed thus. He wore a red scarlet kirtle, and over it a grey cloak (feld), and on his head a bearskin cap (húfa). He wore in his hand a large sword. It was not adorned with silver, and its blade was keen and broad and no rust on it. He called the sword Fótbít (foot-cutter), and never let it go out of his hand" (Laxdæla, c. 29).

Fig. 1144.—Cloth with representation of lion or leopard. ⅓ real size.—Mammen find.

Vigaskúta saw "that a large man in a green cloak rode from Thverá (a farm), and knew that it was Glúm. He alighted from his horse. He had on a cloak of two colours, black and white" (Viga Glum's Saga, c. 16).

"Hrút started up in a shirt and linen breeches, and threw over himself a grey cloak, and had in his hand a halberd adorned with gold, which King Harald had given him" (Laxdæla, c. 37).

"The king had on a red cloak (möttul)[1] with bands, and a

---

[1] Here the word *möttul* = mantle, the same garment which elsewhere is called *skikkja*.

spear in his hand. He twisted the cloak-pin off, and leaned upon the blade of his spear. When Heming came down he took hold of the king's cloak, but the king bowed down his head, and let go the cloak, so that Heming flew down off the rock " (Flateyjarbok, iii. 409).

Fig. 1145.—Piece of cloth found in Bjerringhoi mound at Mammen, near Viborg.—⅓ real size.

Fig. 1146.—Fragment of woollen cloth, ornamented with hands and human faces. ⅓ real size.—Mammen find.

Helgi, a Norwegian trader, was invited to stay with Gudmund the powerful, on Mödruvellir, a whole winter. When he left he said to him :—

" ' Now, herra, look at this payment for quarters, though it is less than you deserve.' It was a cloak, the fur of which was lined with pell, with a golden band on the neck-strap, a most costly thing. Gudmund said : ' I thank thee for it, I have never received a better gift.' They parted good friends " (Ljosvetninga Saga, c. 13).

"Ögmund put on a cloak (feld) of two colours, ornamented with bands beneath the shoulder; it was very costly" (Fornmanna Sögur, ii.).

Fig. 1147.—Well preserved bracelet of silk, knitted with gold threads, found in Bjerringhoi mound at Mammen, near Viborg. Real size.

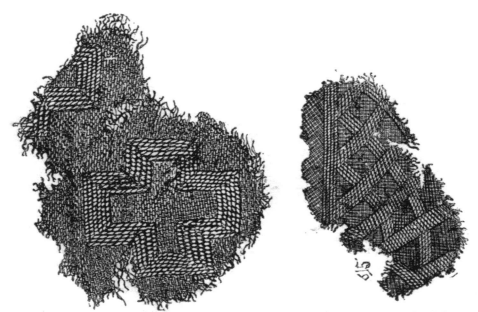

Fig. 1148.—Piece of woven woollen cloth, brownish colour.

Fig. 1149.—Remnant of brown woollen cloth of thin threads and very loose weaving.

"He (Thormód) had covered himself with a double-furred cloak which he owned. It was black on one side, and white on the other" (Fóstbrædra Saga, c. 32).

The different garments were:—

Skyrta, or *serk,* the name given to the shirt worn next the body, which was put on by means of a small opening[1] for the head called *höfudsmátt.*

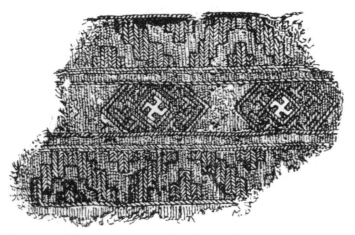

Fig. 1150.—Border of fine woven red silk cloth (1½ inches broad), with gold and silver threads woven into it, and four-cornered pattern with representation of Svastica, found in the mound.

Fig. 1151.—Piece of cloth with two lions or leopards facing each other. ⅓ real size.—Mammen find.

The *kyrtil* shaped like a shirt with sleeves, and put over it. Blue, red, and brown seem to have been the favourite colours for this garment.[2] Sometimes the kirtle is called

---

[1] Laxdæla, 46.　　　　[2] Fornmanna Sögur; Harald Hardradi.

skyrta, or shirt; so both must have been alike in shape. A sleeveless kirtle is mentioned as uncommon.[1]

The *hjúp* which seems to have been a short kirtle without sleeves, sometimes lined with furs, worn sometimes over the coat of mail.[2]

"Sigurd went up on the island. He wore a red kirtle, and a blue cloak with straps on his shoulders; he was girt with a sword, and had a helmet on his head" (Fœreyinga Saga, c. 57).

Linbrækr (linen drawers) which seem to have been often worn, and were kept on at night.

Breeches seems to have been of two kinds:—

Brækr (the more common) were held up round the waist by

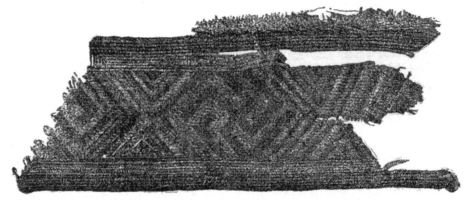

Fig. 1152.—Fragment of woollen stuff, ⅔ real size, found in a tumulus with fragments of a sword, spear points. two axes, a shield boss of iron, and a large number of pieces of stuffs of different qualities, pieces of the skin of a horse still having hair adhering to it.—Norway.

a belt, fastened with a buckle, which was usually wide, but considered more showy when it was narrow.

"He had strange clothes made—hairy breeches (brækr) and cloak, and he had them put into boiling pitch and hardened" (Ragnar Lodbrók, c. 2).

Hosur[3] were a showier kind of breeches; they seem also to have covered the feet, and to have been tight, like high stockings. They were of cloth or skin, and resembled high boots: spurs were often attached to them. Sometimes the

---

[1] Magn. Baref., 8.
[2] Flateyjarbok, i. 481.
[3] In the time of Olaf Kyrri, before 1100, very tight *hosur* were used. Blue trousers and blue and grey *hosur* are mentioned.

breeches were worn outside the kirtle, and a man was then said to be "girt in breeches," the waistband serving as a belt.

" A crowd of men had come to the bœr. Some of these had walked up to Gaulardal. It happened that a broad-shouldered man walked past them; he wore a cloak and white hose, and was alone " (Fornmanna Sögur, v.).

Leistabrækr were breeches and stockings in one, and seem to have been tight-fitting, somewhat similar to those found in the Thorsberg bog, which were of great antiquity. On the relief ornamentation on a superb silver vase of Greek workmanship found at Kertch, representing the capture of wild horses, and the different phases of taming them, the men are represented as wearing such breeches.

Hökulbrækr. Of these there is no description.

Fig. 1153.   Fig. 1154.
Bronze plates found, Björnhofda, parish of Thorslunda, showing man's trousers, &c.

Sokkar (socks) were also used.

Thórodd had been wounded in a fight, and his breeches were all wet from the blood.

" The servant of Snorri was to pull off the breeches, and when he pulled he could not get them off. Then he said: ' It is not a lie about you, the sons of Thorbrand, that you are very showy, as you wear such tight clothes that they cannot be pulled off.' Thórodd answered: ' You do not pull hard enough.' Then the man put his feet against the bedside and pulled with all his strength, and the breeches did not come down. Then Snorri godi came and touched the leg all over, and found that a spear was standing through the foot between the tendon and the leg, and had pierced the foot and the breeches " (Eyrbyggja, c. 45).

U 2

The belts worn round the waist were often very costly, and of silver and gold.

"Thjóf (= Fridthjóf) threw off his cloak; he had on a dark blue kirtle under it, and wore the good ring on his hand (or arm). He wore a broad silver belt round his waist, and a large bag with pure silver money in it, and a sword at his side. He had on his head a large hood made of skin, for he had weak eyes and was hairy all over his face" (Fridthjóf's Saga, c. 11).

These cloaks were the most costly part of their dress; they were made of materials called *gudvef*, *pell*, and *baldakin*.[1] Among the many kinds of cloaks mentioned were—

The *Kapa*, or hood-cloak, the usual colour of which for everyday use was grey; for feasts, scarlet; sometimes lined with fur.

The *Feld*, identical with the Kapa, both sides of which were sometimes of different colours.

There were also rain or dust cloaks, and cloaks made of reindeer-skin.

The finest were the *skikkja*[2] and *möttul*, which were only worn by the high-born chiefs, being a characteristic of birth, just like the paludamentum or military cloak of the Romans, or the chlamys of the Greeks, which were of scarlet bordered with purple. The cloaks and mantles (möttul) were fastened round the neck or held up by bands or straps, which were so long that they could be put on the head.

The cloak seems to have been long enough for a sword to be carried under it without being seen.

"Then Thorólf put off his strap-mantle (*seilamöttul*), which was of scarlet, lined with grey fur. He laid it over Thorstein, but it did not reach lower down than his waist when he rose. He then took it off and told him to wear it himself, and give him another garment, though it might not be as fine. Thorólf then fetched a hairy cloak (lod-kápa), and told him to put it on. He threw it over him, and it was neither too long nor too short" (Svarfdæla Saga).

"He (Sigurd) wore blue breeches, a shirt, and **a mantle**

---

[1] Baldakin, stuff or skin from Bagdad.
[2] It seems to have been the custom to fold up the edges of the skikkja (Magnus Erlingson, ch. 13, 37; Magnus Barefoot, 8 Flateyjarbók, iii.).

(*möttul*) with straps (*tygil*) for over-garment. He looked down and kept the mantle-straps in his hands, and by turns put them on and off his head. When they had passed the cape they had got merry and drunk, rowed hard and kept little guard. Sigurd rose and went to the gunwale, and his two guards did the same, and both took his mantle and held it up as was the custom to do with highborn men " (Magnus Blind, c. 16).

" Halldor had on a cloak on which were long brooches [1] as was then customary " (Laxdæla, ch. 75).[2]

The Slœdur was a trailing gown of costly stuff embroidered with gold and ornamented with bands.

In the time of Olaf Kyrri (the Quiet, 1066–93) the men's gowns had trains, laced on the side, with sleeves 10 feet long, so tight that they had to be pulled on with a leather thong, and jerked up to the shoulder. These gowns were soon considered old-fashioned : it was also customary to wear gold rings round the legs.

" In the days of King Olaf Kyrri, drinking at the inns and parting-bouts began in the trading-towns, and the people became fond of show ; they wore costly breeches laced tight to the leg, and some fastened gold rings round their legs ; the men wore trailing gowns (drag-kyrtil), laced on the sides, with sleeves ten feet in length, and so narrow that they had to be put on with a running-string and laced tight up to the shoulder ; the shoes were high, sewed with silk, and some of them ornamented with gold. There was much other display at this time " (Olaf Kyrri, c. 2).

This sort of sleeve belonged to the old-fashioned kind of clothing.

" He (Arinbjörn) gave Egil as Yule-gift a gown (*slœdur*) of silk, largely embroidered with gold, and set with gold-buttons all the way down the front ; he had this made so as to fit Egil. Arinbjörn also gave him a new cut suit of clothes, of many-coloured English cloth " (Egil's Saga, 70).

Erling jarl was tall and brawny, somewhat high-shouldered, with a long and thin face and light complexion ; he was very

---

[1] Brooches = fibulæ.
[2] Cf. also for cloaks.—Egil's Saga, c. 77 ; Eyrbyggja, c. 37 ; Vigaglum's Saga, c. 6 ; Ljosvetninga Saga, c. 17.

grey-haired, and carried his head on one side. He was amiable and high-minded, and wore old-fashioned clothes, high-necked and long-sleeved, kirtles and shirts, and foreign cloaks (valas-kikkja) [1] and high shoes. Thus also he dressed King Magnus while he was young, but as soon as he had his own way he dressed very showily " (Magnus Erlingsson's Saga, c. 37).

Shoes made of leather or skins were used, and made fast by strings, sometimes adorned with fringes : silk strings were wrapped round the leg to the knees, and sometimes very high shoes were worn, often seamed with silk and partly covered with gold, but they were old-fashioned.

" It is told about his (Sigurd's) dress, that he wore a blue kirtle and blue hose, high shoes laced round his legs, a grey cloak (kápa) and a grey broad-brimmed hat and a hood over his face, a staff in his hand with a gilt silver-mounting at the upper end, from which a silver ring hung " (St. Olaf's Saga, [2] c. 31).

" Sigurd jarl had a brown kirtle and a red cloak, the skirts of which were folded up ; he wore shoes made of the skin of sheep's legs ; he had a shield and the sword called Bastard " (Magnus Erlingsson's Saga, c. 13).

" The king (St. Olaf) and his men went into the bath and laid their clothes on the ground, and a tent was pitched over it. At that time it was common to wear silk strings like garters, which were wound round the leg from the shoe to the knee ; the first and high-born men always wore them, and the king and Björn had the same . . . Björn always had these thongs around his legs while he lived, and was buried with them " (Bjarnar Saga Hitdælakappa).

Magnus Barefoot (1093-1103) adopted the Scotch custom (then also used in Ireland) of having *bare legs* and *plaids*, but this fashion was antiquated a hundred years later.

" It is told that when Magnus came from *Vestrviking* (warfare in the west), he and many of his men adopted the customs in dress that were common in the western lands (Scotland and Ireland). They walked bare-legged in the streets, and wore short kirtles and over-garments " (Magnus Barefoot, c. 18).

On the hands gloves (*glófar*) of skin, especially hart's-skin,

---

[1] Valaskikkja = Welsh (foreign) cloak. | [2] Cf. also Eyrbyggja Saga, c. 43.

sometimes stitched with gold, were worn; occasionally they were lined with down. In the hand a staff was generally carried, with or without an axe.

"Bard sat in a high-seat; he was bald and dressed in scarlet clothes, and wore gloves of hart-skin" (Fornmanna Sögur, ii. 148).

On the head a *hött* (hat) was worn. *Skálhatt* (a hat formed like a bowl) is mentioned, also black, grey, and white hats. Another head-covering mentioned is a silken cap ornamented with lace; those from Gardariki seem to have been most appreciated.

After a battle at sea between King Ingi and Sigurd Slembidjákn, a pretender to the crown of Norway, in which Ingi got the victory, Sigurd jumped overboard and took off his coat-of-mail while swimming under his shield. The king's men nevertheless found him.

"Thjóstólf Alason went to him (Sigurd) where he sat and struck off his head a silk cap ornamented with lace bands."[1]

"Thorkel Sursson had on his head a hat from Gardariki, a grey fur cloak, with a gold buckle on the shoulder, and a sword in his hand" (Gisli Súrsson, p. 55).

Karl and Leif saw a man approaching, "who had in his hand a cudgel (*refdi*), wore a broad-brimmed hat, and a green woollen cloak; he was barefooted, but had linen breeches tied (with a band) round his legs" (St. Olaf's Saga, c. 153).

"The everyday dress of Án was a white fur-coat, so long that it touched his heels; a grey short fur-coat over it reached down to the middle of the calf of his leg; over it was a red kirtle, which reached below the knee. Over this was a common trading cloth blouse (stakk), which reached to the middle of his thigh. He had a hat on his head, and a chopping-axe in his hand" (Án Bogsveigi's Saga, c. 5).

The wearing of moustaches by warriors seems to have been very common from the earliest time; this is seen from the bracteates and antiquities belonging to the earlier and later iron age. The custom, which continued to the end of the Pagan era, and which is also well illustrated in the Bayeux

---

[1] Cf. Svarfdæla Saga, c. 5, and Magnus Barefoot, c. 8.

tapestry, was so common that it is but seldom mentioned in the Sagas.

Laughed then Jormunrek,
Put his hand on his moustaches;
He did not want tumult,
Was drunk with wine;

Shook his brown hair,
Looked on his white shield;
Let the golden cup
Turn in his hand.

(Hamdismál, 20.)

After the burning of Njal, Skarphedin, his son, was found dead.

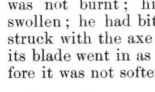

Fig. 1155.—Man with moustache; reverse of silver coin with ship.

" He had been standing at the gable, and the greater part of his legs were burnt up to his knees, but the rest of his body was not burnt; his eyes were open and not swollen; he had bitten his moustache, and had struck with the axe so fast into the gable that its blade went in as far as its middle, and therefore it was not softened " (Njala, c. 132).

A peculiar story is related of Ögmund Eythjófsbani, a famous Viking, full of witchcraft and devilry, who often fought against Örvarodd.

" When Ögmund left Odd he went into Austrveg (eastern lands) and married the daughter of Geirröd the Jötun, and made all the kings in Austrveg pay tax to him; every twelve months they were to send him their lower and upper moustache. From these Ögmund had a fur cloak made " (Orvar Odd's Saga, c. 23).

The men wore their hair long, hanging over their neck; their foreheads were ornamented with a gold band like a diadem, and from the finds we learn that they parted their hair in the middle.

" Kjartan, Olaf's son, grew up at Hjardarholt; he was the handsomest of men born in Iceland. He had fine and marked features in his face, with most beautiful eyes and fair complexion; he had much hair as fine as silk, which fell down in locks. He was large and strong as his mother's father Egil (Skallagrimsson), or Thorolf had been. He was better shaped than any man, so that all wondered who saw him; he also fought better than most other men; he was a good smith, and swam better than any other man; he surpassed others greatly in all idrottir; he was better liked and more humble than any other man, so that every child loved him; he was merry and open-handed. Olaf (the Irish) loved him most of all his children" (Laxdaela Saga, ch. 38).

"He (Hakon jarl) was the most handsome man that men had seen, with long hair, fine as silk, and a gold band on his head" (Fornmanna Sögur, iv.).

"Odd was dressed every day in a scarlet kirtle, and had a *gullhlad* (gold band) tied round his head" (Orvar Odd, c. 1).

Fig. 1156.—Fragments of the upper part of a bronze kettle (the eyes had probably been adorned with stones), showing how men parted their hair.—Bog find, Fyen.

Fig. 1157.—Ornaments inside the kettle on another plate of bronze.

"He (Gunnar of Hlídarendi) looked handsome, and had a light complexion, a straight nose, slightly turned up, blue and keen eyes, and red cheeks. His hair was long, thick, and yellow, and sat well" (Njala, c. 19).

Chiefs seem to have often set the fashions.

"One summer a seagoing ship owned by Icelanders came from Iceland. It was loaded with trade-cloaks (*varar-feld*), and they went with it to Hardangr, for they heard that many people were there. When they began to sell none wanted to buy the cloaks. The steersman went to King Harald, for he had spoken to him before, and told him this difficulty. Harald said he would come down, and did so. He was a condescending and very merry man. He came on a fully-manned skúta. He looked at the goods, and said to the steersman: 'Wilt thou give me one of the grey cloaks?' 'Willingly,' answered the steersman: 'more than one.' Harald took one cloak and put it on, and then went down into the skúta. Before they rowed away every one of his men had bought a cloak. A few days after there came so many who all wanted to buy cloaks that not half of them got any. Thereafter the king was called Harald gráfeld (grey cloak)" (Harald Gráfeld's Saga, c. 7).

The fashion in the time of King Sverri is thus described:—

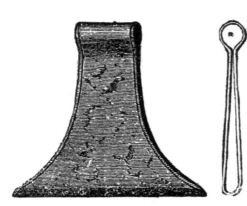

Fig. 1158.   Fig. 1159.
Iron tweezers, ⅔ real size, found in a quadrangular stone setting, with a bent sword, a bent spear head, both of iron, and burnt bones.—Öland.

" Thou shalt always choose brown cloth for hose; it is not wrong to use black skin for hose or other kinds of cloth except scarlet. Thou shalt also have a brown or green or red kirtle of good and beseeming cloth. Thy linen clothes thou shalt have made of good linen, but not much of it; have thy shirt short and all thy linen-clothes light. Always have thy shirt a good deal shorter than thy kirtle, for no good-mannered man can make himself look well with flax or hemp. Thy beard and hair thou shalt have well prepared before thou comest before the king, after the customs prevailing at the time in the hird.[1] When I was in the hird it was customary to cut the hair shorter than the lobes of the ears, and comb it so that each hair would lie flat, and a short lock of hair be over the eyebrows. It was customary to cut the beard and the moustaches short and have whiskers like the German custom; it is not likely that there will be any better or more becoming fashion for warriors" (Konungs Skuggsjá, p. 66).

---

[1] The *hird* or hirdmen were so called because they guarded their lord or king; the word being derived from *hirda*, to guard or preserve. The hird of a king was often very considerable: King Harald Fairhair sometimes had a hird of 400 men.

THE DRESS OF KINGS.

From the earlier Edda and the Sagas we find that kings or warriors were easily recognised by the splendour of their accoutrements. They wore gilt spurs.

" When the king (St. Olaf) had said this, he sat down and let his shoes and stockings be pulled off, put cordovan hose on his feet and put on gilt spurs. Then he took off his cloak and kirtle and dressed himself in clothes of pell, and over these a scarlet cloak. He girded himself with an ornamented sword, put a gilt helmet on his head, and mounted his horse " (St. Olaf's Saga, c. 32).

" King Hakon was easily recognized before all others; his helmet glittered when the sun shone upon it " (Hakon the Good's Saga, c. 31).

" Kjartan Olafsson took up the scarlet clothes which King Olaf (Tryggvason) gave him at their parting and dressed himself magnificently; he girt himself with the sword which was the king's gift; he wore on his head a gilt helmet, and had a red shield at his side with the holy cross marked thereon in gold, and in his hand a spear with a gilt handle. All his men were in coloured clothes; they were more than twenty " (Laxdæla, c. 44).

" The king (Hakon) put on his dress of war; he wore a coat of ring-mail, and was girt with the sword *Kvernbit*; he had on a gilt helmet, a spear in his hand, and a shield at his side. Then he arrayed in ranks his hird and the bœndr, and raised his standard " (Fornmanna Sögur, vol. i., pp. 42, 43).

" One day Gilli and Leif (kinsmen) went from their booths to a hill, which was on the island, and there talked together; they saw many men on the headland on the eastern side of the island . . . . there glittered in the sunshine fine shields and magnificent helmets, axes and spears, and the men looked very valiant; they saw that a man, tall and bold-looking, went in front of the rest in a red kirtle, with a shield half blue and half yellow, a helmet on his head, and a long cutting spear in his hand; they thought they recognized in him Sigurd Thorlaksson. Next to him walked a stout man in a red kirtle, who had a red shield; they thought they recognized him with certainty as Thórd Lági (the low); the third man had a red shield, with a man's face painted on it, and a large axe in his hand; this was Gaut the red " (Færeyinga Saga, c. 48).

While King Olaf was at Stiklastadir a man came to him who was not like other men.

"He was so tall that no other man reached higher than to his shoulders; he was very handsome, and fair-haired. He was well armed; he had a very fine helmet, a coat of mail, and a red shield; he was girt with an ornamented sword and had a large spear inlaid with gold, whose handle was so thick that it could scarcely be grasped with the hand" (St. Olaf's Saga, c. 22).

It was the custom for those who attended the Thing to put on their best clothes.

"The champion Gunnar came to the Althing, so finely dressed that none were dressed as well, and the people came out ot every booth to admire him. He had on the scarlet state[1] clothes which King Harald Gormsson (Denmark) gave him. and a gold ring on his hand from Hakon jarl" (Njala, c. 33).

---

[1] Fignarklœdi = dignity-clothes; clothes of highborn men.

CHAPTER IX.

DRESS OF WOMEN.

The gown—Festive dress—Outer garments—Under garments—Head-dress—
Mode of wearing the hair—Ornaments—Buckles and fibulæ—Numerous
jewels of gold.

THE most important piece of clothing worn by women was the *kyrtil* (gown). It was made very wide, with a train, and was usually provided with long sleeves reaching to the wrists. It was fastened round the waist by a belt, often made of gold or silver, from which a bag was suspended for rings, ornaments, housewife's keys, &c. Sometimes this dress was narrow at the waist, and had a close-fitting jacket. Over the kirtle was wore a kind of apron (*blæja*), which sometimes had fringe at the bottom.

The *slædur*, mentioned in Rigsmál, was a festive dress for women as well as for men; it did not reach so high as to entirely cover the neck and bust; therefore a separate piece of clothing, called *smokk* (collar), was worn with it, and a *dúk* (neckerchief) was also wrapped round the neck. The neck and bust were frequently left bare, and ornamented with a necklace and other ornaments. A kind of shoulder ornament is also mentioned, under the name of *dvergar*.

And the housewife
Looked at her sleeves,
She smoothed the linen,
And plaited them,
She put up the head-dress;
A brooch was on her breast,
The dress-train was trailing,
The shirt had a blue tint;
Her brow was brighter,
Her breast was more shining,
Her neck was whiter
Than pure new fallen snow.

(Rigsmál, 28, 29.)

" Gisli could not sleep, and said he wanted to go from the house to his hiding place, south of the cliffs, and try if he could not sleep there. They all went there (Gisli, his wife Aud, and her foster-daughter Gudrid); they (the women) had on kirtles, which left a track in the dew" (Gisli Sursson's Saga, p. 67).

From the four representations here given, we get an idea of the dress of women, and the peculiar manner in which they arranged their hair. The long trailing dress reminds us of the descriptions in the Sagas. Three of the figures are presenting drinking-horns to some persons unseen. On the Hallingbrö stone [1] a woman, dressed in a somewhat similar way, is presenting a drinking-horn to a warrior on horseback.

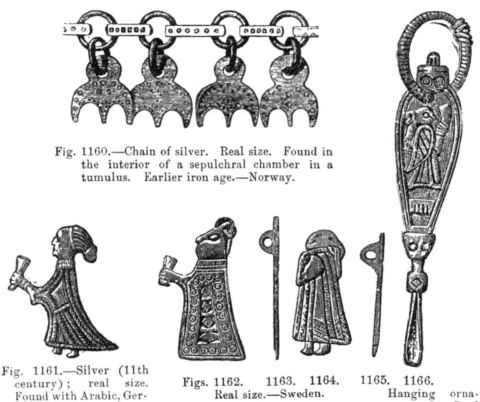

Fig. 1160.—Chain of silver. Real size. Found in the interior of a sepulchral chamber in a tumulus. Earlier iron age.—Norway.

Fig. 1161.—Silver (11th century); real size. Found with Arabic, German, and old English coins.—Öland.

Figs. 1162. 1163. 1164. Real size.—Sweden.

1165. 1166. Hanging ornament. Real size.—Sweden

The women's outer garments were more or less similar to those of men. The principal were the *skikkja* and *möttul*, a kind of cloak worn by high-born women, without sleeves, usually fastened on the breast with a fibula, and the *tygla möttul* (strap-cloak), used by men and women, sometimes with costly borders (*hladbuinn*), and lined with fur; but the term *kvenn-skikkja* (woman's cloak) implies some difference between theirs and those of the men.   When travelling they wore overcoats, like men; the *ólpa*, with hood of felt, and *hekla*.

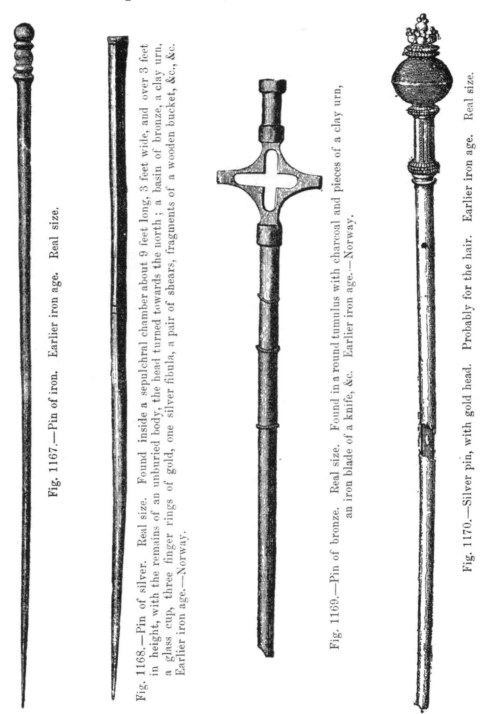

Fig. 1167.—Pin of iron.   Earlier iron age.   Real size.

Fig. 1168.—Pin of silver.   Real size.   Found inside a sepulchral chamber about 9 feet long, 3 feet wide, and over 3 feet in height, with the remains of an unburied body, the head turned towards the north ; a basin of bronze, a clay urn, a glass cup, three finger rings of gold, one silver fibula, a pair of shears, fragments of a wooden bucket, &c. Earlier iron age.—Norway.

Fig. 1169.—Pin of bronze.   Real size.   Found in a round tumulus with charcoal and pieces of a clay urn, an iron blade of a knife, &c.   Earlier iron age.—Norway.

Fig. 1170.—Silver pin, with gold head.   Probably for the hair.   Earlier iron age.   Real size.

"A beggar-woman who died left a hekla, which was embroidered with much gold. The men of King Magnus

(Erlingsson) took the cloak and burnt it, and divided the money among themselves. When the Birkibeinar (Sverris men) heard this they called them *heklungs*" (Sverri's Saga, c. 41 ; Fms. viii.).

Women wore the *skyrta* or *serk* (chemise), either of linen or silk, next to the body. It was so made that the breast was partly uncovered. They slept in night-shirts, as we find from

Fig. 1171.—From Bayeux tapestry. Woman with long dress.[1]

the frequent occurrence of the word *nattserk*, which in earlier times had long sleeves.

When the house of the chief Gissur at Flugumýri was burnt by enemies, Ingibjörg, daughter of Sturla, escaped out of the fire.

"She was dressed only in a night-shirt (*natt-serk*), and was barefooted ; she was then fourteen winters old, tall and fine.

---

[1] The name of Ælgyva, mentioned on the tapestry, is evidently the same as the Northern Alfifa.

"Svein, son of King Knut and Alfifa, daughter of Alfrun jarl, had been put in Jomsborg to rule Vindland " (St. Olaf's Saga, c. 252).

A silver belt was round her legs when she jumped out of her bed; a bag containing many of her precious things was hanging on it " (Sturlunga, ix., c. 3).

King Hakon went to tell his queen the news that her father, Skúli, had assumed the title of king.

" He went to the bed, and the queen stood in a silk shirt, and threw over herself a red *möttul*; she received him well, and he was kind to her. She took a silk cushion and asked the king to sit down; he said he would not. She asked for news. ' There is little news,' the king answered; ' there are two kings in Norway now.' "

Women's socks or hose were called *skoklædi* (shoe clothes); they are still worn in Sœtersdal in Norway, and are often richly embroidered.

Married women generally had their head covered with a *höfudduk* (head-cloth). High-born women wore a gold band, or diadem of gold, round the head, a fashion occasionally adopted by men.

" One day Án met Drifa, Karl's daughter, and with her three women. She was handsome, and well dressed in a red kirtle with long sleeves, narrow below, and long and tight at the waist. She wore a band (*hlad*)[1] round her forehead, and her hair was very fine " (Án Bogsveigi's Saga, c. 5).

One kind of head-dress was called *fald* (fold); others were *sveig*, *motr*, and *krókfald*. The last word probably means a crooked head-dress, perhaps somewhat similar to those now worn in Normandy and Iceland. It must be concluded that the so-called *fald* was often made of linen, and it was considered stately to wear this head-dress high.

Skupla was another head-dress, which fell down over the face.

" Once when the famous chief and Saga-writer Snorri Sturluson was travelling, he met a woman who wore a blue jacket (*ólpa*) with a felt hood, which was fastened round her head; she wore it instead of a hat " (Sturlunga, iv., c. 36).

---

[1] *Hlad* seems to mean band rather than lace, as it is sometimes translated; the finds show that gold bands or diadems were worn.

X

Girls wore the hair, when long, wrapped round their belt; widows also wore their hair hanging down. Long yellow hair, and a delicate complexion, were considered essentials of beauty.

Bui once went to Dofrafjöll (Dovrefjeld) on an errand for King Harald Fairhair, and there met a woman of large stature.

"She was fair to look at, and dressed in a red kirtle, ornamented all over with lace; she wore a broad silver belt; she wore her long and fine hair loose, as is the custom of maidens; she had beautiful hands, and many gold rings on them" (Kjalnesinga Saga, c. 13).

Ermingerd, a queen in Valland, at a feast which she gave to Rögnvald jarl,

"came into the hall with many women. She had in her hand a drinking-vessel of gold, and was dressed in the finest clothes; her hair was loose, as is the custom of maidens, and

Fig. 1172.—Bone comb, a little less than ⅓ real size, found in a round tumulus, with an iron kettle, glass beads, charcoal, and burnt bones.

on her forehead she had placed a golden band" (Orkneyinga Saga, p. 280).

"Helga was so beautiful, that wise men say she was the most beautiful woman in Iceland. Her hair was so long that it could cover her whole body, and was as fine as gold; no match was then thought equal to her in the whole of Borgarfjord and many other places" (Gunnlaug Ormstunga, c. 4).

"Then Hallgerd was sent for, and came with two women. She wore a blue woven mantle (*vefjarmöttul*), and under it a scarlet kirtle with a silver belt; her hair reached down to her waist on both sides, and she tucked it under her belt" (Njala, c. 13).

When Gunnar went to the Althing he met the widow Hallgerd, daughter of Höskuld, who

"was dressed in a red ornamented kirtle, and over it a scarlet cloak ornamented with lace down to the skirt. Her long and fair hair reached down to her bosom" (Njala, c. 33).

Fig. 1173.—Fibula in silver gilt, adorned with niello and two green glass pieces. $\frac{1}{2}$ real size.—Gillberga, Nerike, Sweden.

Fig. 1174.   Fig. 1175.

Beads of bronze, real size, found in a stone cist, Sojvide, Götland. There were 500 of these used to be fastened on a garment. Found with buckle.

Fig. 1176.

Ring and ornament of bronze, with rivets of iron. $\frac{2}{3}$ real size.

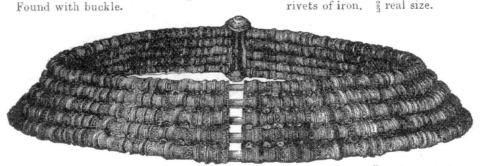

Fig. 1177.—Necklace of gold, weight about $1\frac{1}{2}$ lbs., Thorslunda, Öland, consisting of tubes fastened one above the other and ornamented with filigree work. Two other of these have been found in Vestergötland—one on the slopes of the Alleberg Hills, near Falköping, the other near Möne Church, about seventeen miles from the former. A similar one was found in Southern Russia, now in the Hermitage Museum, with upper and lower end, ending in well formed long head of snake.

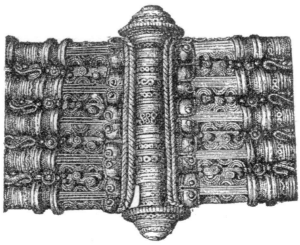

Fig. 1178.—Back of the necklace.   Real size.

X 2

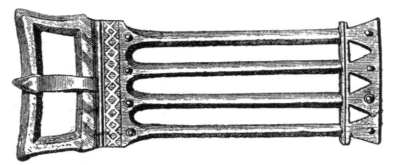

Fig. 1179.—Belt buckle of bronze.   Real size.—Götland.

Fig. 1180.—Belt hook of bronze.   ½ real size.

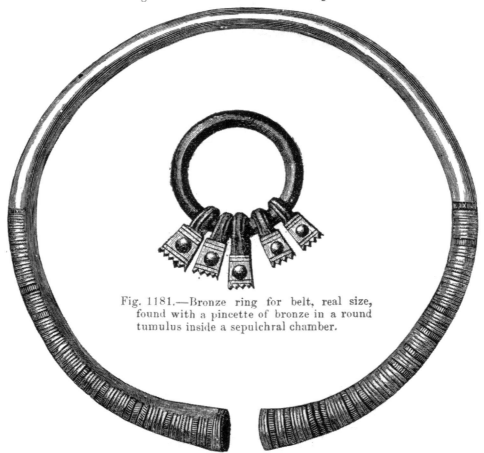

Fig. 1181.—Bronze ring for belt, real size,
found with a pincette of bronze in a round
tumulus inside a sepulchral chamber.

Fig. 1182.—Heavy gold arm-ring; weight, 1 lb. 7 oz.   ⅔ real size.   Found in a very
large tumulus, with fragments of a two-edged sword, with a magnificent
scabbard of wood and bronze mounted with silver gilt, and partially ornamented;
a gold ring, six small rings of gold, a gold pin, fragments of bronze kettle and
vases, pieces of a bronze sieve, ornaments of silver of drinking horn, fragments of
spear-heads of iron, &c.

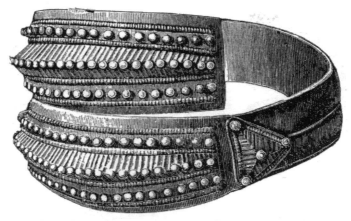

Fig. 1183.—Bracelet of silver plated with silver gilt with the exception of the heads of the small nails.—Norway.

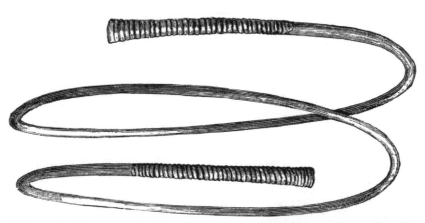

Fig. 1184.—Spiral bracelet of gold. Real size. Weight, over 1½ oz. Found in the lower part of a stone cairn with a gold spiral ring. A little below the soil of the cairn were found charcoal, pieces of bone, and fragments of iron destroyed by rust.—Norway.

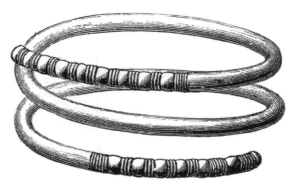

Fig. 1185.—Spiral bracelet of gold, ⅔ real size, found in a mound inside a cist. Weight, nearly 3 oz.—Norway.

Fig. 1186.—Ring of gold.   Real size.—
Norway.

Fig. 1187.—Gold ring, found in a mound
with a bronze vase, pieces of a large
spiral gold bracelet, &c.—Norway.

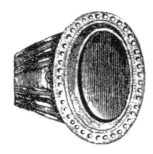

Fig. 1188.—Finger ring of gold with a
cornelian.   Real size.—Karneol Sneda,
near Ystad, Scania.

Fig. 1189.—Spiral finger ring. Real size.
—Bohuslan.

Fig. 1190.

Fig. 1191.

Gold ring, real size, found in a tumulus with fragments of a two-edged sword with
its bronze mountings, &c.—Norway.

Fig. 1192.

Fig. 1193.

Gold ring, real size, found in a round mound with four other gold rings, &c.   The
stone in the middle is a flat cornelian, the one above a piece of convex glass;
the lower one is missing.—Verdalen, Norway.

Fig. 1194.—Ring of gold. **Real size.—**
Norway.

Fig. 1195.—Ring of gold.
Real size.—Norway.

Fig. 1196.—Necklet of gold, weight over 4 oz., found under a large stone.—
Södermanland, Sweden. ⅔ real size.

Fig. 1197.—Diadem of gold, found while digging potatoes; weight slightly over 6 oz.
¾ real size.—Öland.

Fig. 1198.—Diadem or necklet of gold, weight 6½ oz., found in a ditch near the city
ot Abo, Finland. ½ real size.

These types of diadems in spiral bracelets have been found in bog finds of the
Thorsberg, and also with Valoby graves.

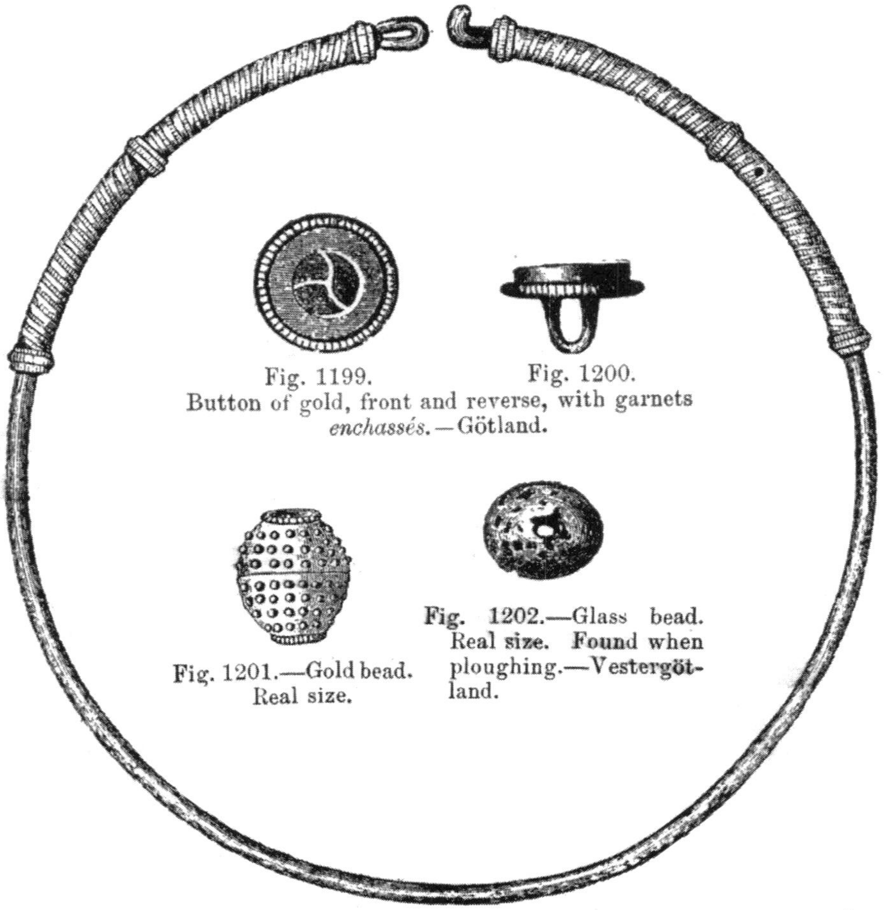

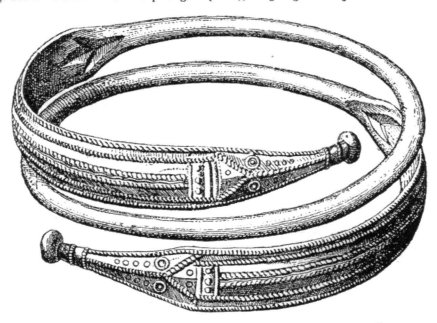

Fig. 1199.
Button of gold, front and reverse, with garnets
enchassés.—Götland.

Fig. 1200.

Fig. 1201.—Gold bead.
Real size.

Fig. 1202.—Glass bead.
Real size. Found when
ploughing.—Vestergöt-
land.

Fig. 1203.—Necklet of almost pure gold (99·5), weighing 6 oz. ⅔ real size.—Öland.

Fig. 1204.—Spiral bracelet of gold ; weight, 7 oz. Real size.—Öland.

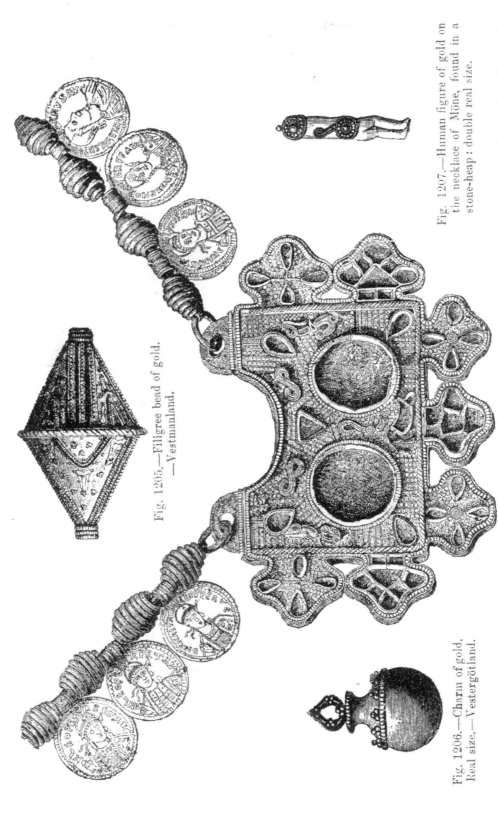

Fig. 1205.—Filligree bead of gold.—Vestmanland.

Fig. 1206.—Charm of gold. Real size.—Vestergötland.

Fig. 1207.—Human figure of gold on the necklace of Möne, found in a stone-heap : double real size.

Fig. 1208.—Necklace of gold, ornamented with filigree work and Roman and Byzautine coins of the 5th century ; ⅓ real size.—Scania, Copenhagen Museum.

155

Fig. 1209.—Bracelet of bronze, found in a mound at Husby, Erlinghumdra, Upland. Real size.

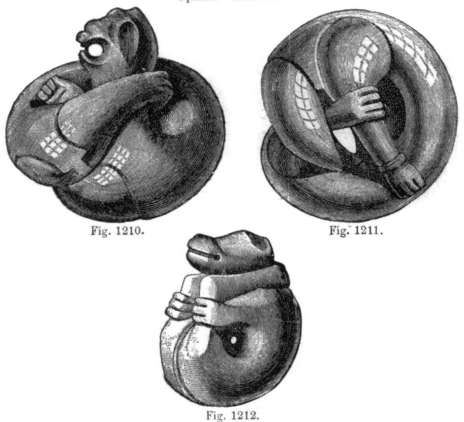

Fig. 1210.　　　　　　　　　　　Fig. 1211.

Fig. 1212.
Figures of animals, real size, in amber, found in a tumulus.—Indersöen, Norway.

Fig. 1213.—Diadem of gold. ½ real size. Found under a big stone in a heap of stones; weight, 8 oz.—Norway.

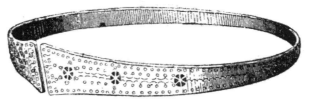

Fig. 1214.—Probably a diadem of gold melted with silver ; weight over 2 lbs. ½ real size.—Medelpal. Sweden.

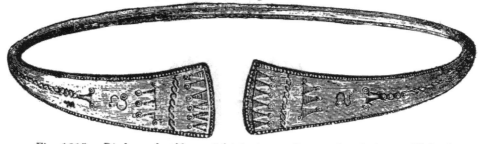

Fig. 1215.—Diadem of gold ; weight just over 6 ozs. ⅔ real size. —Götland.

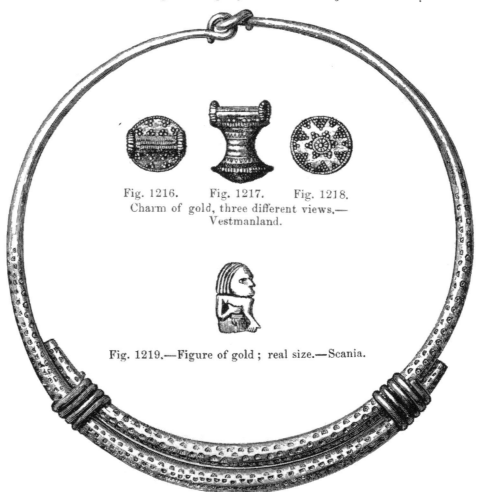

Fig. 1216.   Fig. 1217.   Fig. 1218.
Charm of gold, three different views.—
Vestmanland.

Fig. 1219.—Figure of gold ; real size.—Scania.

Fig. 1220.—Neck-ring of gold. ⅔ real size. Found under a big stone. Weighs 11¼ oz.—Norway.

Fig. 1221.—Pendant of gold, found
in a field. Real size.—Öland.

Fig. 1222.—Neck-ring of almost pure gold, forming part of one of the largest
finds of gold ornaments ever made in Sweden, which weighed over 27 lbs.;
weight, 2½ lbs. ⅔ real size.—Thureholm, Södermanland, Sweden.

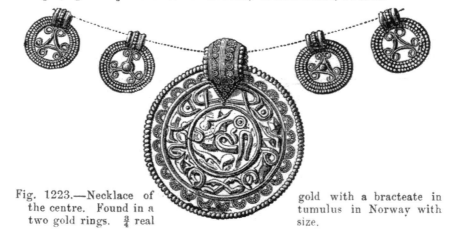

Fig. 1223.—Necklace of   gold with a bracteate in
the centre. Found in a   tumulus in Norway with
two gold rings. ¾ real   size.

Fig. 1224.—Necklace of silver. ½ **real size.**

Fig. 1225.—Pendant on necklace as seen from below. Real size. Found in a tumulus, in a deep hole, made on purpose, with a fragment of a silver gilt fibula, a small spiral ring of gold having been used as money, five clay vessels, a glass cup, fixtures of iron for two wooden buckets, one lever balance of spindle in clay, &c.—Norway.

Fig. 1226.—Real size. Fig. 1227.

Fig. 1228. Fig. 1229.
Bracteates of gold found **with other** bracteates. ⅔ real size.—Norway.

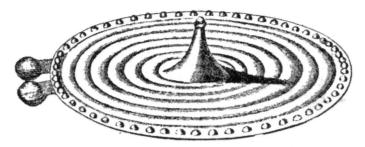

Fig. 1230.—Bronze fibula having the form of a tumulus; the pin of iron has been destroyed by rust.—Helgö, Smaaland. Collection Wittlock, Vexio. ½ real size.

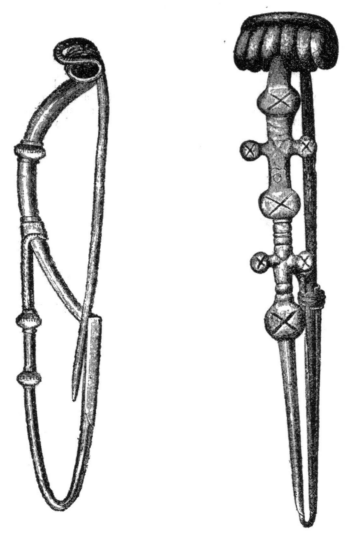

Fig. 1231.—Fibula of iron, found with burnt bones in a clay urn.—Tanum, Bohuslan. ¾ real size.

Fig. 1232.—Fibula of iron, found in a stone cist by the side of a skeleton, with a clay urn and an iron sword, &c., &c., in Stora Dalby, Öland. ⅔ real size.

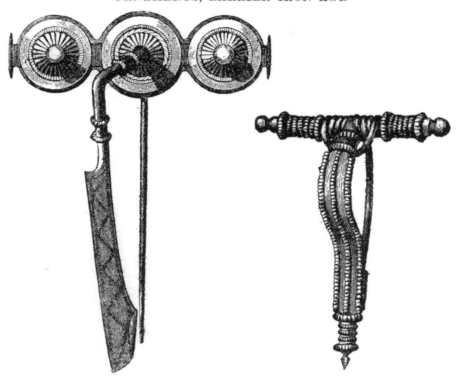

Fig. 1233.—Fibula of silver, plated with gold, found in a stone cist with a skeleton seated. ¾ real size.—Vestergötland.

Fig. 1234.—Fibula of silver, plated with gold, found under a stone with several glass and silver beads. Collection of Captain Ulfsparre, Stockholm.—Götland. Real size.

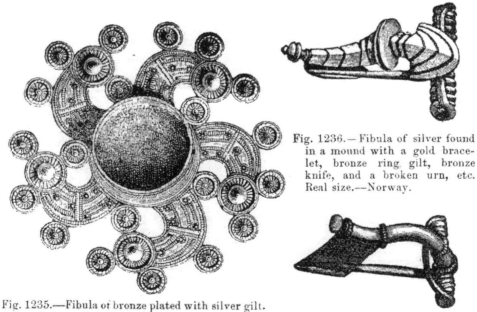

Fig. 1236.— Fibula of silver found in a mound with a gold bracelet, bronze ring gilt, bronze knife, and a broken urn, etc. Real size.—Norway.

Fig. 1235.—Fibula of bronze plated with silver gilt. ½ real size. Found in a large sepulchral room built of slabs, with a bronze kettle, two clay urns, &c.—Aak, Norway.

Fig. 1237.—Silver fibula. Real size. In a mound with burnt bones and charcoal.—Norway.

161

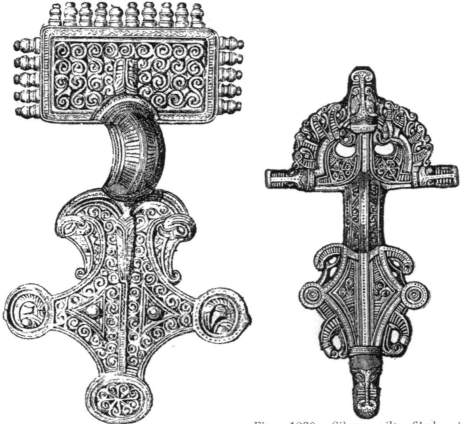

Fig. 1238.—Fibula of silver gilt. $\frac{2}{3}$ real size. —Scania.

Fig. 1239.—Silver gilt fibula in tumulus. $\frac{1}{2}$ real size. — Hagby, Öland.

Fig. 1240.—Fibula of bronze. Real size. Found in a mound with a wooden bucket ornamented with bronze, pieces of iron scissors, a flat ring of gold, &c., &c.—Near Stavanger, Norway.

Fig. 1241.—Fibula of bronze found in a clay urn with burnt bones near the border of a tumulus. Real size.—Norway.

Fig. 1241A.—Fibula of bronze inlaid with silver. In a mound with shield boss, spear-point and arrow-points of iron, belt ring, and knife handle of bronze, and an ornamented leather belt. ⅔ real size.—Norway.

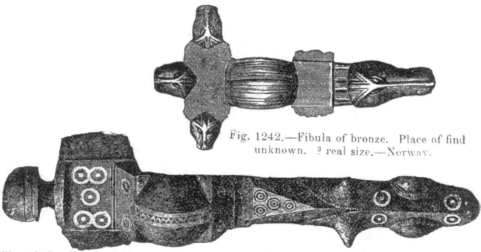

Fig. 1242.—Fibula of bronze. Place of find unknown. ⅔ real size.—Norway.

Fig. 1243.—Fibula of bronze inlaid with silver, found in a tumulus with three other bronze fibulæ, fifteen gilt buttons, &c. ⅔ real size.—Norway.

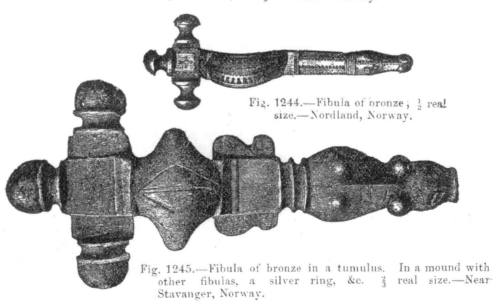

Fig. 1244.—Fibula of bronze; ½ real size.—Nordland, Norway.

Fig. 1245.—Fibula of bronze in a tumulus. In a mound with other fibulas, a silver ring, &c. ⅔ real size.—Near Stavanger, Norway.

Y

Fig. 1246.——Fibula of silver gilt. The most elevated flat parts are niellés. There are many blue stones here and there, some fastened with gold. ¾ size. Found in a mound, with three gold bracteates, a spiral ring of gold, three small fibulæ of silver gilt of the same type, a bronze key, pieces of a two-edged sword, a small spear-head, &c., &c., unburnt bones and teeth of a cow and other animals, &c., and a quantity of burnt grain (rye).

Fig. 1247.—Fibula of bronze plated with silver work, found with a bronze kettle filled with burnt bones, and covered with a slab; a gold chain, and a spiral ring. Real size.—Norway.

Fig. 1248.—Fibula of bronze. Real size. Found in a funeral chamber of stone, with two clay urns with burnt bones, a belt, ring, &c.—Lödingen, Norway.

Fig. 1249.—Earring of bronze with glass beads. Real size. Found in a round mound under a bronze kettle, glass beads, &c. The kettle contained burnt bones, and was in a bed of charcoal and calcined earth.—Norway.

Fig. 1250.—Fibula of silver gilt, partly niellé. ⅔ real size.—Norway

Fig. 1251.—Fibula in bronze. Real size. Found when ploughing over an ancient tumulus. Nearly similar in form to the fibulæ found at Camirus, Rhodes. Not very archaic pottery.

Y 2

Fig. 1252.—Fibula, real size.—Bornholm, Denmark.

Fig. 1253.—Fibula, real size.— Bornholm, Denmark.

Fig. 1254.—Fibula, plated with gold, only a little of the metal remaining. **Real** size.—Southern Jutland.

Men and women loved to adorn themselves with jewels and objects of gold;[1] the ornaments for both sexes seem to have been somewhat similar; rings, bracelets, fibulæ (used to fasten together on to the right shoulder the ends of

Fig. 1255.—Buckle of a belt in silver and bronze, ornamented with garnets *enchassés*. Real size. Earlier iron age.—Norway.

cloaks), brooches, clasps and buckles, pins, hooks, pendants round the neck, bracteates, diadems, necklaces, beads of silver,

---

[1] Among the objects made of gold were spurs, see Völsunga Saga, c. 27; gold chairs, Hrolf Kraki's Saga, c. 18; gold chests, Fornmanna Sögur, vii.; gold horse-shoes, Fornmanna Sögur, vii.; gold dog-collars, Gautrek's Saga, c. 9; gold ring-coats of mail, Sigurdarkvida, iii.; gold tablets, Orvar Odd's Saga, c. 26; cows' horns occasionally seem to have been covered with gold, as we see from Thrymskvida, st. 23, Helgakvida Hjörvardssonar.

gold, and glass, &c., and gold rings worn round the legs, were most common.

The numerous illustrations of jewels and ornaments seen throughout the pages of this work show the taste of the people, and the different forms worn by them, even in very early times.

To gold the poets gave many figurative names which are derived from either the myths or history of the people, and which often show in their metaphors the different uses to which gold was applied:—The fire of the hand, or arm; the beacon of the hawk-seat (the wrist); the fire of the top of the masthead, &c.

Some of the rings and necklaces were of such remarkable workmanship that they had special names, and their fame was known far and wide. Among the more celebrated rings were the *Sviagris*,[1] *Draupnir*, and *Hnitud*; and among the necklaces that of Freyja made by the Dvergar.

"Ulf the Red was always accustomed to be with King Olaf during midwinter. Ulf brought the king many precious things which he had acquired during the summer. And one gold ring he had got called *Hnitud* (the welded). It was welded together in seven places. It was of much better gold than other rings. This ring had been given to Ulf by a bondi named Lodmund" (Thatt of Norna Gest).

Beads are often mentioned.

Bardi, a good champion, was going to a fight, and when his foster-mother took leave of him

"she took out of her shirt a large necklace of beads, and put it round his neck over his shirt.[2]

"Thorbjörn ran at Bardi and struck his neck; a very loud crash was heard; the blow hit the bead in the necklace, which had moved when Bardi gave his knife to Njal's son. The bead burst asunder, and blood gushed out on both sides of the necklace, but Bardi was not wounded. Thorbjörn said: ' Thou art a tröll, as irons bite thee not '" (Viga-Styr and Heidarviga c. 23).

---

[1] Cf. Hrolf Kraki's Saga, c. 10–12.

[2] This was probably given him as an amulet to protect him in the fight.

Towards the later centuries of the Viking **period the** brooches, fibulæ, &c., become coarse and heavy.

Fig. 1256.—Fibula of bronze, ornamented with gold and silver.

Fig. 1257.—Fibula of bronze, ⅔ real size.—Zeeland, Denmark.

Fig. 1258.—Fibula of bronze, ⅔ real size.—Bjornhofda, Öland.

Fig. 1259.—Fibula of gilt bronze, ornamented with walrus tusk and garnets (later iron age). ⅔ real size.—Othemar's, Götland.

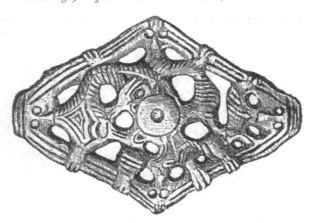

Fig 1260.—Bronze ornament gilt, found with glass beads, fragments of an axe, spears and arrow heads, &c, &c. Real size.—Norway.

Fig. 1261.—Bracelet of massive gold, ¾ real size, found in a field at Vallakra, Scania.

Fig. 1262.—Silver fibula, ¼ real size, with filigree work and ring for a chain.—Öland.

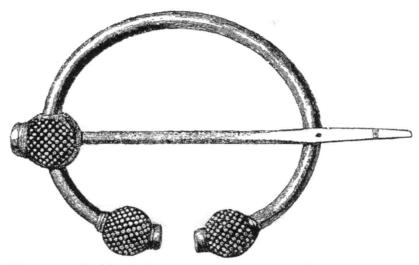

Fig. 1263.—Buckle of silver; ⅓ real size; weight, 13½ ozs.—Björkås, Tanum parish, Bohuslan.

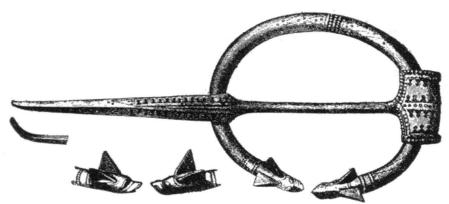

Fig. 1264.—Silver buckle; ⅔ real size; weight, 9 oz.; found in 1739.— Vible, Götland.

Fig. 1265.—Silver chain with Thor's hammer. ½ real size.—Bredsättra, Öland.

Fig. 1266.—Bracelet of gold, real size. Middle iron age.—Gudme, Svendborg Amt.

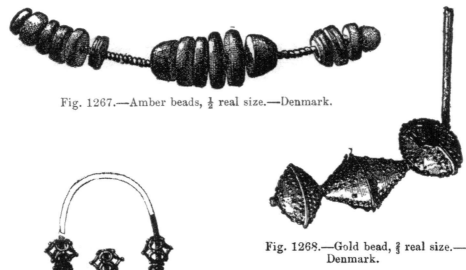

Fig. 1267.—Amber beads, $\frac{1}{2}$ real size.—Denmark.

Fig. 1268.—Gold bead, $\frac{2}{3}$ real size.—Denmark.

Fig. 1269.—Ornament of silver, real size, found in a grave mound, with a large hoard consisting of two neck rings, five bracelets, two finger rings, two fibulæ, &c., &c., of silver, three hanging ornaments of bronze, one representing a human face, three silver and fourteen glass beads, &c., &c. Earlier iron age. —Tuna parish, Helsingland, Sweden.

Fig. 1270.—Silver brooch. $\frac{2}{3}$ real size. Found in a tumulus. The sepulchral chamber was about $13\frac{1}{2}$ feet long, 3 feet wide and high, made of slabs and lined with oak planks and birch bark. There were remains of several other brooches, a large bronze vessel with three handles, remains of a silver-gilt fibula and two small silver fibulæ. Earlier iron age.

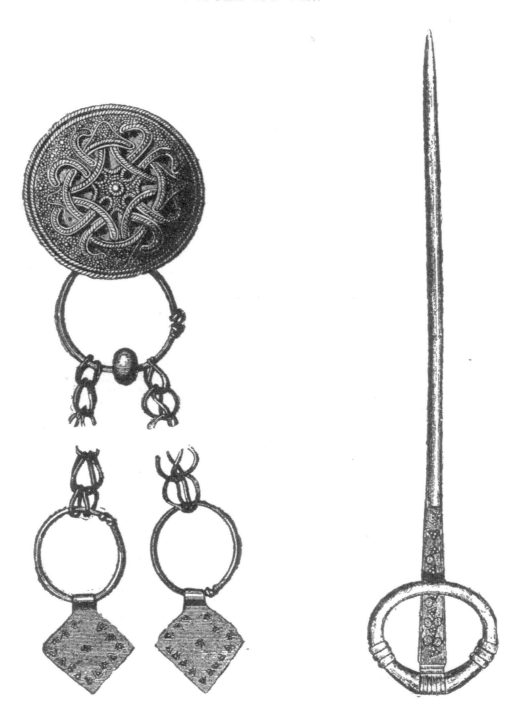

Fig. 1271.—Fibula ornamented with filigree work and chain of silver; length, 10½ inches. Found in a field at Ekelunda, Öland.

Fig. 1272.—Bronze pin. ½ real size.—Aronstorp, Öland.

CHAPTER X.

THE BRACTEATES.

Gold bracteates—Peculiarity of their designs—Mystic and symbolical signs—Earlier runes—The Vadstena bracteate—The svastica, triskele, and triad.

AMONG the most curious and beautiful ornaments that have been discovered in the north are the gold bracteates, which occur in great numbers, but are seldom found in graves, and which were used, as we can see from the loop attached to them, as an ornament to be worn hanging from the neck ; that they were held to be protective amulets, and were used by the temple priests in religious ceremonies, is probable.

They are formed by embossing or stamping upon a disc, and the gold is extremely thin. The peculiarity of their designs, and the mystic and symbolic signs which are used upon them, such as the *svastica*, the *triskele*, the *cross*, the *triad* in dots, birds, snakes, &c., peculiar shapes of animals, and the head-dress of men, are very remarkable ; and the sign in the shape of an S, found also on objects of the bronze age, makes them specially interesting.

We must receive with a great deal of caution the interpretation put upon these signs by some of the archæologists who have tried to unravel their meaning, and have taken the *svastica* for the sign of Thor, for this sign has been found in Greece by Schliemann and other antiquarians ; the *triskele*, or the triad with dots, to mean Odin, Vili, Ve, or Odin, Hœnir and Löd ; the birds to be the ravens of Odin ; the human heads to be representations either of Thor, Odin, or Frey ; the animals to be the goat of Thor, and Odin's horse, Sleipnir. That the representations with the sacred signs and the figure upon them had some peculiar meaning there is, I think, no doubt ;

but what they really meant is a mystery which has not yet been unravelled.

Fig 1273.—Bracteate— with man's head and horned animal below— found at Helsingborg, Sweden.

Fig. 1274.—Bracteate—with man's head with helmet, and horned animal—found at Raflunda, Scania, Sweden.

Fig. 1275.—Bracteate—horse (?) apparently loaded with treasure, probably the horse *Grani* mentioned in Volsunga Saga—found at Eskatorp, Halland, Sweden.

Fig. 1276. — Bracteate— warrior with spear, a two-horned animal, and runes, found in Zeeland, Denmark.

The runic characters stamped upon these ornaments show

them to be peculiarly northern, and to belong to a rune-writing people.

Fig. 1277.—Bracteates forming part of a necklace found at Faxö, Sjælland, Denmark. Real size.

Fig. 1278.—Bracteate—man's head with symbolic signs, a hand, &c.—Lolland, Denmark. Real size.

Fig. 1279.—Bracteate — man, and two-horned animal, and runes—in Stockholm Museum. Real size.

Fig. 1280. Real size.—Scania

Fig. 1281. Real size.—Scania. Bracteates

Fig. 1282. Real size.— Zeeland.

Fig. 1283.   Fig. 1284.—Reverse.

Roman gold coin (Valentinian), real size, found with fragments of a bronze vessel, glass beads, &c.—Norway.

Fig. 1285.   Fig. 1286.—Reverse.

Imitation of Roman gold coin, real size, found in a tumulus with charcoal, gold ornaments, glass and amber beads, &c.—Norway.

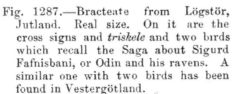

Fig. 1287.—Bracteate from Lögstör, Jutland. Real size. On it are the cross signs and *triskele* and two birds which recall the Saga about Sigurd Fafnisbani, or Odin and his ravens. A similar one with two birds has been found in Vestergötland.

Fig. 1288.—Bracteate. Southern Jutland. A warrior, bird, stag, or horse, and dots. Real size.

Of the hundreds of bracteates [1] which have been discovered, a large number were found together; and those of similar design, which have evidently been struck from the same die, are sometimes found in regions far apart. The bracteates with the peculiar mystic signs above enumerated disappear entirely towards the year 600, and though bracteates are still found they are of quite different designs; for those with representations of dragons, serpents, &c., are of a much later period.

Many of these designs may perhaps represent the deeds of great heroes told in ancient songs, such for example as the scene upon the gold bracteate found under the altar in the ancient wooden church of Gudsdal Troen parish in Gud-

Fig. 1289.—Bracteate. Real size.—Blekinge, Sweden.

Fig. 1290.—Bracteate. Real size.—Vestergötland, Sweden.

brandsdal, Norway, on which an armour-clad warrior on horseback fights a dragon. The purity of their gold is as remarkable as the skill of their workmanship.

The most important bracteate found is one of the two discovered near the little town of Vadstena on the Wettern, in Sweden. It has around its border an inscription in earlier runes, which evidently must be read from right to left. It has been ascertained by the scholars who have made a study of runes that, with the exception of the first division of eight, they represent the runic alphabet in its

Fig. 1291.—Bracteate with runic alphabet. — Vadstena, Sweden. Real size.

earliest form, the letter D being, for want of space, the only one missing.

---

[1] Some magnificent works have been published on bracteates, the finest being ' Atlas for Nordisk Oldkyndighed,' Copen-hagen, 1857; but since then many valuable additions have been discovered.

Fig. 1292.—Bracteate, Lyngby, Jutland, representing a man with a two-horned animal, surrounded by the *svastika*, the *triskele*, and four dots forming a cross, a circle of men's heads, and a circle of animals.   Real size.

Fig. 1293.—Bracteate in Copenhagen Museum. Warrior, with a sword, fighting animals.   Real size.

Fig. 1294.—Bracteate found at Hitterdal, Norway, with *svastica*, and dots on it. Warrior's head with helmet over the face, and crown above the helmet.   Real size.

Z

Fig. 1295.—Bracteate found at Raflunda, Scania. Triangle of heads. **Real size.**

Fig. 1296.—Bracteate ; place of find unknown. Real size.—Stockholm Museum.

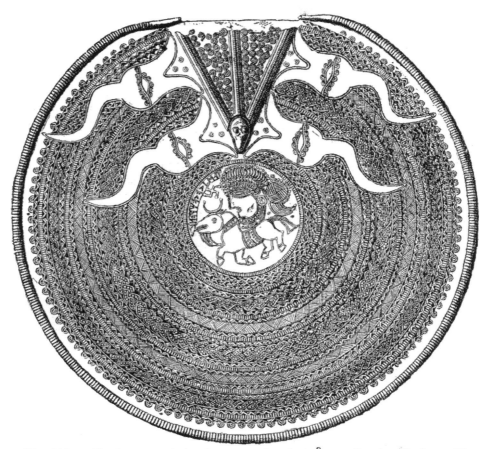

Fig. 1297.—The largest existing bracteate, found at Åsum, Scania, Sweden, with *svastica*, in 1882. ¼ real size.

Fig. 1298.—Bracteate found at Upland, Sweden. Real size.

Fig. 1299.—Reverse, with horseman apparently riding on the bare back of the horse.

z 2

Fig. 1300.—Bracteate found at Gudbrandsdal, Norway. Warrior fighting a dragon. Real size.

Fig. 1301.
Bracteate found at Trollhättan, Sweden.   Real size.

Fig. 1302.—Reverse.

Fig. 1303.

Fig. 1304.

Bracteates found at Slangerup, Zeeland.   Real size.

Fig. 1305.—Bracteate, Zeeland, Denmark.   Real size.

Fig. 1306.—Bracteate found in Scania.   Real size.

Fig. 1307.—Bracteate found in Scania.   Real size.

Fig. 1308.—Bracteate found at Raflunda, Scania.   Real size.

Fig. 1309.—Bracteate found at Lelling, Zeeland.   Real size.

One of the facts which attracts great attention is the different mystic signs[1] found upon bracteates and other numerous objects represented in these pages. These no doubt had some symbolical meaning, just as the Christian cross when used as an ornament, or placed upon a grave as a symbol.

Fig. 1310.—Runic stone with three horns in the shape of triskele.—Snoldelev, Zeeland.

Some of the signs appear to have been common to various nations, who probably adopted the same religion from which

---

[1] We find constant mention of the numbers 3 and 7, 9 and 12, which seem to have been holy :—

Heimdall had ix sisters for his mothers.

Ægir had ix daughters.

In Helgi Hundingsbani, ii., ix Valkyrjas help Helgi in a storm and save his ships.

Halfdan the old had ix + ix sons, of which ix were born first, and ix after.

Dag, one of Halfdan's sons, had ix sons, and from all Halfdan's sons there are ix generations to Harald Fairhair.

Draupnir begets 8 rings every ix night, and is itself the ix. The ring did not get this quality before going through the fire on Baldr's pyre.

The following will show the frequent occurrence of the number Nine in the literature of the North :—

With Harald Hilditönn were ix Scalds (Sögubrot, c. 8).

IX nights had Frey to wait for Gerd.

Njörd and Skadi watched in turns every ix nights by the sea or on mountains (S. E. i. 92, 94).

IX days at a time were Sigmund and Sinfjötli in wolves' shapes.

IX nights in succession comes King Siggeir's mother as a she-wolf and kills ix Volsungas (Volsunga, c. 5).

IX nights did Odin hang on the wind-blown tree (Hávamál, 138).

IX nights did Hermod ride through deep and dark valleys without any sun, when he was going to Helheim.

IX days lasted the battle on Dunheath.

IX times 60 doors there are in Valhalla.

IX times 60 halls in Bilskirnir.

IX paces did Thor go from the Midgard's serpent and die.

IX paces are red-hot irons carried (Fornmanna Sögur, i.).

IX red-hot plough-shares are stepped upon (Fornmanna Sögur, vii. 164, x. 418).

they spring, just as to-day the Christian cross is the emblem of numerous nations or tribes scattered over the globe.

Fig. 1311.—Fibula of silver, plated with gold, in shape of svastica. ⅔ real size.—Woman's skeleton grave, Fyen.

Fig. 1312.—Fibula of gold ¾ real size.—Skeleton grave, Fyen.

The cross with four arms of equal length seems to be one of if not the most ancient of symbolic signs; it is seen on the rock-tracings of Bohuslan (of which several illustrations are

Fig 1313.—Fibula, ⅔ real size; appears to have been gilt.—Norway.

given in this work), sometimes surrounded by a ring, at others a double cross is represented by itself. Such tracings cannot be taken for wheels or shields.

Bronze knives, with a cross surmounted by a ring, are also to be seen.

The *svastika*, or hooked cross, in its various modifications, seen on so many objects in the North, is of very ancient origin, and occurs in the Vedaic religion.

Other remarkable signs are the triad, in the shape of dots placed in a triangle, and the *triskele*, which are seen on many

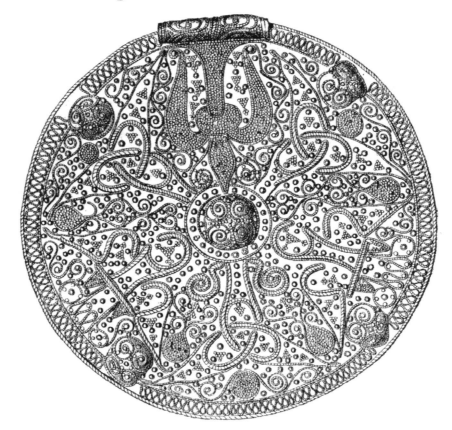

Fig. 1314.—Bracteate of gold, real size, found with the door.—Tuft Church, Sandver.

objects. There was evidently importance attached to the numbers "Three" and "Nine;" but it is impossible to tell what was the true meaning in the mythology of these people of the triad, which is very common on the jewels and other objects illustrated in this work,[1] and it is remarkable that some of the graves are made to represent the above signs.[2]

---

[1] The S sign is also common, especially in the bronze age.

[2] A kind of trinity of the higher deities is represented in Persia, India, Chaldæa, and other countries.

CHAPTER XI.

OCCUPATIONS AND SPORTS OF MEN.

Honour in which work was held —Kings superintend their own estates—Importance of fisheries—Skill of the people in the working of iron, and in shipbuilding—The Thiele find — Sports — Falconry — Retrievers and hounds—Dancing not a favourite amusement—Chess and backgammon —Several varieties—Costliness of chessboards—Games with dice— Jugglers and buffoons — Horsefights — Parables and puzzles —Gest's riddles.

PROMINENT chiefs did not disdain to take part in or superintend the work on their estates, and neither master, mistress nor children of wealthy families were ever idle.

"Harald Grœnski's son, Olaf, was fostered with his step-father Sigurd Syr and his mother Ásta. Hrani Vidförli (the Wide-travelling) was with her, and fostered King Olaf Haraldsson. Olaf soon became an accomplished man, fair of face, of middle stature, and wise and eloquent. Sigurd Syr was a great husbandman; his men were always at work, and he often went himself to look to the fields, meadows, and cattle, and to the smithy, or wherever anything was going on " (St. Olaf, c. 1).[1]

"King Olaf often stayed in the country on the large bœr which he owned. When he was at Haukbœr in Ránriki, he fell sick and died " (Olaf the Quiet's Saga, c. 11).[2]

The well-to-do generally had a very large number of servants, both free and thralls, to assist them in their work.

"It is told that Gudmund Riki was much superior to other men in magnificence, and had 100 servants and 100 cows; it was his custom to have the sons of prominent men with him, and he treated them well; they had not to do any work, but were always to sit with him, though it was their custom when they were at home, high-born though they were, to work " (Ljósvetninga Saga, c. 5).[3]

---

[1] Cf. also Njala, cc. 44, 53.
[2] Cf. also Njala, cc. 44, 53, 111; Ragnar Lodbrok.
[3] Cf. also Vatnsdæla, c. 22.

The bœndr after the spring cultivation went on Viking expeditions, returned at Midsummer and attended to the harvest; then again went on Viking expeditions, from which they did not return until winter, which was spent quietly at home.[1]

"King Sigurd Syr was on his field when the messengers came to him and told him this news (that Olaf was coming) and all the doings of Ásta at the bœr. He had many men there; some cut corn, others tied it (into sheaves), others

Fig. 1315.—Plough of oak wood. Length, 9 feet. Found in Döstrup, Jutland.

Fig. 1316.—Shears. ⅓ real size.—Ultuna. Earlier iron age.

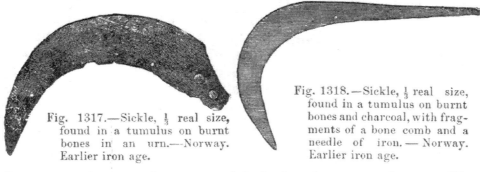

Fig. 1317.—Sickle, ⅓ real size, found in a tumulus on burnt bones in an urn.—Norway. Earlier iron age.

Fig. 1318.—Sickle, ⅓ real size, found in a tumulus on burnt bones and charcoal, with fragments of a bone comb and a needle of iron. — Norway. Earlier iron age.

drove corn home, others stowed it in hay-houses or barns. He, and two men with him, walked sometimes on the field, sometimes where the corn was stacked " (St. Olaf's Saga, c. 31).

The Sagas often mention people possessing sheep, and shears are often found. The one here represented was in the Ultuna ship's find, and had been placed with weapons and other objects belonging to the warrior, who probably owned great estates and large flocks of sheep.

---

[1] Orkneyinga Saga.

The fisheries were of great importance, and much care was bestowed upon them even by great chiefs, among whom were Eyvind Skáldaspillir and Erling Skjalgsson. The seal, herring, and cod fisheries gave occupation to a large number of people.

"Erling always kept at home thirty thralls, besides other bond-people. He allotted to them a certain day's work, and afterwards gave them leave and time to work for themselves at twilight or at night; he gave them land for tillage, to sow grain for themselves and use the produce for getting property. He placed on each one his value and price. Many redeemed themselves in the first or second season, and all who were thrifty did so in three winters. With this property Erling bought himself other thralls; and he sent some of his produce to the herring fishery, and some to other kinds of business; some cleared the woods and made themselves farms; to all he gave some means of support" (St. Olaf, c. 22).[1]

We have seen that the people of the North were great shipbuilders, and the numerous discoveries of various tools as well as weapons show the skill of their smiths and workers in iron, some of whom were high-born men.

"He (Thorolf) had a large long ship made with a dragon's head, and had it fitted out in the best manner. He sailed in it southward, and made a great sweep of the provisions then found in Halogaland. He also sent men herring fishing and cod fishing, and in many places seals were caught and eggs taken; all the produce of this expedition was brought to him. He had never fewer free men than a hundred at his home. He was open-handed and liberal, and became a good friend of the chiefs and all his neighbours; he became powerful, and paid much attention to the outfitting of his ships and weapons" (Egil's Saga, c. 10).

"Skallagrim was a very hard-working man. He had always many men with him, and had fetched many of the provisions and means of subsistence, for at first they had but few cattle in comparison with what was needed for so many. His cattle found their own food during the winter in the forests. He was a great shipwright, and there was no want of drift-timber [2] west of Myrar. He had a bœr built at Alp-tanes, and had another household there; his men went out fishing, seal-catching, and egg-gathering from there, as there was a quantity of these things; he also had drift-timber

---

[1] Cf. also c. 21.　　　　　[2] Forests then existed in Iceland.

brought in. Many whales were there then, and they could shoot as many as they wanted, for the creatures were not used to men. He had a third bœr near the sea, in the western part of Myrar, where it was still easier to procure drift-wood; there he had grain grown and called the farm Akrar. Some outlying islands there were called Hvalseyjar, because whales were found on them. Skallagrim also had his men up at the salmon rivers to fish, and placed Odd Einbúi at Gljúfrá to take care of the catch; he lived at Einbuabrekkur, and Einbuanes is named from him. . . . When the cattle of Skallagrim grew numerous they all went up on the mountains in the summer. He found that those cattle which went up on the heaths became much larger and fatter, and that the sheep kept themselves during the winter in mountain valleys if they were not taken down, so he had a farm made up at the mountain, and had a household there where his sheep were taken care of. Gris took care of that farm, and Grisartunga is named from him " (Egil's Saga, c. 29).

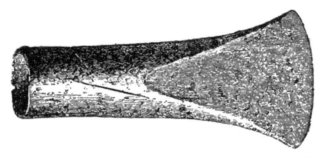

Fig. 1319.—Celt, of iron, ⅓ real size, found with five Roman silver coins (Adrian–Commodus).—Götland.

" Thorstein had built a church on his farm. From this he had made a bridge with great skill; under the beams which supported it were rings with tinkling bells[1] attached to them, so that when people walked over it they were heard at Skarfsstadir, half a sea-mile distant. Thorstein took much pains with this bridge, for he was a great worker in iron. Gretti worked hard in beating the iron that winter, though at times he did not care to do it. He was however quiet that winter, so that nothing happened " (Gretti's Saga, c. 53).[2]

" Then Skallagrim set up a household in Knarrarnes, and there had a farm for a long time after. He was a great iron-smith, and used much red iron ore[3] during the winters. He had a smithy made close to the sea, far from Borg, at Raufarnes " (Egil's Saga, c. 30).

---

[1] Din-bells = dyn-bjöllur.
[2] Cf. also Gisli Sursson's Saga, p. 47.

[3] Extracted much iron out of iron-ore — haematite.

"Ulf was son of Bjalfi and Hallbera, daughter of Ulf Uargi; she was the sister of Hallbjörn Half-Troll in Hrafnista, the father of Ketil Hœng. He was so tall and strong that his like was not found in the land at that time; when he was young he went on Viking expeditions. Berdlu-Kari, high-born, berserk, of great strength and boldness, was with him. He and Ulf had one money-bag together, and the most intimate friendship existed between them. When they returned from their expedition Kari went to his bœr at Berdla; he was very wealthy and had three children, Eyvind Lambi, Ölvir Hnufa, and a daughter Salbjörg. She was one of the fairest of women and very accomplished. Ulf married her, and went to his bœr; he was rich both in lands and movables. He took the rights of a lendr man, as his forefathers had done, and became a powerful man. It is said that he was a great husbandman. It was his custom to rise early in the morning and overlook the work of the men or of his smiths, and see over his cattle and fields, and sometimes to give advice to those who needed it. His

Fig. 1320.—Blacksmith's pincers of iron, found with an urn containing burnt bones, a hammer of iron, 29 small glass beads, &c. ⅓ real size.—Skåggesta, Södermanland, Sweden.

counsel was good in everything, for he was very wise; but every evening he became so peevish that few men could speak to him, and he was then fond of sleep. It was believed that he was a great shape-changer (hamramm = shape-strong), and he was called Kveldulf (evening wolf). Kveldulf had two sons by his wife, the older named Thórolf, and the younger Grim. When they grew up they were both tall and strong like their father. Thórolf was very handsome and accomplished; like his mother's kin, very cheerful and a liberal man in everything, and a great trader; he was beloved by all; Grim was swarthy and ugly, like his father, both in looks and character. He became a great man of business, and was skilled in working wood and iron and became a great smith. In winter he often went herring fishing with a *lagnar skuta* (fishing sloop), and many servants with him" (Egil's Saga, c. 29).[1]

Several finds have been discovered which evidently belonged to a blacksmith. At Thiele, Viborg, Jutland, was

---

[1] Cf. also St. Olaf's Saga, c. 234.

Fig. 1321.   Fig. 1322.

Two of nine different weights of iron, covered with thin plates
of brass. Real size.

Fig. 1323.   Fig. 1324.   Fig. 1325.

Iron tongs, 12 inches   Iron pincers, 6 inches   Iron tongs, 10 inches long.
long. ⅓ real size.   long. ⅓ real size.   ⅓ real size.

Fig. 1326.—Flat iron hammer of peculiar shape, 6¼ inches
long, 1 inch square at the head, and ½ inch broad at the
pointed end. ⅓ real size.

Fig. 1327.   Fig. 1328.

Iron hammers (?) ⅓ real size.

THIELE FIND.

discovered in the ground a great number of objects which

Fig. 1329.

Fig. 1330.—Two mountings of iron and a kind of light-coloured bronze, 5½ inches ; consisting of two parallel twisted iron bars, between which there had been soldered a square iron bar, held together by a bronze ring. ⅔ real size.

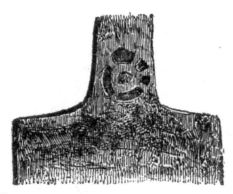

Fig. 1331.—Two-edged sword, in an unfinished state, with trade-mark.—Norway. Found with other objects, which appear to have been quite new when placed there, and some unfinished, among which were two swords with similar analogue trade-mark as those found in the Nydam and Vimose bog finds.

undoubtedly had belonged to one.[1]

Among the different occupations mentioned are those of salt and tar making.[2] Salt making or burning seems to have been one of the humblest of occupations or trades.

" A man is allowed to take bark and birch of his tenant-land for roofing his house and buy food-salt with it, and he shall make salt if he lives by the sea in order to buy birch and bark with it, and as

---

[1] Among the objects belonging to that find which are preserved in the Old-northern Museum of Copenhagen, were :—

A small (2¾ inches long) anvil of iron of the shape common at the present day.

A heavy iron hammer, 6 inches long, of similar shape to those now in use.

A pair of iron shears, 10 inches long, like those used for cutting of metal plates.

Three iron files, from 7¼ to 8¾ inches long. The cutting of the files being straight across the length of the file. Similar files have been found in the Vimose bog find.

An iron chisel, 5½ inches long.

Soldering spoons of iron, containing remains of a very hard melted metal, which, on examination, has been found to be a whitish alloy of base metals.

Seven fragmentary pieces of scales.

Two bronze bells.

An iron axe, 6 inches long.

A 4½-inch long iron point for an arrow or spear.

An iron spike, 7½ inches long, with head.

An iron key, 5 inches long.

An iron buckle, in which the pin is wanting.

A mass of fragments of iron mountings.

Several fragments of bronze plates covered with thin silver-foil, and of bronze mountings, and thin bronze wire ; also lumps of melted bronze.

Three small fragments of bone ; the largest piece has snake ornaments engraved on it.

[2] In N. G. L. ii. 145, tar work on the place where tar is made is mentioned.

much as he needs himself, but not more" (Frostath, xiii. 4).

"A man named Karl had a brother, Björn. They were of low birth, but very industrious men. They had before been salt-burners, and had earned money and become traders. They went on trading-journeys to Saxland and Sudrriki "[1] (Magnus the Good's Saga).[2]

Among the favourite pastimes of the Norsemen were falconry and hunting. Falconry existed in the North from the earliest times, and may have been brought into France, England, and other countries in Europe by the Northmen. Its existence is not, I think, mentioned in the Roman accounts of the countries conquered by them, and the low civilisation of the tribes inhabiting Germania in the Roman period did not admit of such a pastime.

Men had their hawks burned with them and a number of the talons of these birds have been found in several graves.

The inference drawn from the Sagas that men when going on a journey had their hawks with them, is corroborated by the Bayeux tapestry, where numerous chiefs are seen with these birds.

When Hrólf Kraki and his men walked into the hall of King Adils at Upsala, it is said—

"They had their hawks on their shoulders, and it was thought a great ornament in those times. King Hrólf had a hawk called Hábrók "[3] (Hrólf Kraki's Saga, c. 40).[4]

"One day the king (Olaf of Sweden) rode out early with his hawks and dogs[5] and men with him. When they let loose the hawks the king's hawk in one flight killed two heathcocks (*Tetrao tetrix*), and at once he again flew forward and killed three more. The dogs ran underneath and took every bird that fell down on the ground. The king galloped after, and picked up the game himself, and boasted much. He said: 'Long will it be before you hunt like this.' They assented,

---

[1] By Sudrriki seems to be meant the south of Europe.

[2] Cf. also Fridthjof's Saga, c. 11.

[3] Hábrók is mentioned in the earlier Edda Grimnismal, 44, as "the best of hawks."

[4] Cf. also c. 44, *ibid.*

[5] They had many kinds of dogs, some of which were very fierce Irish sheep dogs were known, and their value appreciated at a very early time by the Northmen, and there were penalties for killing dogs.

and answered that they thought no king had such luck in hunting. Then they all rode home, and the king was very glad " (Heimskringla, St. Olaf, c. 90).

Hawks were protected by the laws.

" If a man kills a hawk on a man's hand he shall pay a mark valued in silver, and damages for the outrage, but half a mark if he kills one in another place, all valued in silver " (Earlier Frostathing's Law, xi. 25).

Besides hunting-dogs there were other kinds, among which were shepherd and watch-dogs.

" When Olaf was in Ireland he went on a coast-raid.[1] As they needed provisions they went ashore and drove down many cattle. A bondi came there and asked Olaf to give him back his cows. Olaf replied that he might take them if he could recognise them and not delay their journey. The bondi had with him a large sheep-dog. He pointed out to it the herd of cattle, which numbered many hundreds. The dog ran through all the herds, and took away as many cows as the bondi had said belonged to him, and they were all marked with the same mark. Then they acknowledged that the dog had found out the right cattle. They thought it a wonderfully wise dog. Olaf asked if the bondi would give him the dog. ' Willingly,' answered the bondi. Olaf at once gave him a gold ring, and promised to be his friend. The dog's name was Vigi, and it was the best of all dogs. Olaf owned it long after this " (Olaf Tryggvason's Saga, c. 35).

" If a man kills a lapdog of another he must pay 12 aurar if the dog is a lapdog whose neck one can embrace with one hand, the fingers touching each other; 6 aurar are to be paid for a greyhound (mjóhund), and for a hunting-dog half a mark, and also for a sheep-dog, if it is tied by the innermost ox,[2] or untied by the outermost ox, and also at the gate. One aurar is to be paid for a dog guarding the house, if it is killed " (Frostath, xi. 24).

Chess, among house pastimes, was included in the Idrotter, as was gambling with dice, music, &c.

From an early period the game of chess, or at least a game

---

[1] Lit. a strand-raid.   [2] At the two ends of the cow-stall.

resembling it, was known in the North; skill in playing it was held to be an accomplishment worthy of powerful chiefs. Judging from the numerous finds, the game must have been very common. It must have been of very great antiquity, for it is mentioned in Voluspa.

The game, of which there were several varieties, though in what they differed we do not know, was called *tafl*,[1] and the pieces *toflur*. In *Hnot-tafl*, the pieces were called "*hunar*" (sing. *hunn*, or *huni*).

Hnefa-tafl was played with black and white pieces; one of them, probably the most important, was called *Hnefi*, from which the name of this peculiar game is probably derived. *Skak*, or *Skak-tafl*, was played on a board divided into squares, and seems to have been most like the present chess.[2] The board was like the chessboard of our day. To learn the game was part of the education of the high-born, and was considered idróttir. It must have been a great pastime on board ship, for in many of the pieces found are little holes in the centre for pegs, which made them fast and prevented them from being upset or changing place when the vessel rolled. The placing of the pieces was decided by the throwing of dice.

" After the battle at the river Helga, Ulf jarl made a feast for Knut at Roiskelda. They played skaktafl, but the king was very gloomy. . . . When they had played for a while, the jarl took one of the king's knights; the king put the piece back, and told him to make another move. The jarl got angry, upset the chessboard (taflbord), and went away " (St. Olaf's Saga, ch. 163).

The board itself was often very costly, being sometimes made of gold, and was counted among valuable inheritances, and as worthy of adorning the temple of the gods; it was such a treasure that Hrolf Nefia, at the risk of his life, sought to capture one in the temple of Bjarmaland.

Sturlaug went to Bjarmaland, and with his men walked up to a temple.

" He looked into the temple and saw a very large (image of)

---

[1] Cf. Kormak, c. iii.; Hörd's Saga, c. 21.

[2] Cf. Hervarar Saga, 15.

Thor sitting in a high-seat; in front of him was a splendid table covered with silver. . . . He saw a chess-board and chess-pieces of bright gold "[1] (Sturlaug's Saga Starfsama, ch. 18).

The people often spent their time during the long winter evenings in playing chess.

"In Brattahlid (a farm), in Grœnland, during the winter, they often amused themselves with chess-playing (*tafl*), and

Fig. 1332.—Chess piece of bone.—Norway. ⅔ real size.

Fig. 1333.—Chess piece of bone, found with two other pieces.—Norway. ⅔ real size.

Fig. 1334.—Chess piece of clay, found with three others.— Norway. ⅔ real size.

Fig. 1335.

Fig. 1336.

Chess, backgammon, or draughtsman, of bone, showing hole for peg, found with fragments of a double-edged sword, iron spurs, &c.—Norway. ⅔ real size.

Fig. 1337.—Draught piece of bone.— Ultuna find. Real size.

saga-telling, and many things that could improve their home-life" (Thorfinn Karlsefni, c. 7).

It was customary for women, as well as men, to play at the game.

"He (Gunnlaug Ormstunga) and Helga often amused themselves with chess; they soon liked each other well, as

---

[1] Lýsigull (bright gold) probably meant yellow gold, and we find that red | gold is also often mentioned.

was afterwards seen. They were almost of the same age" (Gunnlaug Ormstunga, 4).

"One night in the spring Thorir could not sleep; he walked out and it rained hard; he heard a loud bleating from where the lambs were separated from the ewes; Thorir walked there and saw that two kids and two lambs were lying tied on the wall of the fold, and in the fold sat two women playing at chess; the pieces were made of silver, but all the red ones were gilded. They were much startled. Thorir got hold of them and seated them at his side, and asked why they stole his sheep. . . . Thorir agreed that they might take the sheep with them, but that he should have the chessboard and what belonged to it; on the strings of the *taflpung* (chess-bag) was a gold ring set with stones, and a silver ring was in the chessboard. Thorir took all this, and they parted" (Gullthori's Saga, ch. 14).

The temper of the players did not always remain unruffled.

"It happened that Thorgils Bödvarsson and Sám Magnússon quarrelled over a game of chess; Sám wanted to move back a knight which he had exposed, but Thorgils would not allow it. Markús Mardarson advised them to move the knight back and not quarrel. Thorgils said he would not take his advice, and upset the chess, put (the pieces) into the bag, rose and struck Sám on the ear, so that blood flowed" (Sturlunga Saga viii., vol. ii. c. 1).

"Fridthjof sat at a hnefa-tafl when Hilding came. He said: 'Our kings send thee greetings, and want to have thy help for battle against King Hring, who wants to attack their realm overbearingly and unjustly.' Fridthjof answered nothing, and said to Björn, with whom he played the game: 'There is an empty place, foster-brother, and thou shalt not make a move but I will attack the red piece (tafla), and see if thou canst guard it.' Björn said: 'Here are two choices, foster-brother, and we can move in two ways.' Fridthjof answered: 'It is best to attack the hnefi (= the highest piece) first, and then it is easy to choose what to do'" (Fridthjof's Saga, ch. 3).

It seems that the pieces that had just been moved were called out in a loud voice.

"The king (Magnus the Good) sat and played at *Hneftafl*, and a man called out the names of the king's pieces when Ásmund came."

2 ▲ 2

Games with dice were of great antiquity, as seen from the finds, which prove even more than the Sagas how common dice-throwing was. The dice-throwing of the three Northern kings about Hisingen shows that the highest throw won.

"On Hising (an island at the mouth of the Gauta river) was a district which had at one time belonged to Norway, and at another to Gautaland. The kings agreed to cast lots about

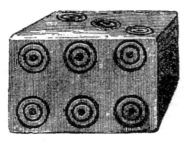

Fig. 1338.—Die of bone. Real size. —Ultuna find.

the possession thereof, and throw dice, and that he should have it who threw the highest. The Swedish king threw two sixes, saying that King Olaf need not throw; but he replied, shaking the dice in his hand, 'there are yet two sixes on the dice, and it is easy for God, my lord, to let them turn up again.' He threw, and got two sixes. Olaf King of Sweden threw and again got two sixes. Olaf King of Norway threw and there was on one die six, but the other burst asunder, and then there were seven. He then took possession of the district " (St. Olaf's Saga).

Dancing does not seem to have been a popular amusement before the end of the 11th century; and it is only referred to in a very obscure manner in the following Saga.

"King Godmund, of Glæsisvellir, was to give his sister in marriage to Siggeir, son of King Harek of Bjarmaland, and had prepared a splendid wedding-feast. Bosi was present, disguised in the garb of King Godmund's councillor Sigurd, whom he had slain. It is not stated how the chiefs were placed, but it is mentioned that Sigurd played on a harp for the brides-maids; and when the horns were brought in the men said that no one was his equal. . . . When the horn consecrated to Thor was brought in, Sigurd changed the tune; then all that was loose, both knives and plates, began to move; many jumped from their seats and moved to and fro on the floor; and this continued for a long while. Then came the horn consecrated to all the Asar. Sigurd once more changed the tune, and played so loud that it echoed all around. All in the hall rose, except the bride and bridegroom and the king, and everyone was moving round the hall, for a long while. The king asked if he knew any more tunes, and he said he still had some left, but he told the people to rest first. The men sat down and began to drink. Then he played the *gygjarslag* (air of jötun-woman), and *draumbut* (dream-piece), and *Hjarrandahljod* (air of Hjarrandi). When the horn consecrated to Odin came, Sigurd opened the harp, which was so large that a man could stand upright in it; it shone all over like red gold; he took from it white gloves embroidered with gold, and played the air called *faldafeykir* (the head-dress blower). At this the head-dresses flew off the women, and moved above the crossbeams; the women jumped up, the men sprang to their feet, and nothing could be kept quiet. When this toast was finished, the toast consecrated to Freyja, which was to be the last, came in; Sigurd touched the string which lay across all the others, and which he had not struck before, and told the king to expect hard playing; the king was so startled that he, as well as the bride and bridegroom, jumped up, and none were more lively than they, and this continued for a long while" (Herraud and Bosi's Saga, ch. 12).

Some of the chiefs or kings had jugglers or buffoons and performing dogs to amuse them and their guests. It seems to have been customary to exercise dogs in jumping over poles. A beggar came to King Magnus Erlingsson.

"The king asked who he was. He answered he was an Icelander of the name Mani, who had come northward from Rúm (Rome). The king said: 'Thou must know some wisdom, Tungli;[1] sit down and sing.' He then sang the *Útfarardrápa* (poem on a voyage to the Holy Land) which Haldór Skvaldri made about King Sigurd Jorsalafari, and the poem was much liked and thought amusing. Two players[2] were in the stofa, who made small dogs jump over high poles in front of highborn men, and the more high-born they were the higher they jumped" (Fornmanna Sögur, viii.; Sverri's Saga).

"Tuta, a Frisian, was with King Harald; he was sent to him for show, for he was short and stout, in every respect shaped like a dwarf" (Harald Hardradi's Saga).

Horse-fights were a favourite amusement with the people. Several mares were kept near in order to make the horses fight more fiercely: each horse was led by the owner or the trainer. When they rose on their hind feet and began to bite each other, the men who followed supported and urged them

---

[1] Tungli has the same meaning as Mani, namely moony; tungl = máni = moon.

[2] "Players" seems to mean jesters, fools.

on, partly by inciting them with a stick. Great chiefs often followed their stallions, and sometimes umpires were chosen, who in doubtful cases decided which horse had the best of it; to own the best horse was a great honour, and in such horse-fights **many** stallions were often led against each other.

" It happened one summer, as it often does, that there was a horse-fight (in Bergen, Norway). A man by name of Gaut of Mel, high of kin, a great friend of the Sturlungar, had received from Sturla a good horse; it was said by many to be the best in Norway. Arni öreyda, an Icelander, had sent the king a horse which he called the best in Iceland; and these horses were to fight. A large crowd of people gathered there. When the horses were led forth, each of them seemed to be very fine; they were let loose, and came together fiercely, and there followed a splendid fight, both severe and long; but when the fight had lasted some time, the king's horse slackened. The king did not like this, as could easily be seen. Gaut went round the circle of men, and made good use of the one eye he had. Aron was present there, and with him Thorarin, his kinsman; they were much displeased at the defeat of the horse. Aron was the friend of Arni, but not of Gaut; he thought he knew why it was defeated. As they saw that the king did not heed his horse, they went to him, and Aron said: ' Do not undervalue your horse, lord, for it must be most precious; but this is not the way of fighting he is used to.' ' What way is that ?' asked the king. ' A man follows each horse, as it is led forth, with a staff in his hand, and strikes the horse's quarters, and supports the horse when he rises.' ' If thou thinkest thou canst make the horse stand,' said the king, 'then go.' Now Aron and Thorarin took off their overcoats, and took sticks in their hands; then they went to where the king's horse stood outside the circle; they touched it with their sticks, and it started as if it knew why they had come; it rushed at the horse of Gaut, and the latter at it, and they came together violently. The horse of Gaut was now much pressed, for the king's horse was supported with strength; and it was said that it so had the best chance. As day declined, the horse of Gaut slackened (its efforts), though it would neither retreat nor run. Aron and Thorarin pushed their horse the harder, till the horse of Gaut fell down from exhaustion and hard fighting, and never afterwards rose. Gaut could not remain quiet on account of his anger, and thought that Aron had killed his horse, and was greatly displeased; but one could see that the king liked it well. Then other horses were led forth, of which there is no account " (Biskupa Sögur, i. ; Aron's Saga, ch. 18).

Some kinsmen of the chief Glúm came to him one autumn, and a feast was made for them.

" When they made ready to go home, Glúm gave his kinsman Bjarni a red stallion, six winters old, and said he would give him another if any horse surpassed this one. They went home from the feast, and Bjarni at once fed it on hay, and it was very well kept there. The next summer he was very curious to know how it would fight. He talked about having a fight against a horse owned by Thorkel Geirason of Skörd, and it was decided that they should make the horses fight at Midsummer at Máfahjalli. Thormód and his son Eyjúlf had a grey stallion with a mane of a different colour, and always sold horses begotten by it, but did not like to use it in a horse-fight. It is said that once the stallions of Thormód and Bjarni met and bit each other so that they were all bloody. The servant of Bjarni came to him and said that he had seen the two stallions bitten, and red all over. . Bjarni sent word to Thorkel that they would not have the horse-fight, as his stallion was no longer able to fight. Bjarni supposed that Eyjúlf and his father Thormód had made the horses fight, as they could not have maltreated each other thus by themselves, and therefore offered to have a horse-fight when eight weeks of the summer had passed. Thormód asked his son to decide whether to do it or not, for he wanted the fight. The horses were led forward, and the fight went on well till eleven rounds had passed. Then Eyjúlf's stallion took hold of the jawbone of Bjarni's, and held on until Bjarni came up and struck it off. Eyjúlf turned round and struck the stallion, and the stick rebounded heavily from the horse and hit Bjarni's shoulder. The horses were parted at once. Eyjúlf went to Bjarni and said this mishap had not been wished by him. I will show whether I did this intentionally or not. I will give thee sixty rams if thou wilt not blame me for this, and then thou canst see that I did not wish this to happen.' Bjarni said that he had caused it himself, and thought they had not made the stallions bloody. Then they went home. In the autumn at the *réttir* (sheep-meeting) Eyjúlf took out sixty rams. Thormód asked what he was going to do with these. Eyjúlf answered that he had given them to Bjarni. Thormód said, 'The blow was heavy, nor is the payment little.' As soon as he had said this Bjarni turned to him and struck him a death-blow, and would not **receive the sheep**" (Vemund's Saga, ch. 23).[1]

These horse-fights ocasionally led to a struggle.

" In the summer a large horse-fight (*hestathing*) was appointed at Langafit above Reykjar, and thither came many men. Atli of Bjarg (Gretti's brother) had a good horse, with a dark stripe along the back, and of Keingála's breed (a famous mare which had been owned by Gretti's father). Father and son thought a great deal of the horse. The brothers Kormak and Thorgils of Mel had a brown horse, fearless in fight. The horse of the brothers and that of Atli from Bjarg were to fight against each other. There were also many other good horses. Odd Úmagaskald, a kinsman of Kormak, was to attend the horse of the brothers during that day ; he had become a strong man, was very proud, overbearing, and reckless. Gretti asked his brother Atli who should attend to his horse. ' I have not quite decided that,' Atli said. ' Do you wish me to stand near it ? ' Gretti asked. ' Be very quiet, then, kinsman,' Atli added, ' for we have to deal with proud men.' ' They will have to pay for their overbearing,' continued Gretti, ' if they do not keep it within bounds.' These horses were now led forward, while the others were standing tied together near the bank of the river, which was there deep.

" The horses bit each other savagely, and afforded the greatest amusement. Odd followed his horse eagerly, while Gretti retreated and seized the horse's tail with one hand, holding in the other a staff, with which he whipped him. . . . The horses while fighting moved towards the river ; Odd thrust at Gretti with the staff, and hit his shoulder-blade, which was turned towards him. The blow was so violent that the flesh was bruised, but Gretti was only slightly wounded. At that moment the horses rose high on their hind legs. Gretti jumped under the haunch of his horse and thrust his staff into the side of Odd, with such force that three of his ribs were broken, and he fell into the river with his horse as well as all the others. Men swam out to him, and he was pulled up from the river. At this there was much shouting. Kormak and his men and those from Bjarg seized their weapons ; when the men from Hrutafjord and those from Vatnsnes saw this they interceded, and they were parted, and went home threatening each other ; but they nevertheless kept quiet for awhile. Atli spoke little of it, but Gretti was rather loud-spoken, and said they would meet again, if he had his way " (Gretti's Saga, ch. 29).

---

[1] Cf. also Njala, c. 59.

" Wherever a man makes the horse of another fight without the owner's permission he shall pay the loss that ensues and *öfundarbót*[1] to the owner, according to lawful judgment. If the hurt is valued at half a mark, he shall pay full rett according to law, as if it were done from hatred or envy. Every man shall answer for himself at a horse-fight, whoever may have the fight. If a man strikes a horse without necessity at a horse-fight, he shall pay öfundarbót to the owner; and if the horse is damaged by it, he shall pay indemnity for damages and rett-of-envy to the owner " (N. G. L., ii. 126).

---

[1] Öfundarbót = indemnity paid for intentional outrage.

CHAPTER XII.

OCCUPATIONS OF WOMEN.

Weaving and embroidery—The housewife's keys—General occupation of
ordinary women—Queens brewing ale and bleaching linen—Looms—
Amazons.

HIGH-BORN women occupied themselves with weaving and
embroidery, participated in the household duties, and took
charge of the estate while their husbands
were absent.

Fig. 1339.—Bundle of
bronze keys in a
large stone cist made
of slabs; found with
two human skeletons
upon a bed made of
birch bark, &c. ¼
real size.—Norway.

The wife had a bunch of keys at her side,
to show her authority over the household;
and in many graves of women keys either of
iron or bronze have been found.

The women had a special habitation called
Dyngja or Skemma, which men were not
allowed to enter, and where their female
friends visited them.

In earlier days it seems to have been the
custom for fathers to have champions outside
keeping guard in order to prevent men from
coming into the women's quarters; and these
champions are described as having taken
animal shape.[1]

The Bayeux tapestry[2] corroborates in
many points the truthfulness of the Sagas;
for example, when referring to the dragon-

[1] Ragnar Lodbrok's Saga.

[2] This valuable piece of work contains
72 distinct scenes, 623 persons, 202 horses
and mules, 55 dogs, 505 divers animals,
41 ships and boats, 49 trees—in all,
1,512 distinct objects. And well worth
while, indeed, is a journey to Bayeux
for the special object of seeing it. The
historical part does not take up more
than 11 inches; in the space above
and below there is a border, where lions,
birds, dragons and fantastic objects are
represented. The most accurate work on it
that has been published is 'La Tapisserie
de Bayeux, reproduction d'après nature
en 79 planches photographiques, avec un
texte historique, descriptif et antique,
par Jules Comte, conservateur du dépôt
légal au ministère de l'instruction pu-
blique et des beaux arts. Paris. J. Roth-
schild, éditeur, 13, Rue des Saints-Pères.
1878.'

ship, ornamented with shields, striped sails, small boats, &c., the ancient wood carvings, some of which are shown in this work, the clothing and cloaks which are only worn by the higher-born, and which are fastened with fibulæ on the right shoulder, and the embroidery.

"Then his foster-daughter Brynhild returned to Heimir. She spent her time in a bower with her maidens, and surpassed in handiwork all other women. She made embroidery with gold, and sewed thereon the great deeds of Sigurd, the slaying of the serpent, the taking of the treasure, and Regin's death" (Volsunga Saga, c. 24).

"Gudrun went on until she came to the hall of King Half, and stayed there with Thora, Hakon's daughter, in Denmark seven seasons (i.e., half-years), and was well entertained; she made embroidery, and worked thereon many great deeds and fine games, which were customary at that time, swords and coats of mail and all the outfit of a king, and King Sigmund's ships gliding along the shore. They also embroidered how Sigar and Siggeir fought on Fyen. This was their enjoyment, and Gudrun now somewhat forgot her grief" (Volsunga Saga, c. 32).

The general occupation of ordinary women was to milk cows, prepare food and drink, serve the men, work in the field, and especially make the hay, card wool, attend to the clothes,[1] wash the men's heads, and pull off their clothes when they went to bed; a custom still prevalent in many parts of Scandinavia.[2]

Women of high rank even superintended the work of the farm, and had at times no small amount of authority.

Fig. 1340.—Needle of iron. Real size.

Fig. 1341.—Needle of bronze. Real size. Found with a pincette of bronze, a fragment of a double-edged sword, an axe of iron, a bronze chain, &c.—Norway.

Fig. 1342.—Silver needle. Real size. Found in an oblong mound with glass and amber pearls and two clay urns, in one of which were burnt bones.—Norway.

---

[1] Eyrbyggja, 51.
[2] Such expressions as "She was well versed in all kinds of accomplishments that belonged to women" are often used. (Heidarviga Saga. 21; Viglund, 17.)

" Thorbjörn Skrjúp lived next to the farm of Thórd in Laxárdal. He was wealthy, mostly in gold and silver : he was also large in stature and of great strength. . . . Höskuld bought a ship from a Shetlandman and equipped it, announcing that he intended to go abroad, but would leave Jórun at home to take care of the farm and their children. He set sail. . . ." (Laxdæla, c. 11).

Grettir had been captured, and they were going to hang him.

" Then they saw six men ride farther down in the valley ; one of them was in coloured clothes. They guessed that Thorbjörg, housewife at Vatnsfjord, was there, and so it was. She was going to the sæter (mountain pasture). She was a highly accomplished woman, and very wise ; she ruled the district, and settled all matters, when Vermund, her husband, who was a godi, was not at home " (Gretti's Saga, c. 52).

One summer, Thorodd, bondi at the farm Froda, in Iceland, rose early one morning—

" And distributed work ; some took the horses, and the women had to dry the hay, and the work was divided between them. Thorgunna had to dry as much as the fodder of a bull, and they did much work that day " (Eyrbyggja, ch. 51).

The mischief caused by gossiping women is occasionally referred to.

" The hall was 100 ells [1] long, and five fathoms broad ; to the south of it was the room (dyngja) of Aud and Asgerd, and they sat there sewing. Thorkel went thither and lay down near it. Asgerd said : 'Help me, Aud, and cut a shirt for my bondi Thorkel.' Aud answered : 'I know no better than thyself how to do that, and thou wouldst not ask me if thou hadst to make one for my brother Vestein.' Asgerd replied : 'What concerns Vestein is a thing by itself ; and thus it will be for some time ; but I love him more than my husband Thorkel, though we may never enjoy each other.' Aud added : 'I knew long ago what Thorkel thought about it, and how it went ; let us talk no more of it.' Asgerd said : 'I think it no fault that I love Vestein, but I heard that thou and Thorgrim often met before thou wast married.' Aud replied : 'No harm was in

---

[1] 1 ell = 2 feet.

that, and I preferred no man to Gisli so there was no dishonour in it; let us leave off this talk.' And so they did. Thorkel heard every word, and exclaimed: 'Hear great wonders! hear words of fate! hear great talk, which will cause the death of one man or more!' Thereupon he went away. Aud said: 'The talk of women often causes evil, and it may be that by this evil will be occasioned; let us think over what we shall do.' Asgerd said: 'I have bethought myself of an expedient.' 'What is that?' asked Aud. 'I will put my arms around the neck of my husband, Thorkel, when we get into bed this evening and be very affectionate; his mind will change at this, so that he will forgive me. I will also tell him that this is such a lie, that it is of no consequence though we have babbled about it. But if he should want to make any fuss about it, give me other advice. Or what expedient art thou going to take?' . . . In the evening Gisli came home from his work. It was the custom of Thorkel to thank his brother Gisli for the work; this time he did not, and spoke not a word to him. Gisli asked: 'Art thou not well, brother, as thou art so silent?' Thorkel answered: 'I am not sick, but this is worse than sickness.' Gisli asked: 'Have I done anything which thou dislikest, brother?' 'Nothing,' said Thorkel. Gisli said: 'It is well, for I would least of all that we should disagree. But nevertheless I should like much to know what is the cause of thy sadness.' Thorkel answered: 'Thou wilt know it, although later.' Gisli went away, and then went to bed. Thorkel retired first. When Asgerd came to bed Thorkel said: 'I do not mean thee to sleep here this night.' She said: 'What is more befitting than that I should sleep with my husband? or why has thy mind changed so soon? But what is the cause?' 'Thou knowest the cause,' said Thorkel, 'and I know it also.' 'What is the need of talking in this way?' added she; 'believe not the foolish talk of us women, for when we are alone we always chatter about things in which there is little truth; and so it is in this case.' Asgerd then put both arms around his neck, and was very affectionate, and begged him not to believe such things. Thorkel told her to go away. Asgerd said: ' . . . I give thee two choices: either to take as unsaid what we have talked about, and not believe that which is not true; or that I at once name my witnesses and declare separation from thee. Then I will do what I like, and it may be that thou then wilt have reason to speak of real enmity. I shall let my father claim my *mund* and dower.' Thorkel was silent, but after a while said: 'I think it is best for thee to creep under there at the bedside to-night.' She got into bed, and they agreed as if nothing had occurred. Aud went to the bed of her husband Gisli, and told him all the talk of herself and Asgerd. She begged him not to be angry, and to give good advice if he thought necessary. 'I know that Thorkel wants my brother Vestein to be killed, if possible.' Gisli answered: 'I cannot give any good advice, but I will not blame thee for this, because some one must speak the words of fate'" (Gisli Sursson's Saga).

Even queens attended to the brewing of ale and bleaching of linen.[1]

"One day when Thordis went out to her linen,[2] the weather was fine, the sun shone and the wind blew from the south" (Ljosvetninga, ch. 5).

"King Alrek, who lived in Alreksstadir, ruled over Hörda-land; he was married to Signy, a king's daughter from Vörs, One of his hirdmen, Koll, followed him north into Sogn, and told him much of the beauty of Geirhild, Drif's daughter; he had seen her at the brewing of ale, and said he wanted him to marry her. Hött, who proved to be Odin, went to visit her when she was at her linen, and bargained with her that Alrek should marry her, but that she should invoke him for all things. The king saw her on his way home, and made their wedding the same autumn. He rewarded Koll well for his faithfulness, and gave him jarldom and residence in Kollsey, south of Hardsæ which is a populous district. King Alrek could not have them both as wives on account of their disagreement, and said he would have the one who brewed the best ale for him when he should come home from an expedition. They vied in the ale-brewing. Signy invoked Freyja, and Geirhild, Hött, who gave his spittle as ferment, and said he wanted for his help that which was between the tub and herself;[3] the ale proved to be good; then Alrek sang:

Geirhild, my maiden,	I see hanging
Good is this ale,	From a high gallows
If no defect	Thy son, woman,
Follows it;	Given to Odin.

In that year, Vikar, the son of King Alrek and Geirhild was born" (Half's Saga, c. i.)

That the people knew the art of weaving[4] we have ample

---

[1] Half's Saga, i.
[2] Implies that her linen lay bleaching.
[3] She was with child.
[4] Looms can be seen in the Museum of Christiania, and were still in use a short time since in the neighbourhood of Bergen.

proofs in the sagas, and also in the finds. From the following description we know what the looms were like.

" It happened one morning, Good Friday, in Kateness (Caithness, Scotland), that a man called Dorrud went out of doors, and saw that twelve men were riding together to a woman's house and there disappeared. He went there and looked through a ' light hole ' and saw other women who had

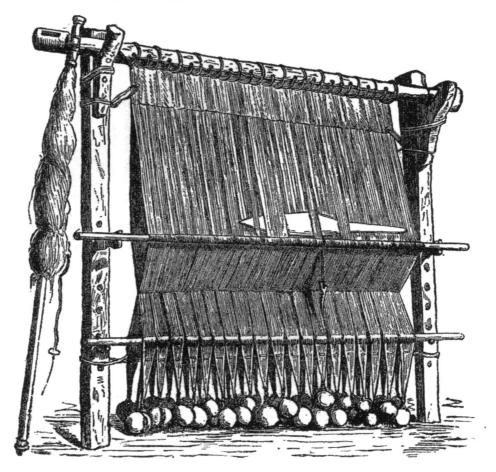

Fig. 1343.——Ancient loom from the Färoes in Bergen Museum.

set up a web on the loom. The weights (whorles) were human heads, but the woof and the warp were intestines of men, a spear was used as a spindle and an arrow as a shuttle " (Njal Saga).

Whorls are very common in the graves.

Many examples occur of women taking to the profession of arms, and often fighting as bravely as the most valiant warriors ;[1] and that this custom was not altogether unknown in some parts of Europe at a later period than that of the Viking age is shown by the appearance of Joan of Arc.

"Svafa, the daughter of Bjartmar jarl, gave birth to a girl; most people thought she ought to be exposed, and said she would not have the character of a woman if she became like the kinsmen of her father.[2] The jarl had her besprinkled with water, and brought up and called her Hervör, and said

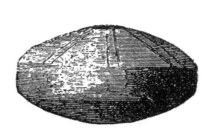

Fig. 1344.   Fig. 1345.

Whorle of spindle of burnt clay, ⅔ real size, found by the side of a clay urn containing burnt bones in an oblong mound —Greby, Bohuslan. From a neighbouring hill one can count about 160 tumuli, sixty of which are oblong —varying from 25 to 36 feet in length, and 15 to 20 feet in width—several have memorial stones upon them, the highest being 14 feet.—Earlier iron age.

Fig. 1346.—Specimen of a peculiar weaving shuttle formed in the shape of a short double-edged blade—the back being formed for putting on a handle. Specimens found in several women's graves. About ¼ real size.—Norway.

the kin of Arngrim's son was not quite dead while she was alive. When she grew up she was fair; she practised more shooting and the handling of sword and shield than sewing and embroidering; she was tall and strong, and as soon as she was able she oftener did evil than good; when she was hindered from that she ran into the woods and slew men in order to take their property. When the jarl knew this he took her home, and there she stayed for a while" (Hervarar Saga, ch. 6; also Herraud and Bosi's Saga, c. 2, and Atlakvida.)

---

[1] In the famous Bravalla and Dunheath battles, and in other cases, Amazons are mentioned; they are called Shield-maidens (*Skjald-mær*, pl. *Skjald-meyjar*).

[2] Angantyr and his brothers were all very fierce tempered.

CHAPTER XIII.

EXERCISES—IDRÓTTIR.

Bodily and mental exercises—Love of athletics—Jumping—Climbing—
Popularity of wrestling—Different modes of wrestling—Running—Games
of ball—Skin-pulling—Swimming—Some extraordinary feats in swimming
—Webbing the fingers—Warlike exercises—Dexterity in the handling of
weapons—Archery—Proficiency of chiefs in athletics and gymnastics.

BODILY as well as mental exercises were known under the
name of *Idróttir.* In no ancient records have we so many
detailed accounts of games as we have in the Sagas. The
education of the Northmen was thoroughly Spartan in its
character. To this day the love of athletic games is one
of the characteristics of their most direct descendants, the
English people; and other countries have lately awakened
to the importance of physical training.

Their exercises or games may be classified under three
heads.

1st. *Athletic* games or gymnastic exercises, such as wrestling,
swimming, running, jumping, leaping, balancing, climbing,
playing at ball, racing on snow-shoes, skin-pulling, &c., &c.

2nd. *Warlike* exercises with weapons, which embraced
fencing, spear-throwing, arrow-shooting, slinging, &c., &c.

3rd. *Mental* exercises, consisting of poetry, Saga-telling,
riddles, games of chess and draughts, and harp-playing.

In those days of incessant warfare, physical training was
considered of the highest importance. Old and young constantly practised games of strength and dexterity; they knew
that it was only by constant exercise that they could become
or remain good warriors. This made the young men supple,
quick of foot, dexterous in motion, and gave them great power
of endurance, insuring a good physique, which told on their
children and future generations. They were thus always
prepared for war, and this is the key to the character of the

old Viking. We see what a healthy and powerful man he must have been, skilful alike to strike the fatal blow, and avoid the treacherous sword, spear or arrow. The result of such education was seen in the powerful and strong bodily frame that was attained by the youth of the country, the young men being of age and ready for war at the age of fifteen.

There were constant competitions for the honour of the championship in each of the particular games or exercises, and young and old competed together on special grounds which were selected for that purpose, where the assembled and admiring multitude came to witness these contests. There seem to have been no prizes given to the successful competitor—at least no mention is ever made of them. All that was desired was the fame which fell to the victor, and every great warrior always excelled in the use of weapons or in athletic exercises.

Their love of physical exercise explains how these dauntless and manly tribes, who had a virile civilisation of their own, contributed to regenerate the blood of the people among whom they settled or whom they conquered.

Jumping was a favourite exercise of the Norsemen. Some men could jump higher than their own height, both backwards and forwards, and this with their weapons and complete armour on.

Agility was absolutely necessary in order to obtain victory or escape from danger; many a man owed his life either to a timely jump to one side, or to a leap from a height, or over a circle of surrounding foes.

" One day as they (Herraud and Bosi) sailed near the land in a strong gale, a man standing on a rock asked to be allowed to go with them. Herraud said he could not go out of his course for him, but if he could reach the ship he might go with them. The man jumped from the rock, and came down on the tiller; it was a leap of thirty feet " (Herraud and Bosi's Saga, ch. 3).

"Sigurd ran down on the single path, but Leif came to where Heri, one of Sigurd's companions, lay, and quickly turned, ran forward on the island, and jumped down to the foreshore, and men say it is ninety feet down to the beach " (Færeyinga Saga, ch. 57).

" Lambi Sigurdson ran at Kari from behind and thrust a spear at him ; but Kari saw him and jumped up, at the same time spreading his legs. The spear came down into the ground, and Kari stepped on the handle and broke it asunder " (Njala, ch. 146).

" Skarphedin stood with his axe on his shoulder, smiling scornfully, and said : ' This axe I had in my hand when I leapt 12 ells (24 feet) over Markarfljót and slew Thrain Sigfusson, and they stood there eight men, and none of them got hold of me ' " (Njala, c. 120).

" Skarphedin (son of Njal, a great champion) started up when he was ready, holding the axe *Rimmugyg* in the air ; he ran forward to the channel of the river, which was so deep that it was completely impassable. Much ice had been forced up on the other side of the river, and it was as slippery as glass ; they (Thrain and his men) stood in the middle of it. Skarphedin swung himself aloft and leapt over the river between the sheets of ice, and did not stop, but ran sliding on the ice. This was very slippery, and he advanced as swiftly as a flying bird. Thrain was going to put on his helmet. Skarphedin came up to them and aimed at Thrain with his axe, struck his head, and cleft it down to the jaw, so that they fell down on the ice. This happened so suddenly that nobody could deal him a blow. He ran away instantly with great speed " (Njala, c. 92).[1]

Climbing was another of their exercises.

" King Olaf once had his ships in a harbour, not far from a very high mountain and most steep rocks. One day two of his *hirdmen* were talking about their *idróttir*, and each thought himself the better, and that he knew more games than the other. They contended as to who could climb the steepest rock ; they disputed about this so keenly, that at last they made a bet, and one wagered his gold ring, and the other his head. After this they both climbed the rock. The first went so far that he was in danger of falling down, and then returned in fear, and could with difficulty save himself from injury ; the other climbed up to the middle of the mountain, but there he dared go neither forward nor backward, nor even move, for he had but little hold either for hands or feet ; his position was so dangerous, that he saw his downfall and death were certain if he should make the least movement where he was. He shouted in great fear for King Olaf or his men to help him. When the king heard his shout, and found out what it was about, he bade

---

[1] Cf. also Sturlunga, i. c. 9; Orkneyinga, c. 18; Njala, c. 120, 145; Færeyinga, c. 37.

2 в 2

them save him, saying that it would be a deed of great bravery if any one should dare to do it. When the king saw that no one stirred, he threw off his cloak and ran up the rock to the man as if it had been a level plain, took him under his arm, and went farther up with him. He then turned to go down with the man under his arm, and laid him unharmed on the ground. All praised this as a great feat, and the fame thereof was widely spread " (Olaf Tryggvason's Saga, vol. ii.; Fornmanna Sögur).[1]

Wrestling was a very popular pastime, and had a beneficial effect on the body, to which it gave suppleness, strength and firmness; it was a great favourite at the Things and festivals. The most simple form of this sport was for the wrestlers to take hold of each other's arms or waists as best they could, and by the strength of their arms to throw each other off their feet. The wrestlers often threw off not only the outer clothing, but also their under-garments, in order to be more free and agile. The competitors were divided by lots into two parties, each of which was drawn up in a row with its leader. These paired off their men to wrestle in the arena or space between the two rows, one after the other. If one side was weaker in numbers, or one man had had all his men defeated, he could challenge his antagonist, and the result of their wrestling decided the game.

A more difficult form of wrestling was that of grappling, and attacking each other (sometimes fastened together by a belt at the waist) according to certain rules, and by systematic turnings and grip movements, with arms and legs, seeking to bring each other to the ground. These combats for the championship sometimes ended fatally.

"The sons of Thórd were the leaders of the games. Thorbjörn Öngul was very overbearing, and quickly forced any one he wanted to take part in the game, seizing him by the hand, and pulling him forward to the field. Those who were less strong wrestled first, and then one after the other, which caused great amusement. When most of them had wrestled, except the strongest, the bœndr talked about who of these should contend against each of the sons of Thord; but no one came forward. They went before different men and challenged them, with the same result. Thorbjörn Öngul looked around, and saw that there sat a man of large size,

---

[1] Cf. also **Gretti's Saga**, c. 78.

whose face could not be clearly seen. Thorbjörn took hold of him, and pulled hard; but he sat still and did not move. Then Thorbjörn said: 'No one has sat so firm before me to-day as thou; but who art thou?' 'My name is Gest' (guest), he replied. 'If thou wilt take part in some game, thou art a welcome guest.' He answered: 'It seems to me, many things may change, and I will not join in games with you, who are entirely unknown to me.' Many said that he would do well if he, though a stranger, would give them some amusement. He asked what they wanted of him. They asked him to wrestle with some one. He said he had ceased to wrestle, 'but,' he added, 'there was a time when I enjoyed it greatly.'"

"Thord rushed at Grettir, but he stood firm without flinching. Grettir then stretched his hand to the back of Thord and got hold of his breeches, lifted him off his feet, over his head, and threw him down behind him, so that Thord's shoulders came down with a heavy thud. Then they said that the two brothers should attack him at the same time, and they did so; there was a hard tussle, and each had the better of it by turns, although Grettir always had one of them under him. They fell by turns on their knees or dragged each other along; they grasped each other so tightly that they were all blue and bloody. All thought this the greatest fun, and when they stopped thanked them for the wrestling; and it was the opinion of all who were present that the two brothers were not stronger than Grettir, though each of them had the strength of two strong men" (Gretti's Saga, c. 72 and 74).

Thórd Fangari challenged Klaufi, who was only ten winters old, to wrestle, and called him a coward if he would not.

"They summoned many people to Hof, for Thórd would wrestle nowhere except there. They began and wrestled long, until a bondmaid came into the door of the women's room and called it bondmaid-wrestling, as neither of them fell, and told them to kiss each other and then stop. Klaufi got angry at this, and raised Thórd up on his breast, and threw him down so hard that all thought he was hurt" (Svarfdæla, c. 12).

"One summer at the Althing men were divided in two parties at the Fangabrekka (wrestling-brink, slope), Nordlendings (men from the northern part of the land) and Vestfirdings (from the western fjords). The Nordlendings were defeated, and their leader was Már, the son of Glúm. Ingolf, the son of Thorvald of Rangárvellir, came there. Már said: 'Thou art a stout man; thou must be strong; be on my side in the wrestling.' He answered: 'I will do it for thy sake.' The man who opposed him fell, and the second and the third also; this pleased the Nordlendings. Már said: 'If thou needest my help in words I will help thee; but what art thou going to do now?' He answered: 'I have not decided on anything, but I would like best to go northward and get work.' Már said: 'I want thee to go with me'" (Viga Glum, c. 13).[1]

Some men were said to run as fast as the fleetest horse. It was often customary to run with loads, especially arms.

"There was in Iceland an outlawed thief named Geir, who was so quick of foot that no horse could overtake him" (Sturlunga, ii., ch. 13).

"Harald Gilli was a tall and slender man, long-necked, rather long-faced, black-eyed, dark-haired, nimble and swift; he often wore an Irish dress, short and light clothes; he spoke Norwegian with great difficulty,[2] and stammered much, and many made much fun of this. Once Harald sat at a drinking-bout, and spoke to another man about Ireland; he said that there were men in Ireland so swift-footed, that no horse when galloping could overtake them. Magnus, the king's son, heard this, and said: 'Now he lies once more, as he is wont.' Harald answered: 'This is true, that men can be found in Ireland whom no horse in Norway will outstrip.' They talked somewhat about this; they were both drunk. Then Magnus said: 'Thou shalt bet thy head that thou canst run as fast as I ride my horse, and I will lay my gold ring against it.' Harald answered: 'I do not say that I can run so fast, but I can find men in Ireland who will, and I can make a wager about that.' Magnus, king's son, answered: 'I will not go to Ireland; let us make the wager here and not there.' Then Harald went to sleep, and did not want to have any more to do with him. The next morning, when the matins were finished, Magnus rode up to the roads; he sent word to Harald to come there. When he came he was dressed in a shirt and strap-breeches, a short cloak (möttul), with an Irish hat on his head, and a spear in his hand. Magnus marked out the race-course. Harald said: 'Thou makest it too long.' Magnus at once made it far longer, and said it was still too short. There were many people present. Then they galloped off, and Harald followed the whole way at the shoulder of the horse. When they came to the end of the courre, Magnus said: 'Thou hadst hold of the strap of the

---

[1] Cf. also Liosvetninga Saga, c. 9; An's Saga Bogsveigis, c. 4; Gunnlaug Ormstunga's Saga, c. 10

[2] He had been brought up in Ireland.

saddle-girth, and the horse pulled thee along.' Magnus had a very fast horse from Gautland. Then they raced again, and Harald ran in front of the horse the whole way. When they came to the end, Harald asked: 'Did I this time take hold of the saddle-girth?' Magnus answered: 'Thou didst begin the race first.' Magnus let the horse breathe awhile; when he had done that he pricked his horse with his spurs, and it soon started off; Harald stood quiet. Then Magnus looked back, and shouted: 'Run now.' Then Harald soon outran the horse far in front of it, and so all the way to the end of the course; he reached the end so long before Magnus that he lay down, jumped up and greeted him when he came. Then they went home to the town. King Sigurd had been at mass during that time, and did not hear of the matter until after his meal that day. Then he said angrily to Magnus: 'You call Harald silly, but I think you are a fool; you do not know the customs of men in other lands; did you not know before that men in other lands train themselves in other idróttir than in filling their belly with drink, or making themselves mad and disabled, and unconscious; give Harald his ring, and never hereafter, while my head is above ground, make fun of him" (Sigurd Jorsala-far's Saga, ch. 35).

There were three kinds of games of ball: *Knattleik, Soppleik,* and *Sköfuleik.* The latter was played with sköfur (scrapers).

"Once the king (Hring) had a game called *soppleik;* it was played with eagerness, and they tried Bósi in it; but he played roughly, and one of the king's men had his hand put out of joint. The next day he broke the thigh-bone of a man, and the third day two men attacked him, while many were harassing him; he knocked out the eye of one with the ball, and he knocked down another man and broke his neck" (Herraud and Bósi's Saga, c. 3).

These games of ball and other athletic games became serious when two districts met, or when two men were jealous of each other, and sometimes ended in bloody fights.

Kolgrim the old, son of Alf hersir in Throndheim, lived at Ferstikla in Iceland; he was one of the first settlers.

"Kolgrim sent word to the men of Botn to have *Sköfuleikar* and *Knattleikar* at Sand, to which they agreed. The games began and continued until after Yule; the men of Botn were usually defeated, for Kolgrim arranged it so that the men from Strandir were the stronger in the game. Many shoes were used up by the men of Botn, as they often walked there ; and the hide of an ox was cut up into shoes.[1] The people thought Kolgrim wanted to know about the disappearance of the ox, and therefore had had these games ; he thought he recognized the hide of the ox on their feet. Then they were called ox-men, and again were ill-used. At home they talked about this ill-treatment, and said they would soon give up the games. Hörd spoke harshly to them, saying that they were great cowards if they dared not to take revenge, and were only ready for evil doings. Then Thórd and Thorgeir Gyrdil-skeggi, an outlaw, had come to Hörd. Hörd had made horn scrapers during the night. Every man was ready to go to the game when Hörd went, though they were rather backward before. Önund Thormódsson of Brekka was to play against Hörd ; he was a popular and strong man. The game was very rough, and before evening six of the men of Strandir lay dead, but none of the men of Botn ; and both parties went home " (Hörd's Saga, ch. 29).

"One day the sons of the King (Njörfi) and of Jarl Viking played at ball ; as usual the sons of Njörfi were very keen, and Thorstein spared his strength. He played against Jökul, and Olaf against Thórir, and the others according to their age. Thus it was during the day. Thórir threw down the ball so hard that it bounded over Olaf and fell a long way off. Olaf got angry· and fetched the ball. When he came back the men were preparing to go home. Then Olaf struck at Thórir with the bat, and when Thórir saw it he ran under the bat, which hit his head and bruised it. Thorstein and others ran between them, and they were parted " (Thorstein Vikingsson, 10).[2]

One day two unknown men came to Thorgnýr Jarl in Jotland, and said they were brothers.

" There often were games of ball ; many asked the brothers to go to the games ; they said they had often been at these games and were rather rough-handed. The Jarl's men said they would take care of themselves whatever might happen. The next morning the brothers went to the games, and generally had the ball during the day ; they pushed men and let them fall roughly, and beat others. At night three men had their arms broken, and many were bruised or maimed ;

---

[1] Their foot-gear was made of un-dressed ox-hide.

[2] Cf. also Göngu Hrolf's Saga, ix.

the Jarl's men now thought themselves ill-treated, and this lasted for several days."

Then Stefnir, the Jarl's son, got Hrólf to go with him against them.

"The next day Hrólf and Stefnir went to the games; the brothers had also come. Hrafn took the ball, and Krák the bat, and they played as they were wont. The Jarl sat on a chair and looked at the game, and when they had played it for a while Hrólf got hold of the ball. He snatched the bat from Krák and handed it to Stefnir. They then played for a long time, and the brothers did not get hold of the ball. Once when Hrafn ran after the ball a young kinsman of the Jarl's, who liked to banter with others, put out his foot so that Hrafn fell. He got very angry, jumped up at once, caught the man, lifted him up, and flung him down on his head so that his neck was broken " (Göngu Hrolf, ix.).

"Once Víglund struck the ball out of Jökul's (of Foss) reach; Jökul got angry, took the ball, and flung it at Víglund's forehead so hard that both his eyebrows hung down. Trausti cut a piece from his shirt and tied up the brows of his brother. When he had done that the men of Foss had gone " (Viglund's Saga, ch. 11).

The most popular of these games was the *Knattleik.* Special places were chosen, generally the ice of a frozen lake. The Breidvikings used to have games of ball during the long winter nights; and where these took place shelters were built for the people, for the games often lasted for a fortnight.

The balls, which were very hard and seem to have been made of wood, were struck by a bat of wood called *knatt-tré.* In this game, which often became serious from the wounds inflicted by ball or bat, two men of equal strength usually played together. *Knattleik* was played as follows: The ball, usually of wood, was thrown with the hand into the air, and then struck with the bat; another person caught it with his hands, or knocked it back with a kind of bat. This the other players sought to prevent by shoving him aside or throwing him down, or by striking the ball away from him. If he let the ball fly beyond the bounds, or fall to the ground, he had to go in search of it.

" It was the custom of the men of Breidavik in the autumn

to have games of ball about the winter nights. Men came there from the whole district, and large halls were raised for the games. Men dwelt there for half a month or more" (Eyrbyggja, ch. 43).

"Games were then held in Asbjarnarnes, and men gathered for them from many districts, from Vididal, from Midfjord, Vatnsnes, Vatnsdal, and all the way from Langadal. There was a crowd of people. All talked about how much Kjartan surpassed others. Then the games were prepared, and Hall managed them. He asked Kjartan to take part in them. ' We want thee, kinsman, to show thy skill in them.' Kjartan answered: ' Little exercise did I have in games during the last time, for King Olaf employed himself with other matters; but this time I will not refuse thee.' He made ready for the play, and the strongest men present were pitted against him. They played during the day, and no man equalled Kjartan, either in strength or skill. In the evening, when the games were finished, Hall Gudmundsson rose and said: ' It is the offer and will of my father that all those who have come the longest way here shall remain overnight and begin the amusement again to-morrow.' This offer was thought chief-like and much praised. Kálf Asgeir's son was there, and was a great friend of Kjartan; Hrefna, his sister, was also there, splendidly dressed. That night 100 men were on the farm besides the household. The following day they were divided for the games. Kjartan then sat and looked on" (Laxdæla, ch. 45).[1]

Skin-pulling, which was like the modern pastime the tug-of-war, is seldom mentioned.

"The king said: ' We (Hörd and himself) will pull a goat's skin across the fire in this hall to-morrow. . . .' Early next morning they went into the hall; a large fire had been made there. A little after the king came, and said: ' I will get Hástigi to pull with thee, Hörd.' Hörd answered: ' It is well for us to try skin-pulling; so make thyself ready, Hástigi.' Hástigi took off all his clothes, but Hörd did not take off his fur-cloak. A very strong walrus-hide was given to them. Then they set to with hard grips and tuggings, and each alternately was successful. They soon pulled the hide asunder between them. The king ordered the ox-hide to be brought to them. Then they pulled with all their might, and so hard, that they were in danger of falling into the fire.

---

[1] Cf. also Egil's Saga, c. 40; Gisli Sursson's Saga.

Hástigi was the stronger, but Hörd was more agile and nimble. The king said: "Thou dost not pull, Hástigi, as thou allowest this child to struggle so long against thee.' Hástigi replied: 'It will not last long if I use all my strength.' While they were speaking, Hjalmter took the sword and the sax, and put them in front of the feet of Hörd; nobody saw this, because the fur-cloak projected. Then Hástigi pulled so hard that Hörd nearly fell into the fire, and thought he had never had such a tug. They both pulled so hard, that all wondered that they were not dead from over-exertion and could endure it. Hörd said to Hástigi: 'Look out; for now I will use my strength, and thou wilt not live long.' 'I will,' answered Hástigi. Hörd then pulled with all his strength, and pulled Hástigi forward into the fire, and threw the hide over him; he jumped on his back, and then went to his bench. The king ordered them to take the man out of the fire; he was much burnt. The king was very angry, though he saw it was chiefly his own fault" (Hjalmter's and Olver's Saga, ch. 17).

To such a maritime people, the idrótt of swimming was most important. There were men who could swim for miles with armour on, or with a companion on their shoulders. Occasionally it happened that a fierce struggle ensued in the water, and that the stronger carried his adversary down to the bottom, holding him until he was almost half drowned, and unable to offer any further resistance.

"One day in fine weather and warm sunshine many men were swimming, both from the long-ship and the trading-ship. An Icelander who was swimming amused himself by taking under water the men who did not swim so well as himself. They laughed at it. King Sigurd heard it and saw; then he threw off his clothes and jumped out, swam to the Icelander, took hold of him and put him under water, and kept him there, and as soon as the Icelander came up again the king put him down again. Then Sigurd Sigurdsson said: 'Shall we let the king drown the man?' A man said that no one seemed very willing to go to them. Then he answered: 'If Dag Eilifson were here, he would be the man to do it.' Then he jumped overboard and swam to the king, took hold of him, and said: 'Do not kill the man, lord; all now see that thou swimmest far better. The king said: 'Let me alone, Sigurd, I shall kill him; he wants to drown our men.' Sigurd said: 'Now let us play first; and thou, Icelander, swim to the land.' He did so. The king let Sigurd loose and swam to his ship; Sigurd did the same" (Sigurd Jorsalafar's Saga, ch. 36).

"They (Olaf· Tryggvason and Eindridi) went to the shore and the men with them. The king and Eindridi undressed. They swam off and played a long time with each other, and alternately dragged each other down, and finally they were so long under water that they were not expected to come up; but at last King Olaf rose and swam ashore. He went up and rested himself, but did not dress; no one knew nor dared to ask what had become of Eindridi. After a long time they saw him; he had got a very large seal, and sat on its back; he clung to it with both hands in its bristles, and thus steered it, and, when he came near the shore, let it go. The king sprang up and swam out to him, thrust him under water and held him down for a long time; when they came up, the king swam ashore, but Eindridi was so exhausted that he could not save himself; when the king saw this, he went to him and helped him ashore. When Eindridi began to recover and they were dressed, the king said: 'Thy swimming idrótt is great, Eindridi; but nevertheless God is to be thanked that thou wast inferior to me, as all could see, when I had to take thee ashore.' 'Thou canst think whatever thou likest about that,' replied Eindridi. 'But,' asked the king, 'why didst thou not kill the seal, and drag it ashore?' 'Because,' answered Eindridi, 'I did not want thee to say that I had found it dead.'" (Olaf Tryggvason's Saga, vol. ii., p. 270; Fornmanna Sögur).

Kjartan, son of the Icelandic chief Olaf, went to Nidaros in Norway.

"One fine day in autumn men went from the town to swim in the river Nid. The Icelanders saw this. Kjartan told his companions that they ought to go to the swimming and amuse themselves; this they did. One man swam far better than others. Kjartan asked Bolli if he would try his powers of swimming with this man of the town. Bolli answered: 'I do not think I am able to do it.' Kjartan said: 'I do not know where thy ambition is now; then I will.' Bolli replied: 'Do as thou likest.' Kjartan threw himself into the river, and swam to the man who was the best swimmer; he took him down at once, and kept him beneath the surface for a while; he then let him come up, and when they had not been long above water the man took hold of Kjartan and pulled him under water, and they were under water as long as Kjartan thought convenient. They came up again, and said nothing. They went down a third time, and were by far the longest time under water. Kjartan did not see how it would end, and thought he had never been so hard tried before. At last they came up and swam to the bank. The townsman asked : ' Who is this man ? ' Kjartan told his name. The townsman said : ' Thou art a good swimmer ; art thou as skilled in other idróttir as in this ? ' Kjartan answered, rather slowly : ' When I was in Iceland it was said that my other idróttir were equal, but now it is of little consequence ' " [1] (Laxdæla, ch. 10).

"Then he (Egil) took his helmet, sword, and spear; he broke off his spear-handle and threw it into the water; he wrapped the weapons in his cloak, made a bundle of it, and tied it to his back. He jumped into the water and swam across to the island " (Egil's Saga, c. 45).

Sometimes, in order to swim better men had their fingers webbed.

" Now Grettir got ready to swim, and had on a hooded cloak, of common cloth, and breeches; he had his fingers webbed together. It was fine weather. He left the island late in the day. Illugi, his brother, thought his journey very dangerous. Grettir swam into the fjord, the current being with him, during a perfect calm. He swam fast, and reached Reykjanes after sunset " (Gretti's Saga, ch. 77).

That warlike exercises should have played such a prominent part in physical education is not surprising.

Some men could change weapons from one hand to the other during the hottest fight, use both hands with equal facility, shoot two spears at the same time, or catch a spear in its flight.

" Gunnar Hámundsson lived at Hlidarendi in Fljótshlid. He was of large size and strength, and more skilled in fight than any other man. He could shoot and strike with both hands equally when he wanted ; he moved his sword so swiftly that it seemed as if three swords were in the air. He shot better with a bow than any one else, and never missed his aim. He could leap as well backwards as forwards, more than his height, in full war-dress. He could swim like a seal, and there was no game in which any man was able to cope with him, and it has been told that no man was his equal " (Njala, ch. 19).

" Sigmund (during his fight with the Holmgard viking

---

[1] Cf. also Gretti, 77 ; Ingi's Saga, 11 ; Olaf Tryggvason, vol. ii., c. 160 ; | Fornmanna Sögur.

Randver) showed his idrótt. He threw his sword and flung it into the air, and caught it with his left hand, and took the shield in his right hand and dealt Randver a blow with the sword, cutting off his right leg below the knee. Randver then fell. Sigmund thereupon struck a blow on his neck, and cut off his head " (Færeyinga Saga, ch. 18).

Archery was another favourite amusement. The Thelemarkians (Norway) and Jomsvikings were in this respect considered as excelling all others, and the former distinguished themselves at the battle of Bravalla.

Of their skill in slinging, stone-throwing, archery, &c., &c., we have most remarkable examples.

" After the fall of Olaf Tryggvason, Eirik jarl gave peace to Einar Thambarskelfir, son of Eindridi Styrkársson. Einar went with the jarl to Norway, and it is said that Einar was the strongest of all men and the best archer in Norway. . . . He shot with a *bakkakólf* (a thick arrow without a point, shot from a crossbow), through a raw ox-hide which hung on a rafter " (Snorri Sturluson ; St. Olaf's Saga, ch. 20).

" The next day they went to the woods, not far from the farm. The king took off his cloak, placed a target on a hill-slope, and marked out a long-shooting distance. Then a bow and arrow were given to him. He shot, and the arrow hit the target near its edge, and stuck there. Eindridi shot farther in on the target, but not in the middle. The king then shot a second time ; they went to the target and the arrow was in the middle, and all called it a famous shot. Eindridi also praised the king's skill, and said he thought it was not worth his while to try again. The king told him to give up if he liked, and acknowledge himself beaten in this idrótt. Eindridi replied that it might be so, but still he would try again ; he shot, and his arrow entered the notch for the bow-string of the king's last arrow, so that both of them stuck there. The king said : ' A very skilled man art thou at idróttir, but this idrótt has not yet been fully tried. That handsome boy shall now be taken whom thou saidst thou lovedst so well the other day, and he shall be a target as I shall direct.' The king let a piece of *hnefatafl* [1] be placed on the boy's head. ' Now we will shoot the piece down from the boy's head,' said the king, ' so that he shall not be hurt.' ' You can do that if you wish, but I will certainly take revenge if the boy is harmed,' replied Eindridi. A long linen

---

[1] A piece belonging to a chess board.

cloth was tied round the boy's head, and two men held the ends, so that he could not move his head when he heard the whistling of the arrow. The king went to the place where he was to stand, and made the mark of the cross before himself and before the point of the arrow before he shot; but Eindridi grew very red in the face. The arrow flew under the piece, and carried it off the boy's head, but so near the skull that blood dripped from the top of his head. The king then told Eindridi to shoot after him if he wished; but Eindridi's mother and sister begged him, weeping sorely, not to try it. Eindridi said to the king: 'I am not afraid if I risked shooting that I should do the boy any harm, but nevertheless I will not shoot this time.' 'Then,' said the king, 'it seems to me that thou must acknowledge thyself beaten'" (Olaf Tryggvason's Saga, vol. ii.; Fornmanna Sögur).

Playing with dirks was a common practice. It consisted in playing simultaneously with three short swords, or dirks, so that one was always in the air, while one was in each hand; as one was thrown up, the player seized the falling one.

A very uncommon accomplishment was to run on the oar-blades around a ship whilst it was being rowed. Among those thus skilled was Olaf Tryggvason, who, while he was walking over his ship, the *Long Serpent*, on the oar-blades of the rowers, could play with three dirks or short swords.

"On the third day the king said to Eindridi: 'Now the weather is fine and calm, and we will try the handsax game.'

"The men went out to look on; each took two saxes, and they played with them for awhile.

"Then a third sax was given to each, and they played so that all the time one was in the air and two in their hands; they always caught them by the handle, and no one could determine who was most skilled. After a long while the king said: 'This game has not yet had sufficient trial.'

"They went down to the shore and out on a large longship, and the king bade his men row the ship, and the king then walked outside the board, on the oars along the side of the ship, and there played with three handsaxes as skilfully as before on land; and Eindridi did the same. The king played first, and Eindridi after him. The king then went again in the same manner along the oars, and thus in front of the stern, not dropping the handsaxes, and not even getting his shoes wet; he came back along the other side on the oars, and up into the ship. No one could understand how he did this. Eindridi stood before the king, when he came upon the ship, and looked at him in silence. The king said : 'Why dost thou stand, and not try after me ? ' Eindridi replied : 'You, lord, could by no means do this with your idrótt alone, without the power of that God in whom you believe ; and from this I see that he is all-powerful, and therefore I shall henceforth believe that he and no one else is the only God'" (Olaf Tryggvason's Saga ; Fornmanna Sögur).

Among such warlike and Spartan-like people the chiefs had to be the foremost in all athletic and gymnastic exercises if they wished to enjoy the respect and confidence of the people, and have rule over them. To talk of what their forefathers had done was not sufficient; they had to show themselves worthy of them, and if incapable of ruling, they were deposed by the people in Thing assembled.

There are several examples in the Sagas of powerful chiefs showing their anger and jealousy when any man excelled them.

"King Olaf was in every respect, of all the men who have been spoken of, the greatest man of idróttir in Norway ; he was the strongest and most skilled of all, and many accounts of this have been written. One is about how he climbed Smalsarhorn and fastened his shield on the top of the rock ; he helped his hirdman who had climbed the rock and could neither get up nor down again ; the king walked up to him and carried him under his arm down to the level plain. . . . He could fight equally well with both hands, and shoot two spears at once " (Olaf Tryggvason's Saga, ch. 92 (Heimskringla)).

"Magnus (the king) exercised himself and was skilled in many games and idróttir even in his youth ; he walked along the gunwales as young men used to at that time, and he did it with great nimbleness, and showed his accomplishments in this as in other things " (Magnus the Good's Saga ; Fornmanna Sögur, vi. 5).

"Olaf was a great man of idróttir in many respects, highly skilled in the use of the bow and spear, a good swimmer, expert and of good judgment in all handicrafts, whether his own or others. Olaf Haraldsson was eager in games and wanted to be the first, as was fitting for his rank and birth " (St. Olaf's Saga, ch. 3 (Heimskringla)).

"One day King Olaf talked to Sigmund in the spring, and

said : 'We will amuse ourselves to-day, and try our skill.' 'I am very unfit to do that, lord,' said Sigmund; 'though this shall, like other things that I can do, be as you wish.' Then they tried swimming and shooting and other idróttir, and it is said that Sigmund was next to King Olaf in many idróttir, though he was surpassed by the king in them all, but nevertheless nearer to him than any other man in Norway"[1] (Fœreyinga Saga, ch. 28–32).

"I (Harald Hardradi) know eight idróttir;
I can make the drink of Ygg;[2]
I can ride fast on a horse;
I have sometimes practised swimming;
I can run on snow-shoes;
I shoot and I row well enough."

(Fornmanna Sögur, vi. 169.)

"The king asked : 'Art thou a man of idróttir?' Heming answered : 'My foster-father and foster-mother thought that I knew many things well, but I have not shown my skill to others, and I think you will find it slight. One idrótt I think I can perform for you.' 'Which?' asked the king; 'I do not care with whom I try running on snow-shoes, for nobody can surpass me in that.' The king added : 'We will see thy skill, and know what it is worth.' Heming replied : 'I shall try to perform what you have had performed first.' 'Let us go out,' said the king, 'and strive against each other.' Aslak went to him and said : 'I have prepared ships for your departure if you please, because I think it is best to have no games.' But the king said : 'We will stay here to-day;' and all went out. The island was very woody, and they went to the forest.

"The king took a spear, and put its point into the ground; then he placed an arrow on the string and shot into the air; the arrow turned itself in its course, came down with its point into the end of the spear-shaft, and stood there upright. Heming took an arrow and shot, it went very high, then the arrow point came down into the shaft of the first arrow. The king took the spear and threw it; he shot so powerfully and so far, and nevertheless straight, that all wondered. Heming threw further than all, so that his spear socket lay on the point of the king's spear. The king took the spear and shot another time, and the whole spear beyond Heming's. 'I will not throw any more, for I see it is useless.' 'Throw,' said the king, 'and further if thou canst.' Heming shot, and far ahead.

"The king placed an arrow on the string, and took a knife and stuck it into an oak. He shot into the back of the knife-handle so that the arrow stuck fast. Heming took his arrows. The king stood near him and said : 'With gold are thy arrows wound round, and a very ambitious man art thou.' 'I did not

---

[1] Cf. also Fœreyinga Saga, c. 13; St. Olaf's Saga, c. 112.   [2] Odin = poetry.

2 C

227

cause these arrows to be made ; they were given to me, and I have not taken any ornaments off them.' Heming shot and hit the knife-handle, and split it ; the arrow point stuck in the upper point of the blade. Then the king said : 'Now we will shoot further.' With an angry look he laid an arrow on the string, and drew the bow so as to bend its tips together. The arrow flew very far, and stopped in a very slender bough. All thought this a most excellent shot. Heming shot somewhat farther, and the arrow went through a nut. All present wondered at this. The king said : 'Now the nut shall be taken, and placed on the head of thy brother Björn, and there thou shalt hit it. Thou shalt not shoot from a shorter distance than before, and, if thou dost not hit, thou hast forfeited thy life.' 'Thou canst decide over my life, but I will never shoot this shot.' Björn answered : 'Thou must shoot rather than choose death, for every man is bidden to prolong his life while he may.' 'Wilt thou stand still, and not shrink, if I shoot at the nut ?' 'Certainly,' said Björn. 'Then the king shall stand at his side,' replied Heming, 'and see if I hit the nut.' The king agreed to stand at his side. He called Odd Ofeiggson, who went to where Björn stood, and said it was a fit trial for him to keep his courage there. Then Heming went to where the king would have him stand, and made the sign of the cross. 'I call God to witness that I make the king responsible for this, and that I do not want to harm my brother.' Heming shot ; the arrow went swiftly, and skipped over the crown of his head and under the nut, and Björn was not wounded. The nut rolled backwards down from his head, but the arrow went much farther. When the king asked if the shot had hit the nut, Odd replied : 'Better than hit, for he shot under the nut and it rolled down, and he harmed not Björn.' 'It does not seem to me that he has shot as I ordered,' added the king. They slept over night.

"In the morning Aslak went to speak with the king, and told him he had again prepared his journey if he wanted to go to the mainland, but he determined to stay that day. When the drinking hour was over, he called his men, and they went down to the shore. The king said to Halldór Snorrason (an Icelander) : 'I entrust it to thee to kill Heming while swimming to-day.' Halldór answered : 'It would be difficult for abler men than I am.' Then the king told Bödvar Eldjarnsson to do it. He replied : 'Though I had all the idróttir of those here present, I would not harm him in anything, but least of all as I know that he surpasses me in everything.'

"The king bade Nikulas Thorbergsson to tire out Heming in swimming. Nikulas was doubtful of success, but consented to try. The king told them both to swim. Heming said :

'Now I need not spare myself, as I should have liked best to contend with him if I did with anybody.' They undressed, and began swimming. Nikulas asked if they should try a long swimming match. 'We may try that as thou hast had the better of it in the other' (modes of swimming). When they had been swimming for a long time, Nikulas seemed anxious to go back, but Heming said: 'I guess you the king's bellies will stop farther from the shore.' Heming kept on. Nikulas swam somewhat slower, and asked shortly after: 'Art thou going to swim longer?' Heming said: 'I thought thou wouldst be able to swim alone ashore, and I will swim farther.' 'That is good, I will risk going back,' said Nikulas, and turned, but had not gone far before he became faint. At last Heming swam to him and asked how it went with him. He told him it did not concern him, and he might go his way. Heming answered: 'I think thou deservest that I do so, but we will nevertheless now go both together.' 'I will not refuse that,' said Nikulas. 'Lay thy hand on my back and thus support thyself;' and in this way they came to land. Nikulas walked up, and had become quite stiff, but Heming sat down upon a stone at the flood-mark. The king asked Nikulas the result of the swimming. Nikulas replied: 'I should not be able to tell any tidings on land if Heming had not been a better man to me than thou art to him.' 'Now thou, Halldór, shalt kill Heming,' said the king. 'That I will not do,' answered Halldór, 'it seems to me that the man who tried the swimming before has won little.' The king threw off his clothes. Aslak went to Heming, and cried: 'Save thyself; the king wants thy death, and there is a short way to the wood.' Heming said: 'Face to face the eagles shall fight with their claws, and he shall not be drowned whom God will exalt; he may go into the water as soon as he likes.' Heming rose from the stone, and the king from another place, and as soon as they met the king swam to him and thrust him down into the deep. Others did not see their doings, but the sea became very restless above them. As it drew towards evening, and when it was almost dark, the sea became quiet and the king swam ashore. He looked so angry that no man dared to speak to him. Dry clothes were brought to him; no one saw Heming, and all thought him dead, but none dared to ask. The king went home with his men, but there was little merriment over the beer. The king was overcome with anger, and Aslak with sorrow. Lights were kindled in the hall, and the king was in his seat, when Heming entered and placed on the king's knees the knife which he had worn on his belt. Everybody knew that he had taken the knife from the king.

2 c 2

"Again in the morning Aslak said to the king: 'We have prepared your journey if you intend to go.' The king replied: 'Now I will not stay, but Heming shall follow us to the mainland.' They made ready and departed.

"They landed at a large mountain, very steep towards the sea, and there was a path along the mountain-side on which only one man at the time could walk. There were precipices beneath and a high mountain above, and the ledges on the

Fig. 1347.—Handle of Shield, iron, in a mound with skeleton. One-third real size—Öland.

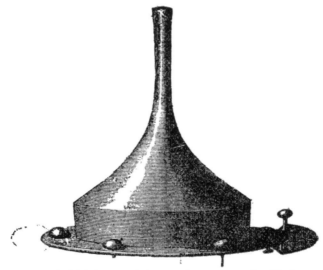

Fig. 1348.—Shield boss, of iron, edges covered with bronze One-third real size—Öland.

mountain-side were only wide enough for one man on horseback. The king ordered him to amuse them by running on snowshoes, Heming said: 'It is now not suitable to run on snowshoes, for there is no snow, but only ice, and the mountain is very hard.' The king replied: 'There would be no danger if all was in the best condition.' 'As you will,' said Heming, and took his snowshoes and ran about the mountain-side, up and down, and all said they had never seen any one run so nimbly. . . ." (Flateyjarbók, iii.).

CHAPTER XIV.

IDRÓTTIR.--POETRY OR SCALDSHIP, MUSIC AND MENTAL EXERCISES.

Poetry a gift from the gods—The scald—Many sagas based on poems—Honour paid to poets—Their moral power—Poets on the battle-field—Recital of poems at feasts—Saga telling—Forms of poetry—The harp—Parables and puzzles—Gest's riddles.

POETRY (or *Scaldship*) was reckoned among the Idróttir, and was considered a gift from the gods. The people looked to their poets to perpetuate in songs and transmit to future generations the deeds of their heroes, and the fame which was to cling to their names when they had gone to Valhalla. From these poets, or *scalds*, we learn all we know of the history of the earlier Norse tribes; from their songs the people heard of the birth of their religion; of the creation of the world, of the wisdom of the past, &c. Without them the history and deeds of the race must have been lost to us, and we would only have had left the antiquities of the early times to ponder over. These songs filled the youth of the country who listened to them with ambition, urging them to emulate the deeds of those whose praises were sung.

In no literature which has come down to us do we see dying heroes such as Ragnar Lodbrok, Hjalmar, Orvar Odd, and others, singing the deeds they had accomplished as life is ebbing away from them, and they are ready to enter into *Hel*. Whether these heroes sang these songs at such a time or not, or whether they were written by poets at a later time, matters little. The people of the land believed in them.

In this peculiar branch of poetry the earlier Norsemen stand wholly apart from those of other lands.

The figurative names given to scaldship [1] by the poets show how the earlier traditions were impressed upon the mind—*Kvásirs blood, Dvergar mead, Suttungs mead, Asar's mead, Odreyris liquid, Odin's gift, Odin's freight, The Dvergar's sea, The Dvergar's ale, Jötnar's mead.*

Bragi was supposed to be the most eloquent scald among the Asar.

The origin of poetry is given in Hávamál; but in the later Edda we have a more minute account of how it was learned by the Asar.

When Hler of Hlessö, who was also called Ægir, came to Asgard to visit the Asar, he made many inquiries, among which was the following :—

"Ægir said : 'Whence has come the idrótt which you call scaldship?' Bragi answered : 'The origin was that the gods (Asar) went to war with a people called Vanir. They appointed a truce thus; both went to a vessel and spat on it. When parting, the gods, unwilling to let this mark of truce be lost, took it, and out of it shaped a man, Kvasir. He is so wise that no one can ask him any question that he cannot answer. He travelled far and wide about the world to teach wisdom to men. When invited home to the Dvergar, Fjalar and Galar, they called him to a secret meeting and slew him. They let his blood run into two tubs and a kettle called *Odreyrir* (song-rearer), but the tubs are called *Són* (sacrifice), and *Bodn*. They mixed [2] the blood with honey, and therefrom came the mead of which whosoever drinks becomes a skald or a wise man. The Dvergar told the Asar that Kvasir had been

---

[1] Skaldskap = scald-ship, derived from skald, a poet.

The leading poets were :—

Bragi Boddason the old (about 800). The earliest who appears within historical periods.

Thjodolf of Hvin and Thorbjörn Hornklofi, Harald Fairhair's scalds.

Eyvind Skaldaspillir, Hakon the Good's greatest poet.

Egil Skallagrimsson.

Kormak Ogmundsson, famous for love songs.

Hallfred Vandrœdaskald, the troublesome scald, Olaf Tryggvason's greatest poet.

Sighvat Thordarson, St. Olaf's greatest scald.

Thjodolf Arnorsson, Harald Hardradi's scald.

The scalds who made songs on Knut the Great were : Thord Kolbeinsson, Sighvat Thordarson, Ottar the black, Thorarin Loftunga (praise-tongue), Hallvard Harekublesi, Bersi Skaldtorfuson.

The greatest masterpiece of scaldic art was composed in 1222–23 by Snorri Sturluson on Hakon Hakonsson, King of Norway, and the jarl Skuli, Bard's son. Hattatal (the list of metres) is its title, and of the 102 strophes each one is in a different metre.

[2] Cf. mixing blood in foster-brotherhood.

suffocated by too much wisdom, because no one was so wise that he could put questions to him. Thereupon these Dvergar invited to them a Jötun called Gilling and his wife, and offered him to row out to sea with them. Rowing along the shore they struck on hidden rocks, and the boat was upset. Gilling could not swim, and was drowned. But the Dvergar turned over their boat and rowed to the shore" (Later Edda 57, Bragarœdur).

Many of the sagas, if not all, were based upon the poetry which is often quoted in them, and both were used and kept as historical records.

"Olaf had been king in Norway fifteen years, including the winter when Svein Jarl and he were both in the land. Yule was past when he left his ships and went on shore, as has been told. This record of his reign was first written by the priest, Ari Thorgilsson, the wise, who was truthful, had a good memory, and was so old that he remembered the saga-telling of those who were so old that they could remember these events. Ari has himself related this in his books, and has named the men from whom he had this knowledge" (St. Olaf's Saga, c. 189).

The scalds were honoured above all men, and married even mighty kings' daughters, and **many** of them **were** great warriors.

"Thórolf, son of Herjolf Hornabrjot, and Olaf, his brother, were kings in Upplönd; with them was the poet Flein Hjörsson, who was brought up in Mæri on an island called Jösrheid where his father lived. Flein went to Denmark to visit King Eystein, and there got so much honour on account of his poetry that the king gave him his daughter" (Landnama v. ch. 1).

King Harald Fairhair had a feast for his friends and followers.

"Of all his hirdmen the king valued his scalds the most. They were placed on the second high-seat bench (*annat ondvegi*). At the furthest end from them sat Audun Illskœlda (thus called because he wrote satirical songs). He was older than any of them, and had been the scald of Halfdan Svarti (black), the father of King Harald. Next to him sat Thorbjorn Hornklofi, and then Olvir Hnufa, and next to him Bard was placed" (Egil's Saga, ch. 8).

"Thereupon Gunnlaug sailed from England (London) with

traders north to Dublin. At that time King Sigtrygg Silkiskegg (silkbeard), son of Olaf Kvaran and Queen Kormlöd, ruled Ireland; he had then ruled only a short time Gunnlaug went before him and greeted him well and honourably. The king received him well. Gunnlaug said: 'I have made a song about you, and I want to get a hearing.' The king answered: 'No man has before delivered a poem to me, and I shall certainly listen to it.' Gunnlaug then sang the *drapa*, and this is the refrain:

Sigtrygg feeds
The horse of Svara (the wolf)
   with corpses.

I know distinctly
Whom I will praise,
The kinsman of kings,
He is the son of Kvaran;

The king will not to me
(He is wont to be liberal,
The champion knows it)
Spare the gold rings;
Let the king tell me
If he has heard made
A more glorious song;
This is the lay of drapa.

" The king thanked him for the song, and asked his treasurer with what it should be rewarded. He answered: 'With what will you reward it, lord?' The king said: 'How will it be rewarded, if I give him two knerrir (trading-ships)?' The treasurer replied: 'That is too much, lord; other kings give costly things, good swords or good gold-rings, as rewards for a song.' The king gave him his own clothes of new scarlet, a lace-ornamented kirtle, a cloak with the finest furs on it, and a gold ring which weighed a mark. Gunnlaug thanked him, and stayed there for a short time, and went thence to the Orkneys " (Gunnlaug Ormstunga's Saga, ch. 8).

The moral power of a renowned poet was often very great.

" Sindri, a high-born man, was renowned among Halfdan the Black's warriors; formerly he had been with King Harald, and was the greatest friend of both. Guthorm was a great scald, and had made a song about each. They had offered him a reward, but he refused it, saying that they must grant him one request, and this they promised. He went to King Harald (to reconcile him and Halfdan), and so much did the kings honour him that they were reconciled at his request " (Olaf Tryggvason, Fms., vol. i. c. 12).

The scalds were always on the battlefield near the shield-burgh, in order to witness the heroism of the combatants, and sing their victory or glorious death. With their *vapnasong* (weapon-song) they encouraged the champions in battle, or with their *Sigrljod* (lay of victory) praised the bravery of the hero.

"It is said that King Olaf (before the battle of Stiklastad 1015–30) arrayed his men, and then arranged the shieldburgh which was to protect him in the battle, for which he selected the strongest and most valiant men. He then called his scalds and bid them go into the shieldburgh. 'You shall stay here,' said the king, 'and see what takes place, and then no Saga is needed to tell you afterwards what you shall make songs about'" (Fostbrœdra Saga, c. 47).

These rulers loved to be surrounded by men who could entertain them and their guests during the long winter evenings, or at festivals, and took great pride in having poems made about them.

"One summer an Icelander came to King Harald, who asked him what he knew. He said he knew some sagas. The king said : 'I will receive thee, and thou shalt join my hird this winter, and always entertain my men when they want it, whoever asks thee.' He did so. He was soon well liked by the hird ; they gave him clothes, and the king himself gave him a good weapon. This went on till near Yule, when the Icelander began to look sad ; the king saw it, and asked him for the reason, and he said it was his variable temper. The king answered : 'That is not the reason, but I will guess it ; I suspect that thy sagas are now all told, for thou hast always entertained every man who asked thee this winter, and often by night and day ; now thou dost not like the sagas to be wanting during Yule, but wilt not tell the same sagas again.' The Icelander said : 'Thy guess is right ; the only saga that remains is one which I dare not tell here, for it is your Utfarar saga' (saga of Harald's voyage to the Holy Land). The king answered : 'That is a saga which I am most curious to hear ; now thou shalt not recite before Yule, for people are now very busy, but the first Yule-day thou shalt begin this saga and tell part of it ; then there will be great drinking, and they cannot sit long listening to it. I will manage that the saga shall last during Yule, and thou wilt not find while thou tellest it whether I like it well or ill.' Accordingly the Icelander began his saga first Yule-day, and after he had told it a short while the king told him to stop. People then began to talk much about this entertainment ; some said it was very bold of the Icelander to tell this saga, and had doubts how the king would like it ; some thought he told it well, others less well. The king took good care that they listened well ; he managed that it lasted as long as Yule. The thirteenth day the king said : 'Art thou not curious to know, Icelander, how I like the saga ?' He answered : 'I am afraid to hear, lord.' The king said : 'I think it very well told, and nowhere is the truth deviated from ; but who taught thee ?' He answered : 'I used in Iceland to go to the Thing every summer, and every summer I learnt a part of the saga which was told by Haldor Snorrason.' The king said : 'It is not strange that thou knowest it well, as thou hast learnt it from him, and this saga shall be of use to thee ; thou art welcome to stay with me as long as thou wilt.' He stayed with the king that winter, and in the spring the king gave him some good wares to trade in, and he became a thriving man " (Harald Hardradi, c. 6).

Saga-telling seems to have taken place also in England.

"Then Játvard the good (Edward Confessor), son of King Adalrad (Ethelred), was chosen king in England. He remembered the friendship of his father Adalrad with King Olaf Tryggvason. He adopted the custom of telling on the first Easter-day the Saga of King Olaf Tryggvason to his chiefs and hirdmen " (Flateyjarbók, i. 506 (Olaf Tryggvason's Saga).[1]

Some poets used poetry as their mode of speech.

"Sigvat scald had been a long time with King Olaf, who had made him his marshal. Sigvat was not quick of speech in *unbound words* (prose), but poetry was so easy to him that song flowed from his tongue as fast as he talked ; he had made journeys to Valland, and during these he had come to England and met Knut the powerful " (St. Olaf's Saga (Heimskringla), ch. 170).

There were two well-known forms of poetry.

The *Drapa*, a heroic laudatory poem, generally written in memory of a deceased man, and *Flokk*, a shorter poem.

The memory of some men was extraordinary ; the blind scald Stuf recited before King Harald Hardradi in one evening thirty songs ; in answer to a question he said that he knew at least half as many more longer drapas.

An Icelander, named Stuf, went to Norway, and stayed with a bondi in Upplönd. To him came King Harald Hardradi on a visit, and sat talking to Stuf.

"Then the bondi came into the stofa, and said the king

---

[4] Cf. Flateyjarbóк, iii.

must find it dull. 'It is not so,' answered the king, 'for this winter guest of thine entertains me well, and I will drink to him this evening'; and thus it happened. The king talked much to Stuf, and he gave wise answers; when the men went to sleep the king asked Stuf to stay in the room where he was to sleep, in order to entertain him. Stuf did so; when the king was in his bed Stuf entertained him, and sang a flokk, and when it was finished he asked him to sing more.

"The king was awake a long time, while Stuf entertained him, and at last said: 'How many songs hast thou sung now?' Stuf answered: 'I intended that you should count them.' 'I have done it,' said the king; 'they are thirty now, but why doest thou only sing flokks? Doest thou not know any drapas?' Stuf answered: 'I know no fewer drapas than flokks, though many flokks which I know are still unsung'" (Fornmanna Sögur, c. 6).

The harp is mentioned in Voluspa, and seems to have been used in early times. Gunnar played his harp with such skill that even champions were moved. He could also play with his toes, and charm snakes with its tones. Rognvald also reckoned harp-playing among his Idróttir. Norna Gest was very skilful on this instrument, and played famous tunes.

"Gest took his harp and struck it long and well that evening, so that every one thought it pleasant to listen; he played Gunnar's tune best; finally he played the old *Gudrúnarbrögd*, which they had not heard before; afterwards they went to sleep" (Norna Gest's Saga, ch. 2 (Fornaldarsögur i.)).

King Hugleik's orchestra consisted of harp[1] and other instruments, and Olaf Skautkonung kept for his table regular performers.

We have no description of the shape or size of the harp. It was no doubt a large instrument, as a little girl, Aslaug, wife of Ragnar Lodbrok, could be hidden in it, and from Herraud and Bosi's Saga we learn that a man could stand in it upright. They sometimes had strings of silver and gold.

The harp shown on the wood carvings give us an idea of its shape.

Mental Exercises.——The unravelling of puzzles seems to have

---

[1] The harp is also mentioned in Atla Kvida, 31; Oddrunargrat, 29; Atlamal, 62; Bard's Saga.

been one of the most favourite pastimes among chiefs and other powerful men, and deep penetration was required to understand them. Heidrek, a king of Reidgotaland, was credited with having been able to unravel any riddle that had ever been propounded to him.

"A man named Gest the blind was a powerful hersir in Reidgotaland, but wicked and overbearing ; he had kept back the tribute belonging to King Heidrek, and there was great enmity between them. The king sent him word that he must come to him and submit to the judgment of his wise men, or fight. Gest did not like either of these terms, and became very uneasy, for he knew that he had committed many offences ; he then resolved to sacrifice to Odin for help, and begged of him to look on his case, and promised a large reward. Late one evening there was a knock at the door, and Gest the blind went to open it ; he asked the name of the man who had come, and he answered his name was Gest ; then they inquired of each other about the tidings. The guest asked if anything grieved him ; Gest the blind told him everything carefully. The guest said : 'I will go to the king on thy behalf, and see how it will go ; let us exchange appearance and clothes ;' and thus they did. The bondi[1] went away and hid himself while the guest went in and stayed there during the night, and every one thought it was Gest the blind. Next day Gest went on the journey to the king, and did not stop until he came to Arheimar (Heidrek's seat) ; he went into the hall and greeted the king well. The king was silent and looked angrily at him. ' Herra (lord),' said Gest, ' I am here in order to be reconciled with you.' The king asked : ' Wilt thou obey the judgment of my wise men ? ' Gest replied : ' Are there no other terms ? ' The king said : ' There are ; if thou wilt come with a riddle which I cannot guess, and thus procure thyself peace.' Gest answered : ' I am little able to do that, and besides the other part (the king) may be heard about it.' ' Wilt thou rather submit to the decision of the wise men ? ' said the king. ' I should prefer,' said Gest, ' to come with some riddles.' The king agreed, and two chairs were brought on which they sat down. Gest then propounded his riddles ' " (Hervarar Saga, ch. 15).

Gest.	Try to know what it was,
I should wish to have	Peace-maker among men !
That which yesterday I had ;	Tamer of words,[2]

---

[1] Hersir is called here a bondi
[2] One who subdues words—an eloquent

man—for every chief was trained to be a good speaker.

RIDDLES.

And starter of words,
King Heidrek,[1]
Think of the riddle.

Heidrek.

Good is thy riddle,[2]
Gest the blind!
It is guessed;
Ale changes the temper
And quickens prattle,
But in others the tongue is wrapped
   around the teeth.

Gest.

I went from home,
I travelled from home,
I looked on the road of roads,
Road was above,
Road was beneath,
And road in every direction.

Heidrek.

A bird flew above,
A fish swam beneath,
Thou walkedst on a bridge.

Gest.

What kind of drink was it
I drank yesterday?
It was neither water nor wine,
Mead nor ale,
No kind of food.
However, I went thirstless thence.

Heidrek.

Thou went'st into sunshine,
Hiddest thyself in the shade;
There fell dew in the valleys;
Then thou didst taste
The night-dew,
Cooling thy throat by it.

Gest.

Who is the shrill one
That on hard roads walks

On which he has been before?
He kisses rather roughly,
Has two mouths;
And walks on gold only.

Heidrek.

The hammer walks
On the fire of Rin,[3]
It sounds loudly
Falling on the anvil.

Gest.

What wonder is that
Which I saw outside
Before the door of Delling?[4]
Two lifeless ones
And breathless,
Seethed wound-leek.[5]

Heidrek.

There is neither breath nor heat
In the bellows of smiths,
They have neither life nor power;
However one can before them
Make a sword
By the wind they give.

Gest.

What wonder is it
I saw outside
Before the doors of Delling?
It has eight feet,
Eyes four,
And bears its knee higher than its
   belly.

Heidrek.

From east thou went'st
To the door of a house
To see the hall;
Thou camest thereto
Where the king of webs [6]
Wove a web from its bowels.

---

[1] These two lines, which are repeated in every stanza in the original text, are omitted in subsequent stanzas here.

[2] These three lines are repeated at the beginning of each stanza, but are omitted in subsequent stanzas.

[3] Rin = Rhine river, fire of Rhine = gold, because hidden in the river.

[4] Door of Delling, a Dverg = the rock; before his door = on the ground.

[5] A sword.

[6] Spider.

Gest.

What wonder is it
I saw outside
Before the doors of Delling?
It turns its head
On the way to Hel
And its feet to the sun.

Heidrek.

The head of the leek turns
Towards the bosom of the earth
And its leaves into the air.

Gest.

What wonder is it
I saw outside
Before the doors of Delling?
Harder than horn,
Blacker than raven,
Brighter than shield,
Straighter than shaft.

Heidrek.

Now thy riddle-making
Begins to slacken;
Why should a ready man tarry?
Thou lookedst on the roads,
There lay raven-flint,
Glittering in a sunbeam.

Gest.

Two bondwomen,
Light-haired maidens,
Carried ale
To the skemma;[1]
It was not touched with hand,
Nor with hammer shaped;
The wave-breasting one who made it
Was outside the islands.[2]

Heidrek.

White-feathered skin
Have the swans
Which by islands
Sit on the sea;
Nests they built,
Had no hands,
With other swans
Eggs begat.[3]

*　　*　　*

Gest.

What beast is that
Which defends the Danes?
It has a bloody back
And shelters men,
Meets the weapons,
Exposes its life,
Man lays his body
Against its palm.

Heidrek.

The shields shine
In the battles,
And protect those who wield them.

Gest.

Who are the play sisters
That pass over lands
And play much at will?
They wear a white shield
In winter,
But a dark one
In summer.

Heidrek.

Ptarmigans call
The sons of men
Feather-wearing birds;
Their feathers become black
In summer-time,
But white during the bear's night.[4]

Gest.

Who are the maidens
That sorrowful go
To seek their father?

---

[1] Woman's house.
[2] On the sea.
[3] The swans swim to their nests and lay eggs; the shell of the eggs is neither made by hand nor shaped by hammer, but the swan with whom they beget the eggs is breasting the waves outside the islands.
[4] The bears of the North sleep all winter.

To many they have
Harm done,
Passing their life therein.

Heidrek.

The evil-minded
Maidens of Eldir [1]
Slay many men.

Gest.

Who are the maidens
Going many together
Seeking their father?
They have light hair,
These white-hooded ones,
Men cannot be safe against them.

Heidrek.

Gymir [2] has
By Ran begotten [3]
Wise-minded daughters;
Billows they are called,
And also waves;
No man can be safe against them.

Gest.

Who are the widows
That go all together
To seek their father?
They are seldom gentle
To men,
And they must be awake in the
wind.

Heidrek.

These are the waves,
Daughters of Ægir,
They let themselves fall heavily.

*   *   *   *

Gest.

Who are the maidens
That walk over the reefs
And journey along the fjords?
These white-hooded women
Have a hard bed,
And make little stir in calm weather.

Heidrek

Billows and waves
And all breakers
At last lay themselves on skerries; [4]
Their beds are
Rocks and stone-heaps,
But the calm sea stirs them not.

*   *   *   *

Gest.

Who lives on high mountains?
Who lives in deep dales?
Who lives without breath?
Who is never silent?

Heidrek.

Ravens live on high mountains;
Dew falls in deep dales;
Fish live without breath in water,
But the sounding waterfall
Is never silent.

Gest.

Four are walking,
Four are hanging,
Two showing the way,
Two keeping dogs off;
One lags behind
All his days,
That one is always dirty.

Heidrek.

A cow is that beast
Which thou didst see
Walk on four feet,
Four teats hang,
And horns defend her:
Her tail hung behind.

Gest.

What kind of wonder is it
I saw outside
Before the door of Delling?
It had ten tongues,
Twenty eyes;
Forty feet
That being moves forward.

---

[1] Ægir.
[2] Ægir = the sea.
[3] Ran, the wife of Ægir. According

to the Prose Edda, Gymir is the same as
Ægir and Hlér.
[4] Rocks.

Heidrek.

If thou art the one thou sayest,
Then thou art wiser
Than I expected;
Thou talkest of
A sow outside
Which walked in the yard;
She was slaughtered
At the king's will,
And she was with nine pigs.

Gest.

Who are those two
That go to the thing?
They have three eyes both,
Ten feet,
And one tail have they both.
Thus they pass over lands.

Heidrek.

It is Odin
When riding along on Sleipnir;
He has one eye,
His horse two,
The drösul[1]
Runs on eight feet,
Ygg[2] on two,
The horse has one tail.

Gest.

Tell me that only,
As thou seemest to be
Wiser than any king;
What did Odin say
Into the ear of Baldr
Before he was carried on the pyre?

Heidrek.

This is wonder and wickedness,
And cravenness only,
Jugglery and trickery only;
But no one knows those words of
    thine
Except thyself,
Thou evil and wretched being.

———

The king burnt with anger,
He drew Tyrfing[3]
And wanted to strike Gest;
But he turned himself
Into the shape of a hawk,
And thus saved his life.
The hawk attempted
To escape by the light-holes,
But the king struck after him;
He cut off the tip of his tail
And shortened his feathers,
Therefore the hawk has a docked tail.

"The sword hit the tail, and took off what it touched, and therefore the hawk has a short tail ever after; then the sword hit a man of the hird, and he was at once slain. Odin then said: 'Because thou, King Heidrek, drewest thy sword and wantedst to slay me, and thyself brokest the truce which thou hadst set between us, the worst of thralls shall be thy slayers.' Then Odin flew away, and thus they parted" (Hervarar Saga, c. 15).

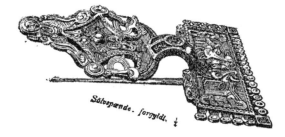

Sölvspænde. forgyldt. ¼

Fig. 1349.—Gilt silver fibula, one-quarter real size—Zeeland.

---

[1] Horse.   [2] Odin.   [3] His sword.

CHAPTER XV.

THE CONDUCT OF LIFE—THE HÁVAMÁL.

Rules of life—The duty of hospitality—Folly of boasting—The wise man keeps his eyes and ears open—Wits are better than wealth—Drink destroys reason—The duty of cheerfulness and bravery—Over-eating—We should not worry—All who smile on a man are not his friends—The value of silence—A guest should not outstay his welcome—The value of a home however humble—No man should be the friend of his foe's friend—Every man has two sides to his character—Man's happiness—Wealth is the most unstable of friends—The fickleness of woman—All is fair in love—Do not neglect your friends—No man is without his faults—Proverbs and wise sayings.

To all great popular leaders and lawgivers are often attributed the dogmas and words of wisdom which form part of their creed. It is not therefore surprising to find the great Norse code of morality, known under the name of Hávamál,[1] attributed to Odin; Hávamál meaning the "Song of the High."

All door-ways
Before one goes forth
Should be looked over,
Should be searched out,
For 'tis hard to know
Where foes sit
On the benches before one.

Hail my host![2]
A guest has come in;
Where shall he sit?
In hot haste is he
Who has to try his luck
On snow-shoes.

Fire is needed
By him who has come in
And is benumbed in his knees;
Food and clothes
Are needed by one
Who has travelled over the mountain.

Water is needed
By the one who comes to the meal,
A towel and a hearty welcome,
Good-will
If he can get it,
Talk and answer.

Wisdom is wanted
By him who travels widely;
Anything is easy at home;[3]
He who nothing knows
And sits among the wise
Becomes a gazing-stock.

A man with a thinking mind
Should not boast,
But rather be heedful in his mood.
When a wise and silent man
Comes to a homestead
The wary man seldom makes a slip,
For a more faithful friend

---

[1] Háva = of the high, namely Odin; mál = song.

[2] Giver in the text = host.
[3] Meaning: anything will do at home.

Will a man never get
Than great man-wit.[1]

The wary guest
Who comes to a meal
Is silent and talks little,
Listens with (his) ears,
Looks on with (his) eyes;
Thus every wise man looks about him.

He is happy
Who gets for himself
Praise and good-will;
That which a man must own
In the mind[2] of another
Is less easy to deal with.

He is happy
Who himself has
Praise and wits while alive;
For evil counsels
Has one often got
Out of another's breast.

A better burthen
A man carries not on the road
Than great wits;
Better than wealth
It is thought at strange places;
It is the strength of the poor.

Better burthen
A man carries not on the road
Than great good sense;
No worse journey-provisions
Weigh him to the ground
Than too much ale-drinking.

The ale of men's sons
Is not so good
As men say it is;
For the more
A man drinks
The less has he his senses.

He is called heron of Oblivion
The one who soars over ale-bouts,

He steals away men's senses;
With the feathers of that bird
I was bound[3]
In the house of Gunnlód.[4]

I got drunk,
I got too drunk
At the wise Fjalar's;
The ale is best when
Every man
Gets his reason back.

Silent and thoughtful
Should a king's son be
And bold in battle;
Glad and cheerful
Should every man be
Till he meet his death.

The unwise man
Thinks he will live for ever
If he shuns fight,
But old age gives him
No peace
Though spears may spare him.

A fool gapes
When he comes into company,
He mutters or sulks;
All at once
If he gets a drink
His mind is displayed.

He alone knows
Who widely travels
And has seen much
What the temper is
Of every man
Who has his wits about him.

A man shall not send away the cup
But drink mead moderately,
Speak usefully or be silent;
No man will blame thee
For ill-breeding
Though thou goest early to sleep.

---

[1] Good sense.
[2] Here the text has breast for mind or heart. The meaning of the stanza is that it is very hard to know another man's mind.

[3] This refers to Odin getting drunk from the mead of poetry which he stole from Suttung. (See later Edda.)
[4] A Jotun woman.

A greedy man
Unless he has sense
Eats ill-health for himself;
A foolish man's belly
Often causes laughter
When he is among the wise.

Herds know
When they shall go home
And then walk off the grass;
But an unwise man
Never knows
The measure of his stomach.

A wretched man
With evil mind
Sneers at everything;
He knows not that,
Which he needed to know,
That he is not himself faultless.

An unwise man
Is awake all night
Worrying about everything;
He is weary
When the morning comes
All the woe is as it was.

An unwise man
Thinks all who smile on him
To be his friends;
He does not know
When he sits among wise men
Though they speak badly of him.

An unwise man
Thinks all who smile on him
To be his friends;
But he will find
When he comes to the thing
That he has few spokesmen.[1]

An unwise man
Thinks he knows everything
If he has shelter in a corner;
He knows not
What he should say
If men test him.

An unwise man
When he comes among people,
Had best be silent;
No one knows
That he nothing knows,
Unless he talks too much;
The man who nothing knows
Knows not of it
Though he talk too much.

He who can ask
And answer questions
Thinks himself wise;
The sons of men
Can hide nothing
That passes among men.

He who is never silent
Speaks too many
Meaningless words;
A glib tongue
Unless it has restrainers
Often does harm to itself.

A man shall not
Have another for a gazing-stock[2]
Though he come into company;
Many one thinks himself wise
If he is not asked questions
And can loiter with dry clothes.

Wise thinks himself
The guest who drives away
Another guest with mocking;
He is not wise
Who sneers at a meal
If he prates among angry men.

Many men
Are kind to one another,
Yet quarrel at the meal;
This will always be
The cause of men's strife;
Guest gets angry with guest.

An early meal
Should a man often take
And not go without it into company;
(Otherwise) he sits and sulks,

---

[1] I.e., supporters.

[2] Make fun of him.

2 D 2

Looks as if he were hungry,
And cannot talk.

It is long out of one's way
To a bad friend,
Though he live on the road;
But to a good friend
There are short paths
Though he be farther off.

One should take leave,
The guest should not stay
Always in one place;
The loved becomes loathed
If he sits too long
In another's house.

A homestead is best
Though it be small;
A man is master at home;
Though he has but two goats
And a straw-thatched hall (house)
It is better than begging.

A homestead is best
Though it be small;
A man is a man (master) at home;
Bleeding is the heart
Of him who must beg
His food for every meal.

A man shall not on the ground
Go a step forward
Without his weapons;
For it is hard to know
When out on roads
If a man may need his spear.

I never met a man
So openhanded or free with his food
That he would not take a gift,
Nor one so lavish
With his property
That rewards were to him unwelcome.

A man
When he has gained property
Should not suffer want;
What was meant for the loved
Is often spared for the hated;
Many things go worse than expected.

With weapons and clothes
Such as are most sightly on oneself
Shall friends gladden each other;
Givers and receivers
Are the longest friends,
If they give with good wishes.

A man should be
A friend to his friend
And give gift for gift;
Laughter for laughter
And lie for lie
Should men return.

To his friend
A man should be a friend,
To him and his friend;
But no man
Should be the friend
Of his foe's friend.

Know if thou hast a friend
Whom thou trustest well
And thou wilt good from him get,
Thou must blend thoughts with him,
And exchange gifts,
Go often and meet him.

If thou hast another
Whom thou trustest little
Yet wilt good from him get,
Kindly shalt thou talk to him,
But think deceitfully
And give lie back for lie.

That is further from him
Whom thou trustest little
And whose mind thou suspectest,
Thou shalt smile at him
And speak contrary to thy thoughts,
The reward should be like the gift.

I once was young,
I travelled alone,
And missed my way;
I thought myself wealthy
When I another met;
Man is the delight of man.

Liberal and valiant
Men live best;

They seldom harbour grief;
But unwise men
Fear everything;
The miser always longs for gifts.

My clothes
Gave I to two wood-men (men of the
    forest)
In the field;
They thought themselves men,
When they got the garments;
Ashamed is a naked man.

The fir withers
That stands on a fenced field;
Neither bark nor foliage shelter it;
Thus is a man
Whom no one loves;
Why should he live long?

Hotter than fire
Burns between bad friends
Friendship for five days;
But when the sixth comes
It is quenched
And all the friendship vanishes.

Much at once
Should one not give;
With little you often get praise;
With half a loaf
And a half-filled cup
I got a companion.

Small are sand grains,
Small are drops of water,
Small are men's minds;
For all men
Were not made equally wise;
Men are everywhere by halves.[1]

Middling wise
Should every man be,
Never too wise;
Happiest live
Those men
Who know many things well.

Middling wise
Should every man be,
Never too wise;
For the heart of a wise man
Is seldom glad
If its owner is all-wise.

Middling wise
Should every man be
Never too wise;
No man ought to
Know his fate beforehand,
Then his mind is freest from sorrow

Brand is kindled from brand
Till it is burnt out;
Fire is kindled from fire;
A man gets knowledge
By talk with a man
But becomes wilful by self-conceit.

Early should rise
He who wants the property
Or the life of another;
Seldom a sleeping wolf
Gets a thigh-bone
Or a sleeping man victory.

Early should rise
He who has few workers
And go to his work;
Many hindrances has he
Who sleeps in the morning;
Half one's wealth depends on activity.

Of dry logs
And thatching-bark
A man knows the measure
And of the fire-wood
Which can last
For meals and for seasons.[2]

Washed and well-fed
Should a man ride to the thing,
Though he be not so well dressed;
Of his shoes and breeches
Let no man be ashamed,
Nor of his horse, though he has not a
    good one.

---

[1] The meaning of this line is somewhat obscure; it probably means that every man has two sides to his character.

[2] The application is missing in the text.

Sniffs and hangs with its head,
When it comes on the sea,
The eagle on the old ocean;
So is the man
Who comes among many
And has few spokesmen.

Ask and answer
Should every sage man
Who wants to be called wise;
One may know
But not another;
All know if three know.

His power
Should every foresighted man
Use moderately;
He will feel
When he comes among the skilled
That no one is the best.

* * * *
For the words
That a man says to another
He has often to pay the penalty.

Much too early
Came I to many places
And too late to some;
The ale was drank
Or it was unbrewed;
An unwelcome man seldom finds the
  ale.

Here and there
Might I be invited home
If I needed not food for a meal
Or if two hams hung
At my trusty friend's
Where I had eaten one.

Fire is the best thing
Among the sons of men,
And the sight of the sun,
His good health
If a man can keep it,
And a blameless life.

A man is not utterly unhappy
Though he be in ill-health;
Some are happy in sons,
Some in kinsmen,
Some in much wealth,
Some in good deeds.

Better is it to live
Than not to live;
A living man (may) always get a cow;
I saw fire blaze
Before a wealthy man
And outside was death at the door.

The lame may ride a horse,
The handless may drive a herd,
The deaf may fight and do well;
A blind man is better
Than a burnt one;
The dead are of no use.

A son is better
Though he be late born,
After a man's death;
Seldom memorial stones
Stand near the road
Unless kinsman raise
Them after kinsman.

Two are of one host
The tongue is the head's bane;
Under every fur-coat
I expect a hand.[2]

He who trusts to his knapsack
Is glad when night comes;
The ship's corners are small;
The autumn night is changeable;
There are many weathers
In five days[3]
And more in a month.

He who nothing knows
Knows not this;
Many are made fools by wealth;
One man is wealthy,

---

[1] The text of part of this verse is missing.

[2] The sense of this stanza is most difficult; the meaning of first part seems to be that tongue and head are of one host, and nevertheless the tongue may be the head's bane. The latter part probably means: the hand of a foe or friend may be hidden under any cloak.

[3] Here we see the custom of counting weeks by five.

And another poor;
Blame not a man for that.

Cattle die,
Kinsmen die,
One's self dies too;
But the fame
Never dies
Of him who gets a good name.

Cattle die,
Kinsmen die,
We ourselves die;
I know one thing
That never dies,
The doom over every dead man.[1]

Full stocked folds
I saw at the sons of Fitjung;
Now they carry beggars' staffs;
Wealth is
Like the twinkling of an eye
The most unstable of friends.

An unwise man
If he gets
Wealth or a woman's love
Grows in pride,
But never in wits;
He goes on further in his conceit.

It will be found
When thou askest about
The god-born runes
Which the high powers made,
And the all wise marked,
Then it is best that he be silent.

A day should be praised at night,
A woman when she is burnt,
A sword when it is tried,
A maiden when she is married,
Ice when crossed,
Ale when drank.

In a gale should trees be cut,
In a breeze row out at sea,
In the dark to a maiden talk,
Many are the eyes of day,

A ship is made for sailing,
A shield for sheltering,
A sword for striking,
A maiden for kisses.

At the fire shalt thou drink ale
And glide on the ice,
Buy a lean horse,
And a rusty sword,
Fatten (thy) horse at home,
And (thy) dog at (thy) farm.

The words of a maiden
Or the talk of a woman
Should no man trust;
For their hearts were shaped
On a whirling wheel,
And fickleness laid in their breasts.

A creaking bow,
A burning flame,
A gaping wolf,
A croaking crow,
A squealing swine,
A rootless tree,
A waxing wave,
A boiling cauldron,

A flying arrow,
A falling billow,
A one night old ice,
A ring-coiled snake,
The bed-talk of a bride,
Or a broken sword,
The play of a bear,
Or a king's child

A sick calf,
A wilful thrall,
The kind words of a volva,
The new-felled slain,[2]

An early sown field
Shall no man trust,
Nor his son too early;
The weather rules the field,
And wit guides the son;
Each of them is uncertain.

---

[1] Doom, judgment passed by men over man = his name.

[2] In a paper MS. of 1684 some verses are found which are not on the skin text.

Let no man be so trustful
That he trust
His brother's slayer,
Though he meet him on the highway,
A half-burnt house,
A very swift horse,
A horse is useless
If a leg be broken.

Thus is the love of women
Whose hearts are false
As riding on slippery ice,
With an unshod,
Wild, two year old,
Badly broken horse,
Or like cruising
Rudderless in a strong gale,
Or like the lame reindeer
On thawing mountain sides.

Now I speak openly
For I know both;
Fickle is the mind of men to women;
We speak most fair
When we think most false;
That beguiles wise minds.

Finely must talk
And offer gifts
He who would win woman's love,
Praise the shape
Of the bright (fair) maiden;
He wins who woos.

In matters of love
Should a man never
Blame another;
The bewitching hues [1]
That do not move the dull
Often move the wise.

A man must not
Blame another
For what is many men's weakness;
For mighty love
Changes the son of men
From wise into fools.

The mind alone knows
What is near the heart;
It alone sees what is near the heart;
It alone sees what is in the breast;
No sickness is worse
For a wise man
Than to enjoy nothing.

I tried that when
I sat in the rushes
And waited for my love;
The gentle maiden
Was like my own flesh and heart;
Yet she was not mine.

I found the sun-bright
Maiden of Billing [2]
Asleep on her bed;
The happiness of a jarl
I thought worth nothing,
Unless living with that maiden.

And near evening (in the twilight)
Must thou come, Odin,
If thou wilt talk with a maiden;
It will fare badly
Unless we alone know
Of such unlawful love.

I went away;
It seemed to me I loved
Out of my wise will; [3]
I thought
I had won
All her heart and love.

When next I came
All the doughty household
Was awake;
With burning lights
And carried torches
That way of woe was marked for me.

Near morning,
When I came again,
The household was asleep;
A dog I found
Tied to the bed
Of the good woman.

---

[1] Lostfagr = so fair as to kindle lust.
[2] Billing occurs in Voluspa as a name of dverg.
[3] This means—as if I was mad with love.

250

THE HÁVAMÁL.

Many a good maiden
If thou searchest well
Is fickle to men ;
That I found
When I the counsel wise maiden
Sought to beguile ;
Every mocking
Showed me the wise maiden,
And from that woman nought had I.

At home shall a man be merry
And cheerful to his guests,
Cautious about himself,
Of good memory and ready speech,
If he wants to be very wise ;
A good man is often talked of ;
A great fool is he called
Who little can tell ;
That is the mark of a fool.

I visited the old jotun ;
Now I have come back ;
Little got I silent there ;
Many words
I spoke for my good
In the halls of Suttung.

Gunnlod gave me
On a golden chair
A drink of the costly mead ;
Ill reward
I gave her afterwards
For her strong love,
For her true love.

The point (mouth) of Rati
I let make its way
And gnaw the rock ;
Over me and under me
Were the ways of jotuns,
Thus I risked my head.

The trick-bought mead
I have enjoyed well ;
The wise lack little,

For Odrerir [1]
Has now come up
On the skirt of the earth of men.[2]

I doubt whether
I should yet have come
Out of the jötun halls,
If I had not had help
From Gunnlod, the good maiden
Round whom I laid my arm.

The next day
The Hrim-thussar came,
To ask about the purpose of Hár [3]
Into his hall ;
They asked about Bólverk [4]
If he was among the gods,
Or Suttung had slain him.

An oath on the ring, [5]
I think, Odin took ;
Shall his plighted faith be trusted ?
He defrauded Suttung
Of his mead,
And made Gunnlod weep.

It is time to speak
From the chair of the wise man
At the well of Urd ;
I saw and was silent,
I saw and pondered,
I listened to the talk of men ;
I heard talk of runes,
Nor were they silent about their plans
At the hall of Hár ;
In the hall of Hár
I heard this spoken.

I advise thee, Loddfafnir,
Take thou my advice ;
Thou wilt profit by it if thou takest
    it ; [6]
Rise not at night
Unless thou goest a spying
Or thou art compelled to go out.

---

[1] Odrerir = song-inspirer or vessel for the poetic mead.
[2] Midgard.
[3] Odin.
[4] Odin.

[5] I.e., the Temple ring which, like the Bible now, was formerly used for oaths.
[6] These three verses are repeated at the head of nearly each stanza but omitted after this stanza.

Thou must not sleep
In the arms of a witch
So that she clasp thee with her limbs.

She (the witch) causes that
Thou dost not heed
The thing or the words of a chief;
Thou wantest not food
Nor the amusement of men;
Thou goest sorrowful to sleep.

The wife of another man
Tempt thou never
To be thy ear-whisperer.[1]

On a mountain or a fjord
If thou to travel wantest
Take thou good store of food.

A bad man
Do thou never
Let thy misfortunes know;
For from a bad man
Gettest thou never
Reward for thy goodwill.

I saw the words
Of a wicked woman
Wound a man deeply;
Her false tongue
Became his death,
Though he had no guilt.

Know this, if thou hast
A friend whom thou trustest well,
Go often to see him;
For with brushwood
And with high grass will overgrown
The road on which no one walks.

Draw a good man to thee
For the sake of pleasant talk,
And learn healing spells while thou
 livest.

Be never the first
To forsake
The company of thy friend;

Sorrow eats the heart
If one cannot tell
All his mind to some one.

Thou shouldst never
Words exchange
With fools.

For from a bad man
Wilt thou never
Get return for good;
But a good man
Will be able to make thee
Liked and praised.

Souls are together blended,
When a man tells to one
All his mind;
All is better
Than to be fickle;
No friend is he who speaks as one
 wishes.[2]

Not even in three words quarrel
Shalt thou with a worse man;
Often the better one yields
When the worse one strikes.

Be not a shoe-smith
Nor a shaft-smith
Except for thyself;
Is the shoe misshaped,
Or the shaft wry,
Then is evil wished to thee.

Where thou canst do harm
Do not keep from it,
And do not give peace to thy foes.

Be never
Glad at evil,
But be pleased with the good.

Never look up
Shalt thou in battle;
Like swine [3]
May become the sons of men;
Let no man spell-bind thee.

---

[1] I.e., mistress.
[2] No man is another's friend who says only what he wishes.

[3] To Odin is attributed the power to make men in battle mad with terror like swine.—'Ynglinga Saga,' ch. 6.

Wouldst thou get a good woman
To talk pleasantly,
And get delight from her,
Promise thou fair things
And firmly keep it;
No man dislikes the good if he can
   get it.

I bid thee be wary,
But not too wary;
Be most wary at ale,
And with another's wife,
And thirdly
That thieves play not tricks on thee.

Thou must never
Mock or laugh at
A guest or a wayfarer.

Often know not well
Those who sit within
Of what kin they are who come;
No man is so good
That a fault follows him not,
Nor so bad, that he is good for
   nothing.

Never laugh
At a hoary wise man;

Often it is good which old men say
Skilled words come often
Out of a shrivelled skin
Hanging among hides,
Dangling among dry skins,
And going among the sons of toil.

Scoff not at the guest,
Nor drive him to the door;
Be kind to the poor.

Strong is the door-bar,
That shall turn
And open for all;
Give a ring,[1]
Or to thy limbs
Will every kind of evil be wished.

Wherever thou drinkest ale,
Take earth's strength;
For the earth acts against ale,
And fire against constipation,
The (corn) ear against spells,
The spurred rye against hernia;
The moon shall be called on against
   curses,
Heather against contagious diseases,
Runes against evil spells;
The mould must receive the liquid.

The following proverbs and wise sayings occur in the Sagas:

Courage is better
Than the power of sword
Where the angry must fight;
For I saw a bold man
Win . . . . .
Victory with a blunt sword.

'Tis better for the bold
Than cowards
To be in the game of Hild;[2]
It is better to be merry
Than to be downhearted
Whatever may come to hand.

                  (Fafnismal.)

When Heidrek, the son of Hofund, was outlawed by his father for his misconduct, he asked to have advice given him:

"King Hofund said: 'Little advice will I give him, for I think he will make bad use of it; but, since you ask, I will give him first the advice never to help the man who has betrayed his master; the second is never to spare the life of (always to slay) a man who has murdered his companion; the third is not to let his wife visit her kinsmen often though

---

[1] Something as alms. | [2] War.

she ask; the fourth not to tell his concubine all his secrets; the fifth not to ride on his best horse when in a hurry; the sixth never to raise the child of a more high-born man than he is himself; the seventh never to break his truce; the eighth never to take with him many captured thralls. If he follows all this advice he will be a man of luck, though I outlaw him now for breach of the law " (Hervarar Saga, c. 8).

" A tree falls not at the first blow," said an Icelander to the priest Thangbrand, who was going to christianize Iceland. (Njala, ch. 103.)

" Cold (fatal) are the counsels of women," said the chief Flosi to his kinswoman Hildigunn, who urged him to revenge her husband. (Njala, ch. 116.)

" You have much of a swine's memory " (a very short memory), said Gudrún, when she was urging her brothers to slay Kjartan, her former lover. (Laxdæla, ch. 48.)

" It must be worse before it gets better." (Fms. v. 199.)

" A sheepless household starves."

" The bondi is bú-pillar; the bú is the pillar of the land."

Sigrdrifa gives the following counsels to Sigurd:

Sigrdrífa.

First, I advise thee
Do no wrong to
Thy kinsmen;
Do not avenge thyself
Though they harm thee.
It is said to be good after death.

Secondly I advise thee,
Swear not an oath,
Unless it be true;
Cruel roots
Strike perjury;
Wretched is the wolf of plighted faith.

Thirdly I advise thee
That thou at a thing
Do not quarrel with fools;
For an unwise man
Often says
Worse words than he knows.

All is difficult
If thou art silent,
Then thou art thought to be born a
    coward,

Or his (the fool's) words to be true;
The home-judgment is dangerous
Unless thou gettest a good one.
The next day
Thou shalt slay him (the fool),
And thus reward people for their lie.

Fourthly I advise thee, .
If a witch
Full of evil lives on the way,
It is better to walk on
Than lodge there
Though the night overtake thee.

Eyes of foresight
Need the sons of men
In the angry fight;
Often wicked women
Sit near the road,
Who blunt both sword and sense.

Fifthly I advise thee
Though you seest
Fair brides on the benches;
Let not the goddesses of silver
Hinder thy sleep,
Do not entice women to kisses.

Sixthly I counsel thee,
Though among men be
Evil ale-talk;
Thou shalt not quarrel
With drunk battle-trees;[1]
Many a one's wits wine steals.

Strife and ale
Have caused
Grief of mind to many men,
Death to some,
Curses to others,
Many are the evils of men.

Seventhly I advise thee,
If thou hast to fight
Against fearless men,
It is better to fight
Than to be burnt
In the house.

Eighthly I advise thee
That thou beware of evil
And shun false words;
Do not beguile a maiden,
Nor a man's wife,
Nor entice them to overmuch pleasure.[2]

Tenthly I advise thee,
Do thou never believe
The plighted faith of an outlaw's son,
Whether thou art the slayer of his brother
Or hast killed his father;
There is a wolf in a young son
Though he be cheered (comforted) with gold (wergild).

I think
That strife and hate (are not sleepy),
Nor the grief;
Wisdom and weapons
Are not easy to get
For a chief that would be the foremost among men.

Eleventhly I advise thee
That thou beware of evil
In every way from thy friends;
I think I know
The chief's (Sigurd's) life will not be long;
Strong contests have arisen.

---

[1] Men.   [2] Two stanzas missing, see vol. i. p. 322.

Fig. 1350.—Roman gold coin (solidus) of 5th Century (Libyus Severus), found with many Byzantine and Roman coins. Real size —Öland, Sweden.

Fig. 1351.—Coin from Tyre.

Fig. 1352.—Coin from Sidon with Greek and Phœnician inscriptions.—Gotland, Sweden.

CHAPTER XVI.

SORROW AND MOURNING.

Egil's sorrow—Egil's song—The first song of Gudrun—The second song of Gudrun—Halls draped with black and grey.

THERE are several beautiful examples in Northern literature showing how strong were the affections in the hearts of the people, even among the bravest warriors. Conspicuous amongst these examples are Egil's and Gudrun's songs of sorrow, the former mourning the death of a son, the latter that of a husband.

" When Egil returned from his last journey to Norway and Vermland, Bödvar, his son, was full grown. He was a most promising man; handsome, tall, and strong as Egil or Thorol had been at his age. Egil loved him greatly, and Bödvar also was fond of him. One summer a ship came into Hvita (white river), where there was a large gathering for trade. Egil had bought much wood there, and had it brought home. The *huskarls* went in an eight-oared boat which Egil owned. Bödvar begged to go with them, and this they granted him; he went to Vellir with the huskarls, who were six in number, in an eight-oared boat. At the time fixed for their departure the high tide was late in the day, so they waited for it and left late in the evening. Then came a violent south-west gale, and the ebb tide was opposed to it; the sea rose high in the fjord, as often happens there, and the boat was swamped in the heavy sea, and all were drowned; the bodies were thrown ashore the next day. That of Bödvar came ashore in Einarsnes, but others on the southern shore of the fjord, where the boat was driven, and were found at Reykjarhamar. Egil heard of it the same day, and forthwith rode to search for the bodies. He found that of Bödvar outstretched: he took it up, and put it on his knee, and rode with it out to Digranes to the mound of Skallagrim. He had the mound opened, and laid Bödvar at the side of Skallagrim, the mound was then closed, but this was not done until sunset. Egil rode home to Borg (his farm),

and there went at once to the locked bed-closet where he was
wont to sleep; he laid himself down and locked himself up,
and nobody dared talk to him. When they laid Bödvar
down in the mound, Egil wore hose fitting tight to the leg; a
fustian-kirtle, red, narrow, small at the upper end, and laced
on the side, but he swelled so much from grief that the kirtle
as well as the hose were rent. The next day Egil did not
unlock the door, nor did he take any food or drink. He lay
there that day, and the night following it; nobody dared speak
to him. The third morning at dawn Asgerd made a man take
horse and ride as swiftly as he could west to Hjardarholt, and
tell Thorgerd (daughter of Egil, wife of Olaf Höskuldsson)
all these tidings. He arrived there about noon, and said that
Asgerd asked her to come as soon as possible to Borg. Thorgerd at once had a horse saddled, and two men followed her.
They rode that evening and all night till they reached Borg.
Thorgerd at once went into the hall; Asgerd greeted her, and
asked if they had supped. Thorgerd said loudly " I have had
no supper, and shall have none until with Freyja.[1] I know of no
better resolve than to do like my father. I will not live after
my father and brother." She went to the bedroom, and shouted,
'Father, open the door. I want you to go with me.' Egil
drew back the latch. Thorgerd went up and shut the door;
she laid herself down in another bed which was there. Then
Egil said 'Thou didst well, daughter, in wishing to follow
thy father. Thou hast shown me much love. Who can expect
me to live with this grief?' Then they were silent for a while.
Then Egil said 'What is that, daughter? Dost thou chew
anything?' 'I am chewing *samphire* (sea-weed),' she answered,
'and I think that I shall suffer for it; otherwise I think I shall
live too long.' 'Is it hurtful?' asked Egil. 'Very much so,'
said she; 'wilt thou eat?' 'What does it matter?' said he.
Soon after she called and asked for drink. Water was then
given her to drink. Then Egil said: 'When one eats
samphire, one gets more and more thirsty.' 'Wilt thou
drink, father?' said she. He took deep draughts from a horn.
Then Thorgerd said: 'We are deceived, this is milk.' Egil
bit from the horn what his teeth clutched, and threw it away.
Thorgerd said: 'What shall we do, now that this plan is upset?
I should like, father, to lengthen our life, so that thou mightest
compose a funeral poem on Bödvar, and I will carve it on a
stick of wood; then let us die if we like. I think thy son
Thorstein will be slow in making a poem on him, but it is not
proper that there should be no funeral feast, for I do not think

---

[1] Meaning that she would have no
meals before she came to the gods, as
she intended to die with her father.

we shall sit at the drinking at his *arvel.*' Egil said it was unlikely that he could make a poem then, even if he tried, but he would make an attempt " (Egil's Saga).

I give the leading stanzas of the poem.

SONA-TORREK (the loss of sons).[1]

It is very difficult
To move my tongue,
Or the heavy air
Of the steel-yard of sound.[2]
Now there is little hope
Of the theft of Vidrir,[3]
Nor is it easy to draw it
Out of the hiding-place of the mind.[4]

The silent find[5]
Of the kinsmen of Thriggi,[6]
Brought of yore
From Jötunheimar
Is not easily driven
From the abode of the mind.
Heavy sorrow
Is the cause.

The blameless Bragi
Got famous
On the boat
Of Nokkver (a Dverg);[7]
The wound[8] of the neck of the Jotun
Roars
Down at the door
Of the house of my kinsman.[9]

For my kin
Has come near to its end
Like the death-beaten
Branches in the forest.
The man is not merry
Who carries
The bones of his kinsmen
From the place of dead bodies.[10]

Nevertheless
I recall first
The death of my father,
The death of my mother.
That timber of song,[11]
With words for leaves,[12]
I bring out
Of the temple of speech.[13]

Cruel was the gate
Which Hronn[14] broke
On the kin-wall[15]
Of my father.
I see the place of my son,
Made waste by sea,
Stand empty
And open.[16]

---

[1] He had a son called Gunnar, who had died a short time before. The best stanzas only are given.

[2] I.e., tongue. The heavy air of the tongue = breath.

[3] Odin's the t = poetry.

[4] The breast. The people believed that thought came from the breast.

[5] The mead, stolen by Odin, poetry, song. See the later Edda.

[6] The kinsmen of Odin are the Asar.

[7] Boat of the Dvergar, the poetical mead.

[8] Ymir's blood, the sea. Egil thinks he hears the roar of the surf near the mound of the drowned son; it intensifies his sorrow.

[9] House of my kinsmen, the mound where his son with other kinsmen was buried.

[10] The shore bringing the bodies of the drowned.

[11] As timber is the material for workmanship, so "timber of songs" means the subject from which the song is made.

[12] As the leaves hang on the branches of the trees, so the words hang on the timber of song.

[13] The mouth.

[14] Daughter of Ægir.

[15] Meaning that his kinsmen are round him like a sheltering wall.

[16] I.e., he sees the seat of his son empty.

The want of brothers
Comes often
Into the mind
Of the women of Björn.[1]
I look round
When the battle thickens;
I heed this
And look to see if

Any other Thegn
Daring in fight
Stands
At my side;

I need it often.
Such are the tempers of men;
My flight becomes faint
When my friends get few.

It is also told
That no one gets
The equal of his son
Unless he begets another;
Nor a kinsman
Who is to him
Like the man
Who is his born brother.

THE FIRST SONG OF GUDRUN.

The brothers of Gudrun, daughter of Gjuki, had slain her husband, Sigurd Fafnisbani, in his bed. Gudrun sat over Sigurd when he was dead; she did not weep, as other women, but almost died from grief. Both men and women came to comfort her, but did not find it easy to do so.

Gudrun was
Near to death
When she sat, full of grief,
Over Sigurd;
She did not weep,
Nor wring her hands,
Nor wail
Like other women.

Very wise jarls
Came forward,
Who tried to soothe
Her heavy heart;
Though Gudrun was
Unable to weep;
She was so sad;
Her heart almost broke.

The high-born
Brides of jarls
Sat, gold adorned,
By Gudrun;
Each of them
Related her woes,
The bitterest sorrow
She had suffered.

The sister of Gjuki,
Gjaflang, said:
No women on earth
Lack love more than I;
I have felt the loss
Of husbands five,
Of daughters two,
Of sisters three,
Of brothers eight,
And yet I live alone.

Still Gudrun
Could not weep,
So full of grief was she
For her dead husband,
And heavy-hearted
O'er the king's corpse.

Then said Herborg,
The Queen of Hunaland:
I have a harder
Sorrow to tell;
My seven sons
And my eighth husband
Fell among the slain
In the southern lands.

---

[1] Björn = Thor. The women of Björn = the Troll women.

2 E

My father and mother,
My four brothers;
The wind played with them
On the deep;
The wave dashed them
Against the gunwale.

I myself had to wash,
I myself had to bury,
I myself had to handle
Their corpses;
All that I suffered
In one year,
And no man
Gave me help.

The same year
I became a bondwoman;[1]
I had to dress,
And to tie the shoes
Of a hersir's wife
Every morning.

She threatened me
Because of jealousy,
And struck me with
Hard blows;
Nowhere found I
A better house-master
Nor anywhere
A worse housewife.

Still Gudrun
Could not weep,
So sad was she
For her dead husband
And heavy-hearted
O'er the king's corpse.

Then said Gullrönd,
The daughter of Gjuki:
Little comfort
Canst thou, foster-mother,
Wise though thou art,
Give the young wife.
She bid them uncover
The king's corpse.

She drew the sheet
Off Sigurd
And threw it on the ground,
Before the knees of the wife:—
Look on thy beloved one,
Put thy mouth to his lips,
As if thou did'st embrace
The living king.

Gudrun looked
At him once;
She saw his hair
Dripping with blood;
The flashing eyes
Of the king were dead;
His breast[2]
Was cut with a sword.

Then Gudrun sank down
Upon the pillow;
Loose was her hair,
Flushed was her cheek
And a tear-drop
Fell on her knee.

Then wept Gudrun,
The daughter of Gjuki,
So that the tears
Flowed through her tresses;
And the geese
Screamed in the yard—
The good fowls
Which the maiden owned.

Then said Gullrönd,
The daughter of Gjuki:
I never knew
A greater love
Among all men
Upon earth
Than that of you two.
Thou wast never happy,
My sister,
Indoors or out,
Unless with Sigurd.

---

[1] We see the custom of slave-women.

[2] Breast, called here the burg of the mind.

Then said Gudrun,
The daughter of Gjuki:
Such was my Sigurd
Among the sons of Gjuki,
As a garlic [1]
Grown high among grass,
Or a shining stone
Set on a band,
A precious gem,
So was he above the high-born.

I seemed also
To the king's champions
Higher than any
Dis of Herjan; [2]
Now I am lowly
As a willow leaf,
After the king's death.

I miss in the seat
And in the bed
The talk of my friend;
The sons of Gjuki cause
My misery,
And the sore weeping
Of their sister.

So shall you
Lose your land
As you kept not
The sworn oaths;
Thou, Gunnar, wilt not
Enjoy the gold;
Those rings
Will be thy death,
As thou to Sigurd
Did'st falsely swear.

Oft was it merrier
When my Sigurd
Saddled Grani
In the grass-plot (tun),
And they went
To woo Brynhild,
The cursed being
With bad luck.

Then said Brynhild,
The daughter of Budli:
May that being lack [3]
Husband and children
Who made thee
Weep, Gudrun,
And to thee this morning
Gave power of speech. [4]

Then said Gullrönd,
The daughter of Gjuki:
Speak not these words,
Much hated one;
Thou hast always been
The Urd [5] of the high-born;

Every man disowns thee,
Thou evil being!
Sore sorrow
Of seven kings,
And the greatest spoiler
Of wives' friends. [6]

Then said Brynhild,
The daughter of Budli:
Atli alone causes
All the misery;
The son or Budli,
My brother,

When we in the hall
Of the Hunnish people
Saw with the king
The fire of the serpent lair [7]
I have paid since
For that journey;
Of that sight
I was not afraid.

She stood at the door-post;
She clasped the alder-tree; [8]
Fire flashed
Out of the eyes
Of Brynhild, Budli's daughter;
Venom gushed from her
When she saw the wounds
Of Sigurd.

---

[1] Geirlauk.   [2] Odin.
[3] To be an old maid seems to have been looked upon as a curse.
[4] Speech runes.

[5] One of the Nornir, representing the past.   [6] Husbands.
[7] The gold of Fafnir's lair.
[8] The door-post.

2 E 2

261

Gudrun's second song to King Thjodrek at the hird of Atli.

I was a maiden of maidens,
My bright mother
Raised me in her house;
I loved my brothers well,
Till Gjuki endowed me with gold,
And gave me to Sigurd.

So was Sigurd
Among the sons of Gjuki
As a green leek
Grown high in the grass,
Or a long-legged hart
Among the swift deer,
Or ruddy gold
Amidst grey silver.

Until my brothers
Begrudged me
A husband,
Who was the foremost of all;
They could not sleep
Nor judge law-cases
Till they had slain Sigurd.

Grani[1] ran from the Thing;
The noise (of his hoofs) was heard;
But then Sigurd
Himself did not come.
All the saddle-deer[2]
Were soiled with blood,
And wearied
Under their murderers.

I went in my tears
To talk to Grani;
With wet cheeks
I asked him to speak.
Grani drooped his head,
Bowed it down to the grass;
The steed knew
His owner was no more.

A long while I wavered,
Long was my mind divided
Before I asked

The people-defender
For news of the king.

Gunnar drooped his head;
Högni told me
The painful death
Of Sigurd:
The slayer of Gothorm
Lies slain
Beyond the water,
Given to the wolves.

Seek for Sigurd there,
On the southern road;
Then thou wilt hear
Ravens croak,
Eagles scream,
Glad at their booty,
Wolves howl
Over thy husband.

Why wilt thou, Högni,
Such sorrows tell
To me so joy-bereft?
The ravens should
Tear thy heart
In far-off lands,
Where thou art a stranger.

Högni answered:
Some day, Gudrun,
With heavy mind,
With great grief;
More cause wilt thou have
To weep,
If my heart
By ravens be torn.

I went alone thence
From this talk
Into the forest
To gather what the wolves had left.[3]
I did not moan
Nor wring my hands,
Nor wail,

---

[1] Sigurd's horse.
[2] Horses.
[3] Probably Sigurd's body had been thrown into the forest after he was slain in his bed.

Like other women,	Over Sigurd;
When I sat over	I should have liked
The dead Sigurd.	The wolves far better
	Had they taken my life,
Pitch dark	Or I
The night seemed	Had been burnt
When I sat sorrow-stricken	Like birch-wood.

In the following remarkable account of a battle between Knut and Harald, the two sons of King Gorm, in which Knut was killed, we find that when a family was in mourning the halls were draped with black and grey.

"After this Harald and his men proceeded until they reached King Gorm's farm late at night, and went ashore fully armed. It is said, by some who know, that Harald did not know how he should tell his father, for he had made a vow that he would die if he heard of the fall of his son Knut, and would kill the man who told him of his death.

"Harald sent his foster-brother, Hauk, to his mother, Queen Thyri, and requested her to find some way to give him the news. She bade him go himself and tell the king that two hawks had been fighting, one of which was entirely white, the other grey, and both brave. At last the white hawk was killed, which was thought a great pity. Hauk thereupon returned to Harald, and reported what his mother had said. Harald thereupon went to the hall, where King Gorm and his men were drinking, went up to his father, and told him about the hawks, as his mother had advised, ending by saying that the white hawk was dead. He said no more. It is not stated where Harald and his men took up their quarters that night. King Gorm did not appear to comprehend this. The men sat drinking as long as they liked that night, and then went to bed; but after they had left the hall Queen Thyri took down the hangings, and instead put up black and grey cloth until all was covered. She had done this because it was the custom in those days when tidings of grief came to do as she did.

"King Gorm, the old, rose in the morning, and went into his high-seat, intending to begin drinking. He looked at the walls of the hall; the queen sat in the high-seat with him. He said: 'Thou, Queen Thyri, must have ordered the hall to be thus prepared.' 'For what purpose should I?' she asked. 'Because,' the king added, 'thou wishest now to tell me of the fall of my son Knut.'[1] 'Thou now tellest it thyself,' said

---

[1] Knut Dana-ast was the brother of Harald Bluetooth.

the queen. He had been standing in front of the high-seat while they were talking, but now sat down suddenly, answered nothing, fell back against the wall of the hall, and died. He was carried to burial, and a mound was thrown up over him by order of Thyri. She then sent word to her son Harald to return with all his men and drink *arvel* after his father. This he did, and it was very splendid.

"After this Harald took possession of the kingdom and all the lands of his father, and held a Thing with the men of the country, at which the Danes chose him as king over the whole of Denmark" (Flateyjarbok, vol. i.; Jomsvikinga Thatt).

Fig. 1353.　　　　　Fig 1354.　　　　　Fig. 1355.

Small clay urns, with burnt bones and objects of bronze, buttons, needles, knives, etc. In a mound, Zealand. ¼ real size.

Fig. 1357.—Small clay urn. ½ size.

Fig. 1356.—Clay urn, in a mound with burnt bones. Björkö, Lake Mälar. ¼ size.

CHAPTER XVII.

CHAMPIONS AND BERSERKS.

The warrior's aim to be a Berserk—Berserk frenzy—The twelve sons of Arngrim—They fight without coats of mail—Hrolf's champions—Hakon
Jarl's Berserks—The life of a Berserk—Disregard for death.

To be considered the foremost champion or *Kappi* was the greatest ambition of every warrior; and to attain this proud position was no easy task among so many men who were equally brave and perfectly reckless of their lives, and thoroughly skilled in the handling of weapons.

After such a reputation had been acquired, the champion had either to challenge or be challenged by those who vied with him, and these duels or trials of strength and skill generally took place before a large assembly.

The aim of every champion was to become a "Berserk" (so called, probably, because they fought without serk (shirt)), who was regarded as the bravest of men. When within sight of their foe Berserks wrought themselves into such a state of frenzy, that they bit their shields and rushed forward to the attack, throwing away their arms of defence, reckless of every danger, sometimes having nothing but a club, which carried with it death and destruction.

"In the time of Hákon, Æthelstan's foster-son, there lived in Norway Björn the Pale, who was a Berserk. He went round the country and challenged men to *holmganga* (duel) if they would not do his will" (Gisli Sursson's Saga, p. 1).

This berserk-fury was not only utilised in war, but for the performance of hard feats which were held to be out of the power of ordinary people. In some cases this fury seems to have come over the Berserks apparently without cause, when they trembled and gnashed their teeth.

"The Berserk Arngrim of Bólm had twelve sons; Angantýr was the oldest, the second Hervard, the third Seming, the fourth Hjörvard, the fifth Brani, the sixth Brami, the seventh Barri, the eighth Reytnir, the ninth Tind, the tenth Bui, the eleventh and the twelfth both called Hadding. They were both together equal to one of the others, but Angantýr was equal to two, and was a head taller than any of them; they were all great Berserks. They went on warfare when they were quite young and ravaged far and wide, but met with no equal in strength and courage; thereby they got renown and victory. The twelve brothers went together on one ship with no others; but they often had more ships. Their father had taken in war the most excellent weapons; Angantýr got Tyrfing, Hervard Hrotti, Seming Mistiltein (Mistletoe), which Thráin [1] afterwards took out of his mound. All the brothers had excellent holmganga-swords. It was their custom if they were only with their own men when they found the *berserks-gang* (berserk-fury)[2] coming over them, to go ashore and wrestle with large stones or trees, otherwise they would have slain their friends in their rage. Never did they engage in battle without gaining the victory; therefore great sayings were told of them. There was no king who would not give them what they wanted rather than suffer their overbearing. They were on warfare during the summer, but during the winter they remained at home in Bólmey with their father" (Hervarar Saga, c. 3).[3]

In the following Sagas we have an example of the stuff the men of the North, or the Vikings, were made of.

"When Fridthjof landed after a storm .... in the Orkneys, one of the Berserks of the jarl said: 'Now we will try if it is true that Fridthjof has made a vow that he will never be the first to ask peace of another.' They were ten wicked and greedy men, and often had berserk-rage; when they met (Fridthjof) they took their weapons. Atli (one of the Berserks) said: 'Now it is best, Fridthjof, to look us in the face, for the eagles must fight with their claws face to face, and now it is best to stand by one's words, and not be the first to ask for peace'" (Fridthjof's Saga, c. 7).

It was believed that neither fire nor weapons could harm

---

[1] Thráin, some unknown champion.
[2] Berserks-gang = going like a Berserk into fits of frenzy.
[3] Cf. also Ynglinga Saga, 6; Njal, 104;

Egil, 27, 40; Vatnsdæla, 46; Fornmanna Sögur, i. 132; Svarfdæla, 7; Orvar Odd, 14; Droplaugar Sona Saga, 19.

the Berserks. In war they fought without coats of mail in a bare shirt or kirtle ; hence their name.

"King Hálf went up to King Asmund's farm, where there were many men, with one-half of his men. The entertainment was good, and the drink was so strong, that Hálf's champions fell fast asleep. King Asmund and his hird set fire to the hall. The one of Hálf's champions who awoke first saw the hall nearly full of smoke. He called out : 'Now it will smoke round our hawks,' and then again lay down to sleep. Then another woke and saw the hall burning, and said : 'Wax will now drip from our saxes,' and then lay down.

"But then King Hálf awoke, rose and roused the warriors, and told them to arm themselves. They then rushed at the walls with such strength that the joints of the timbers broke" (Half's Saga).

They were also believed to change shape, and in their greatest fury to take the outward shape of an animal[1] of great strength and ferocity.

It was the aim of every great chief to gather round him the greatest champions of the land, and if he was renowned for bravery, liberality, and convivial qualities, they would come to him from even the remotest parts of the North. When a new champion came who wished to be the foremost, he asked his future companions if they objected to his becoming so among them, and if any one objected, he would at once challenge him to a holmganga to assert or prove his claim. In some cases the fame of a new-comer was so great that he was at once recognised to be foremost.

Among the great champions whose fame and name were sung for generations were the champions of Hrólf Kraki and King Hálf.

Hrólf's champions flocked to him from every part of the North ; among the most celebrated were Bodvar Bjarki, from Norway, and Svipdag, from Sweden. Other kings seem to have had twelve Berserks in their train.

"King Hrólf made himself ready for his journey with one hundred men, besides whom he had his twelve champions and

---

[1] Landnama, Part V., ch. 5 ; Hrolf Kraki's last fight, 50, 51.

twelve Berserks. Nothing more is told of their journey before they came to a bondi " (Hrolf Kraki's Saga, c. 39).

"Haki and Hagbard were the names of two very famous brothers. They were sea-kings and had a large host; sometimes they went together, sometimes each went by himself; many champions followed each of them. King Haki went with his host to Sweden against King Hugleik, who gathered a host; two brothers, Svipdag and Geigad, both far-famed and great champions, came to help him. Haki had with him twelve champions, among whom was Starkad the old; Haki himself was a very great champion. They met on the Fýris-vellir (plain of Fýri) in a great battle; Hugleik's men fell fast. The champions Svipdag and Geigad then made an onset, but six of Haki's champions went against each of them and they were captured. Then Haki went into Hugleik's shieldburg and slew him and his two sons. Thereupon the Swedes fled, and Haki conquered the land and became king over the Swedes. He stayed at home for three winters, and during that time his champions went away on viking-expeditions and thus earned property " (Ynglinga, c. 25).

The twelve Berserks of Hrólf Kraki followed King Adils of Sweden in a battle against King Áli of Norway, on condition that they were to get pay, and be allowed to choose three costly things for Hrólf.

"After the battle, each of them asked three pounds of gold as pay, and to take with them three costly things which they might choose for Hrólf: they were, the helmet *Hildigölt* (war-boar), the brynja *Finnsleif*, which was impenetrable to weapons, and the gold ring *Sviagris* (the Svia-pig) which the fore-fathers of Adils had owned " (Prose Edda (Skáldskaparmál), c. 44).

"With Hákon Jarl were two brothers of Swedish kin: one was named Halli, the other Leiknir. They were much taller and stronger men than were to be found in Norway or in other places. They went a-berserking, and when they were angry lost their human nature and went mad like dogs; they feared neither fire nor iron, but in everyday life they were not bad to have intercourse with if they were not offended, though they were most overbearing if offended. Eirik Sigrsæli (the victorious), King of Sweden, had sent the Berserks to the Jarl, and told him to be careful to treat them well, and said, as was true, that they could be a great help if regard was had to their tempers " (Eyrbyggja, c. 25).

A CHAMPION'S LIFE.

The following account gives a picture of the life of these champions :

"The bóndi Svip lived in Sweden far away from other men; he was wealthy and had been the greatest champion and not all he looked, as he knew many things. He had three sons, Svipdag, Geigad, and Hvitserk, who was the oldest; they were all well skilled, strong, and fine-looking men. When Svipdag was eighteen winters old he said one day to his father : 'Our life here in the mountains, in far-off valleys and unsettled places, where men never visit nor receive visits, is dull; it would be better to go to Adils and follow him and his champions, if he will receive us.' Svip answered : 'I do not think this advisable, for King Adils is a cruel man and not trustworthy though he uses fair words, and his men are jealous and strong, but certainly he is powerful and famous.' Svipdag said : 'A man must risk something if he wishes to get fame ; he cannot know, before he tries, when luck will come to him.' His father gave him a large axe and said to his son, 'Be not greedy ; do not boast, for that gives a bad reputation, but defend yourself if attacked, for a great man should boast little and behave well in difficulties.' He gave him good war clothes and a good horse. Then Svipdag rode and at night came to the burg of King Adils; he saw that games were taking place outside the hall, and Adils sat on a large gold chair and his Berserks near him. When Svipdag came to the fence [1] the gate of the burg was shut, for it was then customary to ask leave to ride in ; Svipdag did not take that trouble, and broke open the gate and rode into the yard. Then the King said : 'This man comes here recklessly, as this has never been done before. It may be that he has great strength and has no fear.' The Berserks at once got very angry and thought that he asserted himself too much. Svipdag rode before the King, and saluted him well in a skilful manner. Adils asked who he was, and he told him. The King soon recognized him, and every one thought he was a great and high-born champion. The games were continued ; Svipdag sat on a fallen tree and looked on. The Berserks eyed him angrily, and said to the King that they wanted to try him ; the King answered : 'I think that he has no little strength, but I should like you to try whether he is such a man as he considers himself.'

"When men gathered into the hall the Berserks walked towards Svipdag and asked him if he was a champion, as he

---

[1] The wall of the burg is called here fence.

made so much of himself: he answered that he was as great a one as any of them. At these words their anger and eagerness (to fight) increased. But the King told them to be quiet that night; they began to frown, and howled loudly, and said to Svipdag: 'Darest thou fight us? Then thou wilt need more than mere big words and boasting. We will try how much there is in thee.' Svipdag answered: 'I will consent to fight one at a time and will see if more can be done.' The King was well pleased that they should do this. Queen Yrsa said: 'This man shall be welcome here.' The Berserks answered her: 'We knew before that thou didst want to send us all to Hel, but we are too big to be killed by words alone or ill-will.'

"In the morning began a hard *holmganga*, and there was no lack of heavy blows; the new-comer knew how to use his sword with great strength and the Berserks gave way. Svipdag killed one, and another wanted to avenge him but suffered the same fate, and Svipdag did not stop before he had slain four; then Adils said, 'Great loss hast thou caused to me, and now thou shalt pay for it,' and he asked men to rise and kill him. The Queen got men and wanted to help him, and said that the King could see that there was much more skill in him alone than in all the Berserks. The Queen made peace between them, and every one considered Svipdag to be a man of great prowess. Now he sat on the lower bench opposite the King, by the wish of Queen Yrsa. He looked round and thought he had not done harm enough to the Berserks, and wished to urge them to fight, and thought it likely that if they saw him alone they would attack him; it was as he thought, for they began at once to fight. The King came when they had been fighting for a while and parted them. Afterwards the King outlawed the remaining Berserks as they could not all together fight a single man, saying he had not before known that they were great only in boasting. They had to go, but threatened to make warfare in the realm of King Adils. The King replied that he did not care for their threats.

"Adils asked Svipdag to help him as much now as all the Berserks had done before, especially as the Queen wanted him in their place. Svipdag stayed there for some while" (Hrólf Kraki, c. 18, 19).

"Now the winter passed, and the time came when the Berserks of King Hrólf were expected home. Bödvar asked Hjalti about their customs; he answered that it was their habit when they came home to the hird to walk first up to the king, and then to every man, and ask if the man thought himself their equal. The king used to answer, that is hard to tell as you are such valiant men, and as you have won renown in bloody battles against several people in the southern and northern half of the world. He gives this answer more from his good-will than unmanliness, for he knows their temper and they win great victories and much property for him. They then walk up to every man in the hall and put the same question, and no one answers that he is their equal. Bödvar said: 'Few good warriors are here with Hrólf, as they are all cowed by the Berserks.' No more was said. Next yule-eve Bödvar had been one year with Hrólf, and when they sat at table the door of the hall was thrown open, and in came twelve Berserks, all over grey with iron (coat of mail), which looked like broken ice. Bödvar asked Hjalti in a low voice if he dared try himself against one of them. 'Yes,' said Hjalti, 'not against one, but against all of them, for I cannot get frightened though there is an overwhelming strength against me, and not one of them shall scare me.' The Berserks first walked up the hall, and saw that the champions of Hrólf had increased in number since they left. They looked carefully at the new men, and thought that one of them was no small man, and it is told that the one who walked foremost was a little startled. They went as they used before King Hrólf, and asked him the customary question; he answered what he thought fit, as he was wont. They walked up to every man in the hall, and last up to the comrades (Bödvar and Hjalti); the foremost one then asked Bödvar if he thought himself his equal. Bödvar said he thought himself not equal, but superior to him in anything they might try; that foul son of a mare should not treat him like a sow. He jumped up at the Berserk who was in full war dress, and threw him down so strongly that he came near breaking his bones; Hjalti did the same, so that a great tumult arose in the hall, and the king saw that a great loss was likely to take place if his men were to be killed. He rushed from his high seat to Bödvar, and asked him to take it all in a quiet and friendly manner. Bödvar said the Berserk should lose his life unless he acknowledged himself to be a lesser man than he. The king said that would be easily done, and allowed the Berserks to rise to their feet. Hjalti did the same after the king's order. Every man sat down in his seat, and the Berserks likewise in theirs with grief in their mind. The king spoke long to them, and told them that now they might see that no one was so great, strong, or renowned but that he might find his equal, and said: 'I forbid you to cause any trouble in my hall, and if you do not obey that you will forfeit your lives; be as fierce as you can when I fight my enemies, and thus win fame and renown to yourself. Now I have so chosen champions that I need not depend upon you. All agreed with the king's words and were fully reconciled. They were then seated thus that Bödvar was most honoured. He sat next to the king on the right hand; at his side sat Hjalti the Bold-minded, which name the king gave him. . . . Bödvar was so highly honoured by King Hrólf that he married his only daughter Drifa " (Hrolf Kraki's Saga, c. 37).

"Thereafter King Adils had his hall cleaned ; the dead men were carried out, for many of Adils' men were slain and wounded. He said : 'Now we will make long fires (on the floor) for our friends, and treat well such men as they are. Now men were put to kindle the fire. Hrólf's champions always sat with their weapons, and never let hold of them. The fire was soon burning, for pitch and dry firewood was not spared. King Adils seated himself and his hirdmen on the one side of the fire, and Hrólf Kraki and his champions opposite. They sat on long benches, and spoke very friendly together. King Adils said : 'The bravery and hardihood of the champions of Hrólf is not exaggerated ; you think yourself better than others, and no lies have been told about your strength ; now increase the fire, for I do not see distinctly where the king is, and though you may be warmed somewhat you will not flee from the fire.' This was done. He wanted to see where King Hrólf was, for he knew that he could not stand the heat as well as the champions, and thought he would get at him more easily when he knew where he was, for truly he wanted to slay him. Bödvar and others saw this and sheltered him from the heat as well as they could, but not in the way that he could be known. As the fire advanced very rapidly King Hrólf remembered the vow he had made neither to flee from fire nor iron weapons ; he saw that King Adils tried to burn them or let them break their vow. They saw that Adils' seat had moved (of itself) to the door of the hall, and also those of his men. The fire advanced fast and they saw they would get burnt if they stayed. Their clothes were much scorched, and they threw their shields on the fire. Böd-var and Svipdag said : 'Now let us increase the fire at Adils' burg (hall). Each of them took one of the men who had kept up the fires and flung them into them, and said : 'Now warm yourselves at it for your work and toil ; we have got warmth enough ; now warm yourselves, as you were so busy for a while to make fire for us. Hjalti took the third one and flung him into it where he sat, and then he did the same with all those who kept up the fires, and they were burnt to ashes, and not helped, for no one dared to come so near. When they had done this King Hrólf said : 'He flees not the fire who jumps (leaps) over it.' Then they all leapt (on their shields) over the fire, and wanted to take King Adils. When he saw this he saved his life, and ran to the tree which stood in the hall, and was hollow inside, and thus he got out with witchcraft and sorcery. He came into the hall of Queen Yrsa and talked to her, and she received him disgracefully, and spoke many big words to him : 'Thou first didst slay my husband Helgi, and betray him and keepest the property from its owner, and besides this thou wantest to slay my son, and thou art much crueller and worse than any other ; now I will in every way help Hrólf to get the property, and thou wilt get shame as thou deservest.' Adils answered : 'Here neither will trust the other, and hereafter I shall not come before their eyes.' Thereupon they ceased to talk " (Hrólf Kraki's Saga, c. 41).

In those days of incessant warfare, the life of the warrior was a magnificent drama from the beginning to the end ; his death the closing of a grand career ; and his entrance into Valhalla the reward for a life of bravery, in which he showed entire disregard of death, and in which he often exhibited the highest qualities of manhood. As he saw life ebbing away he sang the deeds he had accomplished, and when his eye became dim, and darkness was for ever to close from him the light of the sun, he could hear resounding in his ears the lay of the scald recounting the deeds of his life.

No other literature that has come down to us from ancient times describes so vividly and minutely as that of the North the deeds of the grand heroes of old. We can imagine ourselves on the battle-field, can hear the clatter of arms, and the whistling of arrows and spears, the blows resounding against helmet, shield, or coat-of-mail, and the fierce onslaught ; and see before our eyes the boarding of vessels and the carnage on deck.

In the Sagas which speak of the earliest times we find a magnanimous and chivalrous spirit, for the contest had to be equal, ship against ship, man against man. In a great battle chief was against chief, champion against champion, while the combatants of both sides were looking on, and he who was successful had to fight with the rest, himself at last falling mortally wounded, or standing victorious over all. In these deadly fights, more than anywhere else, do we see this cool daring and courage of the hardy Norsemen, men looking death in the face calmly and unflinchingly, feeling that it was better to die with honour or fame than live with shame, as is so often told in the Sagas; for it is only towards later times that we see the decay of this spirit of chivalry.

Fig. 1358.—Bracteate of gold
found in a field, Jutland.

Fig. 1359.   Fig. 1360.

Gold bracteates, Norway, ⅔ size, found with many
other gold bracteates.

CHAPTER XVIII.

SOME EXPEDITIONS AND DEEDS OF GREAT VIKINGS.

Harald Hilditönn's claim to England—King Hring in England—Battle of Brávöll—Battle of Dúnheidi—Warlike character of the Race.

IN the preceding chapters we have dealt with the customs of the forefathers of the English-speaking nations of to-day, and will now proceed to give extracts from those Sagas which deal with the lives and deeds of some of the earlier kings of the North who claimed to own part of England, and which mention events that relate to, or took place in, England, France, Ireland, Scotland, and other countries in later times. In quoting from the different Sagas there is necessarily a certain amount of repetition.

Among the earliest kings who claimed to own or have possessions in England were Ivar Vidfadmi, Harald Hilditönn, Sigurd Hring, and Ragnar Lodbrok.

"When Sigurd Hring (7th and 8th centuries, A.D.), father of Ragnar Lodbrok, King of Sweden and Denmark, had made peace in both, and placed over them tax-kings and jarls, he bethought himself of the kingdom which his kinsman Harald Hilditönn (war-tooth) had possessed in England, and before him Ivar Vidfadmi; but it was then ruled by King Ingjald, who it is said was brother of Petr, Saxon king" (Forrmanna Sögur).[1]

"Ingjald was a powerful king.

"King Hring summoned a great levy from his kingdom, went westward to England, and, when he came to Northumberland, asked for help, which many people gave him.

"But when King Ingjald heard of this, he gathered a large host and went against him, and they fought several battles,

---

[1] Two other manuscripts, Vestra Saxa king.

in the last of which King Ingjald and his son Ubbi, with many of their warriors, fell. Hring thereupon took possession of Northumberland and the whole of Ingjald's kingdom.

"King Hring left England, placing as tax-king over Northumberland Olaf, son of Kinrik, who was said to be a nephew of Moalda the Stout, mother of Ivar Vidfadmi.

"Then King Hring returned to his realm, and Olaf ruled over Northumberland, until Eava (or Eana), son of Ubbi, gained the throne. He and Olaf had many battles; after the last one King Olaf fled, and Eava won the kingdom.

"Olaf went to Sweden to see King Hring, who then made him chief of Jutland, and for long afterwards he was tax-king there, first under King Hring, and afterwards under Ragnar Lodbrok.

"He was called Olaf the English, and his son was Grim the grey, who got the kingship after his father.

"Grim was father of Audulf the strong, who was tax-king in Jutland under Ragnar Lodbrok; Audulf's son was Gorm, who was also tax-king in Jutland, and was named Gorm the childless.

"King Gorm had many thralls, and some of these had been sent to Holtsetaland (Holstein) to buy wine, which they carried on many horses" (Fornmanna Sögur, vol. i.).

Among the most renowned and powerful chiefs and Vikings of the North in the Sagas, who sailed far and wide, are Ragnar Lodbrok [1] and his sons, whose deeds are closely connected with the earlier history of England.

The Saga which follows shows that the Northmen went to England long before the time mentioned by the English Chronicles.

It is, as we have shown, vain to try to reconcile the English or Frankish Chronicles with the Sagas. It is therefore obvious that the men of the chronicles, whose names were similar to the names of Ragnar and Lodbrok, are not Ragnar Lodbrok, while on the other hand the so-called sons of Lodbrok, who

---

[1] Ragnar Lodbrok's Saga is only a continuation of the Volsunga Saga, and especially dwells upon the subject that Ragnar's wife Aslaug was descended from Sigurd Fafnisbani. The other story seems to be a fragment of the same large Saga about Harald Hilditonn and his descendants, which describes the end of Ivar Vid- fadme and the Bravalla battle" (Munch: 'History of Norway').

Trustworthy registry of relationship in ancient Northern writings unite in putting Ragnar Lodbrok three generations earlier than the discovery of Iceland, which took place between 870–880.

plundered England, could not be sons of the above-named Ragnar. We must therefore suppose either that the name Lodbrok's sons was used as a family name, both by Ragnar's grandsons and following descendants, or that in a family nearly related to his own there appeared a *Lodbrok* named after him, who did not rule any realm in the North, but whose sons were the mightiest and most valiant Vikings England had ever seen.

That several Ragnars existed at different periods is as certain as that there were several Halfdans, Sigurds, Haralds, Ivars, Knuts, Olafs, &c. The custom of calling children after their father and grandfather still prevails to this day in Scandinavia.

Sigurd Hring, the victor of Bravöll, who succeeded Harald Hilditönn, was a mighty chief; his realm included the whole of the present Denmark, Sweden, the countries bordering the Baltic, and others westward, among them England. As was the custom of those times, the vast possessions of great and powerful chiefs were ruled by under or tax-kings.

Sigurd Hring had a son, Ragnar. When old enough he obtained ships and men, and became the greatest of warriors.[1]

"Sigurd Hring was king over Sweden and Denmark after Harald Hilditönn; his son Ragnar grew up in his hird; he was the largest and strongest man ever seen, and was like his mother and her family in looks. It is known from all old sayings about the people called Alfar that they were much handsomer than other men in the Northern lands, for all the forefathers of Alfhild his mother and all their kindred were descended from Alf the old; they were called Alfar, and the two large rivers which are called Elf[2] are named after him; the one divided his realm from Gautland, and was therefore called Gautelf; the other separated it from the land now called Raumaríki, and is called Raumelf. Ragnar was like his father and his kinsmen in size, like Harald Hilditönn or Ivar vidfadmi. When Hring began to grow old and unwieldy his realm began to lessen, and the remote parts were first lost. King Adalbrikt (Adalbrecht) was descended from King Ella,[3] whom Hálfdán Ylfing (Wolfing) had slain. He subjugated

[1] Ragnar Lodbrok's Saga, c. ii.
[2] They seem to have believed that Elf (river) was derived from Alfar.
[3] Apparently there were two kings of the name Ella.

2 F 2

that part of England which is called Nordimbraland (North-umberland); this part was owned by King Hring, and before him by Harald (Hilditönn). Adalbrikt ruled over it for a long while; his sons were called Ama and Ella, and were kings of Northumberland after their father."

Two of the most famous ancient battles of the North, accounts of which have been handed down to us, were those of Brávöll and Dunheidi.

"Sigurd Hring got the kingship in Denmark. He fought against King Harald Hilditönn on Brávöll[1] in Eastern-Gautland, and there King Harald and a great many men were slain. This battle, and the battle between Angantýr and his brother Hlöd in Dúnheidi (Dúnheath), have been most mentioned in old Sagas, and most men have been slain in them (have been more spoken of in old Sagas, and more men have been slain in them than in any other battle)" (Hervarar Saga, c. 16).

Battle of Brávöll.—In this battle the champions of King Harald seem chiefly to have come from Denmark and from England and Ireland (the west), also from Saxland, which was tributary to him; the champions of King Hring from Sweden, Norway, and the east.

"One autumn he (Sigurd Hring) went to visit King Harald, his father's brother, was well received, and remained there for awhile in good favour. As King Harald was getting old, he placed Hring, his kinsman, over his host to defend his lands, and he dwelt a long time with Harald. When old age was heavy upon the king, he made Hring king over Uppsalir, and gave into his power the whole of Sweden and West Gautland, but he himself retained the rule over all Denmark and Eastern Gautland (East Gotland). King Hring married Alfhild, daughter of King Alf, who possessed the land between the rivers Gautelf and Raumelf, which then was also called Alfheim; these were great forest-lands. Hring had one son, Ragnar (Lodbrok), by his wife. King Harald had two sons by his wife, Hrærek *Slöngvandbaugi* (Ring-slinger) and Thrand the old.

"When King Harald Hilditönn (war-tooth) was 180 winters old, he lay in bed, unable to walk; Vikings disturbed his realm with war far and wide. His friends thought the people

---

[1] The date of the battle was probably about the year A.D. 700.

fared badly, as there was no rule in the land; many thought that he was too old. Some chiefs resolved when he was bathing in a tub to cover it with timber and stones, intending to choke him therein. When he found that they wanted to kill him, he asked to be allowed to leave the bath, saying: ' I know that you think I am too old; that is true, but I would rather die my fated death. I do not wish to die in the bath, but in a much more kingly way.' Then his friends came and took him away. A little while after he sent word to Sweden, to King Hring, his kinsman, that he should gather a host from all the lands he ruled over, and meet him on the frontier and fight against him, and told him all about the reason, namely, that the Danes thought him too old.

" Hring gathered men from all Sweden and Western Gautland, and many from Norway; it is said that when Swedes and Norwegians went with the levy out of Stokksund the ships were two thousand and five hundred. Hring rode with his hird and the West Gotlanders higher up past Eyrasund, and then westward, to the forest Kolmörk which separates Sweden from Eastern Gautland. When he reached a place called Brávik his ship-host met him, and he encamped on Brávöll near the forest, between it and the bay.

" King Harald gathered men from all Denmark, and a great host came from Austrriki (the eastern realm) and all the way from Kœnugard [1] and Saxland. When his host had gathered on Selund, at Kögja, the passage to Skáneyri from Landeyri could be made on ships only; the whole sea seemed to be covered with his ship-host. He sent Herleif with his Saxon host to King Hring, in order to stake out the field chosen for the battle, and declare the truce and peace broken. King Harald was seven days on his journey eastwards to Bravik. Both made ready for the battle, and arrayed their hosts.

" It is said that in the host of King Harald and with him there was a chief named Brúni, the wisest of all his men, whom he bade to draw up the host, and assign to the chiefs their places under the standards; that of the king stood in the midst of the array, and his bodyguard was placed around it.

" With Harald were: Svein, Sám, Gnepi the Old, Gard, Brand, Blæng, Teit, Tyrving, Hjalti; these were his scalds and champions. In his hird were these champions: Hjört, Borgar, Beli, Barri, Beigad, Tóki. There were the shield-maidens Visma and Heid, each of whom had come with a numerous host. Visma carried Harald's standard, and with her were the champions Karri and Milva. Another shield-

---

[1] Kœnugard (Kief).

maiden was Vebjorg, who came from the south from Gotland, and many champions followed her, of whom the most valiant and renowned were Ubbi Friski (the Frisian), Brat Irski (the Irish), Orm Enski (the English), Búi Bramuson, Ari the One-eyed, and Geiralf.

"Many Vindar (Vends) were in the train of Visma; they were easily recognised, for they had long swords and bucklers,[1] but not long shields like the other men. On one wing was Heid with her standard, and one hundred champions; these were her Berserks, and many chiefs were there too. On the other wing was Haki Höggvinkinni (the cheek-cut one), and the standards were carried in front of him; there were many kings and champions with him, amongst them Alfar and Alfarin, the sons of King Gandalf, who had before been hirdmen at home with Harald. Harald was in a waggon, for he was not able to fight on foot in the battle. He sent Brúni and Heid to see how Hring had arrayed his host, and if he was ready for battle. Brúni said: 'It seems to me that Hring and his host are ready; but he has arrayed them in a strange way; he has drawn up his men in a *swine-array*,[2] and it will not be easy to fight against him.' Harald asked: 'Who has taught Hring to draw up his men in a wedge shape? I thought nobody knew this except myself and Odin; or is Odin going to fail in giving the victory to me? That has never happened before, and even now I ask him not to do it; if he does not want to grant me victory, may he let me fall in the battle with all my host; if he does not wish that the Danes should gain the victory as formerly; all the men who fall on this battle-field I give to Odin.' It was as Brúni had told. Hring had arrayed his men in wedge-shape, so the array looked all the deeper for this; nevertheless it was so broad that one flank reached to the river Vatá, and the other to Bravik.

"Hring had many kings and champions with him; the foremost was King Ali the valiant, who had a great many men and many other famous kings and champions; with him was the champion whose renown is the highest in old Sagas, Störkud the Old Stórverksson, who had been brought up in Norway, in Hördaland, in the island Fenring, and had travelled abroad far and wide, and had been with many kings."

Many other champions had come from Norway to this battle.

---

[1] *Buckler*, probably a smaller shield.
[2] The "wedge shape" was the same as that called *cuneus* by the ancient Romans, and was very old; it is mentioned by Tacitus.

"Thrand from Thrandheim, Thorir from Mœri; Helgi the White, Bjarni, Hafr, Finn from Firda fylki; Sigurd; Erling the Snake, from Jadar; Saga-Eirik, Holmstein the White, Einar from Egda-fylki; Hrut the Rambler, Odd the Wide-travelling, Einar, Ivar.

"The following were the great champions of Hring: Aki, Eyvind, Egil the Squinting, Hildir Gaut, Gudi, Tollus, Stein from the Venern lake, Styr the Strong.

"These also had a host of their own: Hrani Hildarson, Svein Reaper, Hlaumbodi, Soknarsoti, Hrokkel Hœkja, Hrolf the Woman-loving. There were besides: Dag the Stout, Gerdar the Glad, Duk the Vend, Glum the Vermlander, Saxi the Plunderer, Sali the Gautlander.

"These from the Swedish realm: Nori, Haki, Karl Kekkja, Krokar, Gunnfast, Glismak the Good.

"There were from Sigtunir: Sigmund, the Kaupang champion, Tolufrosti.

"Adils the Gay from Uppsalir stood in front of the standards and the shields and not in the Fylkings; Sigvaldi, who had come with eleven ships; Tryggvi and Tvivivil were there with twelve ships; Lœsir had a skeid all manned with champions; Eirik Helsing had a large dragon, well filled with warriors. Champions had also come to Hring from Thelamörk (Thelemarken) and they were least honoured, for they were thought slow-speaking and slovenly; these were: Thorkel the Stubborn, Thorleif Goti the Overbearing, Hadd the Hard, Gretti, Hroald Toe. There was yet one more who had come to Hring: Rögnvald the Tall, or Radard Hnefi, who was the greatest of all champions; he was foremost in the point of the wedge; next to him were Tryggvi and Lœsir, and then the sons of Alrek and Yngvi; then were the Thelemarkians, whom none wanted to have, as they were thought to be of little use; they were great archers.

"When these hosts were ready for battle, both had the horns sounded, and raised the war-cry. The arrays met, and the battle was so severe, that it is said in all old Sagas that no battle in the Northern lands was ever fought with so many and so valiant picked men. When it had raged a little while, Ubbi the Frisian, a champion, advanced in front of the host of Harald, and attacked the snout of the array of Hring, and first of all Rögnvald; their fight was very hard, and terrible blows could be seen in the host where these dauntless champions rushed at each other, dealing many and heavy cuts. Ubbi was such a great champion that he did not cease until their single fight ended by Rögnvald's fall; then he rushed at Tryggvi, and gave him his death wound. When the sons of Alrek saw his appalling rush into the host, they went against him; but he was so hardy and skilled that he slew them both; then he killed Yngvi; and rushed so furiously into the ranks that every one fled before him; he slew all who were foremost in the snout, except those who were fighting other champions.

"When Hring saw this he urged the host not to let one man overcome all, such proud men as there were. He shouted: 'Where is Störkud, who till now always has borne the highest shield (gained victory)?' Störkud answered: 'We have enough to do, lord, but we will try to gain a victory if we can, though where Ubbi is, a man may be fully tried.' At the urging of the king he rushed to the front against Ubbi, and there was a great fight between them with heavy blows, as each of them was fearless. After a while Störkud gave him a large wound, and himself received six, all of them severe, and he thought he had rarely been so hard pushed by a single man. As the arrays were dense they were torn from each other, and so their hand-to-hand fight ended. Then Ubbi slew the champion Agnar, and cleared a path in front of himself, dealing blows on both hands; his arms were bloody up to his shoulders; thereupon he attacked the Thelemarkians. When they saw him they said: 'Now we need not go elsewhere, but let us shoot arrows at this man for awhile, and little as everybody thinks of us let us do the more, and show that we are valiant men.' The most skilled of the Thelemarkians began to shoot at him, namely Hadd the Hard, and Hroald Toe; these men were such excellent archers that they shot twenty-four arrows into his breast; this much was needed to destroy his life. These men slew him, but not before he had slain six champions and severely wounded eleven others, and killed sixteen Swedes and Goths who stood in the front of the ranks. Vebjörg, shieldmaiden, made hard onsets on the Swedes and Goths; she attacked the champion Soknarsoti; she had accustomed herself so well to the use of helmet, coat of mail and sword, that she was one of the foremost in chivalry,[1] as Störkud the Old says; she dealt the champion heavy blows and attacked him for a long while, and with a blow at his cheek cut through his jaw and chin. He put his beard into his mouth and bit it, thus holding up his chin. She performed many great feats. A little after Thorkel the Stubborn, a champion of Hring, met her, and they fiercely attacked each other; finally she fell with many wounds and great courage.

"Great events happened here in a short time; and first one, then the other array got the better; many a man from both

---

[1] Riddaraskap = equestrian exercises.

hosts never returned home, or was maimed. Störkud then made an attack on the Danes, and on the champion Hún, and at last slew him, and a little after one who tried to revenge his death, by name Ella. Then he attacked Borgar, and after a hard fight slew him. Störkud rushed through the ranks with a drawn sword and killed one after another; he cut down Hjört; whereupon Visma, shieldmaiden, who carried the standard of Harald, met him. Störkud made a fierce attack on her. She said to him : 'The fierceness betokening death is over thee, and now thou shalt die, Thurs!'[1] He answered : 'First thou shalt nevertheless let the standard of Harald fall,' and cut off her left hand. Then Brai, Sækalf's father, tried to avenge her, but Störkud pierced him with his sword. In the host in many places could now be seen large heaps of slain and fallen men. A little after Gnepja, a great champion, attacked Störkud ; they fought hard, and Störkud gave him his death-wound. Afterwards he slew Haki, but received many large wounds himself; he was cut on the neck at his shoulders so that one could see into his chest, and on his breast he had a large wound so that his lungs were hanging out, and he had lost one finger on his right hand. When Harald saw that so many of his hird and champions fell, he rose on his knees and took two saxes, whipped fast forward the horse which drew the waggon, and thrust the saxes with both hands and slew many a man with his hands, though he was not able to walk or sit on horseback. The battle went on thus for a while, and the king performed many great deeds. Towards the end of the battle Harald Hilditönn was struck on the head with a club,[2] so that his skull was broken ; and that was his death-wound, and Brúni slew him. When Hring saw the waggon of Harald empty, he knew that he had fallen ; he had the horns blown and shouted that the host should stop. When the Danes became aware of this the battle ceased, and Hring offered truce to the entire host of King Harald, which all accepted "[3] (Sögubrot, c. 9).

Then follows the grand and imposing **funeral of King** Harald, given in Vol. I., page 326.

The Battle of Dúnheidi. —It arose out of a quarrel between Hlöd, son of Heidrek, and the latter's brother, Angantyr, in

---

[1] The word Thurs is used as an abusive term.

[2] *Kylfa.* In several places in the Sagas the use of heavy clubs as weapons is mentioned.

[3] For continuation **see chapter** on "Burials."

regard to the inheritance claimed by the former ; he went to his mother's father, King Humli of Hunaland, who was also his foster-father, and both went to war against Angantyr.

" In the spring they (Hlöd and Humli) gathered a host so large that no man able to fight was left in Húnaland. All from twelve winters old up to sixty went; the host was so large that it could be numbered by thousands, and no less than thousands were in the fylkings. A chief was put over every thousand, and a banner over every array ; five thousand were in every fylking, and thirteen hundred in every thousand, and in every hundred four times forty (160) ; and the fylkings were thirty-three. When this host had gathered it rode to the forest called Myrkvid (the dark wood), which separates Húnaland and Reidgotaland. When they came out of the forest there were level plains, and the land was much cultivated ; on the plains there stood a fine burgh, which Hervör, the sister of Angantyr, and Hlödver and her foster-father Ormar ruled. They were there to defend the land against the host of the Hunar, and had many men.

" One morning at sunrise, as Hervör stood on a tower over the burgh-gate, she saw such large clouds of dust in the direction of the wood that the sun was hidden for a long time ; . then she saw so distinctly through the dust-clouds that it looked as if all were gold under them, with fine and gold-covered shields, gilded helmets, and white *brynjas* ; she saw it was the Huna-host,[1] and a large mass of men. Hervör went quickly down, called her horn-blower, and told him to summon her men together. Then she said : 'Take your weapons and make ready for battle ; and thou, Ormar, shalt ride to the Hunar, and challenge them to battle in front of the southern burgh-gate.' Ormar answered : 'The Hunar have so large a host that we cannot withstand it ; therefore I advise that thou shalt ride to thy brother, King Angantyr, and tell him how matters stand.' Hervör asked : 'Art thou afraid, Ormar, to meet the Hunar ? Do as I said, and challenge them to battle.' Then Ormar rode out of the town towards the Hunar ; he shouted loudly, and told them to ride to the burgh and in front of the southern gate. 'I challenge you to battle there ; those who come first shall wait for the others.' Ormar rode back to the town ; then Hervör was ready for battle, and they

---

[1] The numbers of the Huna-host are differently given in different texts. It is difficult to find the exact numbers, as Latin letters are used, and sometimes forty and sixty (XL., LX.) seem to be confused ; this may be due to the carelessness of the scribe.

rode with all their host out of the burgh against the Hunar. Horns were blown, and thereupon a great battle began, and soon more men fell on Hervör's side, for the Hunar had a far larger host. Ormar rode forward into the host of the Hunar, and slew so many that it would take a long time to enumerate them, and none whom he could reach with the sword had any chance of living; both his arms were bloody up to the shoulders. When Hervör saw that her men fell she became exceedingly angry, and slew men and horses to the right and left; she always slew six men at each blow, and all fled from her. She was more like a lion than a man to look at. Were a man ever so valiant, if he met her, he met his death; she could not, however, withstand the great odds she fought against. When ten thousand of her men had fallen, she shouted to Hlöd and said: 'Come to single fight against me, Hlöd, if thou hast the bold heart of a man.' Hlödver answered: 'I am not thirsty for thy blood, sister.' He entreated his men to take her, 'for she must be first in our power.' When Hervör heard this she spared no one, and slew all that met her, and thus it went on for a long time; then the host attacked her, but she slew all who came near her, until she fell dead from her horse. Large streams of blood gushed out of her mouth, and every man thought she had died from exhaustion; none had ever heard that a woman had fought so valiantly. Hlödver had her laid in a mound with great honour. When Ormar saw that Hervör fell, he galloped much wounded out of the battle, and did not stop until he came to Arheimar; the remnant of Hervör's men fled to the town. When Ormar found King Angantyr, he received him well and asked for tidings. Ormar sang:

'From the south I have come
To tell this tale;
Burned is all
The heath of Myrkvid;
The whole Goth-thjód
Is besprinkled with blood of men.

I know the maiden of Heidrek,[1]
. . . .
Thy sister,

Sank to the ground;
The Hunar have
Slain her,
And many others
Of your thegns;
She was better at ease
In the fight
Than talking with a wooer
Or going to the bench
In a bride-walk.'[2]

"When Angantyr heard this he curled his lips, and it was a long time before he spoke; at last he said: 'In an unbrotherly

---

[1] Part of the text of this stanza is missing.

[2] Walking with her bridesmaids.

manner wast thou treated, my famous sister.' Thereupon he
looked over his hird, and there were not many.   He sang—

' Very many were we	Who would ride
When we drank the mead ;	And carry a shield,
Now we are fewer	And go to meet
When we should be more ;	The Huna-host,
I do not see one	Though I entreated him
Among my men	And paid him with rings.'

" Gizr the Old said—

' I will not	But will however ride
Ask for an eyrir [1]	And carry a shield
Nor a sounding	To challenge the Huna-thjód
Piece of gold,	To the fight.'

" It was the law of King Heidrek, that if a host of foes came
into a land, and the king of the land enhazelled a battle-field
and appointed the place of the battle, the Vikings should
not plunder before the battle was fought.   Gizr war-dressed
himself and took good weapons ; he mounted his horse as if
he were a young man.   He said to the king : ' Where shall
I tell the Hunar to fight ? '
   " Angantyr sang—

' Tell them on Dylgja,	There the Gotar often
And on Dun-heath,	Carried the spear and fought,
And on all	And the renowned got
The Jossar-mountains,	A fine victory.'

   " Gizr rode onwards till he came to the Huna-host ; he rode
so near that he could speak to them, and shouted with a loud
voice—

' Your king is full of fear,	The Jossar-mountains ;
Your king is death-doomed,	May Odin slight you
Your standard floats high,	In every fight,
Odin is angry with you.	And may he let
I challenge you at Dylgja,	The arrow fly,[2]
And at Dun-heath,	As I foretell.'
To battle under	

   " When Hlöd heard the words of Gizr, he sang—

' Take Gizr	(Who has) come from Ar-
The man of Angantyr	heimar.'

---

[1] Money.
[2] The custom of throwing a spear over   the host to give it to **Odin.**

286

" King Humli said—

' We shall not	Who alone
Slay the messengers	On a journey go.'

"Gizr said: 'The Hunar cannot, nor can their hornbows make away with us.' He pricked his horse with his spurs, and rode to Angantyr, went before him and greeted him. The king asked if he had found the Huna-host. Gizr replied: 'I spoke to them, and summoned them to battle-field on Dun-heath in Dylgja-dales.' Angantyr asked how many warriors the Hunar had. Gizr answered: 'Great is their mass; thirty-three fylkings, five thousand men in each fylking, thirteen hundred in each thousand, a hundred and sixty men in each hundred.'

"King Angantyr then had a war-arrow sent, and sent men in every direction, and summoned every one who was willing to help him and could wield weapons; thereupon he went to Dun-heath with his men, and had fifty thousands; the Huna-host came against him, and it is said that the odds were so great at first, that seven were against one of Angantyr's men. Both raised their war-booths, and slept during the night.

"Next morning they prepared for battle and drew up their arrays; the horns were blown so that they were heard twenty miles away in every direction, and the land shook as if hanging by a thread. Then the array closed; first spears and arrows, shafts and gaflok (a kind of arrow), cross-bows and pole staffs (poles with iron points) were shot, and all that could kill a man was aloft, and that went on for a long time. When the shooting ceased they drew their swords, and a hard hand-to-hand fight began, and kept on all that day; then they went to their war-booths in the evening. Now a third of Angantyr's men had fallen, but few of the Hunar; warriors gathered round Angantyr by night and day from every direction. Early in the morning they began the fight, and it was no less hard than the first day; there was many a shield broken, many a brynja torn, and many a good rider lost his life; thus it went on all day; again more men fell on Angantyr's side, and the night ended the fight. In the same way it went on the third day; they fought till night, and the Hunar had better success. The fourth day they called all their men by the blowing of horns to the battle-field, and began the fight with an immense beating of drums and sounding of horns, and then there was a great slaughter among the men of Angantyr. Gizr the Old saw this, and could not stand it; he rode forward into the Huna-host, as if he were very young, and slew so many that it would take a long time to enumerate them; no shield was so hard, and no armour so safe, that it could resist his blows. Ormar also fought exceedingly well in the Gota-host, though the wounds he had got in the former battle were scarcely cured. Wherever Angantyr went among the host all drew back; no one whom he was able to reach with *Tyrfing* had a chance to live; now so much blood was on the battle-field that it reached up to the belt (of the warriors).

"At the end of the day they went to their tents, and dressed the wounds of their men. The Gotar grumbled much, for the Hunar always had the best of it. Still they went to the battle the fifth day, and defended themselves valiantly, for Angantyr always fought most bravely. Late in the day they heard a war-blast and beating of drums; Herlaug was there with sixty thousand men to help Angantyr. Angantyr said he was welcome in his need; then they raised war-booths for themselves, and the host slept during the night. When it was light enough for fighting they began the battle; so many fell that day that no one knew their number, and the horses waded in the blood up to the saddle-girths; they could no longer fight in the battle-field because of the bodies of the dead, and the battle turned much against the Hunar. The ninth day Hlöd sent Angantyr word that they should rest themselves that day in order to make handles to the spears and repair their shields. Angantyr assented. None of the chiefs were then wounded. Angantyr had no fewer men than when the battle began (fifty thousand) for warriors had gathered to him all the time by night and day; Hlöd had no more left of his host than forty thousand, and of his men three times one hundred thousand, and eight hundred had fallen. It is not told how many Angantyr had lost, and old sagas name this battle only as the greatest north of the sea.

"When the tenth day came, they wanted to fight it out, so the one or the other should be free at night. Hlödver urged the Hunar on as well as he could, and said it would not be easy to ask the Gotar to spare their lives; 'I want to find Gizr the Old before this battle is ended, for we have something to talk over.' On the other side Angantyr said to his men: 'Let us go forward like warriors, and defend our freedom and foster-land.' Herlaug replied he would willingly follow him, and he had to take revenge on the Hunar for his sister's daughter. Then both the hosts put horns to their mouths and blew a war blast, so that the mountains echoed it, and it could be heard more than twenty miles away when they rode to the battle. Then they drew their swords and began fighting, and no man's courage needed to be sneered at. Hlöd rode forth foremost of his men, and slew warriors to right and left like the most savage lion; and wherever he met a thick array he killed twelve with one blow; fear entered many breasts, and they said that none in the host was his like; he had his arms bloody up to his shoulders, and never ceased with this onset till near mid-day. King Humli fought best of the Hunar next to Hlödver, and none to whom he dealt a sword blow had a chance of living. Of the Gota-host, King Angantyr, Herlaug, and Gizr the Old fought best; Angantyr always slew twelve at a blow if he found them standing together; for a long time the brothers did not look at each other, and rode past each other. Many a thick helmet was cleft, and many a strong brynja torn; there one could see many riders cut asunder and many horses running with their saddles empty. The arrows and the spears flew so thickly that the sun could not be seen, and the din of weapons was so loud that no man understood what was spoken; many events took place, though few are mentioned here.

"King Humli and Ormar met in the battle, and exchanged hard blows, and at last Ormar fell dead. Gizr the Old saw this, and struck at King Humli; the sword hit his shoulder, and cut off his arm and his side; the king fell dead from his horse. Hlöd saw this, and rode to Gizr and smote on his helmet with all his strength, and cleft the head, the brynja, the body, the saddle and the horse through the middle; the sword stuck in the ground. Herlaug was near, and rode to Hlödver and said: 'I am daring enough to slay this Troll, or I will get a blow from him like that which Gizr got.' He struck at Hlödver with all his strength, and hit his helmet and cut off the part he hit; then his sword was turned to the shoulder, and cut the brynja, and Hlödver was slightly wounded; then he smote at Herlaug, who retreated; nevertheless the sword-point touched his breast, and cut his brynja and his belly open. Angantyr saw this, and riding forward between them, struck at Hlödver with Tyrfing. Hlödver parried with his sword, and Tyrfing hit it in the middle; it gave a loud clang; they fought thus long during the day that Angantyr could neither hit him with thrust nor blows; then Angantyr cut both the guards off Hlödver's sword with *Tyrfing*, but he did not slacken at that. Now Hlöd smote on Angantyr's helmet, but it was so hard that the blow did no harm; the sword broke in two where Tyrfing had hit it before. Once more Angantyr struck at Hlödver, but he parried with the rest of his sword; Tyrfing hit his shoulder at the breast, and its point went inwards; Angantyr did no more, and they parted thus; the battle at once ceased. So many were slain of the Huna-host that only three hundred men lived of all the great number, and these were all wounded and tired; fifteen thousand lived of Angantyr's and Herlaug's men. Angantyr offered peace to the Hunar, which they willingly accepted. He went to search for Herlaug, and at last found him; he had ridden far away from the battle-field to the war-booths, and lay near to the king's tent; he had wrapt clothes round his belly, and could not speak; the king carried him to his tent, and sewed his belly together with a silken thread, and then laid him in a silk-bed; it had become dark and they went to sleep during the night.

"Next morning the king caused the battle-field to be searched, and no man was found living; all who could not leave the battle-field were drowned in the blood. The king searched for Hlödver, and found him dead on a high hill; then he sang—

' I offered thee, brother,
  Uncut rings,
Property and many treasures
For which thou didst yearn most;
Now thou hast neither
  Bright rings
Nor land
As reward for this battle.
We are cursed, brother,
I have become thy slayer;
That will never be forgotten;
Evil is the decree of the Nornir.'

"Angantyr had him laid in a mound on the hill where he had fallen, and three of the foremost men before named with him; but all the common men were heaped together into large piles, and covered with mould; the place where the slain lay was eight miles in circumference; the mounds may be seen this day. It is said that Reidgotaland and Hunaland are now called Thydskaland (the Scandinavian name for Germany); Thydskaland numbers twelve kings' realms as Norway. It is not mentioned whether Angantyr subjugated Hunaland or not. King Angantyr ruled Reidgotaland till his death, and was very like his grandfather, King Höfund; his son was Heidrek Ulfsham (wolf-skin), who got the kingship after his father, and held it for a long time " (Hervarar Saga, c. 17).

The whole Saga literature teems with figurative expressions and expressions showing the warlike character of the race.

In no other language do we find such poetical and forcible expressions for battles, weapons of offence and defence, ships, blood, &c., as those given by the people of the North. The following are a few of the figurative expressions used for battles:

The Odin's storm, Odin's rain, the Valkyrjas' storm, the weapon's wind, the song of the spears, the din of spears, the weapon's-thing, the sword's game, the Ran's battle (the goddess of the sea), the Thing of Gunn (a Valkyrja), the judgment of the weapons, the storm of weapons, the storm of wounds, the iron voice, the trial of helmets, the ground reddener, the storm of war-kings, the rattling wind of Göndul, the spell song of Odin, the song of Brúni (Odin), the anger of Ódin, the Yule of Hugin (one of the ravens of Odin), the thaw of Göndul, the shower of Ali (a sea-king), and other celebrated sea Vikings, the uproar of the sea.

Warriors were often called :

The thegn of the rain of swords, the helmet heeder, the diminisher of peace, the lord of the battle, the trier of weapons, the feeder of the wolf, the raven-feeder, the servant of the High one (Odin), the oak of Odin, the dyer of hedges, the bush of Odin, the field-reddener, the reddener of the mouth of Hugin (Odin's raven), the dyer of the brynias, the waterer of the wolves, the reddener of eagles' soles (claws), the breaker of brynias, the urger of swords' play, the crane of battle, the cheerer of the wolf, the raven starver, the steerer of the shield.

Blood is called :

The dew of the sword, the dew of Skogul, the dew of arrows, the wine of the corpse, the surf of the wound, the wine of the wolf, the sweat of the wounds, the drink of Hugin, the beer of the battle-ground, the lather, foam, froth of weapons, the mighty fjords of swords, the tears of the sword, the ale of the wolf, the rain of the wound, the stream of the sword, the liquid of life, the feast of the birds of battle, the wine of the hawk, the rivulet of the wound.

The raven and eagle were called :

The oath brother of the eagle, the wound-bird, Odin's hawk, the gull of the wound.

The wolf was called :

The grey deer, the boar of the slain, the dog of the nornir, the horse of the Jotun, the dog of Odin, &c.

Horses were sometimes called :

The bloody-hoofed one, the silver-maned, the gold-maned, the galloping fire, the deer of the saddle, the ship of the ground, the wind, the gilded hoofed, the noisy goer, &c.

Fire, so often used for burning houses, is called :

The brother of the wind, the thief of the house, the wolf of the hall, the dog of the embers, the noise maker.

2 G

CHAPTER XIX.

SOME EXPEDITIONS AND DEEDS OF GREAT VIKINGS.

(*Continued.*)

Ragnar Lodbrok—His voyages and wars—His death in England—The sons of Ragnar Lodbrok—Ivar revenges his father's death—Wide extent of the expeditions of Ragnar's sons—Ivar king in England.

AFTER King Hring's death his son Ragnar **assumed** the sovereignty of Sweden and Denmark, whereupon several kings threw off their subjection and claimed independence, because he was a young man and appeared to them little fitted for counsels or ruling the land.

There was then a jarl in Western Gautaland called Herraud; he was the jarl of King Ragnar. He was a wise man and a great warrior. He had a daughter, who was called Thora Borgarhjort (the hart of the burgh). Ragnar Lodbrok [1] was married to Thora. Their children were Agnar and Eirik, and Alof,[2] who was married to Hunda-Steinar Jarl in England. Their son was Bjorn,[3] father of Audun Skokul, father of Thora Moshals, mother of Ulfhild, who was married to Gudbrand Kula; their daughter was Asta, mother of St. Olaf.

---

[1] Lod-Brók = Hairy breeches. He made a dress of hairy breeches and a hairy cloak, which he boiled in pitch and then hardened: this was done in order that he should be able to attack the serpent which watched over Thora, who was said to surpass all other women in beauty as the hart does other animals, and was most accomplished in all handiwork. Afterwards he appears to have married Aslaug, the daughter of Sigurd Fafnisbani by Brynhild. They begat several children. The oldest, Ivar, had no bones in his body, but was very wise; the others were Bjorn, Hvitserk, Rognvald, and Sigurd (Snake-eye).

[2] From Landnama we find that Ragnar had been previously married, and had other children in addition to those already enumerated.

[3] Another son of Hundasteinar and Alof was named Eirik, father of Sigurd Bjódaskalli, father of Vikinga Kári, father of Bödvar, Vigfús and Eirik, who was the father of Ástrid, mother of King Olaf Tryggvason. (Landnama, p. 234.)

" Now it is told that Ragnar sat at home in his realm, and knew not where his sons were; nor did his wife Randalin know, and he heard every one of his men say that no one could equal his sons, and he thought that no men could equal them in renown. He pondered on what fame he might seek which would be as lasting. At length he resolved to engage craftsmen, and had wood felled in the forest for two large ships, and men saw that they were two knörrs[1] so large that none equal to them had been built in Northern lands; he also made great war preparations all over his realm. By this men saw that he was going on an expedition out of the country, and the rumour of it spread widely in the neighbouring lands, so that their rulers, fearing that they would not be left at peace in their realms, proceeded to guard their lands against the invader, in case he might come. Randalin asked Ragnar whither he was going. He told her he intended to go to England with only two knörrs, and as many men as they could hold. Randalin answered: 'This expedition seems to me rash. I think it better for thee to have more and smaller ships.' He said: 'It would be but a poor exploit to win lands with many ships, but there is no example of a land like England having been conquered by two ships; if I am defeated, the fewer ships I take out of the country the better.' Randalin said: 'It seems to me as costly to make ready these ships as to have many longships for this expedition; thou knowest that it is difficult to land with ships in England, and if thy ships are lost thy men cannot defend themselves, though they get ashore, if an army attacks them, and longships are more convenient for effecting a landing than knerrir.' Then he had his ships prepared and got men so that they were fully manned; people talked much about his intention. When his ships and men were ready and a fair wind came, he said he would go down to his ships. When he was ready she led him down to the ships, and before they parted she said she would reward him for the shirt he had given to her. He asked her how, and she sang:

'I give thee the long shirt, Wounds will not bleed
  Nowhere sewn, Nor will edges bite thee
  Woven with a loving mind In the holy garment;
  Of hair——[2] It was consecrated to the gods.'

" In making his voyage to England he met with adverse

---

[1] In Ragnar's Sons' Saga, ch. ii., the two are said to be built in Norway. Ragnar says to Aslaug: "I have had two knörrs built in Vestfold, because his realm extended to the Dofrafjalls and Lidandisness."

[2] Following word obscure.

gales, so that both his ships were wrecked on the coast of England, but all his men got ashore with their clothes and weapons. Thereupon he succeeded in taking villages and burghs and castles, one after the other. King Ella, who ruled England, had heard that Ragnar had left his country; he sent men to tell him when he had landed; they came and brought news of Ragnar. Ella sent messengers all over his realm, summoning every man to come that could wield a shield and ride on a horse and dared fight; he thus gathered such a large host that it was a wonder, and made ready for battle. Ella said to his men: 'If we gain the victory in this battle, and you see Ragnar, you must not attack him with weapons, for he has sons who sooner or later will avenge his death.' Ragnar made ready for battle, and used the cloth which Randalin had given him to be used as a coat-of-mail, and had the spear in his hand with which he slew the serpent that lay round the hall of Thóra, which no other man dared to face; he had no armour except a helmet. When they met the fight began. Ragnar had far fewer men. Many of Ragnar's men fell after a short time, but where he went himself his foes drew back, and that day he walked through their ranks; whenever he cut or thrust at shields, coats-of-mail or helmets, his blows were so heavy that nothing stood against them, but never did any blow or shot harm him; he got no wounds, and slew many of King Ella's men. In the end, when all Ragnar's men had fallen, he was surrounded by shields and taken. He was asked who he was, but was silent and gave no answer. Ella said: 'That man must be punished if he will not tell who he is; now throw him into a snake-pit and let him sit there a long time, and if he says anything by which we can see that he is Ragnar, he shall be taken away as soon as possible.' So Ragnar was taken there and sat there a long time, and the snakes did not attack him. People said, 'This is a great man; the weapons did not wound him to-day, and now the snakes do no harm to him.' Ella told them to take off his outer garment, and when they had done so the snakes attacked him all over his body. He said: 'The pigs would grunt now if they knew what the old one[1] is suffering;' and though he said this they yet knew not that he was Ragnar or any other king. He sang:

'I have fought battles
Fifty and one
Which were famous;
I have wounded many men.

I little thought that snakes
Would cause my death;
Often that happens
Which one least expects.

---

[1] The old one = Ragnar; the pigs = his sons.

The pigs would grunt
If they knew the hog's suffering;
The gnawing hurts me;
The snakes thrust in their snouts
And stick to me cruelly;
They have sucked me;
Soon shall I be a corpse;
I will die among them.'

"He died, and was taken away. Ella saw that it was Ragnar. But Ella pondered how he should succeed in retaining his realm, and wondered how the sons of Ragnar would receive the news of their father's death. He had a ship made ready, and appointed a wise and hardy man to command it; he manned the ship well, and told the men that he sent them to Ivar and his brothers to tell them of the fall of their father; most of them had little mind to go. Ella said: 'Notice carefully how each of the brothers receives this news; then go your way when you get a fair wind.' He had them so well equipped that they needed nothing; their journey was prosperous.

"The messengers (of Ella) came with their men to the burg, where the sons of Ragnar were enjoying a feast, and went into the hall where they drank, and to the high-seat, in which Ivar (the eldest of Ragnar's sons) sat. Sigurd (snake-eye) and Hvitserk the bold sat playing chess, while Björn jarnsida (ironside) was sharpening a spear-shaft on the floor. When the messengers came up to Ivar they greeted him respectfully; he answered their greeting, and asked whence they were and what tidings they had to tell. Their leader said they were Enskir menn (English men), and that Ella had sent them with the tidings of the fall of their father Ragnar. Hvitserk and Sigurd immediately dropped the chessboard, and listened attentively to this news. Björn stood on the floor of the hall, leaning on his spear-shaft. Ivar inquired of them minutely how his death had occurred. They told all that had taken place after he came to England till he lost his life. When it was told that Ragnar had said 'the pigs would grunt,' Björn moved his hands on the spear-shaft, and grasped it so firmly that the print of his fingers could be seen on it afterwards; when the messengers had finished, Björn shook his spear so that it brake in two. Hvitserk had in his hand a chess-piece which he had taken, and squeezed it so hard that blood started out from under each of his nails; and Sigurd had a knife in his hand and was trimming his nails at the time, and listened so attentively that he felt nothing until the knife had cut him to the bone, and did not move. Ivar inquired about everything as minutely as he could, while his face became red, blue and pale by turns, and his features were so distorted that all his skin became swollen on account of the anger in his breast. Hvitserk began to speak, and said they could most speedily commence their revenge by killing the messengers of King Ella. Ivar said : 'That shall not be; they shall go in peace wherever they like, and if they lack anything they may tell me, and I will give it to them.' When they had performed their errand they went out of the hall to their ship, and with a fair wind sailed out to sea, and returned in safety to Ella.

"When the messengers of Ella had gone, the brothers met to talk over how they should avenge their father. Ivar said: 'I will not take part in or gather men for that, because Ragnar met with the fate I anticipated. His cause was bad; he had no reason to fight against King Ella, and it has often happened that when a man wanted to be overbearing and wrong others it has been the worse for him; I will take wergild from King Ella if he will give it.' When his brothers heard this they became very angry, and said they would never so disgrace themselves, even on his recommendation. 'People will say that our prowess is departed if we do not avenge our father. We have been all over the world on warfare, and slain many innocent men. That shall not be; we will fit out every seaworthy ship in Denmark; every man who is able to carry a shield against Ella shall go with us.' Ivar said he and the ships he commanded, except his own ship, should remain behind. When people heard that Ivar was not going, the brothers obtained fewer men, but nevertheless went. As soon as they landed in England Ella heard of it, and had his horn blown, and bade all who were willing to follow him; he got so many men that no man could number them, and went against them. They met, and Ivar was not in that battle, the end of which was that Ragnar's sons fled, and Ella got the victory. During the flight Ivar said: 'I will not go back; I will try whether King Ella will give me some honour or not; I will rather take wergild from him than be again defeated like this.' Hvitserk said they could not prevent him from doing what he liked, but they would never take wergild. Ivar said he would leave them, and asked them to rule over their realm and send him as much movable property as he wanted. When he had said this he took leave of them and went to Ella, and when he came before him he saluted him, and said : 'I have come to you and want to be reconciled to you, and get as much honour as you will give me; I see that I cannot defeat you, and will rather get from you such honour as you will give me than lose more men or my own life.' Ella answered : 'Some say thou art not to be trusted, and that thou often speakest fair when thou thinkest foul, and it is not easy to be a match for thee and thy brothers.' Ivar said: 'I ask for little; if thou grantest it I swear never to go against thee.' The king asked what he wanted. Ivar answered: 'I want thee to give me as much of thy land as an oxhide stretches over, and this ground shall be marked out; I want no more, and thou wilt do me no honour if thou wilt not do this.' Ella said: 'I cannot see that it will do us harm if thou ownest so much of my land, and I will give it thee if thou wilt swear not to fight against me; I fear not thy brothers if thou art faithful to me.' It was accordingly agreed that Ivar should swear not to fight against him, nor give any advice to harm him, and in return he obtained as much English land as the largest oxhide he could procure stretched over. Ivar got the hide of a bull, and had it soaked and stretched three times; then he had it cut into very thin strips, and the fleshy side separated from the hairy side; and when the strips were joined the length of the thong was astonishing. He stretched this out on a broad field, and the ground surrounded by it was so large that a great burgh could stand on it, and on the outskirts he had ground marked out for large burgh-walls; he engaged many workmen, and had many houses built on that field, and raised a great burgh called[1] Lundúnaborg,[2] which is the greatest and most famous of all burghs in all the Northern lands. He used all the loose property for making this burgh; he was so liberal that he gave gifts with both hands, and his wisdom was so renowned that all came to him for advice in difficulties; he settled all disputes to the satisfaction of the parties, and was so beloved that he had a friend in every man; he helped Ella much in ruling the land, and settled many matters for him without the king requiring to look at it afterwards. And when he was thought to be the owner of all wisdom he sent men to his brothers to ask them for gold and silver, as much as he wanted to have. Messengers came to the brothers, told their errand, and how it had fared with Ivar, for no one knew what devices he had in his mind; the brothers saw that his mind was not as it used to be. They sent as much as he wanted; and when the messengers returned to Ivar, he gave all that he had received to the leading men in the country, and thus drew them away from King Ella, so that they all promised to be quiet in case of war. When he had done this he sent men to tell his brothers that he wanted them to levy a host in all the lands which belonged to their realm, and bring every man they could get. When the brothers got this message they knew that he now thought it likely they would be victorious. They

---

[1] In another the name is given as Jorvik or York.

[2] It may have been a suburb of the present London.

gathered men from Denmark, Gautland, and all the realms they ruled over, and having drawn together an enormous host, they sailed to England, and stopped neither night nor day, as they did not want their journey to be heard of. The news, however, reached Ella, who summoned his men, but got few, for Ivar had drawn many from him. Ivar went to him and said he would do what he had sworn, but could not rule over his brothers' doings, though he might see them and find out if they would withdraw the host and do no more harm. He went to them and urged them to go forward and engage in a battle, for the king had much fewer men. They answered that he need not urge them on, as their mind was the same. Ivar told King Ella that they were so eager and incensed that they would not listen to his words. 'When I wanted to reconcile you they remonstrated; I will do as I swore, and not fight against thee; I and my men will be quiet while the battle goes as it may.' Ella saw the host of the brothers, which ran forward in great haste. Ivar said: 'Now, King Ella, array thy men, as I foresee they will make a severe attack for some time.' When they met there was a great fight, and the sons of Ragnar rushed fiercely forward through the ranks of Ella's host, and they were so eager that they only thought of doing as much as they could, and the battle was both long and hard. At last Ella and his men fled, and he was taken. Ivar was present, and told them how to slay him. He said: 'Now it is time to remember what kind of death he chose for our father; the man who is best skilled in wood-carving shall mark an eagle as deep as he can on his back, and that eagle shall be reddened with his blood.' The man who was told to do this did as Ivar said. Ella got so deep a wound by this that he died, and now it seemed to them they had avenged their father. Ivar said he would give them his part in their realm, but rule England himself.

"Thereupon Hvitserk, Björn and Sigurd went home to their realm, and Ivar remained and ruled over England. After this their host was less concentrated, and they made warfare in various countries. Once Hvitserk, when his mother Randalin was old, made warfare in eastern lands, and such an overwhelming force met him that he could not raise his shield, and was captured. He chose as the means of his death that a pyre should be made of human heads, and he be burnt on it; and thus he died. When Randalin heard this, she sang:

'A son whom I owned   He was warmed by the heads
Met death in the eastern lands;   Of men slain in battle;
Hvitserk was he called,   The strong-minded chief
Nowhere willing to flee;   Chose that death before he died.'

"From Sigurd Snake-eye there descended a great family; his daughter was Aslaug, mother of Sigurd Hart, who was father of Ragnhild, mother of Harald Fairhair, who first ruled all Norway alone. Ivar ruled England till his death from disease. When on his death-bed he told them to carry him to a certain spot exposed to attacks, and said he was confident that those who landed there would not obtain a victory. When he died they did as he said, and he was buried in a mound. It is told by many that when Harald Sigurdsson came to England he landed where Ivar was, and he was slain in that expedition. When Vilhjálm bastard (William the Conqueror) came ashore, he went there and broke Ivar's mound, and saw that his body had not decayed. Then he had a large pyre made and Ivar burned on it. Thereupon he landed and got the victory. Björn Ironside had many descendants, among them Thórd, a great chief who lived at Höfdi in Höfdaströnd (Iceland)" (Ragnar Lodbrók's Saga, cc. 10–19).

After the battle just mentioned on the preceding pages we have an account of the doings of Ragnar Lodbrók's sons; and here again we are reminded that their kinsmen owned part of England before them.

"After this battle Ivar[1] became king over the part of England which his kinsmen had owned before. He had two brothers born of a concubine, Yngvar and Hustó; they tortured King Játmund the holy at Ivar's bidding, and then conquered his realm. The sons of Ragnar made war in many lands—in England, Valland, Frakkland, and Lumbardi. It is told that they came furthest when they took the burg called Luna, and secretly intended to go to Rome and take it; their expeditions were the most famous throughout all the Northern lands of the Danish tongue. When they came back to Denmark they divided the lands. Björn Ironside got Uppsalir, the whole of Sweden, and what belonged to it. Sigurd Snake-eye[2] got Selund (Zeeland), Skani, Halland, the whole of Vik (Christianiafjord), Agdir to Lidandisness, and a great part of Upplönd; but Hvitserk got Reidgotaland and Vindland" (Ragnar's Sons' Saga, c. 3).

---

[1] Ivar, who, according to the Sagas, did great things in England, is no doubt the same man who is called in the chronicles Ingvr, Lodbrók's son, who in 870 killed King Eadmund the Holy.

The English writers mention Ingvar and Ubbi, the sons of Lodbrók, as having taken a leading part in killing the king; and as the Sagas don't speak of any son of Lodbrók who fought in England other than "Ivar," Ingvar and Ivar must be one and the same person.

[2] Sigurd Snake-eye was married to Blœja, daughter of King Ella; their son was Knut, or Horda-Knut, who acquired the realm after his father, and Selund, Skani, and Halland.

From the Sagas we find that even in the times of their father their renown was very great, and their expeditions extended far and wide.

"The sons of Ragnar Lodbrok went thence till they came to a town called Luna, having destroyed nearly every burgh in all Southern realm (Sudrriki); they had become so famous all over the world that there was hardly a little child that knew not their name. They intended not to cease until they came to Romaborg, for they were told that this town was both large, populous, and famous and wealthy; they did not exactly know how far distant it was, but they had so many men that food was not to be procured. In Luna they consulted about the expedition. There came thither an old and grey man, who said he was a beggar, and had been travelling all his life. 'Thou must be able to tell us many tidings we wish to know.' He answered: 'I know of no lands you can ask about, about which I cannot tell you.' 'We want thee to tell us how far it is from here to Romaborg.' He said: 'I can tell you one thing as a mark; you see these iron shoes which I wear? They are now old, and those which I carry on my back are also worn out. When I left Rome I tied on my feet these worn-out ones on my back. They were new then, and I have been on the journey since.' When they heard this, they thought they could not carry out their intention of going to Rome, and so they returned with their host, taking many burghs on their way which had never been taken before, the traces of which are seen to this day" (Saga of Ragnar Lodbrok, c. 13).

"Sigurd was married to Heluna, daughter of King Ella. The sons of Ragnar, after having ravaged in England, Valland, Saxland, and all the way to Lombardy (Lungbardi), Sweden, Denmark, and Vindland, returned home; they divided between themselves the lands which they had won. Björn Jarnsida (ironside) got in his share both Sweden and Gautland; Sigurd Snake-eye, Eygotaland, Halland, and Skaney; Hvitserk, Reidgotaland (probably some part of Northern Germany), and Vindland.

"When Sigurd Snake-eye was in Denmark, his wife bore a son named Knut; he was born at Hord in Jutland, and on that account was called Horda Knut. King Gorm brought him up. Gorm died on a bed of sickness, while Horda Knut became king of Eygotaland, Skaney, and Halland, for these had been the share of his father Sigurd Snake-eye" (Flateyjarbok; Jomsvikinga Thatt.).

"Ivar the Boneless was long King in England, but had no children, as his nature was such that he had no love lust; but he did not lack wisdom or cruelty, and died from old age in England, and was mourned there. Then were all the sons of Lodbrok dead.

"After Ivar, Adalmund Jatgeirsson got the kingship of England; he was a brother's son of Jatmund (Edgarson) the holy, and he christianized England widely; he took taxes for Northumberland, because it was heathen. After him got the kingship his son Adalbrigt (Ethelbert); he was a good king, and became old. In his old age a Danish host came to England, and their leaders were Knut and Harald, sons of King Gorm. They underlaid (subdued) a large realm in Northumberland which Ivar had owned. King Adalbrigt went against them, and they fought north of Kliflönd (Cleveland), and many Danes fell. The Danes went ashore at Skardaborg (Scarborough) and fought there and got the victory; then they went south to Jorvik (York) and all the people became their men and they were not afraid of themselves (were secure).

"One day in hot weather the men went to swim, and as the king's sons (Gorm's sons) were swimming between the ships men came running down on the shore and shot at them; Knut was struck to death with an arrow; they took the body out to the ships. When the men of the country heard this they gathered so that the Danes could not get ashore any more because of the great number of people (against them), and went back to Denmark. Gorm was then in Jutland. When he heard the news he sank backwards and died of grief the next day after at the same time as he had got the news the day before. Then Harald got the kingship after him over the Dana realm; he was the first of his kinsmen who was baptized" (Ragnar's Sons, c. iv.).

"Sigurd Hjort (hart) was king in Hringariki; he was larger and stronger than any other man, and one of the handsomest men. His father was Helgi Hvassi, and his mother Aslaug, daughter of Sigurd Snake-eye, son of Ragnar Lodbrok. It is told that when Sigurd was twelve winters old he slew Hilde-brand, berserk, in single fight, and twelve berserks in all. He performed many great deeds, and there is a long Saga of him. Sigurd had two children; his daughter Ragnhild surpassed other women and was twenty years old while her brother Guttorm was young. It is told of King Sigurd that he rode alone into unsettled places (deserts) and hunted big and dangerous animals; he always was very eager in that. One day, as was his wont, when he had ridden a long distance, he came to a clearing near Hadaland; here he met the berserk Hake with thirty men, and a fight took place, in which fell Sigurd Hjort and twelve of Hake's men. Hake himself lost one hand, and received three severe wounds. Hake then rode with his men to Sigurd's farm, and captured his daughter. Thus Harald Harfagr, on his mother's side, was descended from Ragnar Lodbrok.

"Halfdan married Ragnhild, and she became a powerful queen. The mother of Ragnhild was Thyri, daughter of Klakk-Harald, King of Jutland, sister of Thyri Danmarkarbot, the wife of Gorm the old Dana king, who then ruled Denmark" (Halfdan the Black's Saga, c. 5).

Here we have an account of a terrible battle, which nevertheless has not been considered as great as that of Bravoll and Dunheath by the people of the North.

"Sigurd Snake-eye, Björn Ironside, and Hvitserk had made warfare widely in Frakkland (France); thereupon Bjorn went home to his realm. Thereafter Ornulf Emperor fought against the brothers and one hundred thousand men fell of the Danes and Northmen. There fell Sigurd Snake-eye and another king, Gudrod, who was the son of Olaf, son of Ring, son of Ingjald, son of Ingi, son of Ring, after whom Ringariki is named; he was the son of Dag and Thora, mother of warriors; they had nine sons, and the family of the Doglings has sprung from them. Helgi the bold, Gudrod's brother, took out of the battle the standard and the shield and the sword of Sigurd Snake-eye. He went home to Denmark with his men and found Aslaug, Sigurd's mother, and told her the tidings.[1] But as Hordaknut was young, Helgi stayed there long with Aslaug to defend the land. Sigurd (Snake-eye) and Blœja had a daughter, who was a twin-sister of Hordaknut. Aslaug gave her her own name and then raised her. Afterwards Helgi the Bold married her; their son was Sigurd Hart; he was the finest, largest, and strongest man seen at that time. But when Sigurd was twelve winters old, then he killed in a single fight (Einvigi) the berserk Hildibrand. After that Klakk Harald gave him in marriage to his daughter Ingiborg. They had two children, Gudthorm and Ragnhild. Then Sigurd heard that King Frodi, his father's brother, was dead, and went northward to Norway, and became king over Ringariki, his kin-inheritance. About him there is a long Saga; for he performed many great deeds. But of his death it is told that he rode out into uninhabited places to hunt game, as was his custom, and there came to him Haki Hadaberserk (berserk from Hadaland) with thirty fully armed men, and fought with him. There Sigurd fell, but had before that slain twelve men, and King Haki had

---

[1] Stanza omitted; corrupted, cannot be made out.

lost his right hand and had besides three other wounds. Thereupon Haki rode with his men to Stein in Ringariki, which was Sigurd's farm, and took away his daughter Ragnhild and his son Gudthorm and a great deal of property home with himself to Hadaland ; and a little later he had a great feast prepared, and intended to keep his wedding, but that was delayed, because his wounds would not get cured. Ragnhild was then fifteen winters old, but Gudthorm fourteen winters. Thus passed the autumn and winter to Yule, while Haki lay sick from his wounds. Then was King Halfdan the Black in Heidmork at his farms. He sent Harek Gand (the wolf, the wizard) with a hundred men, and they crossed on the ice of the Mjors (Mjosen) to Hadaland one night and arrived at dawn to King Haki's farm and took possession of all the doors in the skali, in which the hirdmen slept, and then they went to King Haki's sleeping-chamber (skemma) and took Ragnild and Gudthorm her brother, and all the property that was there and carried away with them, and burned the skali with all the hirdmen and then went away. But King Haki arose and dressed himself and walked after them for awhile, and when he came down to the ice, then he turned the guards of his sword downward and threw himself upon its point and died therefrom, and is moundlaid on the brink. King Halfdan saw that they were driving across the ice with a tented waggon, and therefore thought that they had performed his errand as he wanted it. He then sent word all around the neighbourhood, and invited all the prominent men of Heidmork, and that day had a great feast and held his wedding with Ragnhild, and they then lived together for many days. Their son was King Harald Fairhair, who was the first sole king of Norway " (Ragnar Lodbrok's Sons, c. 5).

"There ruled in Denmark two kings, Sigrfrodi and Halfdan, and after them Helgi ; the latter had a fight with Olaf King of Sweden in which he fell, and Olaf afterwards ruled long over Denmark (Danmork) and Sweden, dying on a sick bed. After him Gyrd and Knut took the kingship in Denmark, and after them Siggeir, followed by Olaf Kinriksson, who was a nephew of Moallda the Stout (digra), mother of Ivar Vidfadmi ; he ruled long as king over Jutland, and was called Olaf Enski (the English). His son Grim Gani, who took the kingship after his father, was father of Audulf the Rich, tax-king in Jutland of Ragnar Lodbrok's sons. Audulf's son Gorm, who also was tax-king in Jutland, was called Gorm the Childless. He was powerful and well loved by his men. He had long ruled over the country at this time " (Flateyjarbok, vol. i.).

CHAPTER XX.

SOME EXPEDITIONS AND DEEDS OF GREAT VIKINGS.

(*Continued.*)

The first Jarl of Normandy—His banishment from Norway—Genealogy of the Jarls of Normandy—Political connection between kings of the North and of England—Jealousy between Athelstan and Harold Fairhair—Hákon of Norway educated in England—Northern chiefs come to the help of English kings—Battle of Brunanburgh.

VERY little is said in the Sagas of Göngu Hrolf, the first jarl of Normandy, for he, like all those who left their country to settle in foreign lands, was forgotten by the scalds at home, as these did not take part in their expeditions. We give here different sagas which confirm each other in regard to him. But the little we have concerning him is extremely interesting, as his descendants conquered England and part of France. All the different Sagas agree in calling him a son of Rognvald jarl of Norway.

The causes which led to his banishment are simply and clearly related.

" Rögnvald Mæra jarl was a very great friend of King Harald, and was much valued by him. Rögnvald was married to Hrolf Nefja's daughter Hild,[1] and had by her the sons Hrolf and Thorir. . . . Hrolf was a great Viking, and so large that no horse could carry him, so that he walked wherever he went, and for this reason he was called Göngu Hrolf (walking Hrolf). He made much warfare in the east. One summer when he returned from ' Vikingry,' or a raiding expedition in the east, he committed acts of depredation in Vikin. King Harald, who was then in Vikin, was very angry when he heard of this, for he had strictly forbidden robbery within his land. He therefore announced at a Thing that he made Hrolf an outlaw from Norway. When Hrolf's mother Hild[1] heard this, she went to

---

[1] Hild is here an abbreviation for Ragnhild.

him to ask for pardon for Hrolf, but the king was so angry that her prayers were of no avail. Then she sang :

Disgrace not Nefja's namesake [1]	It is bad to worry
Nor drive the wolf from the land,	Such a wolf of Ygg's, [3]
The wise kinsman of Höld, [2]	He will not be gentle toward
Why dealest thou thus with him, king?	The king's herds if he runs into the woods. [4]

Göngu Hrolf then went westward across the sea to the Sudrey-jar (Hebrides), and thence west to Valland, and made war there, and got a large jarl's realm, where he induced many Northmen to settle down. It was afterwards called Nordmandi.

"Göngu Hrolf's son 'William' (Vilhjálm) was father of Richard (Rikard), father of Richard the Second, father of Robert Longsword, [5] father of Vilhjalm (William) the Bastard, king of the English, from whom all subsequent English kings are descended. The jarls in Normandi are also of Hrolf's family" (Harald Fairhair's Saga, c. 24).

"Rögnvald jarl of Mæri was married to Ragnhild, daughter of Hrólf Nefja; the first of their sons was Ivar, who fell in the Hebrides on an expedition with Harald Fairhair; the second was Göngu Hrolf, who won Northmandi; from him are descended the Ruda-jarls (Rouen jarls), and the Engla-kings (English kings); the third was Thórir jarl the Silent, who was married to Alöf Arbot, the daughter of Harald Fairhair, and their daughter was Bergljot, mother of Hakon jarl the Power-ful" [6] (Landnama, iv., 8).

"Rögnvald jarl conquered the country with Harald Fair-hair, who gave him the rule over the two Mæri's and Raumsdal. He was married to Ragnhild, daughter of Hrolf Nefja; their son was Hrolf, who won Northmandi. He was so large that no horse could carry him, and he was therefore called Göngu Hrolf. From him are descended the Rouen jarls, and the kings of England" (Flateyjarbok, vol. i.).

"Rögnvald, jarl of Mæri, was the son of Eystein Glumra, son of Ivar Uppland jarl, son of Halfdan the old; Rögnvald was married to Ragnhild, daughter of Hrolf Nefja.

"The sons of Rögnvald were : Ivar, who fell in the Hebrides when with King Harald Fairhair; Göngu Hrolf, who won Northmandi, and from whom the Ruda (Rouen) jarls are

---

[1] Hrolf.

[2] The higher class of landowners.

[3] Ygg (Odin). A wolf of Ygg means a champion.

[4] If he becomes a viking he will not spare Harald's men.

[5] The name Longsword is usually given to Hrolf's son William (Löngumspada).

[6] Then Hákon the Great was the son of the daughter's daughter of Harald Fairhair.

descended, as well as kings of England; and Thorir jarl the Silent, who was married to Harald Fairhair's daughter Arbot, their daughter was Bergljot, mother of Hakon jarl the Great" (Landnamabok, iv. 8).

"King Olaf had been on warfare west in Valland two summers and one winter. Two jarls were then in Valland, Vilhjalm and Rodbert; their father was Rikard Ruda-jarl (jarl of Rouen); they ruled Northmandi.[1] Their sister was Queen Emma, who was married to Adalrad (Engla-king); their sons were Jatmund, Jatvard the Good, Jatvig and Jatgeir. Rikard Ruda-jarl was the son of Rikard son of Vilhjálm Langaspjót (longue epée); he was the son of Göngu Hrölf jarl who won Nordmandi; he was the son of Rögnvald Mæra jarl the Powerful. as before is written. From Göngu Hrölf have sprung the Rúda jarls, and long after they reckoned themselves to be the kinsmen of the chiefs of Norway, and thought so for a long time, and were always great friends of the Northmen, and all of these men had a peace-land in Normandy who would accept it. For the autumn King Olaf came to Normandy, and stayed during the winter in Signa (Seine), and had peace-land there" (St. Olaf's Saga, ch. 19).

Here is the genealogy of the jarls of Normandy.

"King Harald was the son of Halfdan (the Black), king in Uppland; Halfdan the Black's father was Gudröd Veidikonung (hunting king), son of Halfdan, who was called the liberal and food-stingy, for he gave his men as much pay in gold as other kings theirs in silver, but he kept them short in food. The mother of Halfdan the Black was Åsa, daughter of Harald Granraud, King of Agdir.

"The mother of Harald Fairhair was Ragnhild, daughter of Sigurd Hjört (Hart), whose mother was Aslaug, daughter of Sigurd Snake-eye, son of Ragnar Lodbrok.

"Sigurd Snake-eye's mother was Åslaug, daughter of Sigurd Fafnisbani. Sigurd Hjört was married to Thyri, daughter of Klakkharald of Jutland and sister of Thyri, Denmark's improver (Danmarkarbot), who was married to Gorm (the Old) King of Denmark" (Flateyjarbok, vol. i., ch. i.).

The testimony of the Sagas, as we see, is here unmistakable, clear, and to the point. When we compare them with the Frankish annals and their fabulous and strange stories and discordant dates, we cannot but give the preference to the Sagas.

---

[1] Northmandi; *th* is here in the place of the soft Icelandic *d* or *ð*.

" Alfred the Powerful (*riki*) ruled over England; he was the first of his kinsmen who was absolute king in the days of Harald Fairhair, King of Norway. After him his son Edward was king; he was the father of Athelstan the Victorious (the foster-father of Hakon the Good), who was king after his father. There were several brothers, sons of Edward. When Athelstan became king those chiefs who had lost their lands through his forefathers rose against him, thinking it would be easier to regain their lands from so young a king. These chiefs were Bretar (Britons) and Skotar (Scots) and Irar (Irish). Athelstan gathered a host, and gave pay to every man, both foreigners and natives, who wanted it. The brothers Thórólf and Egil were going southward past Saxland and Flæmingjaland (Flandre); when they heard that the King of England needed men, and as there was likelihood of getting much property, they decided to go thither with their men. They went in the autumn to the king, who received them well, for he thought that their following would be a great help; he offered them pay for their service to defend his kingdom; they made an agreement and became his men. England had been Christian for a long time when this happened; the king was a good Christian, and was called Æthelstan trufasti (constant in belief). He asked Thórólf and Egil to be *prime-signed*, as was then very usual, both among traders and those who went into the service of Christians; for those who were prime-signed had full intercourse with both Christians and heathens, but at the same time believed what they liked best. Thórólf and Egil did so at his request. They had three hundred men in the service of the king " (Egil's Saga, c. 50).

The following shows the jealousy that existed between the two kings, Æthelstan and Harald Fairhair of Norway.

" At this time Æthelstan, who was named the victorious and the faithful, had taken the kingdom in England. He sent to Norway a messenger, who went in before King Harald and handed him a sword with golden guards and hilt, and its scabbard was ornamented with gold and silver, and set with gems. The messenger turned the handle of the sword towards the king, and said: ' Here is a sword, that King Æthelstan said thou shouldst take.' The king took hold of the hilt, and the messenger added: ' Thou didst take hold of this sword, as our king wanted thee to. Thou shalt now be his *thegn* (subject), because thou didst take it by the hilt.' Harald then saw that this had been done to deride him, for he did not want to be the *thegn* of any man. He nevertheless remembered his habit,

2 H

whenever he got angry, to first keep quiet and let his anger subside, and then look at the matter calmly. He did thus, and brought the matter before his friends; and they all thought it right to do as had been done by. He thereupon allowed King Æthelstan's men to depart unharmed.

"Hauk Hábrok (high breeches) was with King Harald. He was a good messenger on all difficult errands, and dear to the king. The summer after this King Harald entrusted his son Hakon to the hands of Hauk, and sent him westward to England to King Æthelstan. Hauk found him in London, at a great feast. He went into the hall with thirty men, and said to them: ' We will so arrange that the one who enters last shall go out first, and we will all stand in a line before the king's table, and each one shall have his shield on his left side, and hide it under his cloak.' He took the boy Hakon on his arm, and they entered; he saluted the king, who bid him welcome; then he seated the boy on King Æthelstan's knee. The king looked at him, and asked why he did this. Hauk replied: 'King Harald of Norway asks thee to foster for him this child of his bond-woman.' King Æthelstan at this became very angry, seized a sword near him, and drew it as if he wanted to slay the boy.

"Hauk then said: 'Thou hast now seated him on thy knee, king; and murder him thou mayest if thou wilt; but by this thou wilt not exterminate all King Harald's sons.' Hauk and his men walked out and went to their ships, and when they were ready they set sail and returned to Norway. King Harald was well pleased with the result of their errand, for it is said that the man who fosters the child of another is of lower rank. By these doings of the kings it could be seen that each wanted to be greater than the other; but nevertheless each retained his rank, for each was over-king over his kingdom until his dying day" (Olaf Tryggvason's Saga, pp. 16, 17).

The following Saga corroborates the story of Hakon being sent over to England for his education, and indirectly shows the intercourse which existed between England and Norway.

"King Æthelstan had Hakon baptized and taught the true creed, good habits, and all kinds of courtesy. He loved him more than any one else, kinsman or not, and every one who knew him liked him. He was afterwards called Æthelstan's foster-son. He was larger and stronger and handsomer than other men, and the greatest man of *idróttir,* wise and eloquent, and a good Christian" (Olaf Tryggvason's Saga, vol. i.; Fms.).

We see how insecure at the time of Æthelstan was the position of a king or a sub-king, and how much they depended on the help of the powerful and independent warriors by whom they were surrounded, and without whom they could not have ruled.

"When Eirik (blood-axe), a Norwegian, saw that he could not resist the host of (his brother) Hákon, he sailed westwards across the sea with those who wished to follow him; he went first to the Orkneys, and took many men with him thence. Then he sailed to England and made warfare in Scotland wherever he landed; he also made warfare in the North of England. Adalstein, king of the English, sent word to Eirik offering him a realm in England, as his father King Harald had been a great friend of his, and he wished to show that to his son. They made an agreement, so that King Eirik got *Nordimbraland* (Northumberland), in order to keep it for King Adalstein, and defend it against the Danir and other vikings. Eirik was to be baptized, and his wife and his children, and all the men that had followed him there. Eirik agreed, was baptized, and adopted the true belief. *Nordimbraland* is one-fifth of England. He sat in *Jórvik* (York), where the sons of Ragnar Lodbrók are said to have sat before. *Nordimbraland* is for the most part inhabited by Northmen, since the sons of Ragnar won it; the Danir and the Northmen often attacked the land after they had lost it. Many of the names of the land are in the *Norræna* (Northern tongue): *Grimsbær* (Grimsby), and *Hauksfljót* (Hauks-fleet), and many others" (Heimskringla, Hakon the Good, c. 3).

"King Eirik bloodaxe kept many Northmen, who had come westward with him, and his friends continued to come from Norway. As he had little land, he went on warfare during the summer, ravaged in Scotland and the Hebrides, Ireland, and Bretland, and thus won property. Æthelstan died on a sickbed (A.D. 940); he had been king fourteen winters, eight weeks and three days. Thereupon his brother Edmund became King of England; he did not like the Northmen, and was not fond of Eirik, and it was said that he wished to place another king over Northumberland. When Eirik heard this he went on a western viking expedition, taking with him Arnkel and Erlend, the sons of Torf-Einar, from the Orkneys. Then he sailed to the Hebrides, and there many vikings and hostkings joined him. He went first to Ireland, then he crossed to Bretland,

and plundered there. After this he sailed south to England,[1] and ravaged there, as in other places; but all the people fled wherever he went. As he was a very valiant man and had a large host, he trusted so much to this that he went far up into the land, and plundered and searched for men. The king whom Edmund had set to defend the land there was named Olaf; he gathered an overwhelming host, and went against Eirik. There ensued a great battle. . . . Eirik and five kings with him fell; . . . and there was a great slaughter of North-men; those who escaped went to Northumberland, and told Gunnhild and her sons the tidings " (Hakon the Good, c. 4).

" When (Eirik's wife) Gunnhild and her sons became aware that Eirik had fallen, and had first plundered in the realm of the Engla-king, they knew they could not expect peace there, and at once made ready to leave Northumberland with all the ships which Eirik had owned; and also took with them all those who wished to follow them. They also carried away what property had been gathered from taxes in England, as well as what had been won in warfare. They sailed with their men north to the Orkneys, and stayed there awhile. Thorfinn Hausakljuf (head-cleaver) was then jarl. The sons of Eirik subdued the Orkneys and Shetlands, and took taxes from them; they remained there during the winter, but went on western viking expeditions in the summer in Scotland and Ireland " (Hakon the Good, c. 5).[2]

The following account gives us an insight of the manners of the time during Æthelstan :—

" Eirik saw no other choice than to leave the land (Norway), and departed with Gunnhild his wife and their children. Arinbjörn hersir was a foster-brother of King Eirik, and the foster-father of his children, and dearest to him of all lendirmen. . . . They went first westward across the sea to the Orkneys. Then he married his daughter Ragnhild to Arnfin jarl, and went with his host south, past Scotland, and made war there, and thence south to England, ravaging there. King Æthel-stan heard this, and gathered men and went against Eirik. When they met, words of reconciliation were carried between them, and it was agreed upon that King Æthelstan gave Eirik Northumberland (Northymbraland) to rule over; and he was to be his land-defender against the Scotch and the Irish. Æthelstan had made Scotland tributary after the fall of King

---

[1] This shows that Bretland must have been Wales.

[2] Cf. also Egil's Saga, c. 62.

Olaf, but the people were constantly faithless to him" (Egil's Saga, c. 62).

Battle of Brunanburgh.—This battle is interesting and important in its details. It illustrates in many instances the customs of the people at the time of Athelstan, and shows that many customs were identical in England and the North, and that these Northmen were continually coming to England to help their friends or kinsmen.

Of Egil, the hero of this important battle, we read:

"When Egil grew up it could soon be seen that he would be ugly and like his father, with black hair. When he was three winters he was tall and strong as other boys of six or seven. He was early talkative and wise in words, but was rather hard to deal with in games with other youths" (Egil's Saga, c. 31).

"Olaf Raudi (the red) was a powerful king of Scotland. His father was Scotch, while his mother was Danish, descending from Ragnar Lodbrok. Scotland was said to be a third of the size of England; Nordimbraland (Northumberland) is called a fifth part of England, and is northernmost, next to Scotland, on the east. The Danish kings had held it in former times: Yorvik (York) was the head burg. This Æthelstan owned, and had placed two jarls to rule it; one was named Alfgeir, the other Gudrek. They were there to defend it, both against the attacks of the Scots and those of the Danes or Northmen, who ravaged there much. They thought they had great claims to it, for in Northumberland were only men whose fathers or mothers were of Danish kin, and, in many cases, both. The brothers Hring and Adils ruled Bretland (Wales), and paid a tribute to Æthelstan. When they were in the king's host, they and their men were to stand foremost in the ranks, in front of the banners. They were among the greatest of warriors, though not very young. Alfred the Great had deprived all tributary kings of their title and power; they who had been called kings or kings' sons were called jarls; this continued while he and his son Edward lived. Æthelstan came young to the kingship, and did not inspire much dread. Many who were faithful before then became faithless.

"Olaf, king of the Scots, gathered a large host, and went south to England. When he reached Northumberland, he went with [1] war-shield all over the land. But the jarls who

---

[1] = Ravaged.

ruled there heard of it, and gathered men, and went against him. There ensued a great battle, which ended in a victory for Olaf. Gudrek fell, and Alfgeir fled with most of their men who got away from the battle. Alfgeir could stop nowhere, and Olaf conquered the whole of Northumberland. Alfgeir went to Æthelstan and told him of his defeat, but as soon as he heard that so numerous a host had entered the country he summoned men, and sent word to his jarls and chiefs. He at once departed with his host against the Scots. When it was reported that Olaf, King of the Scots, had been victorious, had conquered a large part of England, and had a far greater force than Æthelstan, many chiefs went to him. Hring and Adils had gathered many men, and went over to King Olaf, who then had a very large army. Æthelstan then had a conference with his chiefs and counsellors to see what was most expedient. He told the whole assembly distinctly what he had heard about the Scottish king, and his great number of men. All agreed that Alfgeir jarl had been most to blame, and it seemed to them right to remove him from his place. It was agreed that the king should go back to the southern part of England, and gather men northwards throughout the whole land, for they saw that the great number needed would gather too slowly if the king himself did not call them together. He made Thorolf and Egil leaders of the host there; they were to lead the men whom vikings had taken to the king, and Alfgeir had still the command of his own men. The **king** also made those it pleased to him chiefs of detachments (Sveit). When Egil came from the meeting, he was asked what news he could tell about the king of the Scots. He sang . . . .

"Then they sent men to Olaf with the message that Æthelstan would fence a field with hazels to offer it as a battlefield to him on Vinheidi (= Vin-heath), at Vinuskogar (= Vinu-forest); that he did not want them to ravage in his land, and that the one who gained the battle should rule over the realm, England; they were to meet in the course of one week, and he who should arrive there first was to wait one week for the other. It was customary then, after a battlefield had been enhazelled, to consider it a disgrace for a king to plunder until after the battle. Olaf therefore stopped his host, and did not ravage, but waited for the appointed day; then he moved his force to Vinheidi. There was a town north of the heath, where he took up his quarters; he had there the greatest part of his host, for large provinces (herad) lay up to it, and he thought it was easiest there to obtain necessary supplies for the host. He sent some of his men to the heath where the battle was appointed, to find a place for the tents and prepare everything in advance. When they came to where the field was to be fenced, hazel poles were put up all round to mark the place where the battle was to take place. Care was taken that it should be even, as a large number of men was to be arrayed there. The battleplace was a level heath; on one side a river, and on the other a large forest. There was a very long distance between the forest and the river, where it was shortest, and where the tents of Æthelstan reached all the way from the one to the other. There was no one in every third tent, and even few in those that were occupied. When the men of Olaf came to the tents they had many men in front of all the tents, but did not allow them to go in. The men of Æthelstan said that all their tents were full, and that their whole host had not room in them; the tents stood in so high a place that it was impossible to look over them and see whether they were many or few in a cut through, and they thought there must be a great host. They pitched their tents north of the hazel poles, on a gentle slope. The men of Æthelstan said day after day that their king was coming or had arrived to the town south of the heath, and men gathered to them both by day and by night.

"When the appointed time was past they sent a message to Olaf that Æthelstan was ready for the battle, with a very numerous host, but that he did not wish such a great slaughter as was likely to take place, and bade him rather go home to Scotland and he would allow him as a friendly gift a shilling (skilling) in silver for every plough in all his kingdom, and that they should become friends. When the messengers came to Olaf he was preparing for battle, but on the announcement of their errand he stopped his advance that day, and with his chiefs sat in council. Different advices were given; some urged him much to accept this offer, thinking it most honourable to go home, having received so large a tribute from Æthelstan; others dissented, and said that he would offer much more next time if this was not accepted. This was agreed upon Then the messengers asked Olaf to grant them time to see King Æthelstan, and try if he would pay more to get peace. They asked for truce; one day to ride home, another for deliberation. the third for returning. This was granted; the messengers went home, and came back the third day and told Olaf that Æthelstan would give all he offered before, and besides to his host a shilling to every freeborn man, and a mark to every leader who had command over twelve men or more, one mark in gold to every leader of hirdmen (courtiers), and five marks in gold to every jarl.

"The king had this announced to his men, some of whom desired it, and others opposed it. At last the king decided that he would accept these conditions if King Æthelstan let him have the whole of Northumberland with the taxes and tributes thereto belonging. The messengers asked for a further delay of three days, and that Olaf would then send to hear from Æthelstan if he would accept these terms; they said that they thought King Æthelstan was very anxious to conclude the agreement. Olaf consented, and sent his messengers, who found Æthelstan in the burgh which was nearest south of the heath. They spoke of their errand, and the offer of reconciliation; the men of Æthelstan told also what they had offered to Olaf, and that it was the advice of wise men thus to delay the battle, as the king had not arrived. Æthelstan quickly gave decision, and said to the messengers: 'Carry these my words to Olaf, that I will allow him to go back to Scotland with his men if he pays back all the property he took wrongly here in the land. Let us then make peace between our countries, and let neither make war on the other. Olaf shall become my man, and hold Scotland from me, and be my under-king. Go back and tell him this.' The messengers went back that evening, and came to Olaf about midnight. They awoke him, and delivered their message. The king immediately called the jarls and other chiefs, and had the messengers tell the result of their errand and the words of Æthelstan. As this was made known among the warriors, all said that they must make ready for battle. The messengers also told that King Æthelstan had a great many men, and that he had arrived to the burgh the same day as they. Adils jarl said: 'Now my words have proved true, king, that you would experience the cunning of the English. We have remained here a long time, and waited while they have gathered all their men, and their king has probably not been anywhere near here when we came. They must have gathered many men since that time. It is my advice that I and my brother ride at once in advance of you this night with our men. It may be that they have now no fear about themselves, as they have heard that their king is near with a large host. Then we will attack them, and as they flee they will lose many men, and be less bold afterwards in fighting against us.' The king thought this a good advice, and agreed to make his army ready at dawn and meet him. They decided upon this and then parted.

"Hring, and Adils his brother, made ready and went in the night south to the heath. When it became light the sentinels of Thorolf saw the host; there was blown a war-blast, and the men put on their armour; they began to array them in battle order in two fylkings. Alfgeir commanded one of them, and had a standard carried in front of him; in this one was the force which had followed him, and also those who had gathered from the herads (provinces). It was a much larger host than that which followed Thorolf. Thorolf had a wide and thick shield, a very strong helmet on his head, a sword which he called Lang (the long), a large and good weapon. He also had a spear (= kesja) in his hand, of which the blade was four feet long, the point four-edged, the upper part of the blade broad, and the socket long and thick; the handle was no longer than one could reach with the hand to the socket, but very thick; there was an iron peg in the socket, and the whole handle was wound with iron. These spears were called brynthvari. Egil had the same outfit as Thorolf. He had a sword he called Nadr (= viper), which he had got in Kurland; it was an excellent weapon. Neither of them had on a coat of mail. They set up their standard, and Thorfinn the Hard carried it. All their men had Northern shields, and their whole equipment was Norwegian. All Northmen who were there were in their ranks. Thorolf and his men arrayed themselves nearer to the forest, but the array of Alfgeir along the river. Adils jarl and his brother saw that they could not come on Thorolf and his men unawares. Then they began to array their men in order of battle, and had also two fylkings and two standards. Adils arrayed his men against Alfgeir, and Hring his against the vikings. Then the battle began, and both sides went well forward. Adils pushed hard forward until Alfgeir let his men retreat; the men of Adils then fought more boldly, and it was not long before Alfgeir fled. He rode away southward off the heath with a detachment of men, till he approached the burgh in which the king was stopping. The jarl said: 'I do not think it is safe for us to go into the burgh. We got a great scolding last time we went to the king, when we had been defeated by Olaf, and he will not think that our honour has improved after this journey. We need not expect any honour where he is.' Then he rode southward day and night until they came west to Jarsnes, There he got passage southward across the sea. and went to Valland (France), where he had one half of his kindred. He never since came back to England.

"Adils first pursued the fleeing men, but not far before he returned to the battle and then made an attack. As Thorolf saw this, he sent Egil against him, and ordered the standard to be carried thither; he bid his men follow each other well, and stand closely together. 'Let us move toward the forest,' said he, 'that it may shelter our back, so that they cannot attack us from all sides.' They did so, and a sharp fight followed. Egil advanced against Adils, and they had a hard encounter. The difference in numbers was very great, but nevertheless more fell on Adils' side. Thorolf became so furious that he threw his shield on his back, and taking the spear with both hands, rushed forward and struck or thrust on both sides. Men turned away from him, but he killed many. Thus he cleared his way to the standard of Hring, and nothing could stand against him. He killed the men who bore it, and cut down the standard pole. Then he thrust the spear into the breast of the jarl through the coat of mail and his body, so that it came out between his shoulders; he raised him on the spear over his head, and put the shaft down into the ground. The jarl expired on the spear, in sight of foes and friends. Then Thorolf drew his sword, and dealt blows on both hands. His men also made an onset; many of the Britons and Scots fell, and some fled. When Adils saw the death of his brother, and the great fall and flight of his men finding himself severely pushed, he turned and fled, running into the forest, as did his men. The entire host of the jarls began to flee. Thorolf and Egil pursued them, and many more fell; the fugitives scattered widely over the heath. Adils had dropped his standard, and nobody knew him from his men. It then quickly began to get dark, and Thorolf and Egil went back to their camp, and at the same time Æthelstan came with his entire host. They pitched their tents and encamped. Shortly afterwards Olaf came with his host, and did the same. Olaf was told that both his jarls Hring and Adils had fallen, and a great number of men with them.

"Æthelstan had been, the night before the battle, in the burgh mentioned before, and there heard that a battle had been fought on the heath. He at once made ready with the entire host, and went northwards up on the heath. He then was told minutely how the battle had gone. Thorolf and Egil went to meet him. He thanked them greatly for their valour and the victory they had won, and promised them his full friendship. They all rested there together during the night. Æthelstan awoke his host early in the morning; he had a talk with his chiefs, and told how his host should be arrayed. He placed his own fylking first, and put at its breast those detachments which were the most dashing, with Egil as leader. 'Thorolf,' said he, 'shall lead his host and the other men I may put there in another fylking. They shall go against those of the enemy's men who are scattered and outside the fylking, for the Scots are usually not in serried ranks; they run to and fro, and come forward in various places; they often become dangerous if not guarded against, but do not stand firm on the field if they are faced.' Egil answered: 'I do not want that Thorolf and I shall be separated in the battle, and it seems best that we be placed where it is most needed and hard to stand.' Thorolf said: 'Let the king decide where he wishes to place us. Let us assist him so well that he is pleased. I would rather be where thou art placed, if thou hast no objection.' Egil replied: 'You must have your will, kinsman, but this change I shall often regret.' After this the men went forward into the fylkings as the king had ordered, and the standards were raised. The king's fylking stood in the open field at the river, while that of Thorolf was higher up along the forest. Olaf began arraying his men, when he saw that Æthelstan had arrayed his. He had also two lines, and he had his fylking and his standard, led by himself, against Æthelstan. They were equal in point of numbers, but the other line of Olaf went nearer to the forest, against that which Thorolf led. The chiefs of this numerous host were Scotch jarls, and most of the men Scots. The lines met each other, and soon a great battle ensued. Thorolf made a hard onset, and had his standard carried along the forest, intending to advance thus that he might attack the king's array on the flank. The men of Thorolf carried their shields in front, while the forest protected them on their right side. Thorolf went so far forward that few of his men were in front of him. But, when he expected it least, Adils and his men rushed out of the forest; they pierced Thorolf with many spears at the same time. He fell, but Thorfinn, who carried the standard, retreated to where the warriors stood thicker. Adils attacked, and there was a hard fight. The Scots raised a shout of victory when they had killed the leader of their enemies. When Egil heard that shout, and saw that the standard of Thorolf drew back, he knew that Thorolf himself did not follow it. He rushed forward between the arrays, and soon knew the tidings when he met his men. He urged the warriors much to attack, and was foremost with the sword Nadr in his hand. With this he strided forward slashing on both sides of himself, and slew many a man. Thorfinn carried the standard after him, and the men followed it. There ensued a most sharp fight. Egil went forward until he met Adils; they exchanged but few blows before the latter fell, and many around him. After his fall, the host which had followed him fled. Egil and his men pursued, and killed all they got hold of, for it was then useless to ask for life. The Scottish jarls did not stand long when they saw that their companions fled, but at once took to their heels. Egil then went to where Olaf's array was, and attacked it in the rear,[1] and made a great slaughter. The line began to waver, and was all broken up; many of Olaf's men fled, and the vikings raised a shout of victory. When Æthelstan saw that the ranks of Olaf began to break up, he urged his men, and had his standard carried forward. He made such a fierce attack that the force of Olaf recoiled with a heavy loss. Olaf fell there, and the greatest part of his host, for all who were caught in the flight were slain. Æthelstan gained a very great victory.

" Æthelstan left the battlefield, while his men pursued the fugitives. He rode back to the burgh, and there spent the night. Egil pursued for a long time, and killed every one he could overtake. When he had slain as many as he wanted, he went back to the battlefield, and found his brother Thorolf there, dead. He took his body, washed it, and prepared it as was customary; they dug a grave and put Thorolf therein, with all his weapons and clothes. Egil fastened a gold ring on each of his arms[2] before he left him. Then they piled stones upon him, and threw earth over. Then Egil sang:

The slayer of jarls who could not fear (Thorolf)
Went valiantly forward;
The strong-minded Thorolf fell
In the great *din of Thund* (= Odin)
  (= battle);
The ground will be green near the Vina (= a river)
Over my famous brother;
But we must hide our grief;
That is death-pain (= pain of Hel (= death)).

" Egil went with his men to Æthelstan, and at once went before him where he sat drinking in loud merriment. The king saw that Egil had entered, and said that place should be given to them on the lower bench, and that Egil should sit there in the high-seat opposite to him. Egil sat down, and flung his shield down before his feet. He had a helmet on his head, and placed his sword on his knee He at times drew half of the blade out of the scabbard and then slammed it back again. He sat upright, with his head bent forward. Egil had prominent features, a wide forehead, heavy eyebrows; his nose was not long, but extremely big, the lips thick and long, the chin and jaws wonderfully broad; he had a thick neck and large shoulders, exceeding other men's in size. He looked hard and fierce when he was angry. He was well shaped, and taller than other men; his hair was wolf-grey and abundant,

---

[1] In open shields, or the hollow of the shields; the rear.

[2] Hönd = hand or arm.

and he became bald early. As he sat thus, as before written, he made one of his eyebrows move down on his cheek and the other up to the fringe of his hair. He was black-eyed and swarthy (of a dark complexion). He would not drink the drink that was carried to him, but moved his eyebrows one at a time, up and down. Æthelstan sat in his high-seat with a sword on his knee. As they had sat thus for a while, the king drew his sword from its scabbard, and took a large and fine gold ring from his arm and hung it on the point of the sword blade, rose, walked on the floor, and handed it to Egil across the fire. Egil rose, drew his sword, and walked forward also. He stuck his sword into the ring, drew it to him, and went back to his seat. The king sat down in his high-seat. When Egil sat down he put the ring on his arm, and his brows became smooth, and he laid down his sword and helmet, took a deer-horn which was carried to him, and drank from it. He sang (on the ring). . . .

"Thereafter Egil drank his share, and talked to men. The king had two chests brought in; two men carried each, and both were filled with silver. He said: 'These chests thou shalt have, Egil; and if thou goest to Iceland, thou shalt give this property to thy father. I send it to him as indemnity for his son. But some of it thou shalt divide among the kinsmen of thyself and Thorolf, whom thou considerest the foremost. But thou shalt receive indemnity for thy brother here; land or loose property, whichever thou pleasest. If thou wilt stay with me long, I will give thee the honour and rank thou mayest choose thyself.' Egil accepted the property, and thanked him for his gifts and friendly words. Egil then began to be merrier, and sang:

The towering peaks of the eyelids
  (= the eyebrows)
Did droop on me for sorrow.
Now I found the one who smoothed
These wrinkles on my forehead.

The king has lifted up the
Rocks fencing the ground of the hood,[1]
Of me with the arm-band (= gold-
  ring);
The frown has left my eyes.

"Those wounded men who were fated to live were healed. Egil remained with the king the winter after the fall of Thorolf, and was greatly honoured by him. The men who had followed the brothers, and had escaped from the battle, were there with Egil. Egil made a drapa (= laudatory poem) on the king, who gave him two gold rings, each of which weighed one mark, and a costly cloak which he himself had worn. When spring began, Egil announced to the king that

---

[1] Ground of the hood = forehead; its rocks = the eyebrows.

he intended to go away in the summer to Norway to find out how the affairs of Asgerd, the wife of his brother Thorolf, stood. 'There is much property, but I do not know if there are any children of theirs alive. If there are, then I have to take care of them.[1] But all the inheritance is mine if Thorolf has died childless.' The king answered: 'Thou mayest go if thou thinkest thou hast a necessary errand, but I like it best that thou remainest here on such conditions as thou demandest thyself.' Egil thanked him. 'I shall go first where it is my duty to go, but it is likely that I return if I can to claim these promises.' The king told him to do so. Egil made ready, and with one longship and a hundred men, sailed for Norway."

The widow of Thorolf Skallagrimsson, brother of Egil, who fell in the battle of Brunanburgh, was named Asgerd. Egil told her of the killing of his brother.

"Egil grew melancholy in the autumn, and drank little, but sat often drooping his head in his cloak. Arinbjörn (his friend) once went to him and asked what caused his sadness, 'though thou hast lost thy brother it is manly to bear it well, for man must live after man.'"

"Egil sang a stanza, in which he expressed obscurely the name of Asgerd, and then asked Arinbjörn's help to a marriage with her. Then he was married to her, and was merry the remaining part of the winter" (Egil's Saga, chs. 51–56).

Fig. 1361.—Fire-Steel. ⅔ size. In a grave, Götland.

Fig. 1362.—Key of bronze. ⅔ size. Norway; found with buckles, pearls, etc.

---

[1] Brother inheriting brother.

CHAPTER XXI.

SOME EXPEDITIONS AND DEEDS OF GREAT VIKINGS.

(*Continued.*)

Harald founds Jomsborg—Svein—His vow to drive Æthelred from England —Creation of the *Thingamannalid*—Svein's death—Massacre of Northmen in London—Olaf comes to the help of Æthelred the Second—Attacks the Danes at Southwark—Captures Canterbury—Defends the shores of England, and sails up the New River—His other expeditions.

"HARALD GORMSSON (c. 940–986) was made king in Denmark after his father; he was a powerful king and a great warrior, and conquered Holstein in Saxland, and possessed a great Earldom in Vindland. There he founded *Jomsborg*, and placed in it a large garrison, which was under his laws and pay, and which subjugated the country. During the summer they went on expeditions, remaining at home in the winters, and they were called Jomsvikings " (Knytlinga, c. 1).

"Svein (c. 986–1014 A.D.) took possession of the Danish kingdom after his father (Harald Gormsson); he was called Svein Tjúguskegg (fork-beard), and was a powerful king. In his days jarl Sigvaldi and other Jomsvikings went to Norway and fought against Hakon jarl in Mœri in Hjörungavag; there fell Bui the Stout, but Sigvaldi fled. After that the power in Norway was lost to the Danish kings, and a little later Olaf Tryggvason came to Norway and got the rule.

"King Svein was married to Gunnhild, daughter of Burislaf, King of the Vends, and their sons were Knut (the Great) and Harald. Svein was afterwards married to Sigrid-Storráda (the Proud), daughter of Sköglar-Tosti, and mother of the Swedish king Olaf. She had before been married to King Eirik Sigrsæli (the Victorious) of Sweden.

"The daughter of King Svein and Sigrid was Ástrid, married to jarl Ulf, son of Thorgils Sprakalegg (woman's leg), who had two sons, Svein and Björn. Gyda, a daughter of King Svein Tjúguskegg, was married to jarl Eirik Hakonsson of Norway; their son was jarl Hakon, whom St. Olaf took prisoner in Saudung's Sound.[1]

---

[1] This Hakon was a grandson of the great Hakon jarl.

"King Svein was at the fall of Olaf Tryggvason with King Olaf the Swedish, his stepson, and with jarl Eirik, his son-in-law. They fought at Svold, and after the fall of Olaf Tryggvason, King Svein of Denmark, King Olaf of Sweden, and jarl Eirik of Norway divided Norway between themselves" (Knytlinga Saga, c. 5).

In the chapter on inheritance we have seen that King Svein made the vow to drive Æthelred from England.

"King Svein was a great warrior and a most powerful king; he made warfare far and wide, both in the east and in Saxland. At last he went with his host west to England, ravaged in many places there, and fought many battles; Adalrad Yatgeirsson was then king there. Svein and he fought many battles, and were alternately victorious. Svein won the greatest part of England; he lived there for many winters, and ravaged and burnt widely in the land; they called him the foe of the English. In that war King Æthelred fled from Svein out of the land" (Knytlinga Saga, c. 6).

"King Svein stayed at home in Denmark; his son Knut was brought up there; Thorkel the high fostered him. Svein made warfare in the land of King Æthelred, and drove him out of the land south across the sea; he put *Thingamannalid* [1] in two places. The one in London (Lundunaborg) was ruled by Eilif Thorgilsson, the brother of Ulf (jarl); he had sixty ships in the Temps (Thames). The other Thingamannalid was north in Slesvik, over which Heming jarl, the brother of Thorkel the high, was ruler also with sixty ships.

"The Thingamen established a law that no report should be spread, and no one should stay away a whole night; they attended the Bura-church, in which was a large bell, that was to be rung every night when only a third of the night was left; then every one was to go to church, but without weapons; such laws as these they had in Slesvik.

"He who had the command in the town (Lundunaborg) was Alrek Strjóna, a brother of Emma, the daughter of Richard (Rikgard of Normandy), the father of Vilhjalm (William); King Æthelred was married to her. Ulfkel Snilling [2] ruled over the northern part of England; he was married to Ulfhild, the daughter of King Æthelred. King Svein died in England, and the Danes took his body to Denmark, and buried him in

---

[1] The *Thingamen* seems to have been a kind of standing army, like the Værin-gians in Constantinople.

[2] Snilling = master of speech.

Hróiskelda near his father. . . ." (Jomsvikinga Saga, cc. 50, 51).

"Svein was found one night dead in his bed, and the English say that King Edmund the Saint killed him, in the manner in which the holy Mercurius killed Julianus the Apostate" (Knytlinga Saga, c. 6).

"After the death of Svein the Danish kings retained that part of England which they had won. War then began anew, for when King Svein was dead, King Æthelred, with the assistance of Olaf the Saint (of Norway), returned to the country and regained his realm. At that time the Danes established the host of the Thingamen in England; they were paid warriors, and very valiant. They fought many battles against the English on behalf of the Danes" (Knytlinga Saga, c. 7).

"Knut was then ten winters old. The power of the Thingamen was great. There was a fair there (London) twice in every twelvemonth, one about midsummer and the other about midwinter. The English (Enskir) thought it would be the easiest to slay the Thingamen while Knut was young and Svein dead. Each winter about Yule, waggons went into the town with goods which they were wont to bring to the market. So it was this winter, and they were all tented over; this was according to the treacherous advice and will of Ulfkel Snilling[1] and the sons of Æthelred. The seventh day of Yule Thord (a man of the Thingamannalid) went out of the town to the house of his mistress. She asked him to stay there that night. 'Why dost thou ask for that which is liable to punishment?' 'I ask it,' said she, 'because I think it important.' He answered: 'I will stay here if thou tellest me why thou askest this.' 'Because I know that the death of all the Thingamen is planned.' 'How canst thou know it,' he added, 'when we do not know it?' 'Because men drove waggons to the town, and pretended that they contained goods; but in each waggon there were many men and no goods, and they have done the same thing north,[2] in Slesvik. When a third part of the night has passed bells will be rung in the town; then warriors and also the townsmen will make themselves ready about midnight. When a third of the night is left, the bell of Bura church will be rung. You will go unarmed to the church, which will then be surrounded.'

"'It is likely,' said Thord, 'that thou hast many friends,

---

[1] He was married to Æthelred's daughter (see preceding page).

[2] In the north of England.

2 I

and I will tell Eilif, though it will be thought a rumour. But this farm thou shalt own.' Thord went into the town; he met his companion, Audun; they went and told it to Eilif. He bade the men be on their guard. Some believed it, others said it was only an alarm. They heard the bell-ringing as usual, and many thought the priest was ringing. Those who believed Thord went armed, and all the others unarmed. When they came into the churchyard there was a great crowd. They could not get their weapons, for they could not reach their houses. Eilif asked for their advice, but they could give none; he added, 'It does not seem to me good advice to run into the church if it gives no shelter and we show fear. I think it will be better to jump on the shoulders of those who stand outside the churchyard wall, and thus try to escape to the ships.' And they did so. Most of those who were slain fell at the ships. Eilif escaped with three ships, but none escaped from Slesvik, and Heming fell there. Eilif went to Denmark. Some time after this Jatmund (Edmund) was made king over England. He ruled nine months. During that time he fought five battles against Knut Sveinsson. Alrek Strjona, whom some called Eirek, a brother of Emma, who had been married to Æthelred, the king of the English, was the foster-father of Edmund. At that time Thorkel the High was the most powerful man in Denmark. They had a Thing in the spring after the slaying of the Thingamen; Eilif urged to go and take revenge, but Thorkel answered: 'We have a young king, and it is not proper to make warfare without the king partaking in it, but after three years I think he will be valiant enough, and it will take the English by surprise.' Eilif answered: 'It is not sure that those will remember it for three winters, who now do not care for it at all.' He went to Mikligard (Constantinople), and became chief of the Væringjar, and at last fell there. After three winters, Knut, Thorkel, and Eirik went with eight hundred ships to England. Thorkel had thirty ships, and slew Ulfkel Snilling, and thus avenged the death of his brother Heming, and married Ulfhild, the daughter of King Æthelred, who had been married to Ulfkel. With Ulfkel was slain every man on sixty ships, and Knut captured Lundunaborg. Thorkel went along the coast, and found Queen Emma on board a ship. He took her ashore and urged Knut to ask her in marriage; and the king married her. She gave birth to a son in the winter, who was named Harald, a natural son of Knut; Hörda-Knut was their son. The son of Knut and Alfifa was named Svein; his daughter Gunnhild was married to the Emperor (of Germany) Heinrek Konradsson:

Knut went to Rome with him" (Jomsvikinga Saga, cc. 51, 52).

King Olaf Haraldsson, surnamed Digri (the Stout), known also under the name of St. Olaf, was a great warrior, and made wars in the Baltic, in Friesland, England, France, and other countries. Fifteen of these expeditions are described in his Saga.

The Northmen under Olaf came to help Æthelred against the Danes.

"King Olaf then sailed westwards to England. It was reported that Svein Tjúguskegg, Danish king at this time, was in England with the Danish host, and had stayed there awhile and ravaged the land of King Æthelred. The Danes had spread far and wide over the country, and King Æthelred had fled from the land and gone to Valland. The same autumn that Olaf came to England it happened that King Svein Haraldsson died suddenly during the night in his bed; and it was said by the English that Edmund the saint had slain him, in the same manner as the holy Mercury slew Julian the Nithing (Apostate). When Æthelred heard of this in Flæmingjaland (Flandres), he at once returned to England. When he came back, he sent word to all who wanted to get property to come and win the land; and a mass of men joined him. Then Olaf came to his assistance with a large following of Northmen. They first sailed for London (Lundúnir), and entered the Thames, while the Danes held the burg. On the other side of the river there was a large trading-town, which is called Sudvirki (Southwark); there the Danes had made great fortifications, dug large ditches, and built inside them walls of wood, stones, and turf, and there had a large force. Æthelred caused a fierce attack to be made on it; but the Danes defended it, and the king could not capture it. There were such broad bridges across the river between the city and Southwark, that waggons could pass each other (on them). On the bridges were bulwarks, which reached higher than the middle of a man, and beneath the bridges piles were driven into the bottom of the river. When the attack was made the whole host stood on the bridges, and defended them" (St. Olaf's Saga, c. 11).

"Olaf was leader of the host when they went to Kantarabyrgi (= Canterbury), and they fought there until they took it, slew many, and burned the town. Then Olaf had to defend the shores of England, and coursed along them with warships, and sailed up into Nyjamoda (= Newmouth). There was a host of Thingamen. He fought a battle, and got the victory. Then he went far and wide about the country, and received taxes from the people, making warfare if they paid not. At that time he stayed there three winters " (St. Olaf's Saga, c. 14).

" Olaf had large hurdles made of withies and soft wood, so cut as to make a wicker-house, and thus covered his ships, so that the hurdles reached out over their sides ; he had posts put beneath them so high that it was easy to fight beneath them, and the covering was proof against stones thrown down on it. When the host was ready they rowed up the river ; as they came near the bridges they were shot at, and such large stones thrown down on them that neither their helmets nor shields could withstand them ; and the ships themselves were greatly damaged, and many retreated. But Olaf and the Northmen with him rowed up under the bridges, and tied ropes round the supporting posts, and rowed their ships down stream as hard as they could. The posts were dragged along the bottom until they were loosened from under the bridges. As an armed host stood thickly on the bridges, and there was a great weight of stones and weapons upon them, and the posts beneath were broken, the bridges fell with many of the men into the river ; the others fled into the city, or into Southwark. After this they attacked Southwark, and captured it. When the townsmen saw that the river Temps (Thames) was taken, so that they could not hinder ships from going up into the country, they became afraid, gave up the town, and received King Æthelred.

" King Olaf stayed during the winter with King Æthelred ; then they fought a great battle on Hringmara-heath in Ulf-kelsland, owned by Ulfkel Snilling, and the kings gained the victory. Then a great part of the land was subdued by Æthelred, but the Danes and the *Thingamenn* held many towns, and a large part of the country " (St. Olaf's Saga, cc. 12, 13).

" The third spring King Ethelred died, and his sons Edmund and Edward received the kingship. Then Olaf went southward across the sea, fought in Hringsfjord, and took and destroyed the castle at Holar, held by vikings " (St. Olaf's Saga, c. 15).

The Eleventh, Twelfth, and Thirteenth Battles.

" Then Olaf went with his men westward to Grislupollar, and there defeated the vikings before Vilhjalmsbær (Williamsby). After that he fought west in Fetlafjord. Thence he went south to Seljopollar, and there took a large and old town called Gunnvaldsborg, with the jarl, Geirfinn, who ruled it. He laid taxes on the town and on the jarl for his ransom, twelve thousand gold shillings (gull skillingar). The money demanded was paid by the town" (St. Olaf's Saga, c. 16).

The Fourteenth Battle and Dream of King Olaf.

"Thereafter Olaf went with his men westward to the Karlsa,[1] plundered, and fought a battle there. While he lay in the Karlsa, and waited there for fair wind, wishing to sail to Norvasund (= Straits of Gibraltar) and thence to Jorsalaheim (Jerusalem), he had a remarkable dream, that a handsome and nobly-looking but awe-striking man came and spoke to him. He asked him to give up the intention to go into far countries (= to the Holy Land). 'Go back to thy odals, for thou wilt be king over Norway for ever.'[2] He understood by this dream that he and his kinsmen would rule over the land for a long time" (St. Olaf's Saga, c. 17).

The Fifteenth Battle.

"On account of this vision he changed his journey, and steered his ships up to Peituland (Poitou), plundered here, and burnt a town called Varrandi" (St. Olaf's Saga, c. 18).

Fig. 1363.—Coin coined in Sigtuna. King Anund Jakob, c. 1020, A.D. 1050.

Fig. 1364.—A Kufic coin, Gotland, Sweden.

---

[1] Karlsa, or Karl's river, said to be Garonne.

[2] After his death he was the saint or patron of Norway.

CHAPTER XXII.

SOME EXPEDITIONS AND DEEDS OF GREAT VIKINGS.
(*Continued.*)

Knut the Mighty—His appearance—His liberality—His battles in England—
Besieges London—His numerous expeditions—The successors of Knut.

KNUT THE MIGHTY (1014–1035), or the Great, is, with Charlemagne, one of the greatest geniuses of that epoch; he ruled his three kingdoms with great ability, and died young (at thirty-seven). The appearance of this great and powerful king is thus described:—

"Knut was very tall and strong, and a very handsome man, except that his nose was thin, prominent, low, and somewhat crooked; he had a fair complexion, with fair and long hair; he had finer and keener eyes than any man. He was liberal, a great warrior, very valiant and victorious, a man of great luck, in everything connected with power. He was not very wise, neither were King Svein, Harald, nor Gorm" (Knytlinga Saga, c. 20).

"King Knut was the most liberal of kings in the Northern lands; for it is truly said that he surpassed other kings no less in the property he gave in friendly gifts every year than in taking much more in taxes and dues from three great lands than any other king who ruled one realm; and moreover England is richest in movable property of all the Northern lands" (Knytlinga Saga, c. 19).

King Knut sent messengers to Olaf the Stout (Olaf Haraldson) of Norway to claim obedience from him.

"Sigvat went to the messengers of Knut, and asked for news. They told him what he desired, their talk with King Olaf, and the result of their errand. They said, 'The king had taken the matter angrily; and we do not know in whom he trust when he refuses to become the man of Knut, and go to him; that would be best, for Knut is so mild, that never do the chiefs do so much against him that he does not forgive at once, when they come to him and yield to him. It was only a short time ago that two kings north from Fifi (Fife) in Scotland came to him, and he forgot his wrath and gave them all the lands they had owned before, and also great friendly gifts ' " (St. Olaf's Saga, c. 140).

"Knut fought many battles in England against the sons of Æthelred, King of the English, and they were defeated by each other in turns. He came to England during the summer when Æthelred died, and then married Queen Emma; their children were Harald, Hordaknut, and Gunnhild. Knut made an agreement with Edmund, that each of them should have half of England. In the same month Heidrek Strjona slew Edmund, and thereafter King Knut drove away all the sons of Æthelred " (St. Olaf's Saga, c. 24).

"A long time after this Knut was at a feast with Thorkel the High, saw Ulfhild, and thought Thorkel had cheated him in the sharing of the women (taken the finer one), and therefore had him slain. Knut and Edmund fought some battles against each other, after which both the Danes and the English asked them to come to terms, and this they did; the one who lived longer was to have the land of the other. One month afterwards Edmund was slain by his foster-father Alrek Strjona, and then Knut got the whole of England, and ruled it for twenty-four winters "[1] (Jomsvikinga Saga, c. 52).

"That summer the sons of King Æthelred went from England to Ruda (Rouen) in Valland,[2] to their uncles, when Olaf Haraldsson came from viking expeditions in the west; they were all in Normandy that winter, and entered into an agreement that Olaf should have Northumberland if they got England from the Danes. In the autumn Olaf sent his foster-father Hrani to England to get men there, and the sons of Æthelred sent with him tokens to their friends and kinsmen, and Olaf gave him much loose property wherewith to win men over. Hrani stayed during the winter in England, and obtained the confidence of many powerful men, among them those who preferred having their countrymen to rule over them; but the power of the Danes in England had then become so great, that all the people were subject to them " (St. Olaf's Saga, c. 25).

---

[1] Cf. also Knytlinga Saga, c. 7 to 9; St. Olaf, c. 23.

[2] This shows that Valland was in the west of France.

"In the spring Olaf and the sons of King Æthelred went to England, and arrived at a place called Jungufurda, where they went on shore. There were many who had promised to help them; they took the town with great slaughter. When the men of Knut became aware of this, they gathered such a numerous host that the sons of Æthelred could not resist them, and they saw it was best to return to Rouen; but Olaf parted with them and would not go to Valland. He sailed northwards along England all the way to Northumberland; he landed in the harbour called Valdi, and there he defeated the townspeople and traders, and got a great deal of property " (St. Olaf's Saga, c. 26).

"Knut, the son of King Svein Tjuguskegg, was ten winters old when his father died; then he was made king over Denmark, for his brother Harald was dead. The Danish chiefs who remained in England, and held the land which King Svein had won, sent word to Denmark that King Knut must come west to England with the Danish host to help them. As King Knut was then a child, and not used to command in war, his friends advised him to send a host to England, and place a chief over it, and not go himself until he stood better on his legs; he was three winters in Denmark after he became king. Then he summoned together a host,[1] and sent word to Norway, to his brother-in-law Eirik jarl, to gather a host and go to England with him; for Eirik jarl was very famous for his bravery and skill in warfare, as he had gained the victory in two of the most famous battles in Northern lands, one when King Svein Tjuguskegg and Olaf the Swedish king and Eirik jarl fought against Olaf Tryggvason at Svold, the other when Hakon jarl and Eirik fought against the Jómsvikings in Hjörungavag. King Knut went with a very numerous host west to England. Many chiefs went with him; Ulf jarl Sprakaleggsson, his brother-in-law, who was then married to his sister Astrid, Svein's daughter, also Heming and Thorkel the High, the sons of Strutharald jarl, and many other chiefs. Knut came to England, and landed at a place called Fljót (Fleet); he ravaged the land, slew the people, and burned their houses. The people of the land gathered a host and went against the Danes. Knut fought his first battle in England at Lindisey (Lindsey), and many fell there; he then took Hemingaborg in England, and there also slew many. Thereafter he fought great battles in Nordimbraland at Tesa (Tees). There he slew many, while some fled and

---

[1] Knút the Great's English campaigns are told by three poets, Sighvat, Ottar the Black, and Thórd Kolbeinsson.

perished in swamps or ditches; he then went farther south, and underlaid himself the land wherever he went "[1] (Knytlinga Saga, c. 8).

"King Knut fought another battle at a town called Brandfurda (Branford); it was a great battle, and he got the victory; the sons of Æthelred fled, and lost many men, and the Danes took the town. He fought a third great battle against the sons of Æthelred at a place called Essandune, north of the Danaskogar (Danish forests). He fought a fourth against King Jatmund (Edmund) and his brothers at Northvik (Norwich), and there was a great fall of men; the king got the victory, and the sons of Æthelred fled" (Knytlinga Saga, c. 12).

"King Knut then went with all his host to Temps-a (the Thames river), for he heard that Jatmund and his brothers had fled to Lundunaborg (London); when he came to the mouth of the Temps Eirik jarl Hakonsson, his brother-in-law, sailed in from the sea; they met there, and sailed up the river with the host. In the river Temps was built a large castle (tower), and a host put there to defend it so that a ship host might not go up the river. Knut at once sailed up the river to the castle, and fought against them; but the English went with a ship-host from London down the river, and engaged in battle with the Danes" (Knytlinga Saga, c. 13).

"Knut went with all his host up to London, and surrounded it with his camp (war-booths); then they attacked the town and the townsmen defended it. Thus it is told in the poem (flokk) which was made then by the warriors.

The Hlokk [2] of horns **sees every** morning
On the banks of the Temps (Thames)
Blood-dyed body-hurters (weapons).
The corpse-gull (bird of prey) must not starve.

(She sees) how the victory-yearning Dane-king
Violently attacks the burgh-men.
The blood-ice (weapons) sounds
On British [3] (brezk) brynjas.

"King Knut fought many battles there, but could not take the town" (Knytlinga Saga, c. 14).

"Eirik jarl went with a part of the host up into the land, and the Thingamenn followed him against an English host which was commanded by Ulfkel Snilling, a great chief;

---

[1] Knut (Canute) reigned from A.D. 1014–1035, and was succeeded by his son Harald.

[2] Hlokk of horns = valkyrja of horns = woman.

[3] British here means English; otherwise usually Welsh.

a battle was fought, and Eirik gained the victory, and Ulfkel fled. Eirik jarl fought another battle at Hringmaraheidi (heath) against the English and obtained the victory" (Knytlinga Saga, c. 15).

"Æthelred the King of the English died the same autumn or summer that Knut came with his host to England; he had then been King of England thirty-eight winters. Queen Emma after his death at once made herself ready to leave the land; she intended to go west to Valland (France) to her brothers, Vilhjalm (William) and Robert, who were jarls there. Their father was Rikard (Richard), jarl of Rouen, son of Richard, son of William longspear; he was the son of Göngu-Hrolf, who won Normandy, and was the son of Rögnvald, jarl of Mœri. The men of King Knut became aware of the journey of Queen Emma; when she and her men were ready to sail, his men came and took the ship with all that was in it, and took her to him; King Knut's chiefs advised him to marry Queen Emma, and he did so" (Knytlinga Saga, c. 9).

"After the death of Æthelred, his and Queen Emma's sons were taken as kings; Jatmund (Edmund) the Strong was the eldest; Jatgeir (Edgar) the second; Jatvig (Edwig) the third; and Jatvard (Edward) the Good, the fourth. Edmund gathered a large host and went against Knut; they met at a place called Skorstein, and fought the most famous battle which had taken place at that time; very many of both hosts fell. Edmund rode forward into the midst of the Danish host, and came so near his stepfather King Knut, that he touched him with a sword-blow. Knut thrust his shield in front of the neck of the horse on which he sat; the blow hit the shield a little below its handle, and was so heavy that the shield was cleft asunder, and the horse was cut at the shoulders in front of the saddle. The Danes then attacked him so violently that he went back to his men, but not before he had killed many Danes, being very slightly wounded himself. When the king had ridden forward away from his men they thought he had fallen, as they did not see him, and the host fled, for some saw him riding away from the Danes. All who saw this fled, but the king shouted loudly and bid them return to the fight, but no one seemed to hear it; the entire host fled, and there ensued a great fall of men; the Danes pursued the fleeing till night" (Knytlinga Saga, c. 10).

"Ulf jarl was then, as often, one of the foremost of the men of King Knut, and pursued the fugitives farthest; he entered a wood so thick that he did not get out of it until dawn. Then he saw in some fields in front of him sheep which a well-grown boy was driving. Ulf jarl went to him, greeted him, and asked his name. He answered: 'I am called Gudini (Godwin); but art thou one of Knut's men?' Ulf jarl replied: 'I am certainly one of his warriors; but how far is it hence to our ships?' 'I do not know,' said the boy, 'how you Danes can expect help from us, and you have not deserved it.' Ulf jarl answered: 'I will however ask of thee to help me to find our ships.' The boy said: 'Thou hast gone straight away from them, and far inland across wild forests. The men of Knut are not very much liked by the people here, and for good reason, for the slaughter yesterday at Skorstein is known in the neighbourhood, and neither thou nor any other of his men will be spared if the bœndr find you; and if any one help you the same fate awaits him; but I think thou art a good man, and not the one thou pretendest to be.' Ulf jarl took a gold ring off his hand and said: 'I will give thee this ring if thou wilt guide me to our men.' Godwin looked at him for a while, and said slowly: 'I will not take the ring, but I will try to guide thee to thy men, and will rather have the reward thou thinkest right if I can give thee some help; but if I cannot I deserve no reward; now thou shalt first go home with me to my father.' They did so. When they came to the farm (bœr) they went to a little room and Gudini (Godwin) had a table set there, and good drink was given. Ulf jarl saw that it was a good farm. The bondi and the housewife came to them; they were both handsome and well dressed; they received the guest well, and he remained there that day in the best entertainment. Toward night two good horses were prepared with the best riding gear. They then said to Ulf: 'Now, farewell; I give into thy hands my only son; I ask of thee if thou shouldst come to the king, and thy words might have some influence to get him into his service, for he cannot stay with me hereafter, if our countrymen hear that he has guided thee away, in whatever way I may escape myself.' Ulf jarl promised to get Godwin into the host. Godwin was very handsome and talked well. The bondi's name was Ulfnadr.

"Ulf jarl and Godwin rode all that night, and in the morning, when it was light, they came to the ships, and Knut's men were ashore. When they saw the jarl and recognised him, they welcomed him as one who had escaped from death, for he was so popular that every one loved him. Godwin then for the first time knew whom he had followed. The jarl seated Godwin in the high-seat at his side, and treated him in everything like himself or his son, and in short gave him in marriage his sister Gyda; and with the aid and advice of Ulf jarl, King Knut gave him a jarldom for the sake of Ulf jarl, his brother-in-law. The sons of Godwin and Gyda were: Harald the English king, and Tosti jarl, called wooden spear; Maurukari jarl (Morcar); Valthjof (Waltheof) jarl, and Svein jarl; from them have sprung many chiefs in England, Denmark, Sweden, and Gardariki (Russia). They are king's families in the Danish realm. The daughter of King Harald, son of Godwin, was called Gyda; she was married to King Valdamar (Vladimir) in Holmgard (Novgorod); their son was King Harald; he had two daughters, of whom will be told later" (Knytlinga Saga, c. 11).

"Knut besieged Lundunaborg (London), and Edmund with his brothers defended it; then Knut was married to Queen Emma, their mother, and at last hostages were given and a truce was established to talk about full reconciliation; and peace was made on the terms that the realm should be divided between them in halves, each to have one half while he lived, but if either of them died childless, the survivor should have the right to take the whole realm; this was confirmed with oaths. Heidrek Strjóna was a powerful man who got property from King Knut in order to betray King Edmund and murder him, and that was the manner of his death, though Heidrek was the foster-father of Edmund, who believed in him as in himself. Then King Knut drove away from England all the sons of King Æthelred; many battles were fought in consequence, but they did not get many men to help against Knut after Edmund had been slain. The sons of King Æthelred then stayed west in Valland in Normandi for a long time with their uncles (Rodbert) Robert and Vilhjalm (William), as is told in the Saga of Olaf helgi (the saint). Eirik jarl Hakonsson died in England, when he was ready for a journey to Rome. . . . Knut and Queen Emma had three children; Harald was the oldest, and then Hörda-Knut; their daughter was Gunnhild, who later was married to the Emperor Heinrek, (Henry), the Mild, who was the third of his kinsmen of that name. Svein was the third son of King Knut; his mother was Alfifa the Wealthy, daughter of Alfrun jarl" (Knytlinga Saga, c. 16).

"When Knut came back to England (from Rome) he fell sick, first from what is called jaundice; he was sick a long while during the summer, and died in the autumn, on the 13th November, in Morst (Shaftesbury), a large town, and there he is buried. He was then thirty-seven years old; he had been king over Denmark twenty-seven years, over England twenty-four, and over Norway seven years. It is acknowledged by all that King Knut was the most powerful and wide-reigning of kings in Northern lands " (Knytlinga Saga, c. 18).

" Knut the Great, whom some call Knut the Old, was king over England and Denmark. He was the son of Svein Tjugu-skegg, Harald's son. Their kindred had ruled Denmark for a long time. Harald Gormsson, the grandfather of Knut, got possession of Norway after the fall of Harald Gunnhild's son, received taxes from it, and placed Hakon jarl the great to defend the land. Svein, King of the Danes, son of Harald, also ruled over Norway, and put Eirik jarl Hakonsson to defend it. He ruled with his brother, Svein Hakonsson, until Eirik went west to England, owing to the message of Knut the Great, his brother-in-law, and left Hakon, his son, to rule Norway.

" Hakon then went to his uncle, Knut, and had been with him to the time when Knut had won England after a long struggle, and the people of the land yielded to him. When he thought he had fully established his rule over the land he remembered that he owned a country which was not in his possession, and that was Norway. He claimed the whole of Norway as inheritance, but his nephew Hakon claimed part of it, and said that he had lost it. One reason why Knut and Hakon had not made good their claim upon Norway was, that when King Olaf Haraldsson came the people rose, and would not hear of any one else but Olaf as king over the whole land; but later, when they thought they were oppressed because of his overbearing, some left the country. Many chiefs or sons of powerful bœndr had come to Knut under the pretence of various errands; every one who attached himself to him received his hands full of money. There could also be seen far greater splendour than in any other place, both in the mass of men who continually stayed there, and in the outfitting of the rooms in which he lived himself. Knut received taxes and dues from the wealthiest folk-lands in the North; but as much as he surpassed other kings in receiving more than they, as far did he surpass any other king in giving away gifts. In all his kingdom there was such peace that none dared to break it, and the people lived quietly under the old laws of the land. For this he got great fame through all lands. Many who came from Norway complained of their loss of freedom, and told Hakon jarl; and some informed Knut himself that the men of Norway were ready to return to him and the jarl, and through them regain their liberty. This pleased the jarl, who told it to the king, and asked him to see if King Olaf would give up the kingdom, or make some settlement with them. Many pleaded the same with the jarl. Knut sent men eastward from England to Norway, very finely fitted out; they brought a letter and the seal of the King of the English. In the spring they went to Olaf Haraldsson at Tunsberg. When he was told that the messengers of Knut had come he grew angry, and said that Knut was not likely to send men thither with messages that would be of use to him or his people; and for some days he would not let the messengers see himself. When they got leave to speak, they appeared before him and delivered the letter of Knut. They stated their errand—that Knut claimed all Norway, and that his forefathers had had it before him; but as he wished to have peace in every land, he would not wage war upon Norway, if they could settle the matter in any other way; that if Olaf Haraldsson wanted to be king over Norway he should go to Knut, and take the land as a fief from him, become his man, and pay him such taxes as the jarl paid before. Thereupon they delivered the letter, which expressed the same thing. Olaf answered: ' I have heard in old Sagas that Gorm, King of the Danes, was thought to be a great folk-king, and ruled only over Denmark; but these later Danish kings do not think that enough. Knut now rules over Denmark and England, and has subdued a great part of Scotland, and now he claims his inheritance from me. He ought at last to show moderation in his greediness, or does he wish to rule all Northern lands alone, or to eat alone all the cabbage in England? He is more likely to do that than I to bring him my head, or pay him any homage. Tell him my words: that I will defend Norway *with point and edge* while my life lasts, and pay no taxes from my kingdom.' After this decision the messengers of Knut made ready to go away, ill pleased with the result of their errand. . . . The messengers of Knut returned with a fair wind across the sea. They went to Knut and told him the answer to their message, and the last words of Olaf. Knut answered: ' King Olaf is mistaken if he thinks I want to eat alone all the cabbage in England; he shall feel that I have more things within my ribs than cabbage; for henceforth evil shall come to him from under every rib.'

"Olaf summoned his lendirmen, and assembled a great many that summer, for it was reported that Knut would come from England. People heard report from trading ships from the west that Knut was gathering a great host in England; some asserted and others denied that a host would come in the latter part of the summer. Olaf stayed in Vik, and sent spies to find out if Knut was coming to Denmark. In the autumn he sent men eastwards to Sweden to Önund, his brother-in-law, and told him about the message of Knut and the claim he laid to Norway; and hinted that he thought if Knut subjugated Norway, Önund would have short shrift in Swedish realm, and that it would be a good plan if they allied themselves against him.

"Knut went that autumn to Denmark, and remained there during the winter, with many men. He was told that messengers had been sent from the King of Norway to the King of Sweden, and back again, and that some great events were about to happen. Knut sent men in the winter to Sweden to Önund with rich presents and friendly words, and said that it would be to his advantage not to interfere in the quarrels between him and Olaf the Stout, for his country should be at peace with him. When the messengers came to Önund they presented the gifts of Knut, with his offers of friendship. Önund did not receive their message well, and they thought that he was much inclined to friendship with Olaf. They went back and told Knut this, and that he could expect no friendship from Önund" (St. Olaf's Saga, cc. 139–142).

The great chief Erling Skjalgsson and all his sons were with Knut the Great when he fought against St. Olaf and Önund, King of Sweden, in the river Helga.

"In the autumn he went back to Norway with his men, and at parting got large gifts from King Knut. Messengers of Knut went with him to Norway, having a great deal of loose property with them; in the winter they went about the land, and paid the money which Knut had promised the people that autumn. They travelled under the protection of Erling Skjalgsson. Many men became the friends of Knut, and promised to fight against Olaf; some did it openly, and many others secretly" (St. Olaf's Saga, c. 171).

"Knut got together his host, and went to Limafjord (Limfjorden) and sailed to Norway; he hurried onward, and did not stop at the land east of Vik. He sailed past the Vestfold to Agdir, where he summoned a Thing. . . . He was there chosen king over the whole land; he then filled the stewardships (offices) with new men, and took hostages from the land; no man spoke against him. Olaf was in Tunsberg when the host of Knut went past the Fold. Knut went northwards along the shore, and there came to him men from the herads, and all paid homage to him; he stayed in Eikundasund for some while. There Erling Skjalgsson came to him with many men, and he and Knut renewed their friendship; Knut amongst other things promised him that he should rule all the land between Stad and Rygjarbit. Knut then sailed northward to Nidaros in Thrandheim (Throndhjem). He summoned men from eight *fylki* to a Thing, at which he was chosen king over the whole of Norway.

"When Knut had subdued all Norway, he summoned his own men and the Northmen to a Thing. He declared that he would give his kinsman Hakon rule over all the land which he had won in that expedition; he also led his son Hörda-Knut into the high-seat, and gave him the name of king, and also presented him with the realm of Denmark. He took hostages from all lendirmen and great bœndr, and their sons and brothers or other near kinsmen, or those who were dearest to them, as he thought best, and thus he strengthened the faithfulness of the people" (St. Olaf's Saga, cc. 180, 181).

"Hörda-Knut, son of Knut the Old, succeeded to the king-ship in Denmark after his father, and Harald, the other son, ruled over England. At this time Edward the Good, the son of Æthelred, and brother of Harald and Hörda-Knut, came to England, and, as was fit, was well liked there. Two years after the death of Knut the Old his daughter, Queen Gunn-hild of Saxland, died; she had married the Emperor Henry (of Germany).

"Three years later Harald Knutsson, King of England, died, and was buried at Morst (Shaftesbury), at the side of his father.

"Then his brother, Hörda-Knut, got both the realms of England and Denmark; and Magnus, St. Olaf's son, the sworn brother[1] of Hörda-Knut, ruled over Norway, as is written in the lives of the Norwegian kings. Two winters after the death of Harald, Hörda-Knut died, and was also buried at Morst with his father.

"After the death of Hörda-Knut the line of the old Danish kings became extinct. Edward, Æthelred's son, was taken king over England" (Knytlinga Saga, c. 21).

"Svein, son of King Knut and Alfifa, daughter of Alfrun jarl, had been put to rule Vinland in Jomsborg. Then his father sent word to him that he must go to Denmark, and thence to Norway and rule it, with the name of king. Svein had many men with him from Denmark, Harald jarl and many other powerful chiefs. His mother went with him, and he was taken as king at every law-thing" (St. Olaf's Saga, c. 252).

---

[1] Sworn brother = foster-brother.

" Svein, son of Knut the Great, ruled Norway for some winters; he was a child, and his mother Alfifa ruled for the most part, and was greatly disliked by the people. The Thrœndir (men of Thrandheim) were blamed because they had slain Olaf Haraldson the Saint. The chief Kalf Arnason, who had been the leader in the battle against Olaf, had been promised by Knut jarldom over the whole of Norway, and felt disappointed " (St. Olaf's Saga, c. 261).

" As soon as the spring came Kalf Arnason made his own ship ready, and sailed westward to England, for he had heard that King Knut had gone early in the season from Denmark westward to England. Kalf Arnason went to Knut at once when he reached England, and was received by him very well, and had a talk with him. It ended by Knut asking Kalf to head the rising against Olaf the Stout in Norway, if he came back to the land; and then said: ' I will give thee jarldom, and let thee rule Norway. Hakon, my kinsman, shall come to me, which is best for him, for his mind is thus that I do not think he will shoot a spear against Olaf, should they meet.' Kalf listened, and agreed to take the honour, and the plan was arranged by them. Kalf made ready to go home, and at parting Knut gave him costly gifts " (St. Olaf's Saga, c. 194).

The following passage is of interest in connection with the early history of England and its conquest by William the Norman :—

" When Magnus the Good (son of St. Olaf) had got the Danish realm, he sent messengers westward to England. They went to King Edward (Játvard) and delivered the letters and the seal of the king. In the letters this followed after the greeting of King Magnus: ' It is likely that you have heard of the treaty made between me and Hörda-Knut, that the one who lived after the other was dead without sons, should possess the lands and the tegns (subjects) of the other. Now it has happened, as I know you have heard, that I have inherited the Danish realm after Hörda-Knut. He owned, when he died, England no less than Denmark; now I claim England to be mine, according to a lawful agreement. I want thee to give up thy realm to me, or else I will take it with the help of a host both from Denmark and Norway. He who gets the victory will then rule the lands.'

" When Edward had read these letters, he answered: ' It is known to all people in this land that my father, King Æthelred (Adalrad), was rightfully born to this realm, both of yore and of late. We, his sons, were four. After he was

2 K

dead, my brother Edmund got the realm and the kingship, for he was the oldest of the brothers. I was well satisfied while he lived. After him, Knut, my stepfather, ruled; it was not easy to claim it while he lived. After him my brother Harald was king while he lived; when he died, my brother, Hörda-Knut, ruled over the Danish realm, and it was thought the only right division between us brothers that he should be king both over Denmark and England, and that I had no realm to rule. When he died, it was the will of all the people to make me king over England. While I had no king's name I served my chiefs (höfding) not prouder than those who were not born to rule. Now I have been consecrated as king, and have got the kingship as fully as my father had it before me. That name I will not give up while I live. If Magnus comes hither with his host, I will not gather a host against him; he can then take England, and first put me to death. Tell him these words of mine.'

"The messengers went back to Magnus, and told him all. He answered slowly: ' I think it is most just and best to let Edward have his realm in peace for me, and keep this which God has given me '" (Magnus the Good's Saga, cc. 38, 39).

CHAPTER XXIII.

SOME EXPEDITIONS AND DEEDS OF GREAT VIKINGS.
(*Continued.*)

Harald Hardradi—His influence on English history—His appearance and
character—Numerous expeditions—His bravery—His career in England
and Normandy—Jealousy between him and Godwin—His invasion
of England—The battle of Stamford Bridge—The battle of Hastings.

AMONG the great heroes of the North, and one who had a
special influence on the English history of his period—for
without his invasion of England William the Conqueror would
probably not have been victorious at the battle of Hastings—
was Harald Sigurdsson, surnamed Harald Hardradi, whose life
is a fine illustration of the life of a Viking. His forces,
added to those of Harald, son of Godwin, would have proved
very formidable. Here is a description of the appearance of
this hero.

" It was said by all that Harald surpassed other men in
wisdom and sagacity (counsel-skill), whether a thing was to be
done quick or in a long time, for himself or for others. He
was more weapon-bold than any man, as has been told.
(Thjódólf, in a stanza on him, says that ' the mind rules
one half of the victory.') He was a handsome and majestic-
looking man with hair (auburn), an auburn beard and long
moustaches; one eyebrow a little higher up than the other;
large arms and legs and well shaped. His measure in height
three ells. He was cruel towards his foes, and punished all
offences severely. He was very eager for rule, and all prosperous things. He gave his friends great gifts when he liked
them well. He was fifty when he fell. We have no note-
worthy tellings about his youth before he was at Stiklastadir,
fifteen winters old, in the battle with his brother Olaf. He
lived thirty-five winters afterwards; all that time uproar and
war were his pastime. He never fled from a battle, but often
he took precautions when he had to do with an overwhelming

2 K 2

force. All men who followed him in battle and warfare said that when he was in a great danger which came quickly upon him he would take the expedient which afterwards was seen by all to be the best" (Harald Hardradi's Saga, Heimskringla, c. 104).

We cannot follow him through the numerous expeditions which he undertook and which are described in his Saga.

We find that Harald swept all over the shores of the Mediterranean, went to Serkland (land of the Saracens), Africa, Sicily, Italy, Greece, Constantinople, Jerusalem, and Bulgaria. He was present, often as leader, in about eighty battles. There are many examples of his strategy and consummate generalship.

His life ended at the famous battle of Stamford Bridge, the account of which is a masterpiece of description.

From his youth up he was valiant. He joined in the battle of Stiklastadir, to help his half-brother, King Olaf the Stout, when he was fifteen years old. His mother's name was Asta (descended from Ragnar Lodbrok).

"When the array stood with its standards ready to fight, the king said : 'I do not think it right for my brother Harald to be in the battle, for he is a child.' Harald answered : 'I shall certainly be in the battle, but if I am so weak that I cannot wield the sword, I know what to do; my hand shall be tied to the hilt; no man shall have a better will than I to do harm to the bœndr. I want to follow my companions.' It is told that Harald sang this stanza :—

'I shall be daring enough
  To defend the wing in which I stand.
    *   *   *   *
    *   *   *   *

The young battle-glad poet
Will not draw back from the spears
Where the blows rain down ;
When hardest the fight.'

"Harald had his way and was in the battle, and won great renown. He was then fifteen winters old, as has been told. The skald Thjódólf mentions it in the poem he made about King Harald, called *sexstefja* (six-stave); among them is the following :—

I heard that the strong war-storm
Burst upon the king (Harald) close to
  Haug,
But the burner of the Bulgarians
  (Bolgara brennir = Harald)

Supported his brother (St. Ólaf) well.
The king did part against his will
Fifteen winters old
From the dead Olaf
And hid his helmet-seat (head).

" Harald got severely wounded in the battle, and Rögnvald Brúsason took him to a bondi in the night after the battle. The bondi lived in an out-of-the-way place, and kept him secretly, and cured him completely " (Fms. Harald Hardradi's Saga, c. 1).

Prof. Wassiliewsky has published a treatise, in Moscow, in which he gives extracts from a Greek work of the eleventh century.   We here give part of them :—

" *Araltes* (Harald) was a son of the king in Varangia ; he had a brother Julavos (St. Ólaf) who inherited the realm after his father's death, and made his brother Araltes the highest man next after himself.   Araltes was young, and admired the Roman power.   He came and bowed knee before the late Emperor Michael Paflagon ; he had with him a host of five hundred valiant men.   The Emperor received him befittingly, and sent him to Sicily into the war.   Araltes went there and performed deeds of high renown ; and when Sicily was subdued he came back to the Emperor with his host. Thereafter it happened that Delianos made a revolt in Bulgaria, and Araltes with his men, together with the Emperor and his host, went there ; and he performed against the enemies feats worthy of his birth and valour.   When the Emperor had subdued Bulgaria he went home.   I was there too, and fought for the Emperor as well as I could.   On the way home, in Mosynupolis, the Emperor, in reward for his feats, made him *Spatharokandidatos* (a title).   After Michael's death, in the time of the Emperor Monomachos, Araltes wanted to go home to his country, but was not allowed to do so, and he was hindered from going.   Nevertheless he got away secretly, and became king in his own country, instead of his brother Julavos (Olaf).   Even as king he preserved his loyalty and love towards the Romans " (Gustav Storm : Norsk Historisk Tidsskrift, 1884).

We will now give some extracts from the Sagas which contain an account of Harald's remarkable career, and which relate to the English and Norman history of that period.

" Edward, Æthelred's son, was king in England after Hörda-Knut ; he was called Edward the Good, and so he was.   His mother was Queen Emma, the daughter of Rikard jarl of Rouen ; her brother was Rodbjart (Robert), the father of William the Bastard, who was then duke (*hertogi*) [1] in Rouen

---

[1] Her = host, togi = leader.

in Normandy. Edward was married to Gyda, the daughter of Godwin jarl, son of Ulfnadr. Gyda's youngest brother, Harald, Godwin's son, was raised in the hird of Edward. The king loved him very greatly, and looked on him as his son, for he had no children " (Harald Hardradi's Saga, c. 77).

The death of King Edward the Confessor is here referred to :—

"One summer Harald Godwinson had to go to Bretland (Wales), and went there by ship ; when they got out they had head winds, and drifted out to sea. They landed in Northmandi after having experienced a dangerous storm. They sailed up to the burgh of Rouen (Rúda), and met William (Vilhjálm) jarl, who gladly received them ; Harald stayed there a long time, in the autumn, well entertained, for it kept on stormy, and they could not get to sea. Towards winter the jarl invited Harald to stay there during the winter. Harald sat in a high-seat on one side of the jarl, and on the other side sat the jarl's wife ; she was a very handsome woman ; these three often conversed, drinking and amusing themselves. The jarl usually went to sleep early, but Harald sat up long in the evenings talking to his wife. This went on for a long time. One evening she said : 'The jarl has asked me what we have been talking about so often, and now he is angry.' Harald answered : 'As soon as possible we will let him know all our conversation.' The next day Harald wished to speak to the jarl, and they went into the speaking (málrúm) room, where were also the jarl's wife and the councillors. Harald said : 'I must say, jarl, that there are more reasons for my coming hither than I have as yet told you. I want to ask thy daughter for my wife ; I have often spoken of this to her mother, and she has promised to help me in this matter with you.' When Harald had said this, all present thought it well fit, and recommended it to the jarl ; at last the maiden was betrothed to Harald, but as she was young the wedding was to be delayed for some winters. In the spring Harald made his ship ready and went away ; he and the jarl parted with much love. Harald went to England to King Edward (Jatvard) and never came back to Valland to celebrate his wedding. Edward was king over England for twenty-three winters, and died in London the fifth of January (1066) ; he was buried in St. Paul's Church, and the English call him a saint " (Harald Hardradi's Saga, cc. 78, 79).

"The sons of Earl Godwin were then the most powerful men in England. Tosti had been made chief over the king's host, and was the defender of the land and ruler over all the other jarls, when Edward began to grow old. His brother Harald was always in the hird, and was nearest attendant on the king, and had charge of all his money. It is said that when the king was about to die Harald and a few others were with him; he bent down over him, and said: 'I call you all to witness that the king just now gave me the kingship, and the rule over all England.' Then the dead king was carried away from his bed. The same day there was a meeting of the chiefs, who decided whom they would take to be king. Then Harald called forth his witnesses to prove that King Edward gave him the realm on his dying day. The meeting ended by Harald being taken as king, and consecrated the thirteenth day (of Yule = 6th of January, 1066) in St. Paul's Church, and the chiefs and the people made homage to him. When his brother Tosti heard this he was displeased, and thought he had as much right to be king. 'I want,' said he, 'the chiefs of the land to choose the man whom they think most fit to be king.' Harald heard these words, and said he would not give up the kingship, for he had been placed on the king's high-seat in Edward's place, and had been anointed and consecrated. The greatest part of the people favoured him, and he had all the treasures of the king " (Harald Hardradi's Saga, c. 80).

When Harald, son of Godwin, had got the kingship in England his brother Tosti did not like being his underman:

"So he went away with his men southwards across the sea to Flanders. There he stayed for a little while, and went to Frisland, and thence to Denmark to see his kinsman King Svein. Ulf jarl, Svein's father, and Gyda, Tosti jarl's mother, were brother and sister. Tosti asked Svein for help and support, but Svein asked him to stay there, and said that he should have a jarlship in Denmark, over which he might rule as an honoured chief. Tosti answered: 'I long to go back to England, to my homestead; but if I get no support from you, I will rather give you all the help I can give in England, if you will go there with the Danish host to win the land, as your uncle Knut the Great did.' The king answered: 'I am much weaker than my kinsman Knut, so that I can scarcely defend Danaveldi against the Northmen (Norwegians) and Harald (Hardradi). Knut the Old got Denmark by inheritance, and England by warfare and battle, though it was not unlikely for a while that he would lose his life; he obtained Norway without fight. Now I had rather act moderately according to my strength, than follow the deeds of my kinsman Knut.' Tosti said: 'My errand has been less successful than I thought you would let it be, seeing that I am your kinsman. Maybe I shall search for friendship where it is far more undeserved; and I may find a chief who is less afraid to plan great things than thou, king.' Then they parted, and not on very friendly terms " (Harald Hardradi's Saga, c. 81).

"Tosti then changed his journey and went to Norway to Harald Hardradi, who was in Vik. Tosti told the king his errand, and all about his journey since he had left England, and asked him to help him to get his realm there. The king answered that the Northmen were not willing to go to England and make warfare under an English chief. 'It is said that the English are not to be much trusted. Tosti asked : 'Is it true, what I heard in England, that thy kinsman Magnus sent men to King Edward with the message that he owned England as well as Denmark, and had inherited them after Hörda-Knut, as they had sworn.' The King answered : 'Why had he it not if he were its owner ?' Tosti said : 'Why hast thou not Denmark, as Magnus before thee ?' The king answered : 'The Danes need not boast to us Northmen; many marks have we left on those kinsmen of thine (often have we defeated them). Tosti continued : 'If thou wilt not tell me I will tell thee; Magnus got Denmark because the chiefs in the land helped him, and thou didst not get it because all the people were against thee; Magnus did not fight for England, because all the people of the land wanted to have Edward for king. If thou wouldst get England, I can contrive that the greater part of the chiefs there will be thy friends and helpers; I lack nothing but the name of king to equal my brother Harald. All know that a greater warrior than thou has never been born in the Northern lands, and it seems to me strange that thou didst fight fifteen years for Denmark and wilt not try for England, which is easy for thee to get.' Harald thought carefully about the jarl's words, and saw that there was much truth in them, and moreover was willing to get the realm. He and the jarl spoke often together; they decided that they would go in the summer to England, and win it. Harald sent word over the whole of Norway, and made a half levy. This was very much talked about, and there were guesses as to the result of the expedition. Some reckoned up the great deeds of Harald, and said it would not be impossible to him; but others thought that England would be difficult to win, that there was an immense mass of people there, and the warriors called *Thingamannalid* so valiant, that one was better than two of Harald's best men. Tosti jarl sailed in the spring westward to Flæmingjaland (Flanders) to meet the men who had followed him from England; and those who gathered to him from England and Flæmingjaland" (Harald Hardradi's Saga, c. 82).

The following tells of his preparations against England, his invading fleet amounting to over 240 warships, and describes the Battle of Stamford Bridge (Stafnfurdubryggia):—

"The host of Harald gathered in Solundir. When he was ready to leave Nidaros he first went to the shrine of St. Olaf, opened it, and cut his hair and nails; then he shut the shrine and threw the keys out on the Nid (a river), and went southward with his host. So many men had gathered to him that it is said he had nearly 240 ships, besides store-ships and small skutas" (Harald Hardradi's Saga, c. 83).

"When King Harald was ready for the expedition to England and a fair wind rose, he sailed out to sea with all his fleet; he reached Shetland, and lay a short while there, and then sailed southward to the Orkneys, whence he took many men, and the jarls Pál and Erlend, the sons of Thorfinn jarl, but he left there Queen Ellisif, and their daughters Maria and Ingigerd. Then he sailed southward past Scotland till he came off England, to a place called Kliflönd (Cleveland); then he went ashore, and ravaged and subdued the land, meeting with no resistance. Thereupon he sailed to Skardaborg (Scarborough) and fought against the townsmen; he went up on a high rock near the town, and set fire to a large pile which he made. They took large poles and lifted it up and threw it down into the town; soon one house after the other began to burn, and the whole town was destroyed. The Northmen slew many people, and took all the property they could get. There was no other choice for the English who wanted to save their lives but to ask peace and become King Harald's men; thus he subdued the land wherever he went. Then he sailed with all his host southward along the shore, and landed at Hellornes, where a gathered host came against him; he fought a battle, and got the victory. Then he went up the Humra (Humber) to Usa (Ouse), and there he landed; the sons of Godwin, Morcar and Waltheof, Earl of Huntingdon, were at Jórvík (York) with an overwhelming host, which had been gathering all summer. When the host of the jarls came down, Harald went ashore and began to array[1] his men: one wing[2] stood on the river bank, and the other higher up, near a ditch which was deep, broad, and

---

[1] Fylkja; the array itself is called Fylking.

[2] Fylkingar-arm.

full of water. The jarls let their arrays[1] go down along the river, and most of their men; the standard of Harald was near the river; there the ranks were thick; but they were thinnest at the ditch, and least to be depended upon. Thither Morcar came down with his standard. The wing of the Northmen by the ditch retreated, and the English followed them, thinking they were going to flee; but when Harald saw that his men retired along the ditch, he ordered a war-blast to be blown, and urged them on; he had the standard *land-waster* (landeyda) carried forward, and made so hard an attack that all were driven back. There was great slaughter in the jarls' host. Waltheof had had his standard brought along the river downward against the array of Harald, but when the king hardened the attack the jarl and his men fled along the river upward; only those who followed him escaped, but so many had fallen that large streams of blood in many places flowed over the plains When the jarl had fled Harald surrounded Morcar and the men who had advanced along the ditch with him; the English fell by hundreds. Many jumped into the ditch, and the slain lay there so thick that the Northmen walked across it with dry feet on human bodies; there Morcar perished.

"Tosti jarl had come northward from Flæmingjaland (Flanders) to meet King Harald when he arrived in England; he was in all the battles which we have related. It all happened as he had told the king, for many friends and kinsmen of Tosti jarl joined them in England, which was a great support to Harald. After this battle the people of the nearest districts submitted to King Harald, while some fled. Then he set off to take the town of York, and went with the entire host to Stafnfurdubryggja (Stamford Bridge);[2] but as he had won so great a victory over great chiefs and an overwhelming host, they had all become frightened and despaired of resistance. The townsmen resolved to send word to Harald and offer to surrender themselves and the town; it was agreed that the next Sunday the king should hold a Thing and speak to the townsmen; so on this Sunday Harald went up to the town with his host, and had a meeting outside of it at which all the people promised to obey and serve him; they gave him as hostages sons of high-born men whom Tosti jarl pointed out, for he knew all in the town. The king and his men went down to the ships in the evening, having won an easy victory, and they were very merry. It was agreed that on the second

---

[1] Fylking.
[2] In Heimskringla the corresponding passage has Stanfurdubryggja.

day of the week there should be a Thing, at which Harald was to appoint chiefs and give rights and grants. The same evening, after sunset, Harald, son of Godwin, came from the south with an overwhelming host; he was led into the town with the consent and goodwill of all the townsmen; then all the roads and the gates were occupied so that the Northmen should not get any news; the host was in the town during the night.

"On Monday, when King Harald Sigurdarson and his men had had their day meal, he sounded the horns to go ashore; he made his host ready, and selected those who should remain or go ashore;[1] he let two men from each detachment[2] go, and one remain. Tosti jarl prepared himself and his host to go ashore with the king; but Olaf, the king's son, and Eystein Orri (black cock) were left behind to guard the ships; also the son of Thorberg Arnason, who was then the most renowned and dearest of all lendirmen in Norway to the king—Harald had promised him his daughter Maria—the jarls of the Orkneys, Pál and Erlend, remained behind. The weather was exceedingly fine, and the sun so hot that the men left their armour behind, and went up with shields, helmets, spears, and swords; many carried bows and arrows, and they were in high spirits. When they came near the town they saw great clouds of dust, and a large host on horseback, with fine shields and shining brynjas. The king stopped, and, calling Tosti jarl, asked what men those were who were coming against them. The jarl said: 'They are most likely foes, though it may be that they are some of our kinsmen who come to seek friendship and mercy from us, and give us in return their faith and trust.' The king said that they would stop there and find out about this host; they did so, and the nearer the host approached the more numerous it seemed. It was so well armed, and the weapons glittered so, that it was as if one looked at broken shining ice. Then Tosti jarl said: 'Herra (lord), let us take a good expedient. It cannot be doubted that these are foes, and the king himself probably leads them.' The king asked: 'What is your advice?' Tosti answered: 'The first is to go back as soon as we can to the ships to fetch the rest of our men and our coats of mail (brynjas), then let us fight as well as we can; or otherwise let us go on board the ships, and then the horsemen cannot reach us.' The king said: 'I will follow another plan. I will put three brave men on the swiftest horses, and let them ride to our men as fast as they can, and tell them what has happened; their aid will soon come, for the English will have

---

[1] All through the Sagas we see that it seemed the custom that one-third of the men should remain on board of the ships to protect them.　　[2] Sveit.

a hard fight before we are defeated.' The jarl said: 'You shall have your will, lord, in this as in other things; but I am not more eager to flee than any other man, though I said what I thought advisable.' Harald put up his standard, the land-waster, and arrayed his host, and made the line (fylking) long, but not thick; then he bent the wings (arms) backwards, so that they met each other; it was a wide thick circle, equal on all sides; it had shield against shield on all sides, and shields above also.[1] The array was thus formed because the king knew that the horsemen were wont to rush up in small squads (ridil) and draw back at once; the king's guard, very picked men, was inside the circle, the archers also, and Tosti with his men. Then the king ordered the jarl to go forward where it was most needed. 'Those who stand outermost in the array,' he said, 'shall put the handles of their spears down on the ground, and the points against the breasts of the horsemen if they attack; those who stand next shall direct their spear points against the breasts of their horses; keep the spears thus everywhere that they cannot advance; let us stand firm and take care not to break this array.'

"Harald, son of Godwin, had come thither with an overwhelming host both of horsemen and footmen; it is told that King Harald had not the half of his men. Harald Sigurdarson, on a black horse with a white spot on its forehead, rode about his army and examined how it was arranged; his horse stumbled, and he fell forward off it; as he rose, he said: 'A fall bodes a lucky journey.'

"King Harald Gudinason said to the Northmen who were with him: 'Do you know the tall man with the blue kirtle (kyrtil) and the fine helmet who fell off his horse?' 'It is the king of the Northmen,' they said. The king added: 'He is a tall and noble-looking man, but nevertheless it is likely that his luck is now gone.' Then twenty English horsemen[2] rode forth, fully armoured, as were also their horses; when they came to the array of the Northmen, one of them asked: 'Where is Tosti jarl in the host?' Tosti answered: 'It is not to be concealed that you may find him here.' The horseman said: 'Harald thy brother sends thee greeting, and the message that thou shalt have peace, and get Northumberland, and rather

---

[1] It was a shieldburgh, with walls and roof of shields.

[2] In Snorri the twenty horsemen are described thus: "Twenty horsemen of the Thingmannalid rode up in front of the array of the Northmen. They were armoured all over and also their horses.

Then a horseman said: 'Is Tosti jarl here in the host?'" (Snorri Sturluson, Harald Hardradi's Saga, c. 9.)

From this we see that the English, like their kinsmen, had horsemen; and the finds of spurs, &c., prove this.

than that thou shouldst not join him he will give thee one-third of all his realm.' The jarl replied : 'Then something else is offered than the enmity and disgrace of last winter; if this had been offered then, many who now are dead would be alive, and the realm of the King of England would stand more firm. Now if I accept these terms, what will my brother Harald offer to the King of Norway for his trouble?' The horseman answered : 'He has said what he will grant King Harald Sigurdarson : it is a space of seven feet, and it is so long because he is taller than most other men.' : The jarl answered : 'Go and tell my brother, King Harald, to prepare for battle; it shall not be said among Northmen that Tosti jarl left Harald, King of Norway, and went into the host of his foes when he made warfare in England; rather will we all resolve to die with honour, or win England with a victory.' As the horsemen rode back to their host, King Harald asked the jarl : 'Who was that eloquent man ?' 'It was my brother, Harald, son of Godwin.' The king said : 'Too long was this hidden from us, for they had come so near our host that this Harald would not have been able to tell of the death of our men.'[1] The jarl said : 'It is true, lord, that he acted incautiously, and I saw that it might have been as you said; but when he came to offer me peace and great power, I should have been his slayer if I had betrayed who he was; I acted thus because I will rather suffer death from my brother, than be his slayer, if I may choose.' The king said to his men : 'This man (Harald) was little and nimble, and stood proudly in the stirrups.' Then King Harald Hardradi went into the ring (circle) of the shieldburgh and sang this stanza :—

' Forth we go	The helmets shine,
In the array;	I have not mine (brynja, namely)
Armour-less	Now lies our war-dress
Under the blue edge;	Down on the ships.'

"Emma was his brynja called; it was so long that it reached to the middle of his leg, and so strong that never had a weapon stuck in it. The king said : 'This song was badly composed, and I will sing a better one.' He sang :—

' Not that we crouch	To carry the helmet-stem (= the head)
From the clash of weapons	
In the bight of the shield;	High in the din of metals (= fight)
Thus bade to fight the word-true Hild.	Where the ice of Hlokk (sword) met with heads.'
The woman (Hild) asked me early	

---

[1] Meaning that if he had been known he would have been slain.

" Then Thjodolf skald sang—

'Not shall I though the king　　　　Heirs of a king
　Himself sink to the ground—　　　Than these two.
　It goes as God will—leave　　　The hawks (=sons) of Harald are
　The heirs of the king.　　　　　ready for revenge.'
　The sun shines not on sightlier

"It is said by people that Tosti's advice, given first when they saw the landhost, was the best and wisest, namely, that they should go back to the ships; but since a death-fated man cannot be saved, they suffered from the stubbornness of the king, who could not bear that this cautiousness should be regarded as fear or flight by his foes.

"They began the battle. The English horsemen made an attack on the Northmen; the resistance was very hard, for the spears of the latter were so placed that the horsemen could not reach them with their weapons. Then they rode around the array, but as soon as they came near, the archers of the Northmen shot at them as fast as they were able. The English saw that they could effect nothing, and rode back. The Northmen thought they were going to flee, and followed in pursuit; but as soon as the English saw that they had broken their shieldburgh they rode at them from all sides, shooting arrows and spears at them. When Harald Sigurdarson saw that his men were falling, he rushed into the fray where it was hottest. Many men fell on both sides. Harald, King of Norway, fought with the greatest bravery, and became so eager and furious that he rushed forward out of the array, dealing blows on all sides; neither helmet nor coat of mail could withstand him; he went through the ranks of his foes as if he were walking through air, for all who came near him fell back. Then, as the English almost fled, Harald Sigurdarson was hit with an arrow in the throat, so that a stream of blood gushed from his mouth; this was his death-wound; he fell there with all the men who had gone forward around him, except those who retreated and kept their standard. There was yet a stubborn fight, because the Northmen were very eager, and each urged the other on. When Tosti jarl became aware that the king had fallen he went to where he saw the standard aloft, and under the king's standard he urged the men on strongly; a little after both hosts rested themselves, and there was a long delay in the battle.

"Both sides made ready for battle again, but before the arrays met, Harald, son of Godwin, offered peace to Tösti jarl, his brother, and all Northmen who were left alive; but the North-men shouted all at once, and said that sooner would every one of them fall than accept truce from the English. Then the Northmen raised a war-cry, and the battle began a second time. Tosti jarl was then chief of the host; he fought valiantly and followed up the standards, and ere the fight ended fell there with great bravery and renown. At that moment Eystein Orri came from the ships with the men who followed him; they were in full war-dress, and Eystein at once took the standard of Harald, the "landeyda." Then there was a third and very severe battle; many of the English fell and they almost fled; this was called Orrahrid (the tempest of Orri). Eystein and his men had hurried so much from the ships that they were almost disabled by weariness (exhaustion) before they began the fight; but afterwards they were so eager that they did not spare themselves while they were able, and at last took off their coats of mail (ring-brynjas); then the English could easily find places for wounding them. Some died unwounded from over-exertion, and nearly all the high-born Northmen fell there; this was late in the day. It happened as it always does, where many people gather, that all were not equally brave; many tried to escape in various ways. It went as fate would; some were destined to a longer life and escaped. It was dark in the evening when the man-slaughter was over. Styrkar, the stallari (marshal) of King Harald, was a famous man; he got a horse in the evening, and rode away, but it was blowing a strong and cold gale; he had no other clothes than a shirt (skyrta), a helmet, and a drawn sword in his hand; he soon cooled when the weariness left him. A waggoner (vagn-karl) who had on a lined jacket (kösung) met him. Styrkar asked: 'Wilt thou sell the jacket, bondi?' He answered: 'Not to thee; thou must be a North-man; I know thy speech.' Styrkar said: 'If I am a Northman, what will thou then?' 'I will slay thee,' replied the bondi, 'but now it is so bad that I have not got a weapon that I can use.' Styrkar added: 'If thou canst not slay me, bondi, I will try to slay thee.' He raised his sword and smote his neck so that his head dropped down; Styrkar then took the skin-jacket and put it on, jumped on his horse, and rode down to the shore. Arnor jarla skald sang about this battle, now told of, which was the last that Harald and his men fought, in the erfidrapa (funeral song) which he made about the king. Arnor says: 'It is doubtful if any other king under the sun has fought with such a valour and bravery as Harald.'

"It was on the second day of the week (Monday) that King

Harald fell,[1] two nights before *Mikjalsmessa* (Michaelmas) " (Fornmanna Sögur, cc. 115–119).

Here is a short account of the battle of Hastings.   **William** the Conqueror is called *Vilhjalm Jarl.*

"Vilhjalm (William) bastard, jarl of Rouen, heard of the death of Játvard (Edward) his kinsman, and that Harald, son of Godwin, had been made King of England, and been consecrated. He thought he had more right to the kingdom of England than Harald, on account of his relationship to Edward, and he also wanted to pay Harald for the disgrace of having broken his betrothal with his (Vilhjalm's) daughter. William gathered a host in Normandy (Northmandi), with very many men and ships. When he rode from the town to his ships, and had mounted his horse, his wife went to him and wanted to speak to him; he struck at her with his heel and thrust the spur deeply into her breast, and she fell dead, and then he rode on to his ship, and went with his host to England. Bishop Otto, his brother, was with him. When the jarl reached England he plundered and subdued the land wherever he went.

"He was taller and stronger than others, and a good rider; a very great warrior, but rather cruel; very wise, but, it was said, not trustworthy. Harald, son of Godwin, allowed Olaf, the son of Harald Sigurdsson, and those there with him who had survived the battle, to go, and King Harald then turned southward with his host to England, for he had heard that William the Bastard was in the south of England subduing the land. There were with Harald his brothers, Svein, Gyrd, and Valthjóf. Harald and William met in the south of England at *Helsingjaport* (port of Hastings); there was a great battle, where fell Harald and Gyrd his brother, with a great part of their men. That was nineteen nights after the fall of Harald Sigurdsson. Valthjóf, Harald's brother, escaped by flight, and late in the evening met a detachment of William's men, who when they saw the Valthjóf men fled into an oak forest; they were one hundred men. Valthjóf set the forest on fire, and burnt it up altogether.

"William had had himself proclaimed King of England. He sent word to Valthjóf that they should be reconciled, and gave him truce to meet him. The jarl went with few men;

---

[1] "One winter after the fall of King Harald (Hardradi) his body was brought from England north to Nidarós (Throndhjem) and buried in Maria Church, which he had built" (Harald Hardradi's Saga, c. 104).

when he came on the heath north of *Kastalabryggja* (Castle-bridge) two king's stewards met him with a detachment, took him and fettered him, and he was slain; the English call him a saint. William was king over England for twenty-one years, and his kin ever since " (Harald Hardradi's Saga, Hkr. cc. 99–101).

The battle of Hastings was fought on October 14th, 1066. Gyrd played an important part in the conflict.

" Then said Gyrd jarl to his brother King Harald: ' I fear that thou wilt not succeed in the fight against William, for thou hast sworn not to defend England against him.' The king replied: ' It may be, brother, that it will suit thee better to fight against William than me; but I have not been wont to lie in my room when other men have fought, and William shall not hear that I dare not behold him.' After this King Harald had his standard raised, and began the battle against William. The fight was most violent, and it was long thought uncertain which of them would get the victory; but as the battle continued the fall of men turned on the hands of the English (Enskir menn). William had before the attack let the relics of Otmar be tied to his standard; on these Harald had taken his oath. But when the battle began to turn against King Harald, he asked: ' What is tied to William's standard ? ' And when he was told, he said: ' It may be that we need not then expect victory in this battle.' And thus it ended that King Harald and his brother Gyrd fell, and a large part of their men, but all who were alive fled " (Fornmanna Sögur, vi. c. 121).

CHAPTER XXIV.

THE DISCOVERY AND SETTLEMENT OF ICELAND, GREENLAND, AND AMERICA.

Causes leading to the discovery of Iceland—Naddod's expedition—The expedition of Gardar Svavarson—Those of Floki, Ingolf, and Leif—Iceland so named by Floki—Settlers in Iceland—Discovery of Greenland—Thorvald and Eirek the Red—Discovery of America—Bjarni's voyage—Leif's voyage—Thorvald's voyage—Attacked by plague—Thorfinn Karlsefni's voyage—Description of the inhabitants.

From the Sagas and ancient records which relate to the earlier events of the North, we find that the people spread westward and southward to the Mediterranean. Later we see this maritime race seeking out new lands, and crossing the broad Atlantic and discovering a New World.

The policy of the Norwegian King Harald Fairhair, which led to the subjection of many lesser chieftains about the middle of the ninth century, gave rise to an emigration of the more high-spirited chiefs in search of other lands, and resulted in the discovery of Iceland, called in some Sagas Snowland, and afterwards of Greenland and Vinland, or America. The hero of the discovery of Iceland was a sea-rover called Naddod, about the year 861.

"Owing to his (Harald Fairhair) oppression, many people fled from the country, and many uninhabited lands were then settled—Jamtaland, Helsingjaland, and the western lands, Sudreyjar (the Hebrides), Dyflinnar Skiri (the shire of Dublin in Ireland), Katanes (Caithness) in Scotland, and Hjaltland (the Shetlands), Normandi in Valland, Fœreyjar (the Faroes). At that time Iceland was discovered" (Egil's Saga, c. 4).

DISCOVERY AND SETTLEMENT OF ICELAND.

men from Norway, settled there permanently. Their example was followed by many others afterwards.

" It is said that some men were going from Norway to the *Fœreyjar* (Faroes). Some say it was Naddod Viking. They were driven westward into the sea, and there found a large land. They went up on a high mountain in the eastern fjords, and looked far and wide for smoke or some token that the land was inhabited. They saw none. They went back to the Faroes in the autumn, and when they set sail much snow fell on the mountains, and therefore they called the country *Snœland* (Snow land). They praised the land much. The place where they landed is now called Reydarfjall in the Austfjords " (Landnáma, i. c. 1).

Naddod's example was soon followed by others, amongst whom was Gardar Svavarson, a Swede, who called the island Gardarshólmi.

" A man called Gardar Svavarson, of Swedish kin, went in search of Snowland at the advice of a foreknowing (foresighted) mother. He landed east of the eastern Horn. There was a harbour. Gardar sailed round the land, and saw it was an island. He stayed over the winter at Húsauik, in Skjálfandi, and built a house there. In the spring, when he was ready to sail, a man called Náttfari with a thrall and a bondmaid were driven off in a boat. They settled in Náttfaravik. Gardar went to Norway, and praised the land greatly. He was the father of Uni, the father of Hróar Tungugodi. Thereafter the land was called Gardarshólmi (Gardar's island); there was at that time forest from mountain to shore " (Landnáma, c. 1).

The name *Iceland* was first given to the island by Flóki,[1] but neither he, Naddod, nor Gardar, settled there. The first settlers were the foster brothers Ingólf and Leif, who with their followers landed about the year 870.

" The foster brothers made ready a large ship which they owned, and went in search of the land which Hrafna-Flóki (Raven-Flóki) had discovered, and which was then called Iceland. They found the land and stayed in Austfjords, in the southern Alptafjord. The south of the land seemed to

---

[1] For the story of Flóki taking three ravens with him in order to guide him on his expedition to Iceland.

them better than the north. They stayed one winter there, and then went back to Norway.

"Thereafter Ingólf prepared for a voyage to Iceland, while Leif went on warfare in the west. He made war in Ireland, and there found a large underground house; he went down into it, and it was dark until light shone from a sword in the hand of a man. Leif killed the man, and took the sword and much property. Thereafter he was called Hjörleif (Sword-Leif). He made war widely in Ireland, and got much property. He took ten thralls; their names were Dufthak, Geirrod, Skjaldbjörn, Haldór, Drafdrit; more names are not given. Then he went to Norway and met his foster brother there. He had before married Helga, Ingólf's sister. This winter Ingólf made a great sacrifice, and asked what his luck and fate would be, but Hjörleif was never willing to sacrifice. The answer pointed out Iceland to Ingólf. After this both made a ship ready for the voyage. Hjörleif had his booty on board, and Ingólf their foster brotherhood property. When ready they sailed out to sea.

"In the summer when Ingólf and Leif went to settle in Iceland Harald Fairhair had been twelve years king over Norway; 6,073 winters had elapsed since the beginning of this world, and since the incarnation of our Lord 874 years They sailed together until they saw Iceland, then they and their ships parted. When Ingólf saw Iceland he threw over-board his high-seat pillars for luck. He said that he would settle where the pillars landed. He landed at a place now called Ingólfshöfdi (Ingólf's cape). But Hjörleif was driven westward along the land, and suffered from want of water. The Irish thralls there kneaded together meal and butter, saying these caused no thirst. They called the mixture *minn-thak*, and when it had been made there came a heavy rain, and they took water into their tents. When the *minnthak* began to get mouldy they threw it overboard, and it came ashore at a place now called Minnthakseyr. Hjörleif landed at Hjörleifshöfdi (Hjörleif's cape), where there was a fjord. Hjörleif had two houses (skáli) made there; the walls of one are 18 fathoms, and those of the other 19 fathoms high. Hjörleif remained there that winter. In the spring he wanted to sow (corn); he had one ox, and let the thralls drag the plough. When Hjörleif was in his house Dufthak (one of the thralls) suggested that they should kill the ox, and say that a bear of the forest had slain it, and then they would slay Hjörleif if he searched for the bear. Then they told Hjörleif this. When they each went different ways in search of the bear in the forest, the thralls attacked them singly and murdered all the ten. They ran away with their women and loose property and the boat. The thralls went to the islands which they saw south-west off the land, and stayed there a while. Ingólf sent his thralls, Vífil and Karli, westward along the shore to search for his high-seat pillars. When they came to Hjörleifshöfdi they found Hjörleif dead; they then returned and told Ingólf these tidings. He was very angry at the slaying of Hjörleif" (Landnáma, i. cc. 4–6).

"Iceland was first settled from Norway in the days of Harald Fairhair, son of Halfdan the black. . . .

"Ingolf was the name of a Northman, of whom it is truly said that he went first from Norway to Iceland, when Harald Fairhair was sixteen years old, and a second time a few winters later. He settled south in Reykjarvik. In that time was Iceland covered with wood between the mountains and the fjord.

"Then were there Christian men, whom the Northmen call *Papa*, but afterwards they went away because they would not remain with the heathens, and left behind them Irish books, and croziers and bells, from which it could be seen that they were Irishmen" (Islendingabok, c. i.).

"At the time when Iceland was discovered and settled from Norway, Adrianus was Pope at Rome, and John, who was the eighth of that name, in the apostolic seat; Louis (Hlödver), son of Louis, Emperor north of the mountains (i.e. the Alps), and Leo, as well as his son Alexander, of Mikligard. Harald Fairhair was King of Norway; Eirik Eymundsson of Sweden and his son Bjorn; Gorm the old in Denmark; Aelfred (Elfrad) the powerful in England, as well as his son Edward (Jatvard); Kjarval in Dublin (Dyflin); and Sigurd the powerful, jarl of the Orkneys" (Landnama c. i. part i.).

From many places in Landnama we find that people from England, Ireland, Scotland, and Flanders, and from different countries of the North, settled in Iceland.

"Fridleif was from Gautland on his father's side, while his mother, Bryngerd, was Flemish. . . . Fridleif settled in Iceland. Thord Knapp was a Swede, son of Bjorn of Haug. He went with another man, named Nafarhelgi, to Iceland" (Landnama, c. xi. part iii.).

"Örlyg was fostered by the holy bishop Patrek (Patrick) in the Hebrides. He desired to go to Iceland, and asked the bishop to help him. He gave him timber for a church, and also a *plenarium*, an iron bell, and consecrated earth, that he might put it under the cornerstave. (This shows they had stave churches in those days). The Bishop Patrick: 'Thou must land at a place where thou seest two mountains run out into the sea, and a valley in each mountain. Thou shalt settle at the foot of the most southerly mountain; there thou shalt build a church, and dwell there'" (Landnama, c. xii. part 1).

DISCOVERY OF GREENLAND.

About one hundred years later the descendants of these roving Vikings, animated by the same restless spirit and love of freedom so characteristic of their race, set out in search of new lands, and discovered and settled Greenland in A.D. 985. The heroes of this new settlement were a Norwegian chief Thorvald and his son Eirek the Red.

"Thorvald and his son Eirek the Red went from Jadar (Jœderen, in Norway) to Iceland, outlawed on account of manslaughter. Iceland was then to a great extent settled. They first lived at Drangar, in Hornstrandir. Thorvald died there. Eirek then married Thorhild, daughter of Jorund and Thorbjörg Knarrarbringa, who was then married to Thorbjörn of Haukadal. Eirek thereupon moved south and lived at Eireksstadir, near Vatnshorn. The son of Eirek and Thorhild was called Leif. After Eirek had slain Eyjulf Saur and Holmgöngu-Hrafn he was outlawed from Haukadal. He moved westward to Breidi-fjord, and lived at Eireksstadir in Öxney (Ox-island). He lent Thorgest his *seat-pillars*, and did not get them back when he asked for them. Hence arose quarrels and battles between him and Thorgest, as is told in the Saga of Eirek.[1] Styr Thorgrimsson, Eyjulf of Sviney, the sons of Thorbrand of Alftafjord and Thorbjörn Vifilsson, supported Eirek. But the family of Thorgest was supported by the sons of Thord Gellir and Thorgeir of Hitardal. Eirek was outlawed at the Thornes-thing. Thereupon he made his ship ready for sea in Eirek's bay. When he was ready Styr and the others followed him out past the island to bid him farewell. Eirek told them that he intended to search for the land which Gunnbjörn,[2] son of Ulf Kráka (crow), saw when he was driven westward across the sea and found Gunnbjarnarsker (Gunn-

---

[1] A lost Saga.
[2] There is no account of Gunnbjorn's | journey.

björn's rock). He (Eirek) said he would come back to his friends if he found this land. Eirek sailed from Snœfellsjökul. He found the land, and came to it at a place which he called Midjökul (Mid-glacier), and which is now[1] called Bláserk (Blue shirt). He sailed thence southward along the coast to see if the land could be settled on. He stayed the first winter in Eireksey (Eirek's island), near the middle of what later was called the eastern settlement. Next spring he went to Eireks-fjord, and there took up his abode. In the summer he went to the western part of the country, and in many places gave names to it. The following winter he stayed at Hólmar, near Hrafnsgnípa, and the third summer he went north to Snœfell all the way to Hrafnsfjord. Then he said he had got into the inmost part of Eireksfjord. He went home (in Greenland), and stayed the third winter in Eireksey at the mouth of Eireksfjord. The next summer he went to Iceland, and landed with his ship in Breidifjord. He called the land which he had found *Grœnland,* for he said it would make men's minds long to go there if it had a fine name. Eirek stayed in Iceland that winter, and the next summer he went to settle on the land. He lived at Brattahlid in Eireksfjord. Wise men say that during the summer when Eirek the Red went to settle in Greenland, thirty-five ships from Breidifjord and Borgarfjord went there, fourteen got there, while some were driven back and others were lost. This was fifteen winters before Christianity was enacted as law in Iceland "[2] (Flateyjarbók, i. 429).

" On this voyage Eirek discovered Greenland, and remained there three winters, and then went to Iceland, where he remained one winter before he returned to settle in Greenland, (Grænland), and that was fourteen winters before Christianity was established by law in Iceland " (Eyrbyggja Saga, c. 24)

DISCOVERY OF AMERICA.

Between the years 985 and 1011 these enterprising mariners, in the course of their expeditions from the remote and rough coasts of the North, discovered the great continent of America, with the inhabitants of which they seem to have had some struggles ; but such was the transient nature of their expeditions that the benefit of this discovery was for a time lost

---

[1] Fourteenth century.
[2] The laws were, according to Land- náma, enacted A.D. 1000.

both to them and to the rest of the civilised world; yet a remarkable destiny has willed that their descendants, in whose veins the blood of the old Norsemen still runs, should people the country.

Five distinct expeditions are related in the Sagas, the most famous one being that of Thorfinn Karlsefni, who about 1007 determined to settle a colony in the new land, and who on his return to Norway sold some of the wood which he had brought home for a large sum to a merchant from Bremen.

First Journey.

"Herjúlf was the son of Bárd, the son of Herjúlf, who was a kinsman of Ingólf, the settler. Ingólf gave Herjúlf land between Vog and Reykjanes. Herjúlf first lived at Drep-stokk. His wife was Thorgerd, and their son Bjarni was a most promising man. When quite young he longed to go abroad. He acquired much property and honour, and alternately spent a winter abroad and a winter with his father. He soon had a trading ship, and the last winter he was in Norway Herjúlf determined to go to Greenland with Eirek, and made ready. Herjúlf had on board a man from the Hebrides, a Christian, who composed the Hafgerdinga drápa.[1] Herjúlf lived at Herjúlfsnes. He was a man of high birth. Eirek the Red lived in Brattahlid; he was held in the greatest honour there, and all obeyed him. His children were Leif, Thorvald, Thorstein, and Freydís, who was married to Thorvard, who lived at Gardar, where now is a bishop's see. She was very overbearing, and Thorvard was weak minded. She was married to him chiefly for the sake of his property. The people of Greenland were heathen at that time. Bjarni landed with his ships at Eyrar the summer after his father had sailed (in the spring).

"Bjarni thought this important news (the departure of his father), and did not wish to unload his ship. Then his sailors asked what he meant to do, and he answered he wanted to continue his custom of staying over winter with his father. 'I will sail to Greenland on my ship if you will follow me,' said he to his men. All answered they would do as he liked. He said, 'Our voyage will be considered unwise, as none of us have been before in the Greenland Sea.' Nevertheless, when they were ready, they set out to sea, and after three days' sailing land was out of sight, and the fair winds ceased, and northern winds

---

[1] Hafgerding = the walls of the ocean, monster waves on the ocean.

with fog blew continually, so that for many days they did not know in what direction they were sailing. Then the sun came into sight, and they could distinguish the quarters of heaven. They hoisted sail and sailed all day before they saw land. They wondered what land this could be, and Bjarni said he did not think it was Greenland. The men asked if he wished to sail towards it, and he answered that he wanted to go near it; this they did, and soon saw that it had no mountains, but low hills, and was forest-clad. They kept the land on their left, but the corners of the sail were towards the land. Then they sailed for two days before they saw other land. They asked Bjarni if he did not think this was Greenland. He answered: 'No, it is very unlike, I thought, for very large glaciers are said to be in Greenland.' They soon approached the land, and saw that it was flat and covered with woods. Then the fair wind fell, and the sailors said they thought it best to land as they lacked both wood and water, but Bjarni did not want to land, and said they had enough left; at this the men grumbled somewhat. He told them to set sail, which they did, and turned the prow seaward, and sailed in that direction with a southwesterly wind for three days, and then more land came in view which rose high with mountains and a glacier. They asked Bjarni if he would like to go ashore there, but he answered he would not do so as the land had an inhospitable look. They did not furl their sail, but sailed along the shore, and saw it was an island. They once more turned the prow of the ship from the shore, and set to sea with the same fair wind, but the gale increased, and Bjarni told them to take in a reef, and not sail so fast, for the ship and its rigging could not stand it. They sailed four days, until they saw land for the fourth time. They asked Bjarni if he thought this Greenland. He answered: 'This most resembles Greenland from what I have been told, and here we will land. They landed in the evening at a cape where a boat was lying. Herjúlf, Bjarni's father, lived on the cape, and it is called Herjúlfsnes after him. Bjarni now stayed with his father, left off sea-journeys, and dwelt there during his father's lifetime, and after his death" (Flateyjarbók, i. 430–32).

Discovery of Vinland.

"Now it is related that Bjarni Herjúlfsson came from Greenland to Eirek Jarl (son of the great Hákon, 1000–1015) who received him well. Bjarni described his voyage and the lands that he had seen. People thought he had shown a lack of interest as he had nothing to tell about them, and he was somewhat blamed for it. He became the Jarl's hirdman, and went to Greenland the following summer. Now there was much talk about land discoveries. Leif, son of Eirek the Red, of Brattahlid, went to Bjarni Herjúlfsson and bought his ship, and gathered together thirty-five sailors. He asked his father Eirek to lead the expedition as before. Eirek declined it, saying he was too old, and was less able to bear hardship than formerly. Leif answered that even were this so he would still have with him more luck than the rest of his kinsmen. Eirek yielded, and when ready they rode from home. Not far from the ship Eirek's horse stumbled,[1] and he fell and hurt his foot. Then he said : ' It cannot be my fate to be the discoverer of any other lands than the one on which we now live. I will follow you no further.' Eirek went home to Brattahlid and Leif with his thirty-five companions went on board. There was a man from the south with them called Tyrker. When they had made their ship ready they set out to sea. The first land they found was that which Bjarni had found last. They sailed towards it, cast anchor, put out a boat and went ashore, but saw no grass. The whole interior consisted of glaciers, and the land between them and the sea was like a plain of ice, and this seemed to them barren of good things. Leif said : ' Now we have not acted with this land like Bjarni, who did not come ashore. I will give a name to the land and call it Helluland.[2] Then they went on board and sailed out to sea, and found another land. They approached it, cast anchor, pushed off a boat, and went ashore. This land was flat and forest-clad, and the beach was low, and covered with white sand in many places. Leif said : ' This land shall be named after its properties, and be called Markland (Woodland). They then went on board again as quickly as they could. They sailed thence out to sea with a north-east wind for two days before they saw land. They sailed towards it, and came to an island lying north of it, and went ashore in fine weather and looked round. They found dew on the grass, and touched it with their hands, and put it into their mouths, and it seemed to them they had never tasted anything so sweet as this dew. Then they went on board and sailed into the channel, which was between the island and the cape, which ran north from the main-land. They passed the cape sailing in a westerly direction. There the water was very shallow, and their ship went aground, and at ebb-tide the sea was far out from the ship. But they were so anxious to get ashore that they could

---

[1] Cf. Harald Hardrádi at Stamford-bridge.

[2] Hella = a plain of ice, a cover of ice.

not wait till the high-water reached their ship, and ran out on the beach where a river flowed from a lake. When the high-water set their ship afloat they took their boat and rowed to the ship, and towed it up the river into the lake. There they cast anchor, and took their leather-bags (hudfat) ashore, and there built booths. They resolved to stay there over winter, and built large houses. There was no lack of salmon in the river and lake, and they were larger than any they had seen before. The land was so fertile that it seemed to them that no barns would be needed to keep fodder for the cattle during the winter. There was no frost there during the winter, and the grass lost little of its freshness. The length of night and day was more equal than in Greenland or Iceland. The sun set there at eykt [1] and rose at dagmál [2] on the shortest day. When they had finished building their houses, Leif said to his men: 'I will divide you into two parties, as I wish to explore the land. One half shall stay in the *skali* (house), and the other explore the country, but not go so far that they cannot get home in the evenings, and not separate from each other. They did this for some time. Leif sometimes went with them, but at other times remained in the *skali*. He was a large and strong man, of imposing looks, and wise and moderate in everything.

"One evening it happened that they missed one of their men, Tyrker, the southerner. Leif was much grieved at this, for Tyrker had long been with him, and his foster father had been very fond of Leif in his childhood. He upbraided his men harshly, and made ready to go and search for him with twelve men. A short way from the house Tyrker met them, and was welcomed back. Leif soon saw that his foster father was in high spirits. He had a projecting forehead, unsteady eyes, a tiny face, and was little and wretched, but skilled in all kinds of handicraft. Leif said to him : 'Why art thou so late, foster father, and why hast thou parted from thy followers ?' He then spoke for a long time in Thyrska, and rolled his eyes in many directions and made wry faces. They did not understand what he said. After a while he spoke in the northern tongue (Norrœna), and said : 'I did not go much farther than you, but I can tell some news. I found a vine and grapes.' 'Is this true, foster-father ?' Leif asked. 'Certainly it is,' he answered, 'for I was born where there was neither lack of vine nor grapes.' They slept there that night, and in the morning Leif said to

---

[1] *Eykt*—the word is found in the early Christian laws—Kristinrett of Thorlak and Ketil, two bishops in Iceland—where it is defined as the time of the day when the sun has passed two parts of the south-west and the other third is left.

[2] *Dagmal*, the early meal in Iceland, which is now from 8.30 A.M. to 9.0 A.M.

his sailors: 'Now we will do two kinds of work, one day you shall gather grapes or cut vines, the other you shall fell trees so that I may load my ship.' This they did, and their boat is said to have been filled with grapes, and a ship's load of timber was cut. When spring came they made ready and left, and Leif named the land after its fruits, and called it *Vinland*. They sailed out to sea and got fair winds till they saw Greenland and its glaciers. Then a man said to Leif: 'Why dost thou steer the ship so close to the wind?' Leif answered: 'I am attending to my steering, but I am also looking at something else; do you see anything remarkable?' They answered they did not. Leif said: 'I do not know whether it is a ship or a rock which I see.' Then they saw it, and said it was a rock. His sight was so much better than theirs that he saw men on the rock. He said: 'Now I want to keep closer to the wind, so that we may get to them, and we must give them help if they need it. If they are not peaceful they are in our power, but we are not in theirs.' They approached the rock, cast anchor, lowered their sail, and set out a little boat which they had with them. Then Tyrker asked these men who their leader was. The leader answered that his name was Thórir, and he was a Norwegian, but what, he said, is thy name? Leif told his name. 'Art thou the son of Eirek, the Red, of Brattahlid?' Leif answered: 'I am. Now I offer to you all to come on board my ship with as much cargo as it can hold.' They accepted the offer, and sailed to Brattahlid, in Eiriksfjord, with the cargo, where they unloaded the ship. Leif invited Thórir to stay with him, and also his wife Gudrid and three other men, and for his own sailors and those of Thórir he got quarters. Leif took fifteen men from the rock, and was afterwards called Leif the Lucky. He was now rich and respected; that winter a disease came among the men of Thórir, and he and the greater part of his men, and also Eirek, the Red, died. There was much talk about Leif's Vinland journey, and his brother Thorvald thought the land had been explored too little. Leif then said to him: 'Thou shalt go with my ship, brother, if thou likest, to Vinland, but it shall first fetch the timber of Thórir from the rock. This was done" (Flateyjarbók, i. 538).

Third Voyage.

"Now Thorvald made ready (in Greenland, where his father Eirek lived), with the help of his brother Leif, for this voyage with thirty men. They prepared their ship and sailed to sea, and nothing is told of their journey till they came to Vinland, to the booths of Leif. . . . They sat quiet that winter and caught fish for food. In the spring Thorvald told them to make the ship ready, and sent the boat with some men to go west and explore the land during the summer. The country seemed to them fair and covered with forests; there was a short space between the forest and the sea, and the sands were white. There were shallows and many small islets. They found no abodes of men or animals, except in a westerly island, where they found a corn barn of wood. They found no other traces of men, and went back and came to the booths of Leif in the autumn. The next summer Thorvald went with his ship north-east along the coast. A strong gale burst on them off a cape, where they were driven ashore, and the keel of the ship was broken. They stayed there long and repaired it. Thorvald said to his followers: 'I want you to raise the keel upright here on the ness, and call it Kjalarnes (Keel cape). This they did. Then they sailed thence in an easterly direction off the land, into the fjord mouths nearest the cape, which projected there, and which was covered with trees. They cast anchor and took their gangways ashore, and Thorvald walked up with all his followers. He said: 'This is a fine country, and here I should like to raise my bœr.' Then they walked down to the ship, and saw three marks on the sand inside the cape, where they found three *skin-boats* (canoes) with three men under each. They divided their men and took them all, except one who escaped with his boat. They killed the other eight, and then again went to the cape and looked round, and saw some eminences in the inner part of the fjord, which they thought were houses. Thereupon such drowsiness came over them that they could not keep awake, and all fell asleep. Then they heard a voice shouting which roused them all, saying: 'Wake Thorvald and all thy men if thou wishest to save thy life. Go on board thy ship with all thy men, and leave the land as quickly as you can.' Innumerable skin-boats came out along the fjord and attacked them. Thorvald said: 'Let me put war hurdles on the sides, and defend ourselves as best we can, but kill few of them.' This they did, and the Skrœlingjar [1] shot at them for a while, and then fled, each one as quickly as he could. Thorvald asked his men if they were wounded. They said they were not. 'I have got a wound under my arm,' he said, 'an arrow flew between the gunwale and the shield under my arm, and here is the arrow; this will cause my death. I advise you to prepare to go back as soon as you can, but you shall take me to the cape, which appeared to me to be the most habitable. It may be that truth has come out of my mouth, and that I shall live there for a while. You shall bury me there, and put crosses at my head and feet, and henceforward call it Krossanes' (Cross Cape). Greenland was then Christian, though Eirek, the Red, died before the introduction of Christianity. Thorvald died, and they carried out his wish, and then went to their other companions,[1] and told each other the tidings they knew. They lived there that winter, and took grapes and vines on board with them. In the spring they made ready for Greenland, and landed in Eireksfjord, and had great tidings to tell Leif" (Flateyjarbók, i. 541).

"Thorstein, son of Eirek, the Red, desired to go to Vinland to fetch the body of his brother Thorvald. He made the same ship ready, and took on board picked men as to strength and size, twenty-five men, and his wife, Gudrid. They sailed to sea when ready, and the land disappeared. They were thrown hither and thither all the summer, and knew not where they were. When a week had passed of the winter they landed in Lysufjord, in the western settlement of Greenland. Thorstein searched for houses, and got lodgings for all his men, while he and his wife had no lodgings. They two remained on board for some nights. Christianity was then still young in Greenland."

Thorstein the Black, a heathen man, offered them lodgings.

"Early in the winter a disease came among the men of Thorstein, and many of them died. He had coffins made for the corpses, and had them brought on board and prepared, 'for I want to take them all to Eireksfjord in the summer,' said he. After a short time the disease came into the house of Thorstein the Black, and first his wife Grimhild fell sick. She was very large and strong, like men, but nevertheless the disease laid her up. Soon after Thorstein Eireksson fell sick, and they were in their beds, and Grimhild died. When she was dead, Thorstein the Black walked out of the room to fetch a board, and lay the body on it. Gudrid said: 'Do not be long away, my good Thorstein.' He answered he would not. Thorstein Eireksson said: 'Strange does our housewife look now, for she rises on her elbow, draws up her feet, and searches for her shoes with her hand.' Then Thorstein came in, Grimhild lay down, and every timber of the room creaked. Thorstein made a coffin for the body, took it away, and prepared it. He was large and strong, but needed it to take it away. Thorstein Eireksson's illness grew worse,

---

[1] I.e., who had been left at the booths.

and he died. His wife, Gudrid, did not like it well. They were all in one room. Gudrid sat on a chair in front of the bench on which lay her husband, Thorstein. Thorstein the Black took her off the chair in his arms, and sat on another bench with her opposite Thorstein's body. He talked much, and consoled her, and promised to go with her to Eireksfjord with the bodies of her husband and his men, and to have more people stay there for her entertainment and consolement. She thanked him. Then Thorstein Eireksson rose and said: 'Where is Gudrid?' Three times he said this, but she was silent, and said to Thorstein: 'Shall I answer or not.' He said, 'Do not.' He walked across the floor and sat on the chair with Gudrid on his knee. He said: 'What dost thou want, namesake?' Thorstein answered after a while: 'I long to tell her fate.' "

The dead man proceeds to tell that he is in heaven himself, and that she will be married in Iceland. Thereupon these two who were alive, Thorstein the Black and Gudrid, went home to Eirek the Red.[1]

Fourth Voyage.

"This summer a ship came from Norway to Greenland. Thorfinn Karlsefni steered it. He was the son of Thórd Hesthöfdi (horse-head), son of Snorri, son of Thórd. Thorfinn was very wealthy, and during the winter stayed in Brattahlid (West Greenland) with Leif Eireksson. He soon fell in love with Gudrid (widow of Thorstein Eireksson), and asked her in marriage, but she referred the answer to Leif. Then she was betrothed to him, and their wedding took place that winter. The voyages to Vinland were talked over as they had been before, and both Gudrid and others strongly urged Karlsefni to go. He resolved to go, and manned the ship with sixty men and five women. Karlsefni and his men made an agreement that they would divide equally all goods which they might acquire. They took all kinds of cattle with them, for they intended, if possible, to settle in the land. Karlsefni asked Leif for his houses in Vinland, and Leif answered he would lend him the houses, but not give them. Thereupon they sailed out to sea, arrived safely at Leif's booths, and carried their *skin-bags* ashore. They soon found good and plentiful provisions, for a large and fine

---

[1] Evidently the Christian writer, abhorring the heathen people, attributed the plague to them and also the un- natural talk of the dead, which was, perhaps, invented by him.

whale had been driven ashore. They went there and cut up the whale, and there was no lack of food. The cattle walked up on land, and the male cattle soon became wild, and caused a deal of trouble. They had taken with them a bull. Karlsefni had trees felled and cut for his ship, and spread them on a rock to dry them. They used all the produce of the land, grapes, and all kinds of fish and good things. After this first winter the summer came, and they became aware of the presence of the *Skrœlingjar*. A large host of men came out of the forest, near the place where their cattle were. The bull began to bellow out . . . very loudly, and the Skrœlingjar got scared and fled with their burdens, which consisted of grey fur and sable, and all kinds of skins. They went to Karlsefni's house, and wanted to get in. Karlsefni had the door guarded. Neither understood the other's speech. The Skrœlingjar took down their burdens and untied them, and offered to exchange them, chiefly for weapons. Karlsefni forbade his men to sell weapons; but tried a new way, and told the women to carry the produce of the cattle out to them. As soon as they saw it they wanted to buy it and nothing else. The end of the bargaining of the Skrœlingjar was that they carried the produce away in their stomachs, and Karlsefni and his companions kept their loads and skins. Then they went away. Karlsefni now had a strong palisade-wall made round his house, and they made themselves comfortable inside. About this time Gudrid, his wife, bore a boy, who was called Snorri. At the beginning of the second winter the Skrœlingjar came to them in much larger numbers than before, and with the same goods. Karlsefni said to the women: 'Now you shall carry out the same food which was so abundant the last time, and nothing else.' When the Skrœlingjar saw this, they threw their loads in over the wall. Gudrid sat in the door with the cradle of her son Snorri. A shadow appeared on the wall, and a woman entered in a black kirtle, rather short, with a lace round her head, with light brown hair, and a pale face. Gudrid had never seen such large eyes in a human head. She walked to her seat and said: 'What is thy name?' 'I am called Gudrid, but what is thy name?' said Gudrid. 'I am called Gudrid,' she answered. Gudrid, housewife, stretched out her hand to seat her at her side, but at the same moment she heard a loud crack, and the woman disappeared, and a Skrœlingi was slain by one of Karlsefni's men, for he wanted to take their weapons. The Skrœlingjar hurried away, leaving their clothes and weapons there. No one except Gudrid had seen this woman. Karlsefni said: 'Now we must make our plans, for I think they will visit us a third time with war and many men. Now let ten men go out on this ness and show themselves there, and the rest of our men shall go into the forest and make a clearing for our cattle, in order to attack the foe when they come out of the forest. We will also take our bull and let it walk in front of us.' On one side of this place to which they were going was a lake, and on the other a forest. They followed Karlsefni's advice. The Skrœlingjar came to the place which Karlsefni intended for battle. A fight ensued, and many of the Skrœlingjar fell. There was a large and fine man in the Skrœlingjar host, and Karlsefni thought him to be their chief. One of the Skrœlingjar took an axe, looked at it for awhile, aimed a blow at one of his own companions, and struck him so that he fell dead at once. The large man took the axe, looked at it for a while, and then threw it into the sea as far as he could. Then each fled into the forest as quickly as he could, and thus the fight ended. Karlsefni stayed there all that winter. In the spring he declared he would not stay there any longer, but wanted to go to Greenland. They made themselves ready, and took with them many good things, vines, grapes, and skins. They set sail, and landed with their ship safe in Eireksfjord, and stayed there during the winter " (Flateyjarbók, i.).

In another account we read :

" At Brattahlid in Greenland (about 1006–1007) there was great talk about going to look for Vinland the good, for it was said that good choice of land was to be had there. It went so far that two Icelanders, Karlsefni and Snorri prepared their vessel to seek for it in the spring. With them went two men before mentioned, Bjarni and Thorhall, in their own ship. . . . They had altogether one hundred and sixty men when they sailed from Greenland. They sailed southwards for two days and then saw land, put out their boat, and examined the country. They found there large slabs (hella), many of them twenty-four feet wide ; there were also a great many foxes. They gave it the name of Helluland (Slab-land). Thence they sailed for two days, and turning from south to south-east, found a wooded country in which there were many animals. To the south-east of it there lay an island, where they killed a bear, and therefore called it Bjarney (Bear Island), and the land itself Markland (Forestland) (Nova Scotia ?) " (Thorfinn Karlsefni's Saga, c. vii.).

" One of the men who went with Thorfinn Karlsefni to Vinland was called Thorhall the Hunter. He had long been

2 M

with Eirek (the Red, who discovered Greenland), and was his hunter in the summer and his bailiff (= bryti) in the winter" (See Volva. Thorfinn Karlsefni's Saga, 408; Grönland's Historiske Mindesmœrker, i.).

The fifth voyage to America, mentioned in the Sagas, is of least interest: Freydis, a sister of Leif, persuaded two brothers, Helgi and Finnbogi, to go over with her; when they reached America a quarrel broke out among them, and after the brothers had been killed by Freydis' men, she returned to Greenland without having explored the country.

CHAPTER XXV.

THE ORKNEYS AND HEBRIDES.

Early expeditions—The Vikings and the Kings of Scotland—The Vikings in Wales.

WE gather from the Sagas that, even for a long time before Harald Harfagr, the Orkneys and Hebrides were a great rendezvous for Vikings; and in the Orkneyinga Saga we read:

"Thus it is said that in the days of Harald Harfagr the Orkneys were settled; but ere that time there was a Viking rendezvous."

Their geographical position, the prevailing winds during a great part of the year in the North Sea, favourable for vessels going westward from Norway or the Baltic, made these islands of special importance. There met many a Viking fleet, unknown to the enemy, previous to a concerted attack on Scotland, Northumberland, England, or Ireland.

"King Harald (Fairhair) heard that far and wide, in the middle of the land, ravaged the Vikings, who, during the winters, stayed west of the sea. He had a levy out every summer, and searched islands and outskerries; but as soon as the Vikings became aware of his host, they all fled, and mostly out to sea. The king got tired of this, and one summer (about 880) sailed with his host westward. He first came to Shetland (Hjaltland), and there slew all the Vikings who did not flee. Then he sailed southward to the Orkneys, and cleared them of Vikings. After this he went as far as the Hebrides (Sudreyjar) and ravaged there, killing many Vikings who before had ruled over warriors. He fought there many battles, and was always victorious. Then he ravaged in Scotland, and had a battle there. When he went westward to the Isle of Man, the people had heard what

2 M 2

ravages he had before made there, and they fled into Scotland; the country was deserted, and all movable property had been removed, so that the king and his men got no booty there.

" In these battles fell Ivar, son of Rögnvald Jarl of Mœri; as indemnity, King Harald gave to Rögnvald Jarl, when he sailed home, the Orkneys and Shetlands; but Rögnvald gave his brother Sigurd both, and remained behind in the west. When the king sailed eastward he created Sigurd a Jarl. Then joined in companionship with him Thorstein the Red,[1] son of Olaf the White and Aud the Wise. They ravaged in Scotland, and took possession of Katanes (Caithness) and Sudrland (Sutherland) as far as Ekkjalsbakki. Sigurd slew the Scotch Jarl, Melbrigdi, and tied his head to his saddle-straps; the tooth which projected from the Jarl's head wounded the calf of Sigurd's leg, which swelled, and he died therefrom; he is mounded at Ekkjalsbakki. After this ruled his son, Guthorm, one winter; he died childless; and there settled in the country many Vikings, Danes, and Northmen " (Harald Fairhair's Saga, c. 22).

In the following extract we find Irish and Norwegians fighting against Einar Jarl of the Orkneys:—

" The same summer (1018) Eyvind Urarborn went westward on a Viking expedition, and in the autumn came to Konofogor, a king in Ireland. In the autumn the Irish king and Einar Jarl of the Orkneys met in Ulfreksfjord, and there ensued a great battle. King Konofogor had many more warriors and obtained the victory. Einar Jarl fled with one ship, and in the autumn returned to the Orkneys, after having lost most of his men and all their booty. The Jarl liked this journey little, and laid the blame of his defeat on the Northmen, who were with the Irish king " (St. Olaf's Saga, c. 87).

The following extract shows, among other things, the relations which existed between the Vikings and the old kings of Scotland:—

" Thorfinn now became a great chief, and got much land from his grandfather, King Malcolm of Scotland. The latter, however, died, and Karl Hundason became king. He thought himself entitled also to possession of Caithness, and demanded taxes from it as from other parts of his realm; but Thorfinn thought his was the least inheritance he ought to get after his

---

[1] Thorstein the Red was slain by the Scots about 888.

grandfather, especially as it had been given to him, and therefore he refused to pay any tax. King Karl then made his nephew, Moddan, Jarl of Caithness; he gathered many men in Sutherland (Sudrland). When this news reached Thorfinn, he gathered warriors in Caithness, and Thorkel came to his assistance with a large force from the Orkneys. The Scots now found that Thorfinn had more men than they, and retreated; whereupon Thorfinn Jarl subjugated Sutherland and Ross, and ravaged widely in Scotland, and returned to *Dungalsbæ* (Duncansby) in Caithness. Moddan returned to King Karl in Berwick, who became very angry when informed of the treatment his nephew had received.

"He embarked with eleven fully-equipped longships, while Moddan was to march overland to Caithness, where the two forces should meet, thus getting Thorfinn between two fires. The king did not stop until he neared Caithness. When Thorfinn became aware of his presence, he with his five ships stood out into the Pentland Firth, intending to sail to the Orkneys. Thorfinn thereupon sailed along the islands, bound for Sandvik, and reached Dyrnes (Dearness), where he sent word to Thorkel to gather men. As he was lying in under Dyrnes, in the morning when it became light he beheld Karl not far off. He held a consultation with Thorkel about what had best be done, and he advised to abandon the ships and go ashore, and thus escape; but Thorfinn decided to fight with the force he had, and urged his men to behave manfully. They thereupon rowed against the king's fleet, and attacked it fiercely. The battle was long and hard; and when Thorfinn saw the king's own ship, he urged his men to board it; at which he ordered his whole fleet to be cut loose, and his men to take the oars and row away. Thorfinn himself reached the stem of the king's ship, and ordered his standard to be carried upon it, and many brave men followed him up. The king jumped on another vessel with such of his men as were still standing—for most of them had fallen. He rode away, and all the Scots fled.

"King Karl sailed to Breidafjord (Broadfirth), where he went ashore and gathered a fresh host.

"After the battle Thorfinn also retired, and met Thorkel, who had gathered a strong force, with which they sailed southward to Breidafjord (Broadfirth), and began to plunder there. Then they heard that Moddan, with a large force, was at Thorsa (Thurso) in Caithness, and had besides sent to Ireland for warriors. Thorfinn and Thorkel consulted, and agreed that the latter should proceed to Caithness with some of the host, while the former should remain with the remainder, and ravage in Scotland. Thorkel thereupon marched secretly, for all the people of Caithness were true and devoted to them, and no news spread before he reached Thorsa at night and the house of Moddan Jarl, which he set on fire. As he ran out he was killed by Thorkel. Thereupon he rejoined the Jarl, who thanked him greatly for his work.

"King Karl gathered men all over Scotland, and also had the force which came from Ireland to help Moddan Jarl. At Torfnes, south of the Breidafjord, the two armies met; and, although the Scots were far more numerous, they were badly defeated, and the king fled, or, as some say, was slain.

"The Jarl then subjugated Scotland as far south as Fife (Fifi). He sent Thorkel away with some of his men. When the Scots found this out, they went to attack him, who, however, gathered the men he had, and defeated them; whereupon, to avenge their treachery, he ravaged the country, killing all men he could find.

"The Jarl then sailed northward to Caithness, and there passed the winter" (Orkneyinga Saga).

Hence we find the Northern chiefs ruling over Wales.

"It is said that Palnatoki one summer, as usual, was on Viking expeditions, and had twelve well-manned ships. At this time Jarl Stefnir ruled over Bretland (Wales); he had a daughter called Olöf, who was a wise and well-liked woman, and a very good match. It is said that Palnatoki landed his ships there, and wanted to make warfare in the land of Stefnir Jarl. When this was heard of, Olöf, with Bjorn Brezki (the Britisher), who was her foster-brother and often gave her advice, took the resolve to invite Palnatoki home to a feast, with great honours, and he should have there peaceland, and not ravage.

"Palnatoki and his men accepted this, and went to the feast; and at it Palnatoki asked in marriage the Jarl's daughter; he got her easily, and the woman was promised to him, and then betrothed; the betrothal lasted no longer than that their wedding took place at this feast; and moreover, the name of Jarl was given to Palnatoki, and one half of the realm of Stefnir Jarl if he would settle there; and after his death he should have all, for Olöf was his only heir. Palnatoki stayed in Bretland the rest of the summer, and also during the winter. In the spring he announced that he wanted to go home to Denmark; but before he went, he said to Bjorn the British : 'Now I want thee, Bjorn, to stay here with my father-in-law, Stefnir, and rule the land with him on my behalf; for he begins to grow very old, and it is not unlikely that I may not soon come back; and if I do not return, and the Jarl dies, I want thee to take care of the whole realm till I come back.' After this Palnatoki went away with his wife Olöf; he had a good voyage, and came home to Fjon (Fyen) in Denmark, and stayed at home for a while, and was thought the next best man in Denmark, and the most powerful and wisest next to the king.

"It is now told that the next summer after the arvel-feast after King Harald, Olöf, the wife of Palnatoki, fell sick and died. After her death, Palnatoki did not like to live in Bretland, and placed Bjorn the British to take care of that realm. He then made thirty ships ready, and intended to go on Viking expeditions and warfare. He left the land as soon as he was ready to go, and that summer made warfare in Scotland and England, and won for himself much property and fame in his expeditions. He continued this for twelve summers, and got well off both in property and honour" (Jomsvikinga Saga).

APPENDIX.

1. The Testimony of the Frankish Annals.

From the Frankish annals of the time of Charlemagne and his sons, we know that before the period of Harold Fairhair (b. 850; d. 933), and consequently before the conquest by Gangu Hrolf of the country called Normandy, the Sueones (Swedes) and Danes, who were also called Northmen by the Chroniclers, attacked and overran the ancient Gaul in every direction. They captured Paris and many other important cities, and also devastated a great part of the present Germany, and extended their expeditions to the Alps. From a passage in Eginhard we find that the Norwegians are also mentioned; while the Frankish coins found in the present Norway show that its inhabitants had intercourse with the empire of Charlemagne, as they had previously had with Rome.

The Frankish, English, Irish, and Arabian records afford us even a fuller and clearer insight than do the Sagas into the maritime power and great activity of the seafaring tribes of the North, and of their migrations during the ninth and tenth centuries. This maritime power, as we have seen, was already very formidable during the Roman domination of Gaul and Britain. If we have a break in the continuity of these maritime expeditions between the fall of the Roman Empire and the time of Charlemagne, it is on account of the lack of records, owing to the chaos that followed the fall and disintegration of the Roman dominion.

The Sagas supply us to some extent with the needed information; they mention how chiefs like Ivar Vidfamme, Harald Hildetonn, Sigurd Hring, Ragnar Lodbrok, and others engaged extensively in Western and Eastern expeditions, and claimed part of England as belonging to them. From the foreign annals we realize more fully what was implied in the Sagas by the simple phrase that particular chiefs had been, or were, engaged in Eastern and Western expeditions: viz., armaments on the most formidable scale were organized for the subjection of different countries—armaments and expeditions which could only have been possible for a people in an advanced state of civilisation. Of these expeditions the Frankish annals give us the most graphic and detailed accounts.

The particulars concerning the sieges of towns given in the Sagas are very meagre and very rare. We only know that the catapult, called *val-slöngva* (war-sling), or *manga* (" mangonel "), seems to have been used for sieges, &c.

That these were well known to the Northmen at an early time, we have ample proofs.

Great strength of arm was requisite for their use, as several stones at a time were often shot from one catapult.

The Frankish annals, describing one of the sieges of Paris by the Northmen, show us how these machines were used by them. We have minute and graphic descriptions of their mode of warfare, and especially the methods they adopted in besieging towns—subjects that are very little noticed in the Sagas, which generally give only results, and consequently are not of much value to the student of history.

We will proceed to quote a few extracts from the writings of Eginhard, the historian of Charlemagne, which bear testimony to the formidable power of the Northmen in his time.

In 777 Charlemagne had summoned an assembly of chiefs at Paderborn.

" All came before him except Witekind, a Westphalian chief, who, feeling himself guilty of many crimes, and fearing in consequence to present himself, had fled to Siegfried, king of the Danes."

788. " An arm of the sea of unknown length [the Baltic], but exceeding nowhere a hundred thousand paces in width, and in many places much narrower, extends from the western ocean towards the east. Many nations inhabit its shores; the Danes and the Sueones, whom we call Northmen, occupy the northern shore and all the islands; on the southern shore are Sclavonians, the Aistes and other people."

800. " Spring having returned, the king (Charlemagne) quitted Aix-la-Chapelle, about the middle of March, traversed the shore of the Gallic ocean, constructed a fleet on the same ocean, then desolated by the piracies of the Northmen, and placed garrisons along the shores."

804. " At this time Godfrey, king of the Danes, came with a fleet and all the horsemen of his kingdom, to a place called Schlesvig, on the borders of his realm and that of Saxony."

808. " A last war was undertaken against the Northmen, whom we call Danes, and their king, Godfrey, was so inflated with proud hopes, that he promised himself the empire of all Germany. Frisia and Saxony he looked upon as provinces belonging to himself.

"Wishing to assemble a fleet to fight the Northmen, Charlemagne had ships built on all the rivers of Gaul and Germany which flow into the Northern ocean; and, as the Northmen devastated in their continual voyages the coasts of both these countries, he erected solid structures at the entrances of all the harbours and navigable mouths of rivers which could receive vessels, and thus blocked the route of the enemy."

810. "The emperor, then at Aix-la-Chapelle, planned an expedition against King Godfrey. He suddenly received tidings that a fleet of two hundred ships, coming from the country of the Northmen, had landed in Frisia, and ravaged all the islands adjacent to this shore; that this army had gone inland, and that three battles had taken place between it and the Frisians; that the Danish conquerors had imposed a tribute on the conquered; that, under the name of a tax, a hundred pounds of silver had been paid by the Frisians; and that King Godfrey was on his return home. These reports proving true, the emperor was so vexed that he sent messengers in every direction to collect an army, left his palace at once, and joined his fleet. He passed the Rhine at Lippenheim, and resolved to await there the troops which had not yet arrived. His army assembled, the Emperor went as quickly as possible to the river Aller, pitched his tents near the confluence of this river with the Weser and awaited the result of the threats of Godfrey; for this king, puffed up with the vain hope of victory, boasted that he would try his strength with the army of the emperor.

"After he had remained here some time he heard, among other things, that the fleet which had devastated Frisia, had returned to Denmark; that King Godfrey had been slain by one of his servants; that a fort near the Elbe, named Hobbuck (supposed to be Hamburg), in which were Odo, the emperor's envoy, and a garrison of eastern Saxons, had been taken by the Wiltzes. . . . Hemming, son of the brother of Godfrey, king of the Danes, succeeded him, and made peace with the emperor."

From the following we find that the Norwegians and Danes are confounded with each other, as were at times all the tribes of the North. Danish princes are said to live on the shores opposite Britain (Norway).

813. "The emperor sent noble Franks and Saxons into the country of the Northmen, beyond the Elbe, to make peace with the Danes, according to the wish of their kings, and to give back their brother. The Danish nobles came to the place appointed, in number equal to that of the Franks (they were sixteen on each side); peace was confirmed by oaths, and the Franks gave up to the Danes the brother of their kings. These princes were not then in their own country, but had gone to Westerfulde with an army. This country, the most distant of their kingdom, is situated to the north-west, and looks to the north of Britain."

Charlemagne died in 814 and was succeeded by his son Louis le Debonnaire. During the early years of his reign, he appears to have kept on friendly terms with the Northmen, who were suffering from internal dissensions, owing to the succession being disputed between Heriold, and the sons of King Godfrey. Louis espoused the cause of Heriold, and we read that in

828. "Lothaire returned to his father at Aix-la-Chapelle. As they proceeded to occupy the frontier of the Northmen, both in order to renew the alliance between these peoples and the Franks, and to protect the interests of Heriold, and when almost all the counts of Saxony had united for this purpose with the commanders of the marches, Heriold, too eager to hasten the conclusion of the matter, broke the peace pledged and guaranteed by hostages, and ravaged and burned some farms of the Northmen. Hearing this the sons of Godfrey quickly collected troops, marched to the frontier, crossed the Eider river, and falling upon our men, camped upon the bank, who were not expecting such an attack, took the entrenchments, put the defenders to flight, pillaged everything, and returned to camp with all their force."

829. "He received the information that the Northmen contemplated the seizure of the part of Saxony beyond the Elbe, and that, with this design, their army had already approached our frontiers. Greatly troubled at this, he sent into all the countries of the Franks to order the people in mass, to march toward Saxony with all haste, and announced that he, in person, would cross the Rhine at Nuitz in the middle of July."

From the annals of Bertin we take the following extract:—

841. "The Danish pirates, from the shores of the North, made an irruption into the territory of Rouen, and, carrying everywhere the fury of pillage, fire and sword, gave up the city, the monks, and the rest of the people to carnage and captivity, devastated all the monasteries and other places near the Seine, and left them filled with terror, after having received much silver. . . . To Harold who, for his cause and to the prejudice of his father, had brought with the other Danes much evil to the maritime districts, Lothair gave for his services Walcheren and the neighbouring region—a disgraceful forfeit."

842. "At this time a fleet of Northmen came suddenly, at break of day, into the district of Amiens, plundering, capturing, and killing persons of both sexes, leaving nothing but buildings ransomed by silver."

843. "The Northern pirates arrived in the city of Nantes, after having killed the bishop and many of the priests, and laymen, and others, without distinction of sex, and, having pillaged the city, ravaged the lower parts of Aquitaine; finally, reaching a certain island, causing earth to be brought thither, they built houses to pass the winter, and there established themselves as in a permanent abode. . . ."

844. "The Northmen, having advanced by the Garonne as far as Toulouse, plundered with impunity the region on every side; a detachment proceeded thence into Galicia, and there perished—some from the bowmen (arbalêtriers) sent against them, and some in a storm at sea; but others, penetrating farther into Spain, had long and severe battles with the Saracens; but at length were vanquished, and retreated."

845. "The Northmen, with a hundred vessels, on March 20th, entered the Seine, ravaging here and there, and arrived, without resistance, at Paris.

Charles had intended to go against them; but foreseeing that there was no hope of his men gaining the advantage, he let them alone; and, by a gift of seven thousand livres, prevented their advance, and persuaded them to return. . . .

"The Danes, who the year before had laid waste Aquitaine, quietly established themselves therein. . . ."

846. "Eurich, king of the Northmen, advanced against Louis in Germany, with six hundred vessels, along the river Elbe The Saxons went to meet them, engaged them in battle, and by the aid of our Lord Jesus Christ, gained the victory; in their retreat the Northmen attacked and captured a city of the Esclavons. . . .

"The Northmen again descended the Seine, and, returning to the sea, pillaged, devastated, and burned all the districts of the shore. . . . When they had plundered and burned a monastery named St. Bertin, and were returning to their ships laden with spoils, they were so smitten by Divine justice, or blinded by darkness and madness, that only a small number escaped to announce to the others the ways of Almighty God."

846. "The Danish pirates come into Frisia and levy at will contributions, and, victorious in battles, remain masters of almost all the province. . . ."

847. "The Danes come into the lower parts of Gaul inhabited by the Bretons, and gain a victory over them in three battles. Noménoe, vanquished, flees with his men, and then, by presents sent, leads them to leave his country. . . ."

859. "The Danish pirates having made a long circuit by sea, for they had sailed between Spain and Africa, enter the Rhone, plunder many cities and monasteries, and establish themselves in the island called Camargue."

860. "Those of these Danes who had established themselves on the Rhone came, ravaging on their way to the city of Valentia; then, having plundered all the neighbouring regions, returned to the island where they had taken up their abode."

"The Danes on the Rhone go towards Italy, take and plunder Pisa and other cities. . . ."

We might give many more extracts from the Annals of St. Bertin and the Annals of Metz; but the above will suffice to show that in the latter part of the 9th century these Northmen were carrying their incursions, with hundreds of ships and thousands of men, all over Europe, ascending its great rivers, ravaging its coasts, marching through and then settling in its countries, and levying tribute from the people.

In the Narrative of Abbon, we have a striking and graphic description, by an eye-witness, of one of the Sieges of Paris by the Northmen, which lasted from November 885 to May 887. The special value of the narrative to us lies in the minute description which it contains of the methods adopted by the Vikings in attacking a town or fortress. Abbon begins by describing the arrival of the fleet of the Northmen in the river.

"Thy (Paris's) blood was poured out by these barbarians, who came on board of seven hundred sailing vessels, and innumerable smaller ships commonly called barques. The deep-water bed of the Seine was so covered by them that its waters could not be seen for a space of more than six miles: one asked with astonishment in what cave the river had hidden itself; it could not be seen; the pine, the oak, and the alder entirely concealed its surface."

"The Danes then make, astonishing to see, three huge machines, mounted on sixteen wheels—monsters made of immense oak trees bound together; upon each was placed a battering ram, covered with a high roof—in the interior and on the sides of which could be placed and concealed, they said, sixty men armed with their helmets. The besiegers had already finished one of these machines of suitable form and size; a second was soon made, and they were at work on a third; but from the tower they shot accurately, with the whole force of the bowstring and javelin against the workers on them. Thus they were the first to receive the death they were preparing for us; and when one of these cruel machines was destroyed, the other soon followed.

"From the hide torn from the neck and back of young bulls, the Danes then made a thousand large bucklers, which a Latin writer would call *pluteos*[1] or *crates*,[2] each one of which would cover four or six men even. During the night, the enemy gave themselves no rest, and not a moment of sleep; they sharpened, repaired, and forged swift missiles, strengthened their old shields, and made new ones. . . . (At sunrise) suddenly the Danes, the progeny of Satan, armed with their formidable missiles, rushed furiously from their camp, and like light bees, ran toward the tower. Born for our misfortune, they advanced with their backs bent under the bows; the missiles quiver on their shoulders, their swords cover the ground, their shields hide from sight the waters of the Seine; thousands of leaden balls, scattered like a thick hail in the air, fall upon the city, and powerful catapults thunder upon the forts which defend the bridge. Mars, reawaking his fury, extends in every direction his fierce empire. The citizens are terrified, the trumpets give forth violent bursts, and fear seizes on those who guard the towers. Still there were seen many great and bold men; above all, the prelate Gozlio shone conspicuous; then his nephew, the brave Abbé Ebble; admirable also were Robert, Eudes, Ragenaire, Ulton, Herilang; all these were counts; but the most noble of all was Eudes, who laid low as many Danes as he threw javelins. . . ."

January 29, 886.—"The fierce Dane divided his army into three bodies, ranged in the form of a wedge. The largest he opposed to the tower, and the two others, borne on painted ships, he directed against the bridge; thinking that, if he could gain possession of the bridge, the tower would soon be in his power. . . . The tower, reddened with blood, groans under the blows which strike it. . . . At its base are seen at a distance only the painted shields which cover the ground and hide it from sight; in every direction can be seen

---

[1] *Plutei*: machines covered with *claies* and skins of oxen, used to protect sappers.

[2] *Crates*: large bucklers made osiers.

only the fatal stones and cruel missiles which fly in the air like dense swarms of bees ; the sky itself between the tower and the clouds is obscured by them. Loud cries are heard, and everywhere reigns the greatest fear, amid terrible noises. Some attack, others resist : and the Northmen, clashing their arms, add to the already cruel horrors of battle. No child of earth has ever laid eyes upon so many warriors on foot, armed with swords, moving in a single body, under a painted testudo [1] of such immense size. The Danes made of this testudo a roof which sheltered them ; but none dared to raise his head above its protection, though beneath it their weapons caused a frightful slaughter. . . . The fierce nation approached the desolated tower, under the cover of their large bucklers made of wood and the skins of freshly killed bulls ; some pass the night under arms, others sleep, others scour the roads, shooting their feathered arrows, from which is dropped poison."

[A two days' attack followed, but without success ; they tried in vain to fill up the moat around the walls, throwing into it earth, trees, leaves, grass, shrubs, slaughtered animals, and even human beings, their captives.]

"Their ill-omened ranks tried in vain to fill up even a single ditch, or to prostrate the tower by their battering rams. Furious at being unable to get at us in open field, the Northmen take three of their highest vessels, quickly fill them with whole trees with all their leaves on, and set fire to them."

January 31, 886.—"The east wind gently moves these ships vomiting flame, and with ropes they drag them along the banks to destroy the bridge and burn the tower; from the wood which fills them burst out burning flames."

[Then the whole populace call upon their patron saint, St. Germain, and implore him to save them. The enemy's vessels get aground upon a large mass of stones heaped up to render the bridge firm ; no harm is done to it, and the besieged rush out, and sink the vessels in the river Seine. Thus ended the combat for that day, and the night was quietly passed.]

February 1, 886.—"Next day the Danes secretly carry to their camp the large bucklers which formed their testudo ; they abandon two of their rams, vulgarly called *carcamuses*, which they feared to carry away ; and our men took possession of them, and joyfully broke them in pieces. Sigefroy, the king, by whom it was feared the gates of our tower would have been burst in, then led away all his Danes.

"The third day of this battle was that of the 'Purification of the Virgin.' Nevertheless, the fatal cohorts of the Northmen went on board their vessels, swifter than birds, and directed their course to the eastern lands, then subject to the rule of Sad Austrasia, and which had hitherto not suffered from the enemy's ravages."

---

[1] The *testudo* of the Roman armies, in which the warriors' shields are interlocked like the scales of a tortoise, forming a protecting roof for the undermining or attacking of walls.

APPENDIX.

[Destroying in their course the deserted cottages of the famous Robert, whom they slew, and in their turn defeated with great loss, they bravely escaped to their ships without booty; they met with no greater success at the church of St. Germain, miraculously defended by the Saint.]

February 6, 886.—" Alas! during the silence of night the middle of the bridge fell in, carried away by the force of the furious waters. It was not so with the tower, which, built on land belonging to the happy Saint, remained standing on its foundations. Both were on the right side of the city.

" At sunrise the cruel Danes awoke, boarded their vessels, filled them with arms and shields, crossed the Seine, surrounded the unfortunate tower, and assailed it repeatedly with showers of missiles. At last, after a desperate fight, in which the besieged behaved nobly, the infamous besiegers, seeing that nothing could bend these brave hearts, brought before the gates of the unhappy tower a car filled with grains, and set it on fire. Another fierce struggle takes place; the Danes allow the flames to do their work, and retire; from want of vessels for drawing water the tower was destroyed, and the besieged retired to the end of the bridge which was still standing, and maintained the fight till sundown."

(Knytlinga Saga.)

(Landnama, part iv.)

(Viga-Styr's Saga, ch. 35.)

(Hardar Saga Grimkelssonar, ch. 11.)

(Chronological fragment, 12th century.)

(Harlar Saga Grimkelssonar, ch. 3.)

F.

Þtā g. gudmðr grǽm. f. hūr er ſcioldungr ſa er ſcipð ſtyr
lete goyrana gulliŋ ſyt ſtarni þrœia iŋ grip yrarar baði
yerpr vigroþa v̄ vikinga, Siŋioði g. Her ma haðbðr he
lga keŋa ſlocco trauþan yrlova muþið. h hey:i epli eccar
þurar arŋ ſialonga vnð ſic þrugit. Þvi ſvn tlo ar ſire
ka ſteim ſari ſaman v̄ ſakað dœma. mal ec haðbrœðr
heŋnð ar vŋa eŋ v̄ legra lvo lēgi barð. ſiyn mðð gudmð.
geŋŋ vm halda y berg ſarar braçar kliſa. haſa þ iheŋði
hellv kylho þ er þ bliþara eŋ britnis ðōar. Þeŋ é liŋŋio
tli ſemra myclo gvŋi ar heŋia y hlaþa œno. ey onyrð o.a.d.
þoð hildigar heirþð deili. Þuctic rū goſ ſ̄n. ſ. þo.ð.ſ.ſ.a.m.
þr merʒþ h.a.m.r. ac hvg haſa hiœ.a.b.éo. hildigar haoll
tri ſtuall. Helgi þꝛ ſigrvnae ʒarco þu ſono var helga
eŋ gamall Dagr havgna ſ. blorapi opiŋ r̄ ſarð heŋnða oþi
leþi dag greiſ ſinſ. Dagr y:aŋ helga m̄ag ſiŋ þar ſē h.
ar y:ocur lvndi. Klagði y:ognð helga mŋ geirnð. þꝛ ſell
helgi eŋdagr reiþ r̄ y:iatla y ſagði ſigruno tibiðv. Traþ
em ar ſyſſ trega þꝛ ſegia þꝛ ac heſi navþigr nipti gr
ecca. y:ell imœʒð vndriocur lvndi buþlvngr ſa é var
berce þēi y hildigom ahalſi ſtoþ. Þic ſkyli allt eiþar
bica þir é helga haŋ:þ vŋa ar eŋ:no lioſa leiþr varni
y ar vr ſvolom vŋar ſteini. Scriþar þ ſcip é vnð þ
ſcriþv þoi aſea byrr epr. lecis. renia ſa mar é iþ þ reŋi
þoi co y:nndr þiŋa y:œþar eŋ. Brria þ:þ ſlōþ é þu bre
gð nēa ſialþð þ ſyngui v̄.haŋ:ðv. þa vi þ heŋ:it hel
ga deŋa eŋ þv vir vargr aviþð vci. aþſ andvani oc
allz gamanſ. heŋ:þ éŋ mac nēa ahryðū ſpŋŋŋ. d.q.
r̄ erðv ſyſ y érvira eŋ þv bryþ þinð biþ y:œſcapa.
eŋ velde oðiŋ allo baolvi þꝛ mŋ ſyŋŋŋgð ſac runŋœ
bar Her byþ brŋþ barga raiba. vll vandill ve
ʒang olle. haſþv haljiaŋ hel harmt ar gioldom
brŋþ baŋg variþ ʒ þvriſ þiŋ. Srcca ae ð ſǽl

(Earlier Edda, complete page.)

388

(Later Edda.)

(Egil's Saga.)

2 N 2

(List of priests from the 12th century. Two columns.)

(Njal's Saga.—Two columns.)

(Heimskringla.—Two columns.)

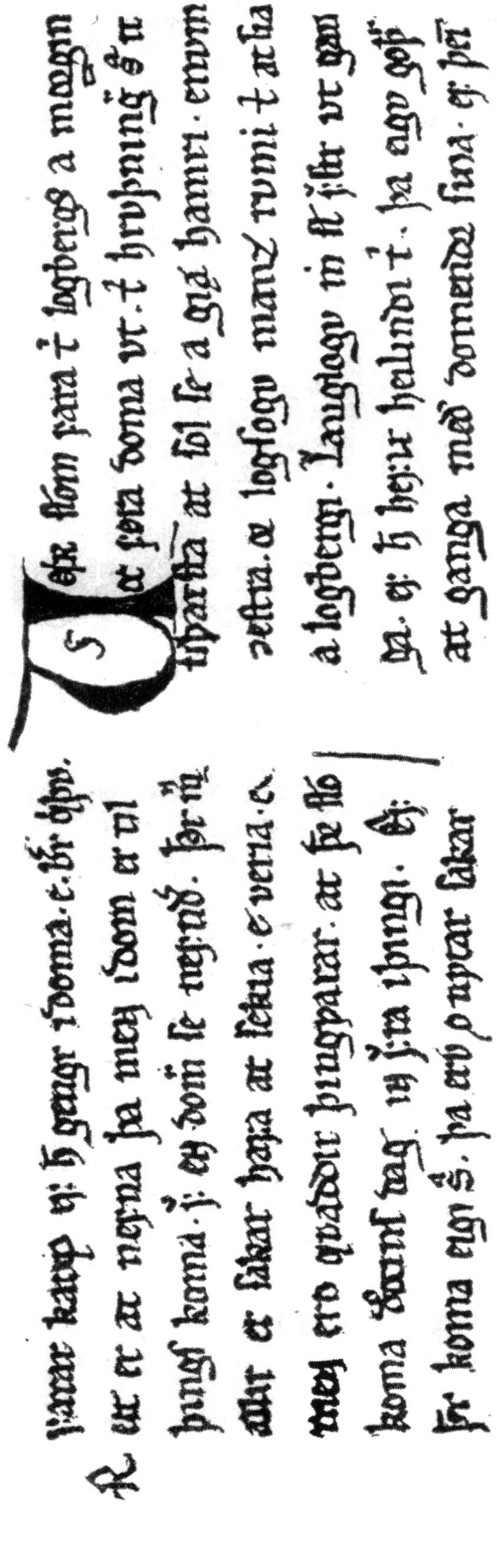

(Part of manuscript of Gragas.)

(Gunnlaug Ormstunga's Saga, ch. 4.)

(Hænsa-Thóris Saga, ch. 5.)

(Saga of Viga-Styr and Heidarvíg.)

APPENDIX III.

ROMAN COINS FOUND IN SCANDINAVIA.

The following is a list of coins found at Hagestadborg, Scania (550); and at Sindarfe, Gotland (1500).

Nero (54–68 A.D.)	.	2	2	Lucius Verus (161–169) .	21	16
Vitellius (69)	. .	0	1	Lucilla, wife of Lucius		
Vespasianus (69–79) .	.	1	16	Verus	11	22
Titus (79–81)	. .	0	5	Commodus (180–192) .	60	91
Domitianus (81–96) .	.	2	10	Crispina, wife of Com-		
Nerva (96–98)	. .	1	7	modus	7	11
Trajanus (98–117) .	.	26	150	Pertinax (193) . . .	0	10
Hadrianus (117–138)	.	33	225	Septimius Severus (193–		
Sabina, wife of Hadrianus		6	11	211)	6	13
Ælius Cæsar (†138) .	.	2	6	Julia Domna, wife of Sep-		
Antoninus Pius (138–161)		136	321	timius Severus . .	1	0
Faustina, wife of An-				Barbaric imitations . .	0	4
toninus Pius . .	.	38	130	Uncertain (worn) . . .	0	72
Marcus Aurelius (161–180)		145	280			
Faustina the younger, wife					550	1,500
of Marus Aurelius	.	52	97			

Roman coins from Augustus up to the death of Alexander Severus.
(29 B.C.–A.D. 235.)

Found up to 1869.

Gotland :

Augustus (29 B.C.–A.D. 14)		
(Silver)		1
Nero (54–68) . . . „		2
Galba (68–69) . . . „		3
Otho (69) . . . . „		2
Vespasianus (69–79) . „		23
Titus (79–81) (1 gold, 4 silver)		5
Domitianus (81–96) . . .		7
Nerva (96–98)		5
Trajanus (98–117) . . .		157
Hadrianus (117–138) . . .		175
Sabina, wife of Hadrianus .		14
Ælius Cæsar (†138) . . .		1
Antoninus Pius (138–161) .		263
Faustina, wife of Antoninus Pius		96
Marcus Aurelius (161–180) .		251
Faustina, wife of Marcus Aurelius		87
L. Verus (161–169) . . .		19
Lucilla, wife of L. Verus . .		18
Commodus (180–192) . . .		86
Crispina, wife of Commodus .		11
Pertinax (193)		1
Manlia Scantilla, wife of Didius		
Julianus		1
Clodius Albinus (†197) . .		1
Septimius Severus (193–211) .		4
Julia Soæmias, mother of Ela-		
gabalus		1
Alexander Severus (222–235) .		1
Effaced and uncertain . . .		184

1 of gold, 1,422 of silver total 1,423

Öland :

Vespasianus (69–79)	(Silver)		2
Trajanus (98–117) .	,,		2
Hadrianus (117–138) .	,,		4
Antoninus Pius (138–161)	,,		19
Faustina, wife of Antoninus Pius (1 brass, 6 silver) . .			7
Marcus Aurelius (161–180)	(Silver)		19
Faustina, wife of Marcus Aurelius	,,		5
L. Verus (161–169) .	(Silver)		3
Lucilla, his wife . .	,,		4
Commodus (180–192) .	,,		9
Julia Mæsa, grandmother of Elagabalus	,,		1
Alexander Severus (222–235) . . .	,,		1
Effaced or uncertain .	,,		6

81 of silver, 1 of brass, total . 82

Recapitulation.—*Entire Sweden* :

Mainland . . . . (gold)		1
,, . . . (silver)		15
,, . . . (brass)		21
Gotland . . . . (gold)		1
,, . . . (silver)		1,422
Oland . . . (silver)		81
,, ... (brass)		1

2 gold, 1518 of silver, 22 of brass 1,542

Zealand :

Vespasianus (69–79) .	(Silver)		3
Trajanus (98–117) .	(Brass)		1
Hadrianus (117–138)	(Silver)		6
Sabina, wife of Hadrianus .,			1
Antoninus Pius (138–161)	,,		16
Faustina senior, wife of Antoninus Pius . .	,,		2
M. Aurelius (161–180) .	,,		5
Faustina junior, wife of M. Aurelius . .	,,		4
L. Verus (161–169)	(Silver)		2

Commodus (180–192) (Silver)			3
Crispina, wife of Commodus	,,		3
Septimius Severus (193–211)	,,		1
Macrinus (217–218) .	,,		1
Effaced or uncertain	,,		728

475 silver and 1 brass, total . 476

Fyen :

Tiberius (14–37) (Solidus, gold)		1
Nerva (96–98) . . (Silver)		1
Trajanus (98–117) . ,,		1
Lucius Verus (161–169) ,,		1
Geta (211–212) . . (Gold)		1

2 of gold, and 3 of silver, total 5

The proportion of effaced or uncertain coins is enormous.

Bornholm :

Nero (54–68) . .	(Silver)		1
Domitianus (81–96) .	,,		1
Trajanus (98–117) .	,,		13
Hadrianus (117–138) .	,,		20
Sabina, wife of Hadrianus	,,		2
Antoninus Pius (138–161)	,,		49
Faustina senior, wife of Antoninus Pius . .	,,		8
M. Aurelius (161–180)	,,		73
Faustina junior, wife of Marcus Aurelius .	,,		11
L. Verus (161–169) .	(Silver)		10
Lucilla, wife of L. Verus	,,		3
Commodus (180–192) .	,,		34
Crispina, wife of Commodus . . .	,,		3
Septimius Severus (193–211) . . .	,,		1
Effaced or uncertain .	,,		7

Total 236

Jutland:

Nero (54–68) . . . (Silver)	1
Vitellius (69) . . . . ,,	2
Vespasianus (69–79) . . ,,	4
Domitianus (81–96) . . ,,	1
Trajanus (98–117). . . ,,	8
Hadrianus (117–138) . . ,,	7
Ælius Cæsar (†138) . . ,,	1
Antoninus Pius (138–161) (1 large brass, 16 silver)	17
Faustina senior, wife of Antoninus Pius . . . . . (Silver)	5
M. Aurelius (161–180) (Silver)	10
Faustina junior, wife of M. Aurelius . . . . . (Silver)	3
L. Verus (161–169) . . ,,	2
Lucilla, wife of L. Verus . ,,	2

Commodus (180–192) . (Silver)	8
Septimius Severus (193–211) ,,	1
Macrinus (217–218) . . ,,	1
72 silver and 1 brass, total .	73

Recapitulation.

Bornholm . . . . (silver)	236
Zealand. . . . . ,,	475
,, ... (brass)	1
Fyen . . . . . (gold)	2
,, ... (silver)	3
Jutland. . . . . (silver)	72
,, ... (brass)	1
2 gold, 786 silver, 2 of brass, total	790

Roman Coins from Claudius to the death of Alexander Severus.
(29 B.C.–A.D. 235.)

Claudius (41–54), Scania (1 gold, 1 brass)	2
Vespasianus (69–79), Scania and Smäland . . . . .(brass)	2
Trajanus (98–117), Halland (silver)	1
Hadrianus (117–138), Scania (brass), Upland (silver), (1 brass, 1 silver)	2
Antoninus Pius (138–161), Scania, near Lund . (2 brass, 1 silver)	3
Marcus Aurelius (161–180), Scania (silver)	2
Lucilla, wife of L. Verus, Halland (silver)	1
Commodus (180–192), 1 Westergotland, 1 Scania . . (silver)	2

Septimius Severus (193–211), Halland . . . . (silver)	1
Julia Domna, wife of Septimius Severus, Scania . . (silver)	1
Caracalla (211–217), Halland ,,	1
Elagabalus (218–222), Halland (silver)	1
Alexander Severus (222–235), Scania . . . (large brass)	1
Effaced or uncertain, Scania (14 brass, 3 silver)	17
1 gold, 15 silver, 21 brass, total	37

Roman coins from the death of Alexander Severus to the death of Theodosius the Great. (A.D. 235–395.)

Found up to 1869.

Norway:

Valens (364–378) . . . (gold)	1
Valentinianus I. (364–375), Lister and Mandal, near Bergen (gold)	1

Gratianus (367–383) (in a grave) (gold)	1
Total . . . ,,	3

Sweden :

Gordianus (238–244), Gotland (silver)	1
Gallienus (253–268), Scania (brass)	1
Probus (276–282), 1 Södermanland, 1 Scania . . . . (gold)	2
Licinius (307–323), Scania (brass)	1
Constantinus Magnus (306–337), 1 Södermanland, 3 Scania, 1 Öland . . (2 gold, 3 brass)	5
Constantinus II. (337–340), Gotland . . . . . (brass)	2
Constantius II. (337–361), 3 Scania, 1 Gotland . . . (brass)	4
Constans (337–350), Scania „	1
Effaced or uncertain, 1 Upland, 4 Scania . . . . . (brass)	5
	—
4 gold, 1 silver, and 17 brass, total	22
	—

Denmark :

Decius (249–251), Fyen . (Gold)	1
Aurelianus (270–275), Fyen „	2
Tacitus (275–276), Fyen . „	1

Probus (276–282), Fyen (Gold)	4
Carus (282–283), Fyen . „	1
Numerianus (283–284), Fyen „	1
Carinus (283–284), Fyen . „	1
Diocletianus (284–305), Fyen „	5
Maximianus (286–305), Fyen „	5
Constantius Chlorus (305–306), Fyen . . . . . (Gold)	2
Helena, wife of Constantius, Fyen (Gold)	1
Licinius (307–323), Fyen . „	2
Constantinus Magnus (306–337), Jutland 2, Fyen 16 (17 gold, 1 brass)	18
Constantinus II. (337–340), Fyen 2, Zealand 1 . . . . (gold)	3
Constantius II. (337–361), Denmark, locality unknown; 2 in Fyen, 1 Jutland (3 gold, 1 brass)	4
Constans (337–350), Fyen (gold)	2
Valentinianus I. (364–375), Zealand 1, Jutland 1 . . (gold)	2
Other gold coins	5
	—
(58 gold, 2 brass)	58
	—

Roman and Byzantine coins from the death of Theodosius the Great to the death of Anastasius. (395–518.)

Found up to 1869.

Swedish Mainland :

Honorius (395–423), Småland .	1
Valentinianus III. (425–455), Småland, Kalmar län . .	1
Anthemius (467–472), Scania .	1
Julius Nepos (474–475), 1 Kalmar län, 1 Blekinge	2
Romulus Augustulus (475–476), Småland	1
Theodosius II. (408–450), Medelpad 1, Upland 4, Småland 1, 2 in Kalmar län, 2 in Blekinge, 3 Scania	13
Marcianus (450–457), Upland .	1
Leo I. (457–474), 3 in Upland, 1 on Hoen	4

Zeno (474–491), 1 in Medelpad, 11 in Upland, 1 in Södermanland, 2 in Scania	15
Anastasius (491–518), 2 in Upland, 1 in Kalmar län, 1 in Scania	4
Unknown, Upland	1
	—
Total . . . (all gold)	45
	—

Öland :

Honorius (395–423)	5
Valentinianus III. (425–455). .	13
Majorianus (457–461)	1
Libius Severus (461–465) . . .	9

Anthemius (467–472)	3
Romulus Augustulus (475–476) .	1
Arcadius (395–408)	2
Theodosius II. (408–450) . . .	20
Ælia Eudoxia, wife of Theodosius II.	2
Marcianus (450–457)	4
Ælia Pulcheria, wife of Marcianus	2
Leo I. (457–474)	19
Leo II. and Zeno (474) . . .	1
Zeno (474–491)	5
Basiliscus (476–477)	1
Unknown	11

Total . . . (all gold) 99

Gotland:

Honorius (395–423)	4
Majorianus (457–461)	1
Libius Severus (461–465) . . .	1
Procopius Anthemius (467–472) .	2
Theodosius II. (408–450) . . .	3
Marcianus (450–457)	1
Leo I. (457–474)	10
Leo II. and Zeno (474) . . .	1
Zeno (474–491)	15
Ælia Ariadne, wife of Zeno . .	1
Basiliscus (476–477)	1
Anastasius (491–518)	17

Total . . . (all gold) 57

Recapitulation.

Sweden, Mainland	45
,, Oland	99
,, Gotland	57
All gold, total	201

Bornholm:

Honorius (395–423)	3
Placidius Valentinianus (425–455)	8
Honoria, sister of Valentinianus .	1
Libius Severus (461–465) . .	1
Anthemius (467–472) . . .	2
Julius Nepos (474–475) . . .	1
Theodosius II. (408–450) . .	16
Marcianus (450–457)	1
Leo I. (457–474)	12
Leo II. and Zeno (474) . . .	3
Zeno (474–491)	13
Basiliscus (476–477)	1
Basiliscus and Marcus	1
Anastasius (491–518)	5

67 of gold, 1 of silver, total . 68

Valentinianus (425–455), Fyen .	2
Majorianus (457–461), Fyen . .	1
Theodosius II. (408–450), 1 Zealand, 1 Fyen	2
Marcianus (450–457), Fyen . .	1
Leo I. (457–474), 1 Jutland, 5 Fyen	6
Zeno (474–491), 1 Fyen . . .	1
Anastasius (491–518), 2 Fyen .	2
Unknown, 1 Jutland, 1 Fyen .	2

All gold, total 17

Recapitulation.

Bornholm . . . . (gold)	67
,, ... (silver)	1
Rest of Denmark . . . (gold)	17
84 gold, and 1 silver, total . .	85

Byzantine coins from the time between A.D. 518–850.

Norway:

Tiberius Constantinus (578–582) 1 gold.
Mauricius Tiberius (582–602)	1
Constantinus V. Copronymus (771–775)	1
Michael III. (842–867) . .	1

Total . . . . . 4 gold.

Sweden (1 Södermanland, 1 Gotland):

Justinianus I. (527–565) . 2 gold.

Denmark (Bornholm):

Justinus I. (518–527) . 1 gold.

In Sweden more than 250 Roman and Byzantine gold coins have been found, and year after year new ones are brought to light.

The whole number of Roman and Byzantine coins of the period before A.D. 850 found up to June, 1872, was—

	From the time before Augustus	Augustus—Alexander Severus (29 B.C.–235 A.D.).	Alexander Severus—Theodosius (235–395).	Theodosius—Anastasius (395–518).	After Anastasius (518–850).	Total
Mainland . .	3	12	4	37	1	57
Scania . . .	—	584	14	19	—	617
Öland . . .	—	88	2	106	—	196
Gotland . . .	9	3,234	4	64	1	3,312
	12	3,918	24	226	2	4,182
Among these coins are—						
Of gold . . .	—	2	6	**226**	2	236
„ silver . .	12	3,894	1	—	—	3,907
„ copper . .	—	22	17	—	—	39

OTHER BOOKS FROM CGR PUBLISHING AT CGRPUBLISHING.COM

1939 New York World's Fair: The World of Tomorrow in Photographs

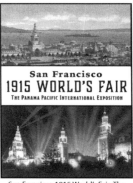

San Francisco 1915 World's Fair: The Panama-Pacific International Expo.

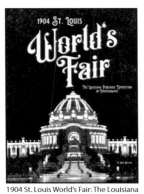

1904 St. Louis World's Fair: The Louisiana Purchase Exposition in Photographs

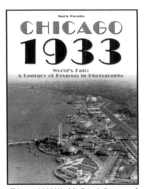

Chicago 1933 World's Fair: A Century of Progress in Photographs

19th Century New York: A Dramatic Collection of Images

The American Railway: The Trains, Railroads, and People Who Ran the Rails

The Aeroplane Speaks: Illustrated Historical Guide to Airplanes

The World's Fair of 1893 Ultra Massive Photographic Adventure Vol. 1

The World's Fair of 1893 Ultra Massive Photographic Adventure Vol. 2

The World's Fair of 1893 Ultra Massive Photographic Adventure Vol. 3

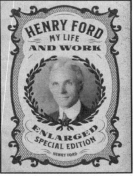

Henry Ford: My Life and Work - Enlarged Special Edition

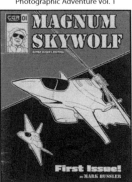

Magnum Skywolf #1

Ethel the Cyborg Ninja Book 1

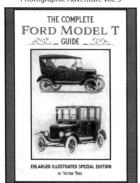

The Complete Ford Model T Guide: Enlarged Illustrated Special Edition

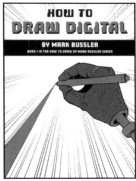

How To Draw Digital by Mark Bussler

Best of Gustave Doré Volume 1: Illustrations from History's Most Versatile...

400

OTHER BOOKS FROM CGR PUBLISHING AT CGRPUBLISHING.COM

Ultra Massive Video Game Console Guide Volume 1

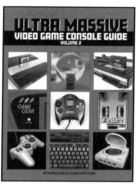

Ultra Massive Video Game Console Guide Volume 2

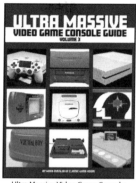

Ultra Massive Video Game Console Guide Volume 3

Ultra Massive Sega Genesis Guide

Antique Cars and Motor Vehicles: Illustrated Guide to Operation...

Chicago's White City Cookbook

The Clock Book: A Detailed Illustrated Collection of Classic Clocks

The Complete Book of Birds: Illustrated Enlarged Special Edition

1901 Buffalo World's Fair: The Pan-American Exposition in Photographs

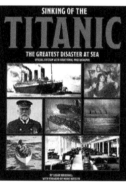

Sinking of the Titanic: The Greatest Disaster at Sea

Gustave Doré's London: A Pilgrimage: Retro Restored Special Edition

Milton's Paradise Lost: Gustave Doré Retro Restored Edition

The Art of World War 1

The Kaiser's Memoirs: Illustrated Enlarged Special Edition

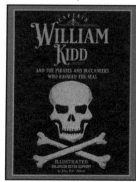

Captain William Kidd and the Pirates and Buccaneers Who Ravaged the Seas

The Complete Butterfly Book: Enlarged Illustrated Special Edition